PATRONS OF ENLIGHTENMENT

EDWARD G. ANDREW

Patrons of Enlightenment

UNIVERSITY OF TORONTO PRESS
Toronto Buffalo London

© University of Toronto Press Incorporated 2006
Toronto Buffalo London
Printed in Canada

ISBN-13 978-0-8020-9064-5
ISBN-10 0-8020-9064-8

Printed on acid-free paper

Library and Archives Canada Cataloguing in Publication

Andrew, Edward, 1941–
Patrons of enlightenment / Edward G. Andrew.

Includes bibliographical references and index.
ISBN 0-8020-9064-8

1. Authors and patrons – Europe – History – 18th century.
2. Philosophers – Europe – History – 18th century. 3. Enlightenment.
I. Title.

B802.A53 2006   190'.9'033   C2005-906296-7

This book has been published with the help of a grant from the Canadian
Federation for the Humanities and Social Sciences, through the Aid to
Scholarly Publications Programme, using funds provided by the Social
Sciences and Humanities Research Council of Canada.

University of Toronto Press acknowledges the financial assistance to its publishing program of the Canada Council for the Arts and the Ontario Arts
Council.

University of Toronto Press acknowledges the financial support for its
publishing activities of the Government of Canada through the Book
Publishing Industry Development Program (BPIDP).

To the patrons of the University of Toronto and to the brave colleagues who have resisted their demands.

Contents

Acknowledgments

I wish to thank Judith Baker, John Beattie, Ronald Beiner, Peter Burke, Roger Chartier, Natalie Davis, Roger Emerson, André Gombay, Dena Goodman, Ian Hacking, Catherine Lu, Iain McCalman, Randall McGowan, James Moore, Caroline Turner, and Tetsuji Yamamoto for helpful suggestions in conversations or communications with me in the course of my writing this book. I owe a particular debt to Sophie Bourgault, a research assistant *extraordinaire*, and Robert Sparling, who improved both my grammar and my understanding of the German Enlightenment in his thoughtful reading of the manuscript while compiling the index. Donna Trembowelski Andrew was extremely helpful throughout the research and writing. Virgil Duff of University of Toronto Press provided friendly and efficient editorial assistance, and Curtis Fahey provided professional and helpful copy editing. Above all, I am grateful to my patrons, the Social Sciences and Humanities Research Council and the Aid to Scholarly Publications Programme, without whom this book would not have been written or published.

PATRONS OF ENLIGHTENMENT

Introduction

How did thinkers subsist before the age of tenured professorships and institutional foundations for advanced thought and research? This study explores how the thinkers of the eighteenth-century Enlightenment earned their living. Although it is a comparative intellectual history of the eighteenth century, the book begins with an examination of the lives of Socrates and Seneca before analysing how eighteenth-century thinkers thought wealth and poverty conditioned the philosophic life. Reflective attention to the lives of a rich philosopher (Seneca) and a relatively impoverished one who was drawn to the rich (Socrates) highlights a structural theme of this work: namely, that philosophers rarely have the wealth and power to do without patrons or political protectors. Socrates was an exemplar for poor philosophers, such as Rousseau and Diderot, and even philosophers who approached Seneca's wealth, such as Voltaire and Montesquieu, had need of political protectors.

Hitherto, there has been no extended study of the patronage of philosophy. In Plato's beautiful allegory of the cave, all persons except philosophers are held in thrall of shadows cast by puppeteers onto an equivalent of our silver screen. The artists who cast these images may be thought to be creators of public opinion but in fact they reshape their images (of, say, a hawk or a dove) in response to the public's approval or disapproval of them. While artists, politicians, and sophists may be sufficiently flexible to accommodate themselves to the demands of patrons and public opinion, the same is not true, according to Plato and Aristotle, of philosophers. Consequently, numerous studies of the patronage of poets, artists, and politicians have been written, but, as of yet, the patronage of philosophy has been studiously ignored. Philosophers, Aristotle wrote, approach godlike self-sufficiency[1] and eighteenth-century *philosophes* prided themselves on their independence. This study will question the Platonic distinction between philosophers and sophists, the Aristotelian view of the contemplative life as self-sufficient, and the Enlightenment's self-understanding of intellectual autonomy.

In *Rameau's Nephew*, Diderot and Rameau agree that everyone has to get into unnatural postures and jump through hoops to please their patrons. But, Diderot added, 'there is one human being who is exempted from this pantomime. That is the philosopher who has nothing and asks for nothing.'[2] Diderot seems to celebrate the self-sufficient Cynic Diogenes who lived from nature: 'Whom does the savage beg from? The earth, the animals and fishes, the trees and plants and roots and streams.' But Diderot knew that Diogenes was not one of Jean-Jacques Rousseau's self-sufficient savages; Diogenes lived from begging from his fellow citizens and taking what he needed from others – for all property is common property for the wise man. Indeed, the honest Diogenes lived much as the truth-telling sponge, Rameau, did. Moreover, Diderot agreed with Rameau's form of Epicureanism – not that money is the chief good but that money is essential for life's vital pleasures. Diderot wrote: 'I am far from despising sensual pleasures. I have a palate too and it is tickled by a delicate wine or dish' as well as beautiful women and drunken parties with his friends.[3] In short, Diogenes' life would not have satisfied Diderot. The more useful model of the philosophic life was the immensely rich Stoic, Seneca. Diderot devoted two of his last and longest works to a justification of the life of Seneca and the place of patronage in living a philosophic life. Diderot was able to obtain relief from his arduous and poorly paid task of editing the *Encyclopédie* by dining six nights a week at the expense of Mme Geoffrin, Mme Helvétius, Baron D'Holbach, and others. But Diderot really separated himself from the living conditions of Rameau's nephew when he accepted Catherine the Great's gracious offer to buy up his library and to give Diderot a life pension as custodian of his own library. Similarly, Seneca's life prospered once he accepted the patronage of Agrippina, Nero's mother, and took on the function of tutor and then adviser to the despotic emperor.

All of the major writers of the eighteenth century were dependent upon royal or aristocratic patronage[4] and they all celebrated independence of thought as the characteristic feature of their time. I shall try to establish connections between receipt of patronage and forms of thought. Patronage often has been thought to be synonymous with corruption and incompatible with republican virtue.[5] For example, John Churchill Wicksted wrote in 1717 of the support of the arts by Augustus Caesar and his minister Maecenas, whose name has become proverbial for patronage:

Their Harps with flattering Sounds repay'd
Th' Imperial Patron's skillful Cost:
But whilst th' applauded Artists played,
The *Roman* Liberty was lost.[6]

Yet these republican sentiments are contained within a poem dedicated to, and celebrating the reign of, George I. Republicanism is a sufficiently supple and transhistorical term to encompass many different strands of eighteenth-century thought that are compatible with constitutional monarchy and commercial empires.[7] Despite the plasticity of the idea of republicanism, this study of patronage in the eighteenth century contests Gordon Wood's claim that 'republicanism was the ideology of the Enlightenment.'[8] A strand of eighteenth-century thought espoused the Aristotelian view that the question of the superiority of republics to monarchies turns on the question of the superiority of the practical to the theoretical life, of the life of the statesman and citizen-soldier to the life of the philosopher – if the latter, then monarchies are superior, if the former, then republics are superior. A widespread but quite different strand took for granted the practical orientation of philosophy and thought monarchies more efficient vehicles to implement enlightened reforms than republics. These different strands or currents of thought converged to form what I have called the Senecan moment of eighteenth-century thought, as opposed to what J.G.A. Pocock has called the Machiavellian moment of eighteenth-century republican thought.[9]

To be sure, many of the *philosophes* supported the American War of Independence; however, since monarchical France allied itself to the Americans to weaken its traditional enemy, England, it can safely be said that Voltaire's greeting of Franklin in 1778 with a salutation of 'God and liberty' did not express Enlightenment views any more than his writing of the invasion manifesto for Bonnie Prince Charlie a generation before signified the Enlightenment's preference for Catholic absolutism. In fact, this book argues that the republican revolutions at the end of the eighteenth century were not the *telos* of Enlightenment – in Isaac Kramnick's words, 'the embodiment and natural home of Enlightenment' or 'the realization of Enlightenment'[10] – but its *eschatos* (end as termination, not as purpose or culmination). Henry Steele Commanger, while agreeing with Gordon Wood and Kramnick that the American Revolution was the *telos* of Enlightenment, provides reasons why it might be considered its *eschatos*: America 'lacked the Courts, the Cathedrals, the Academies, the Universities, and the libraries that provided so large a part of the patronage and nurture of philosophy in the Old World.'[11] Hence, Benjamin Franklin wrote Hume that he intended to return to America because wisdom was in scarce supply there and hence his own wisdom 'may come to a better market.'[12] My argument is, *pace* Franklin's witty formulation, that the intellectual marketplace is not self-subsistent and that the eighteenth-century republic of letters depended upon royal or aristocratic patronage. Indeed, Gordon Wood himself, following Bernard Bailyn, believes that the American Revolution was fought against Old World patronage but that, even so, recognizes the careers of Franklin and Alexander Hamilton depended upon patronage.[13] Our penultimate chapter will attempt to show that the French Revolution, by closing the aristocratic salons and the royal academies, terminated the epoch we know as the Enlightenment.

If patronage appeared incompatible with republican virtue, the practice also encountered an alternative ideal, namely, independence made possible by expanding readership. Men of letters claimed to find their independence as professional writers in the commercial market-place of ideas. David Hume, Adam Smith, Samuel Johnson, and Edward Gibbon, all recipients of patronage, claimed to be independent of patrons other than booksellers and their readers. This claim is repeated by the foremost historian of ideas today, J.G.A. Pocock, who writes that 'the expansion of genteel publishing ... enabled Hume, Robertson and Gibbon to live in affluence off the sale of their copyrights, independent of either patrons or booksellers.'[14] Towards the end of the eighteenth century, the libertarian William Godwin stated: 'It is but lately that men have known that intellectual excellence can accomplish its purpose without a patron. At present, amongst the civilised and well informed a man of slender wealth, but of great intellectual powers and a firm and virtuous mind, is constantly received with attention and deference.'[15] Unfortunately, after marrying Mary Wollstonecraft and taking respon-sibility for her children – he did not dispose of them as Rousseau did to maintain his independence – he was forced to have recourse in the 1830s to a patronage appointment as 'Office Keeper and Yeoman Usher of the Receipt of the Exchequer.'

The ideal of a commercial marketplace of ideas took hold in France only in the nineteenth century, after royal and aristocratic patronage had been disrupted in the French Revolution and authorial rights had been given legal protection.[16] Patronage, as distinct from the ties of kin and friendship, may have emerged from feudal homage and royal favour but came to stand out and be visible in contrast to republican and commercial ideals of independence, whereas these Enlightenment ideals of independence took their point of departure from the reality that *les lumières*, and their British counterparts, depended on patronage. Patronage and Enlightenment ideals of intellectual autonomy are bound together in relationships, both avowed and denied, of attraction and repulsion. What Keith Wrightson writes of manual labourers applies equally to 'intellectual labourers': 'the very ubiquity of patronage and dependency in the hierarchy of domination and subordination placed a premium on the ideal of "independence."'[17]

What is patronage? Patronage, in Burke's definition, is 'the tribute which opulence owes to genius.'[18] Rousseau, as we shall see, strongly deprecated the opulent who did not pay due regard to genius. Although doubtless many people then as now felt that their genius did not receive the tribute owing to it, writers of the eighteenth century both claimed to be independent of patronage and lobbied hard to get it. Jonathan Swift warned the Earl of Oxford that 'if Genius and Learning be not encourag'd under your Lordship's Administration, you are the most inexcusable Person alive.'[19] Letitia Barbauld lamented that, in England in the second half of the eighteenth century, 'genius and learning obtain less personal notice than in other parts of Europe.'[20] Patronage, for eighteenth-century *gens de lettres*,[21] was the consideration and support owing to those who illuminated their age.

The age of Enlightenment, as Immanuel Kant put it, was the age of dawning intellectual autonomy, of men learning to think for themselves without the guidance of priests or spiritual advisers; it was also, Kant dutifully observed, the age of Frederick the Great.[22] In *What Is Enlightenment?* – written after the American Revolution but before the French Revolution – Kant indicated that philosophy flourished more in monarchies than in republics. Moreover, Kant defined Enlightenment as daring to think for oneself in a work that may have been commissioned by, or followed the conceptual framework of, Frederick the Great's *Kultusminister*, Count Von Zedlitz, to whom Kant dedicated his *Critique of Pure Reason*.[23] The eighteenth-century republic of letters, dependent as it was on royal or aristocratic patronage, was a place of imaginary independence or, as Alexis de Tocqueville put it, 'a neutral terrain on which equality was established as a refuge. The man of letters and the great lord met without affectation or fear, and one saw the reign, away from the real world, of a sort of imaginary democracy ...'[24] The Enlightenment ideal was less equality or democracy than independence or intellectual autonomy. As Voltaire wrote, 'it is not inequality which is the real evil, it is dependence.'[25] Enlightenment, as we shall see, was essentially plebeian talent serving royal and aristocratic patrons while professing intellectual independence. England did not have an Enlightenment as France and Scotland did, because, following the English Civil War in the mid-seventeenth century, plebeians were eliminated from the intellectual culture of eighteenth-century England.

This study aims to situate the ideal of independent thought within a context of an expanding middle-class readership, the self-assertion of a secular priesthood, and the Enlightenment's challenge to the monopoly of ecclesiastical 'livings,' or what Paul Bénichou has called the consecration of the writer.[26] Yet the eighteenth century was a period when, as Roger Chartier writes, 'the market for books could not ensure economic independence and when the only recourse for authors without a title, benefice or official post was the protection of the monarch or some other high-placed patron.'[27] The literature of the eighteenth century is to be understood in terms of the conditions of patronal production and consumption. Terry Eagleton argues that: 'every literary text is built out of a sense of its potential audience, including an image of whom it is written *for*: every work ... intimates in its very gesture the kind of "addressee" it anticipates. "Consumption," in literary as in any other kind of production, is part of the process of production itself.'[28] The production of enlightened ideas in the eighteenth century aimed at both the luxury consumption of aristocratic and royal patrons and the 'mass' consumption of common readers. Roger Emerson insists that: 'every Enlightenment depended upon the patronage of the great both to secure places for its members and to insure a hearing for their views. The Enlightenments ... took their shape and orientation from what patrons were willing to countenance.'[29] That Enlightenments were conditioned by what patrons countenanced does not imply that patrons were a conservative drag on the radical mobility of thought. Various patrons, such as the first Earl of Shaftesbury and the Earl of Shelburne, were less conservative than their clients, John Locke and Jeremy Bentham; the liberality of the patrons contributed to the liberalization of their clients.

This study will follow Chartier's suggestion that intellectual production is a collective project, more like the making of a movie (where the director has to cope with actors, producers, and an anticipated audience) than the work of an isolated individual, the *auteur* as Robinson Crusoe constructing his world on a desert island.[30] If the author is like a director, I wish to give especial deference to the producers of the Enlightenment, Frederick and Catherine the Great, the French *salonnières* (Mme de Tencin, Mme du Deffand, Mme Geoffrin, and others), Chrétien-Guillaume de Malesherbes (the liberal head of the 'book police'), the 3rd Duke of Argyll (the chief orchestrator of the Scottish Enlightenment), and Lord Shelburne (the patron of what might be called the radical Enlightenment in England). To cite the greatest of English thinkers, Thomas Hobbes: 'The honour of great persons, is to be valued for their beneficence, and the aids they give to men of inferior rank, or not at all.'[31] If, as Samuel Johnson thought, the chief glory of a people arises from its authors, that glory is to be shared with the patrons of the authors who comprised the Enlightenment.

Frederick wrote, in the French that Voltaire taught him, that German literature will flower when it is properly patronized. Towards the conclusion of his *De la Littérature Allemande*, he declared: 'Let us have some Medicis, and we will have seen the blossoming of German geniuses. Augustuses make Virgils.'[32] Frederick's suggestion that patrons can create geniuses is the opposite of Hume's claim, in 'Rise of the Arts and Sciences,' that government support for the arts and sciences is pointless because it will not result in works of genius.[33] The point of my book is to demonstrate the illusionary character of Hume's position. Hume enjoyed aristocratic patronage and, through the efforts of General St Clair, General Conway, and Lord Hertford, also received government patronage posts and pensions. Moreover, as we shall see, Hume was aggrieved that the 3rd Duke of Argyll did not secure him a university post, as Argyll did for virtually every other member of the Scottish Enlightenment. Certainly, Hume was not blind to the importance of patronage in eighteenth-century Britain. He asserted, in 'The British Government,' that the balance of power in a country rests not simply on its property but on the property made available for patronage: 'a man possessed of 100,000£ a year, if he has any generosity or any cunning, may create a great dependence by obligations, and still greater by expectations.' Hume added: 'The wealth of the MEDICI made them masters of FLORENCE; though, it is probable, it was not considerable, compared to the united property of that opulent republic.'[34]

However, despite his historical awareness of the power of patronage and despite his own experience, Hume maintained his self-image as an independent man of letters earning his living in the marketplace of ideas.

My aim is to compare the patterns of patronage in eighteenth-century England, France, and Scotland as well as the institutions through which enlightenment was diffused, the free press and the Church of England, the royal academies and the aristocratic salons in France, and the aristocratic patronage of Scottish universities. Chartier's view that 'the university as an institution did not enjoy a high reputation with Enlightenment thinkers'[35] was far truer for England and France than it was for Scotland or Germany.

Patronage of the arts and letters has been much more studied than patronage of philosophy. Perhaps, as Viscount Morley suggested in his study of Voltaire, the decorative arts are more suitable candidates for patronage than serious matters, like politics and philosophy. Morley wrote: 'In so far as we consider literature to be one of the purely decorative arts, there can be no harm in this patronage of its most successful, that is its most pleasing, professors by the political minister; but the more closely literature approaches to being an organ of serious things, a truly spiritual power, the more danger there is likely to be in making it a path to temporal station of emolument.'[36] This study will not accept Morley's sharp distinction between pleasing literature, which should be patronized, and serious literature, which should not. Nor will it accept Morley's fear that government patronage of philosophy and scholarship threatens the independence of thought, without balancing the alternative for those without independent means – aristocratic patronage in the eighteenth century and corporate sponsorship today.

Jeremy Boissevain's study of patronage refers to the bias of governmentally funded research; since most researchers 'are generally poorly paid academics who need large sums of money to do research, it would have been surprising if they had bit the hand that fed them.'[37] Personally, I am indeed grateful to the Social Sciences and Humanities Research Council of Canada for the funding to do research on patronage in the eighteenth century. In this connection, I should caution readers that I champion the state's role against a Smithian marketplace of ideas, and some may think that principle and interest coincide in the gratitude I display to my patron. In any case, the model of a free marketplace of ideas, or reliance on competition of commercial presses, may foster conservative or uncritical ideas, ideas that conform to the expectations of readers and advertisers. Samuel Johnson, one of the heroes in my narrative, was an exemplary product of the free commercial press in England but not an Enlightenment figure. This book espouses Michel Foucault's refusal to accept the 'authoritarian alternative' of being for or against the Enlightenment and his suggestion that 'we must try to proceed with the analysis of ourselves as beings who are historically determined, to a certain extent, by the Enlightenment.'[38] This study of patronage and philosophy is a history of the present.

State support for the arts was a central feature of democratic Athens. (Socrates appeared to claim an equal right for philosophy in his *Apology* after the jury had found him guilty of impiety and corrupting youth.) All citizens had a right to attend theatrical spectacles, and the treasurer of the theoric fund was such an important office that it was not filled by lot as was the norm in democratic Athens.[39] Military officers, the superintendent of springs, and the treasurer of the theoric fund were the only elected magistracies; drama, water, and military defence were too vital to be left to chance. I strongly endorse Pierre Bourdieu's concern with the threat to artistic and academic freedom when government cutbacks in the arts and education leave artists and researchers dependent on corporate patronage. Bourdieu writes:

> Research activities, in art as well as science, need the state to exist. To the extent that, *grosso modo*, the value of works is negatively correlated with the size of the market, cultural businesses can only exist and subsist thanks to public funds. Cultural radio stations or television channels, museums, all the institutions that offer 'high culture,' as the *neocons* say, exist only by virtue of public funds – that is, as exceptions to the law of the market made possible by the action of the state, which alone is in a position to assure the existence of a culture without a market. We cannot leave cultural production to the risks of the marketplace or the whims of a wealthy patron.[40]

The eighteenth-century Enlightenment flourished from the competition between the royal patronage of the academies and the aristocratic patronage of the salons. The contemporary form of royal patronage is government support for the arts and sciences, and aristocratic patronage finds its modern parallel in corporate sponsorship of thought and research. The University of Toronto is a privileged site from which to reflect on patronage since governments have withdrawn support for education and corporations have moved in to fill the vacuum. Voltaire and Samuel Johnson, as we shall see, thought royal patronage essential to avoid demeaning dependence on aristocrats, while Rousseau saw royal patronage as fostering servility but accepted the protection of the most blue-blooded of the French aristocracy. Today, the closest approximation to the Enlightenment ideal of independent thought is multiple dependencies, or a variety of patronage opportunities upon which the thinker or scholar can depend. Though complete dependence on the state impaired Soviet intellectuals' ability to live up to the Enlightenment ideal, the diminution of state support for thought and scholarship is most likely to foster not intellectual autonomy but 'corporation men' and their mirror opposites, the mindless followers of an anti-capitalist religious creed.

1 Patronage of Philosophy

Philosophers of the eighteenth century often looked to Socrates as a model of how the philosophic life was to be lived. What is more remarkable is the high regard that philosophers of the eighteenth century had for Seneca, who has not had the esteem of philosophers in centuries before and since,[1] as Socrates had and has. Our study of the conditions of the philosophical life will begin with Socrates and then move on to Seneca's account of the life of Socrates. Seneca's account is contained in *De Benefiis*, a philosophic justification of patronage, written by a client of a royal patron. Diderot, also a recipient of royal patronage, provided the only extensive justification of patronage in the eighteenth century in his accounts of the life of Seneca, which we shall examine in detail in chapter 3.

Socrates was the noblest saint in the philosophic calendar. We know little about him, except what we glean from Aristophanes, Plato, and Xenophon. The question of Socrates, for Friedrich Nietzsche, was how the plebeian Socrates waylaid the patrician Plato from a noble to a base view of life.[2] For Leo Strauss, the fundamental question of Socratic teaching was how to disguise impious thought from the waspish vengeance of the pious masses or 'moral majority.'[3] Neither Nietzsche nor Strauss asked the Marxist question: How did Socrates subsist? Our question is: under what conditions can the philosophic life be lived?

This study of the patronage of Enlightenment attempts to illuminate age-old questions about the relationship of knowledge and power, of thought and wealth. Marx and Engels provided a sociology of knowledge, contending that the dominant ideas in any age reflected the interests of the socially dominant class. I intend to provide a social history of knowledge without the Marxist simplification that thinkers, as leisured or detached from material production, are members of the ruling class. The Marxist position was presented more than two millennia before by the sophist Thrasymachus. In Plato's *Republic*, Thrasymachus asserts that ideas of justice are the idealized expression of the interests of the rulers who justify their dominance in their moral and legal codes. Socrates responds by questioning whether the rulers are infallible or omniscient. If the rulers do not know what their interests are, as well as how they can be satisfied at the expense of the ruled, there is no reason why dominant ideas of justice would in fact correspond to the interests of the ruling class. The Marxist position is also vulnerable to the Socratic challenge. If the ruling class is subject to ideological illusions, its members cannot know their long-term interests and the means to preserve their social dominance. To know the conditions of their social dominance, their relations to subaltern classes, and the means to secure class victory requires the science of society – namely, Marxism – a science not possessed by ideologists of the ruling class.

Thus, the Marxist sociology of knowledge is caught between its polar opposites of science and ideology. If ideology is 'false consciousness', it cannot also truly reflect the interests of the socially dominant class. Thrasymachus and Marx could have said that prevailing ideas of justice correspond roughly to the apparent interests of the ruling classes, but their profession of knowledge or science stood in the way; both were committed to a distinction between opinions about justice (ideologies in Marx's terminology) and knowledge or science.

Socrates' 'refutation' of Thrasymachus' position turns on the Platonic bifurcation of philosophy and sophistry. The philosopher, Socrates, questions the sophist, Thrasymachus, from the horizons of the latter, a professional teacher, one who professes to know and to teach virtue and one who does so for money not love. After Thrasymachus says that real rulers (like real teachers) do not make blunders and enact laws that do not promote their real interests, Socrates assesses the real ruler as a professional, one who is proud of his technical skill and also has an interest in being paid for his skill. Socrates' distinction between the exercise of a skill and the rewards extraneous to its application – the doctor cures his patients and also gets a fee, the ship captain steers the cargo and crew to a safe port and then gets paid – enables him to say that the real ruler cares for the ruled and then gets rewards in the form of money or honour. The basest men rule for money, the honourable for honour, and the noblest rule (and teach) to prevent inferiors from exploiting or corrupting those subject to their rule or teaching. The sophist Thrasymachus could, unchecked by the philosopher Socrates, undermine the aristocratic ethos that one should know one's proper place in relation to superiors and inferiors, subverting justice as the right relationship between classes in the state and the rational and irrational elements of the soul.

If Thrasymachus is a professional, Plato's Socrates is an amateur; he engages in dialectical intercourse for love not money. Thrasymachus, the sophist, is a whore; as the Xenophantic Socrates says, 'those who sell their wisdom for money, to any that will buy, men call sophists, or, as it were, prostitutors of wisdom.'[4] Philosophers, according to Xenophon, are more like courtesans, who make friends, rather than whores, who sell themselves to anyone with money. As the courtesan Theodota says to Socrates (*Memorabilia*, III.xi.4), 'if anyone is my friend and is willing to benefit me, he is my means of subsistence.' Thomas Pangle claims that 'Socrates ... depends on the generosity of others for support and thereby lives a life of freedom from business.'[5] The Xenophantic Socrates (*Memorabilia*, I.ii.6–8) states that the reason he did not take a fee for his conversation is that he remained free, whereas those who took money for their dialectical intercourse 'must of necessity hold discussions with those from whom they received pay.' Rather than being wage slaves or whores, philosophers take part in a gift economy where they give their teaching without pay and receive 'the greatest gratitude towards his greatest benefactor.' Seneca, whose work *On Benefits* is the fullest account of a gift or patronage economy yet written, asserted that Socrates received gifts from rich friends and instilled competition among his friends to see who could benefit Socrates most handsomely (I.viii.1.2). Diderot, in his *Essai sur la vie de Sénèque*, asserted that Socrates received gifts from friends in proportion to their wealth.[6] Following a tradition of eighteenth-century interpretations of the lives of philosophers, Hegel asserted that Crito 'defrayed the cost of Socrates' instruction by masters in all the arts.'[7]

However, the original sources for Socrates's life – Aristophanes, Plato, and Xenophon – are neither clear nor consistent about Socrates' means of subsistence and education. Socrates was the son of a stonemason and a midwife, the latter an occupation for women of humble social origins. Socrates was said to have received an inheritance from his father, rather modest or handsome depending on the source, may or may not have practised his father's craft of masonry, and fought as a hoplite, a station between the aristocratic cavalry and the plebeian light infantry. Although we can infer that Socrates was middle class, we do not know the source of the income with which he outfitted himself in the heavy infantry. In Aristophanes' *The Clouds*, Socrates is presented as a sophist who teaches forensic rhetoric for pay. This view of Socrates as a sophist was flatly denied by both Xenophon and Plato. But Kenneth Dover asks: 'Do we suppose that Aristophanes saw any difference between the fees which Kallias paid to Protagorus and the friendship, patronage, and hospitality which Alkibiades made available to Socrates?'[8]

In Plato's *Apology* (31c), Socrates says that he is poor because he has never accepted fees for his teaching. He has not done so because 'real wisdom is the property of God' and 'my service to God has reduced me to extreme poverty' (23a–c). On account of his poverty, Socrates' rich friends – 'Plato here, and Crito and Critobulus and Apollodorus' – offer to pay a handsome fine of thirty *minae* as an alternative to the death penalty after the jury of Athenian citizens judged Socrates guilty of impiety and corrupting youth (38b). Yet Socrates had antagonized the jurors by claiming 'free maintenance by the state' as the appropriate payment for his philosophizing (37a), and thus the death penalty was chosen rather than the fine offered by his rich friends. Since state pay for public office supplanted aristocratic patronage of political clients in the 5th century BC,[9] Socrates may have been demanding something akin to state support for philosophers, an early form of tenured professorship or an alternative to dependence on the wealthy. Socrates says that he never chased after wealth, but the sons of the wealthy 'have deliberately attached themselves to me' (23c). When Diogenes was taunted with the question why philosophers followed rich men and rich men taunted philosophers, he responded: *'Because the one sort knew what they had need of, & the other did not.'*[10] Plato's account of wealthy men following Socrates differs from Diogenes' retort in that the latter recognized that poor men have need of wealth, while Plato, more the exception than the rule, was independently wealthy and ignored the reality for most thinkers – namely, that they need wealth for the leisure to think. Plato emphasized the nobility of Socrates' poverty and contrasted it with the ignobility of the sophists.

If Aristophanes, Xenophon, and Plato disagreed on the source of Socrates' income, they agreed that sophists, like prostitutes, were shameful. By contrast, Frances Berenson adopts the perspective of Socrates' wife, Xanthippe, and inverts the classical view of the greater dignity of philosophy to sophistry: 'He preferred to accept gifts, like charity, from his friends, rather than earn some money to support his wife with dignity.'[11] Perhaps, indeed, the time has come to challenge the accepted dichotomy between philosophers and sophists as inappropriate to Socrates' time, just as it is to ours.

If the Xenophantic Socrates is more a courtesan free to choose her wealthy friends rather than a sophist-whore, he also freely gave of himself to the common people from whence he came (*Memorabilia*, I.ii.59–60): 'He never required payment for his communication from any one, but imparted to everyone in abundance from his stores.' Plato adds to this portrait of Socrates as promiscuous with his favours. In *Euthyphro* (3d), Socrates says: 'I pour out all I have to everyone, and not merely without pay – nay, rather, glad to offer something if it would induce someone to hear me.'[12] We can see this contrast between the loving and giving Socrates and the sophists who will have intellectual intercourse only for money. However, we may not realize that Socrates' entire argument with Thrasymachus breaks down if ruling, like teaching, can be construed as a labour of love, rather than a skilled profession (the application of which is rewarded by money). If rulers were conceived to have Socrates' superabundant gift-giving quality, the crucial distinction between the exercise of a skill and rewards external to its application would not hold. Thrasymachus' position that ideas of justice correspond to the interests of the ruling class is defeated not refuted, and defeated precisely by likening rulers to Thrasymachus – skilled professionals proud of the exercise of their craft but motivated by money and honour. Plato seems to recognize that Thrasymachus was not logically refuted when Glaucon says that Thrasymachus is like a snake which Socrates has charmed into submission (*Republic* 358b). The serpentine wisdom that justice is the interest of the powerful may have been rendered dormant but it remains alive.

What is at stake in the banal discussion about Socrates' means of subsistence? I wish to emphasize the vulnerability of thinkers in a different way than Leo Strauss has suggested. Basing his argument on his reflections on the life of Socrates, Strauss writes that thinkers are vulnerable to popular religious prejudices. He advances the thesis that readers must take into account the climate of religious persecution and must carefully discern the real intention of the writer beneath the surface of his writing. If Strauss is correct in drawing our attention to the need of thinkers for protection from popular prejudice, he is perhaps insufficiently attentive to thinkers' need for economic protection and its ramifications. Before Socrates, Anaxagoras was charged with impiety and depended on his patron, Pericles, for political protection. But the cry of Anaxagoras to his patron was more elemental; according to Plutarch, Anaxagoras exclaimed: 'Ah Pericles! Those, that have need of a lamp, must take care to supply it with oil.'[13] Enlightenment is the process of converting oil into light.

The Teaching of Virtue, or the Uniting of Theory to Practice

The eighteenth-century Enlightenment turned the fundamental Platonic question about whether virtue is teachable into a program of action, a strategy to educate public opinion and improve public mores. The question – whether or not virtue is teachable – presents moral philosophers with a dilemma. If virtue is teachable, then one should be able to point to people improved by philosophers (as Xenophon and Plato did with Socrates, after Athenian jurors found that Socrates had corrupted youth). But philosophers may not wish to be judged by the fruits of their teaching, if Alcibiades, Dionysius, Alexander, and Nero are held to be the products of the teaching of Socrates, Plato, Aristotle, and Seneca. On the other hand, if they take the position that virtue is not teachable, then, it might be said, philosophy is useless, at best a hobby for idle persons. One could avoid the dilemma by claiming that sophistic teaching does not instill virtue but that philosophers, disciplined by a lengthy education and illuminated by the fundamental knowledge essential for successful practice, can improve people by their teaching. However, philosophers have not been notably successful in imparting virtue to their pupils. Plato's education of the Syracusean tyrant, Dionysius, was a notable failure; Aristotle's connection to the tyrant Hermias was questionable and Aristotle's pupil, Alexander the Great, seemed to have imbibed a Machiavellian ethos of world conquest rather than the Aristotelian teaching on the virtues of the good citizen and the good man; and Seneca, as tutor and adviser to Nero, presents an archetypical case of the relationship between philosophy and political power. Those of us shocked by a thinker of Heidegger's stature serving Hitler may reflect on the long tradition of philosophy serving tyranny. Barry Strauss argues that ancient and contemporary tyrants patronized artists, citing many poets, dramatists, sculptors, and architects drawn to the Syracusean court (but ignoring Plato's, Aristotle's, and Xenophon's relations with tyrants) and the poets, composers, conductors, architects, and actors who did not emigrate from Hitler's Germany (but ignored Heidegger). Strauss's Rousseauan view that 'artists have not only survived in unfree societies, but have sometimes emigrated from a free republic to a tyranny in order to secure the patronage of a tyrant' is one-sided and questionable.[14]

Francis Bacon deprecated Seneca as a 'Trencher Philosopher' (one who served and supped with the great) and moralized that his fortune was not 'a true or worthy end of [a philosopher's] being and ordainment.'[15] Hegel thought Seneca a moralistic rhetorician or sermonizer rather than a philosopher or speculative thinker, a man who corrupted the truth of Stoicism that happiness depends on virtue not fortune, on internal character not external circumstance, by 'his allowing Nero to give him wealth untold, and also the fact that he had Nero as his pupil.'[16] Hegel ignored Seneca's contribution to the central category of his thought – the notion of the will.[17] Hegel also criticized Bacon on the same grounds that Bacon criticized Seneca – namely, that he was an ungrateful and corrupt toady.[18] But, if one eliminates from the history of philosophy all thinkers who kowtowed to power, or were corrupted by wealth, one would drastically thin out the ranks of philosophers. Hegel's criticism of Seneca and Bacon is situated from the comfort of an academic chair. The German, like the Scottish Enlightenment, and unlike the English and French Enlightenment, was centred in the universities. We tenured professors who look back with scorn at the careers of those philosophers who catered to the wealthy and powerful insufficiently consider the condition of those philosophers who are not sheltered economically and politically within academic walls. Moreover, we shall see in our study of the Scottish Enlightenment, patronage operates within as without academic settings.

Seneca's *De Benefiis* was often translated into English and French, and numerous editions and reprintings of the arts of graceful giving, graceful receiving, and graceful requiting were published in the eighteenth century. These three graces made the eighteenth-century world go around. In the gift economy of patronage, liberality is the greatest virtue and ingratitude the greatest vice. Those egalitarians, like Hobbes and Rousseau, who thought justice the greatest virtue and injustice the greatest vice, were condemned by their contemporaries for ingratitude to their benefactors. Seneca was an enormously important source of eighteenth-century thought. La Mettrie, Lagrange, Rousseau, D'Holbach, and Hume shared Diderot's admiration for Seneca.

Yet, if thinkers of the eighteenth century strongly admired Seneca as a man and thinker, they were embarrassed by the results of his education of Nero. The *philosophes* strongly held that virtue was educable, particularly if the educators were backed up by legal enforcement. Diderot himself was appointed by his patron, Catherine the Great, as her educator, as Voltaire had been appointed the king's tutor by Frederick the Great. Enlightened thinkers courted the great with the hope that their teaching might have practical effect; powerful princes or aristocrats could put into effect enlightened reforms. Indeed, Catherine and Frederick generously supported Voltaire's campaign against the persecution of the Calas family, the great infamy that *les philosophes* wished to crush. Samuel Bentham designed the Panoptikon – a prison workhouse whose inmates were to be rehabilitated through constant surveillance – for Catherine the Great and his brother, Jeremy, sought to use Lord Shelburne's influence to promote Samuel's project for various purposes in England. Members of the radical Enlightenment in England, such as Richard Price and Joseph Priestley, saw Shelburne as patron for Price's scheme of reducing the national debt, for funding Priestley's chemical experiments, and for relieving religious dissenters.

The *lumières* understood themselves to be the educators of humanity. Diderot wrote: 'Every writer of genius is born magistrate of his country. He should enlighten it, if he can. His right is his talent.'[19] Indeed, philosophers are not the direct educators of the people but must use the powerful to initiate progressive reforms. In his entry 'Encyclopédie' in the *Encyclopédie*, Diderot wrote that 'the general mass of men are not so made that they can either promote or understand this forward march of the human spirit.'[20] Philosophers must use the powerful to exert a positive impact on the general mass of men. Powerful princes fed this illusion; as we shall see, Frederick the Great wrote to various philosophers offering to serve philosophy and put their theories into practice. Voltaire wished to use powerful monarchs for his project of de-Christianizing the ruling classes of Europe.[21] Philosophy, for Voltaire, is a weapon for action; unlike the dreamy theoretician Rousseau, who 'only writes for the sake of writing, I write in order to act.'[22] Voltaire thought that Montesquieu would have done better to advocate specific legal reforms rather than theorize about the basis of law.[23] In contrast to the republican theoreticians, Voltaire believed that autocrats had divine power to shape and perfect human character. In his *Épître à l'impératrice de Russie* (Catherine the Great), Voltaire wrote:

'Pierre était créateur, il a formé des hommes.
Tu formes des héros ... Ce sont les souverains
Qui font le charactère et les moeurs des humains.'[24]

One might argue that philosophers betray their mission when they
attempt to wed theory to practice, or when they are attracted to
political power; their vocation is as spectators not actors – their concern
is with seeing well, and with the means (whether lamps or mirrors) for
others to see well, not with acting as statesmen or councillors to kings.
Philosophers have no magical powers to make the rains come, can read
no astral signs or animal entrails, can impart no military know-how, no
organizational or administrative technique. However, philosophers
have usually been reluctant to espouse the position that their investiga-
tions are essentially harmless, their teaching remote from political
practice, incapable of doing great harm or great good.

Philosophers are drawn to regal or aristocratic patrons because they
need comfortable subsistence and leisure for the protracted engage-
ment of thinking, they may need political protectors to defend them
against repercussions or reactions to unconventional views, or they may
desire the assistance of the great to implement enlightened reforms.

Enlightenment and Its Patrons

My concern in the following investigation is to examine the conditions
and consequences of different forms of patronage in eighteenth-
century England, Scotland, and France. The approach of comparative
history often emphasizes differences, while Louis Namier's structural
biographies of eighteenth-century politicians emphasizes similarities. I
shall stress different national forms of patronage but also a common
feature of the Enlightenment, namely, the dependence of middle-class
thinkers on royal and aristocratic patronage. The eighteenth century is
particularly interesting for the student of patronage because of three
interrelated factors: first, the marked hostility of Enlightenment
towards the monopoly of 'livings' enjoyed by ecclesiastics; second, the
alleged displacement of aristocratic patronage of letters by a democratic print culture by the 1750s – D'Alembert's *Essai sur la société des
gens de lettres et des grands* and Johnson's letter to Lord Chesterfield are
hailed as manifestos of the modern author;[25] and third, the sanctifying

of the illusion of the independent author, the creative genius serving truth and humanity through his writings.

The idea of the Enlightenment is much contested and its content has become amorphous; in fact, it is in danger of signifying simply the thought of a specific period of time, the long eighteenth century. At the same time, the question of whether England had an Enlightenment comparable to the Enlightenments in France, Germany, and America has been much debated. British philosophers did not appear prominently in Ernst Cassirer's *The Philosophy of the Enlightenment* (1932) and no English philosopher after Locke appeared in Isaiah Berlin's *The Age of Enlightenment: The 18th Century Philosophers* (1963).[26] Two decades ago, John Pocock and Roy Porter wrote that England did not have an Enlightenment because it did not need one; that is, after the Glorious Revolution and the establishment of Lockeian philosophy, there was no infamy to be crushed and thus England stood as a beacon from which other nations could derive light.[27] Their view that England had no need of an Enlightenment has been supplanted by Pocock's more recent vision of Edward Gibbon as 'the English giant of the Enlightenment' and Porter's claim that the English were in the forefront of the Enlightenment.[28]

John Robertson writes that, 'encouraged by the national context approach to discover Enlightenment *even in England,* John Pocock and others have associated the Scots with the English in a common British Enlightenment.'[29] Porter's account of the English Enlightenment does not distinguish the English from the Scots and the Irish; his British Enlightenment smuggles in Scottish and Irish thinkers while also holding British and English to be interchangeable terms.[30] That Scotland had an Enlightenment is not under question. As Linda Colley notes in her analysis of forging the British nation, 'large numbers of people have heard of the Scottish Enlightenment, whereas comparatively few know or care that an English Enlightenment even took place ...'[31] Yet Porter's project of constructing an English/British Enlightenment encounters the problem, which we shall see in chapters 6 and 9, that the Scots and Irish did not think of themselves as English, nor were they so held by the English. David Hume wrote to Sir Gilbert Elliot: 'Am I, or are you, an Englishman? Will they allow us to be so? Do they not treat with Derision our Pretensions to that Name, with Hatred our just Pretensions to surpass & govern them?'[32]

The philosophic expression of English hostility to speculative thought, the fear of people 'too clever by half' or without a sound bottom, whose views are not based on experience, on the evidence of the senses, was provided by a Scot, David Hume, and an Irishman, Edmund Burke. The fullest account by an Englishman of scepticism with respect to speculative philosophy was provided by Samuel Johnson, who was neither a philosopher nor an Enlightenment thinker (and whom we shall examine in chapter 8). An interesting fact in Porter's account of the English Enlightenment is that five of the twelve epigraphs at the beginning of his work are from Samuel Johnson, and three of four epigraphs in chapter 4, 'Print Culture,' are also Johnson's. In the following account of national Enlightenments, Samuel Johnson will be an exemplar of England's free press, Denis Diderot of the patronage of Parisian salons, and Adam Smith of patronage in Scottish universities. If patronage of the Scottish Enlightenment was funnelled through the universities, the French had aristocratic salons that were distinct from British clubs; Johnson and Hume had to pay for their meals, whereas Diderot did not. The English had a freer and more vibrant press than did the French and Scots. The English could readily import light from abroad, while its universities became moribund. Oxford and Cambridge recruited students increasingly from the gentry and aristocracy, dramatically reducing the number of plebeian students, with the goal of producing clerics or 'squarsons' whose livings became increasingly commodious during the eighteenth century.[33] Johnson exemplifies the questionable character of the English Enlightenment: a bookish man who was too poor to afford more than one year at Oxford, who earned his living from the commercial press, but who was too friendly to 'priestcraft' to be comfortably lodged within the Enlightenment.

However, before addressing the question of whether or not the English had an Enlightenment, we must come to some understanding of the character of Enlightenment or Enlightenments, national or subnational, religious or secular. My comparative study of Enlightenment in France, Scotland, and England assumes that there is something to compare, and thus I follow Margaret Jacob, Anne Goldgar, Jonathan Israel, and others who insist on the international character of the Enlightenment.[34] My story with respect to the Enlightenment is that there are different national patterns of patronage, which help to explain national differences in their respective Enlightenments. I have presented the Enlightenment as a secularizing movement in the sense that membership in the republic of letters assumed primacy over citizenship in the Heavenly City, although many retained dual citizenship in both the republic of letters and the City of God; participants in Enlightenment aimed to undermine the authority of priests, looked with resentment at ecclesiastical 'livings,' and wished to replace religion with the authority of a philosophy friendly to scientific experiment and progress. They saw commerce as the vehicle to accelerate religious toleration or, in the case of Hume and *les philosophes*, scepticism and religious indifference. To be sure, Voltaire did not speak for the entire Enlightenment when he wrote to Frederick the Great on 3 August 1775 that his fellow philosophers 'do not dare yet to express themselves openly' but 'are undermining in secret the ancient palace of imposture, founded one thousand, seven hundred and seventy five years ago.'[35] Books on the Catholic Enlightenment, on Enlightenment within the Church of England, within the Popular Party of the Presbyterian Kirk, and on Samuel Johnson as an Enlightenment thinker have been written, contesting conceptions of the Enlightenment as anti-clerical.[36] I do not wish to challenge Brian Young's view that we should reject 'a relentlessly secularizing interpretation of "Enlightenment" based on Hume's "supposed intellectual superiority in eighteenth-century Britain."'[37] As Adam Smith noted, the best minds in England were drawn into the church by its attractive system of patronage, while the best minds of Scotland were attracted into the universities. Bishops Berkeley and Butler were the counterparts of Professors Smith and Millar. However, Young's view that Anglican Enlightenment located 'freedom of inquiry into philosophical and theological questions ... *within* a Christian framework'[38] is problematic, if philosophic freedom of inquiry were to transgress the Christian theological framework.

To be sure, philosophy and blasphemy are not synonymous terms.[39] Indeed, the freethinkers John Toland, Matthew Tindal, and Anthony Collins, often considered stalwarts of the English Enlightenment,[40] will not be considered at length because they are not of philosophical interest. Collins was a wealthy squire with a large library who read widely, wrote numerous anti-clerical works, and was quite widely read by eighteenth-century freethinkers, but he did not question the philosophical, moral, or political implications of his anti-clerical positions.[41] Tindal, who converted to Catholicism during the reign of James II in hopes of becoming warden of All Souls College, was, according to Jonathan Israel, 'not much of a thinker and practically devoid of originality.'[42] Robert Adams states that Toland and Tindal 'were lesser minds than most of Somers's other acquaintances.'[43] Toland, like

Locke, a protégé of Baron Somers and other Whig grandees, 'was read in King William's reign because readers *knew* his patrons, hence, sought to know the views that they wished made public.'[44] Robert Sullivan writes that Toland was more of a hired prizefighter than a scholar or philosopher: 'Toland was equally indifferent to whether the argument from the innocuousness of opinion or that from the sanctity of conscience carried the day for religious liberty.'[45] Toland recognized that the pursuit of truth can be waylaid by poverty, a condition he experienced for most of his life: 'To what sneaking equivocations, to what wretched shifts and subterfuges, are men of excellent endowments forc'd to have recourse thro human frailty, merely to escape disgrace or starving.'[46] Furthermore, Toland cannot be considered a jewel in the crown of English Enlightenment because he was Irish and could depend for support in his final years only on his fellow Irishman, Robert Viscount Molesworth.[47] Toland advocated the subordination of the Irish Catholics to Protestant landlords because their Popish superstition destined them to despotism,[48] and, like Collins and Tindal, he championed a hierarchical Whig order; all were intolerant of their intellectual adversaries and scorned religious limits to the power of the state.[49] Toland is more of interest to students of patronage than to students of philosophy.

In the preface to his *Dictionary*, Johnson asserted, with the calm authority of someone stating a fact, that 'the chief glory of every people arises from its authors ...' Diderot expressed the same thought with Gallic rhetoric: 'Ages without genius are despised. Men will continue to honor the nations where genius thrived.'[50] In accepting Johnson's and Diderot's proposition, I would add my view that philosophy provides the richest and most comprehensive account of experience. By linking philosophy and patronage, I do not intend to deprecate philosophy but rather to examine the conditions of its existence. The grandeur of philosophy does not depend on its historical effects, as if the glory of the French Enlightenment were to be considered its intellectual stimulus to the French revolution. Nor do I claim that the Scottish Enlightenment was great because of its contribution to a sense of Scottish identity or nationality. The converse is more plausible; Robert Darnton's 'high Enlightenment' tended to be more counter-revolutionary than the 'low Enlightenment,' and the enlightened Scottish beneficiaries of Whig patronage did not stand up for Charles Edward Stuart in 1745.[51] Since the French Enlightenment flourished from the competition between royal and aristocratic patronage of letters, and the Scottish Enlightenment was fuelled by government efforts to integrate Scotland into Britain and to purchase loyalty to the Hanovers over the Stuarts, the French Revolution and the integration of Scotland in Great Britain will appear more as the *eschatos* (conclusion) than as the *telos* (purpose) of Enlightenment.

Patronage is the relationship of patrician wealth to plebeian talent. An example was provided in Voltaire's *Lettres philosophiques* when he referred to the Earl of Ilay, who came across one of his boy gardeners reading Newton and subsequently paid for his education as a mathematician.[52] Voltaire did not know that the cultivated Ilay, as the 3rd Duke of Argyll, would become a leading architect of the Scottish Enlightenment and the greatest patron of philosophy in Britain. In addition to *noblesse oblige* or the obligations of the powerful and wealthy to the talented and needy, there is also the interest that the powerful have in supporting the intelligent. Not all patrons were as intelligent and cultivated as Barons Somers, Argyll, or Chrétien-Guillaume de Malesherbes. Samuel Johnson used a vivid image: 'Ignorance to a rich man, is like Fat to a Sick Sheep, it only serves to draw the Rooks about him.'[53] Amplifying Johnson's image with respect to the greatest patron of the English Enlightenment, Ann Holt writes: 'Unlike so many ill-educated persons of wealth and position, Shelburne tried to remedy his own lack of early education by making use of the information of others.'[54] In his stern attack on patronage, Jean D'Alembert said that the great 'are quite happy to be learned on condition that they can become so without trouble, and so wish to be able to judge a work of intelligence without hard study, in exchange for the benefits they promise to the author or for the friendship with which they think they honor him.'[55]

Patrons are not simply friends, nor simply employers, of their clients. Joseph Priestley was a paid employee of Lord Shelburne, Burke's great enemy, as Burke himself was of the Marquis of Rockingham. Price and Bentham did not receive any money from Shelburne, although they both received free food and lodging at Bowood and Shelburne got Bentham a job as tutor to the son of Lady Ashburton. Bentham received more psychic than material income from Shelburne. Bentham wrote: 'Lord Shelburne raised me from the bottomless pit of humiliation – he made me feel that I was something.'[56] Shelburne provided Bentham with connections to statesmen and jurists, French, British, and American thinkers, and his French translator, Dumont. Patron-client relationships were often referred to as friendships, but they were, and are, as Julian Pitt-Rivers puts it, 'lop-sided friendships.'[57] The 2nd Duke of Argyll wrote that his brother Ilay, later the 3rd Duke of Argyll, 'wants to make all his friends Tools of Walpole because he finds his ends in so doing ... My Brother Ilay prefers his Places to all other Considerations; friendship, Honour, Relationship, gratitude & Service to his Country Seem at present to have no weight with him.'[58] Friends as placemen or tools of Walpole were not, according to the 2nd Duke, real friends. The 3rd Duke's 'friends' included Carmichael, Hutcheson, Smith, Ferguson, Millar, and Stewart, all of whom Argyll appointed to their university positions.

If friendship is based on equality, patronage, like feudal homage, is predicated on social inequality. Thus, the homosocial British clubs and French *cercles* of the nineteenth century lacked the patron-client relationship of the eighteenth-century salon, which was usually presided over by a wealthy or aristocratic *salonnière*. Hierarchical relationships were generally deprecated by the radical Whigs John Trenchard and Thomas Gordon, who had no use for master-slave relationships or any other forms of hierarchy unregulated by law, however, patronage and paternal authority were something different – these were just and proper relationships. 'Patron and Client,' Trenchard and Gordon declared, are characterized by 'Protection and Allegiance, Benefaction and Gratitude, mutual Affection and mutual Assistance.'[59]

Sexual love may, like friendship, be associated with equality, but it also may, like patronage, be associated with inequality. In this study of patronage, I shall largely ignore the sexual dimension of the relationship between *patronne* and *philosophe*, however common it was, in order to highlight the relationship between protector and protégé. I will not, however, overlook gender. My analysis will follow Dena Goodman in her emphasis on the *patronnes* of Enlightenment; *les salonnières* protected philosophy in part because it provided women an opportunity for education otherwise denied them.[60] The eighteenth-century pairing of taste and genius was all too frequently gendered, with tasteful aristocratic *patronnes* supporting plebeian male geniuses.

The function of patrons or protectors varied in time and place, although, as the pioneering comparative historian Marc Bloch, writes: 'To seek a protector or to find satisfaction in being one – these are common to all ages.'[61] Linda Levy Peck argues that seventeenth-century 'deferential alliances were designed to bring reward to the client and continuing proof of power or standing to the patron.'[62] The satisfaction of being a patron consists in the sense of having the power to confer benefits or protect clients, or even in acquiring a property in their clients. James ('Hermes') Harris, the classicist and patron of Henry Fielding, Elizabeth Carter, Lord Monboddo and others, wrote the 4th Earl of Shaftesbury to congratulate him on being the patron of Handel, as if he had just acquired an exquisite piece of Dresden china.[63] Hume may or may not have felt himself to be the proud possessor of Rousseau when he acted as the latter's patron, but Rousseau certainly thought that Hume wanted to own him. On the other hand, Rousseau found satisfaction in the patronage of the Duc de Luxembourg and the Prince de Conti, as Diderot did with Catherine the Great and Voltaire with Catherine and Frederick the Great; one's status, as well as one's income, is enhanced by the greatness of one's patrons.

Patrons had a particularly important function as political protectors in eighteenth-century France. Samuel Johnson's *The Vanity of Human Wishes* locates the patron between want and the jail: 'There mark what ills the scholar's life assail\Toil, envy, want, the patron, and the jail.' Although Defoe and many Grub Street writers were jailed early in the century before the Jacobite threat waned, and Henry Fielding was muzzled by the Theatre Licencing Act, English writers were less threatened by state repression than French ones. Voltaire, Marmontel, Diderot, Morellet, and Linguet were jailed and many others were threatened with censorship, jail, exile, or worse. The Marquis d'Argenson, whom Rousseau praised so highly in *The Social Contract*, spirited the Abbé de Prades out of France when he faced prosecution. His brother, the Comte d'Argenson, kept Rousseau from jail during the controversy about the merits of French versus Italian music. Only the protection of Mme de Pompadour and the Duc de Choiseul saved Helvétius in 1758 after the publication of *De l'Esprit*. Voltaire referred to the Duc de Choiseul as his 'hero and protector' and Rousseau called Malesherbes, who devoted his talents and energies to saving the *Encylopédie*, his 'protector friend.' Rousseau thought his protectors – Malesherbes, the Duc et Duchesse de Luxembourg, the Prince de Conti, and so on – would be sufficient to stay prosecution for his *Nouvelle Héloise* and *Du Contrat* social. A patron provides some combination of protection, regard or recognition, connections, and income for his or her clients.

The philosophic anthropologist Ernest Gellner both emphasizes the social gulf between patrons and clients and provides a reason why thinkers of the Enlightenment rarely justified the patronage relationships through which they functioned as thinkers and writers: 'Patronage is unsymmetrical, involving inequality of power; it tends to form an extended system; to be long-term, or at least not reserved to a single transaction; to possess a single ethos; and, whilst not illegal or immoral, to stand outside the officially proclaimed formal morality of the society in question.' Gellner states that patronage 'always belongs to some *pays réel* which is ambiguously conscious of not being the *pays légal.*'[64] Patronage runs counter to norms of universality and impartiality. Burke metaphorically characterized God as 'the universal Patron, who in all things eminently favours and protects the race of man.'[65] For humans, all patronage is particular and personal, not universal. Patrons favour some over others; one is not a favourite if one's patron extends equal protection to others. A patron who favours everyone impartially favours no one. Unlike capitalist contracts or feudal homage, patronage does not have clearly defined terms of reciprocal exchange and is 'anchored only loosely in public law or community norms.'[66]

Several implications for our study of the patronage of Enlightenment flow from these definitions. Since patronage existed in opposition to public norms, it is expressed largely in a state of denial. No thinker sees himself or herself as an intellectual mercenary, hired hand, or proletarian. All thinkers of the Enlightenment prided themselves on their independence of thought even as most depended on powerful patrons for their livelihood. Curiously, thinkers or writers who depended least on patronage, such as Rousseau and Paine, wrote most candidly about the desirability of patronage, while those who loudly affirmed that the days of patronage were over, such as D'Alembert, Johnson, Hume, Smith, and Gibbon, enjoyed royal and aristocratic largesse.

Patronage is often equated with corruption.[67] Gibbon came close to doing just that when he referred to the establishment of peace within the fourth-century Christian church (and perhaps also within the eighteenth-century Church of England): 'Corruption, the most infallible symptom of constitutional liberty, was successfully practiced; honours, gifts and immunities were offered and accepted as the price of an episcopal vote ...'[68] For Burke and Rousseau, however, patronage is not corruption, but a relationship of duty between wealth and talent. Burke wrote to his patron, Earl Fitzwilliam: 'You will certainly so use the sacred trust of Patronage, as to show it is directed, not by humour of affection, but by public principles.'[69] The 3rd Duke of Argyll was performing the duties of a patron in overlooking the claims of friends and kin to advance the prospects of talented recruits to the Whig project of integrating Scotland within the United Kingdom. Patronage, which the 3rd Duke of Argyll wielded, was not nepotism, which the 2nd Duke of Argyll favoured; it was a discretionary relationship to strangers, not duties to family and kin. Burke's use of his position as postmaster general to get his son Richard a position in the Treasury was nepotism, not patronage, as was Franklin's providing jobs to all his kin when he served as postmaster general in America. Patronage is bounded by corruption or nepotism, on the one hand, and charity, on the other. Patronage is not charity to the talented and needy; the patron expects some unspecified service from the client.

An advertisement in the M*orning Herald* on Wednesday, 30 May 1798, headed PATRONAGE, illustrates some of the features of this relationship.

> A Military Gentleman, whose connections, though respectable, have it not at present in their power to promote his interest, hopes, through the medium of this advertisement, to meet with a Lady or Gentleman who may be inclined to make use of their influence in his favour. To any person so circumstanced he would behave with a liberality proportioned to the advantages he might expect to derive from their interest or introduction ... [although] it is impossible, in an advertisement, to state the nature of the services he may expect; but letters addressed to J. Williams, Esq. No 173, Piccadilly, will be attended to in the course of the next day, if possible.

It is not only the forum of an advertisement that prevents Williams from declaring what he will do if some lady or gentleman buys him an office in a regiment. His reticence is rather strategic: he is not offering to challenge an enemy of his patron to a duel if he is awarded an office of colonel, but simply declaring his desire to requite the benefit conferred upon him proportionately to the favour. Occasionally, clients are clear about what they will do for a favour conferred, as when Theophilius Field wrote to George Villiers, Duke of Buckingham, that if Buckingham appoints him to the bishopric of Ely or Bath and Wells, 'I will spend the remainder of my days in writing a history of your good deeds to me and others.'[70] But, generally, the quid pro quo is less clearly spelled out. Patronage is part of a gift economy, not a commercial exchange; it is bad form both to leave the price tags on the gifts exchanged and not to reciprocate as closely as one can to the value of the gift given. Gifts, as Marcel Mauss indicates, are like investments; one spends one's money at the right time to build up one's social capital for later: 'The form usually taken is that of the gift generously offered; but the accompanying behavior is formal pretence and social deception, while the transaction itself is based on obligation and economic self-interest.'[71]

Finally and most contentiously, as John Waterbury writes, 'cronyism, however, based on links between co-equals, is not patronage.'[72] Much of what went by the name of patronage in eighteenth-century England was cronyism, or an exchange of favours between the gently situated, and did not extend to the plebeian classes. Patron-client relationships, or relationships between social superiors and inferiors, were of a different order entirely and constituted genuine patronage. Nevertheless, patronage in common usage connoted 'cronyism' more than patron-client relationships. The 3rd Earl of Shaftesbury wrote that all political parties after the Glorious Revolution were ultimately moved by patronage; politicians are either 'in or out of court, that is in possession of the places, and afraid of losing their daily bread by not being servile enough, or that are out of places, and think, by crossing the court, and siding with good and popular things against it, to get into those places of profit and management.' Historians, such as John Brewer, following Namier's *The Structure of Politics at the Accession of George III and England in the Age of the American Revolution,* asserts that patronage was at the core of eighteenth-century British politics: 'Treasury appointments proliferated under the financial and administrative pressures of war; appointments in the armed forces were increasingly politicized; the diplomatic service, colonial administration and the church were all harnessed to the whig gravy-train. Walpole became a spider at the centre of an elaborate web of patronage which extended to every walk of administrative, political and social life ... [P]atronage was the bedrock of politics and the foundation of political stability.'[73] My contention, however, is that Enlightenment depends on plebeian 'genius' serving patrician 'taste' and thus England did not have an Enlightenment because it did not enlist plebeian energies in the construction of national culture and because the channels of intellectual patronage were monopolized by the Church of England. As late as the 1840s, 'Sir Robert Peel remarked that he had no way to reward achievements in science and scholarship except clerical preferment.'[74] England had cronyism not patronage, or patronage without patron-client relations; after the English Civil War, the aristocracy and crown did not patronize plebeians, and the clerical profession became sufficiently commodious to attract the 'squarsons,' or the younger sons of the gentry and even the aristocracy.

What is commonly called patronage in England was in fact an exchange of favours among the powerful and propertied and, after the opening decades of the century, did not extend to men of letters. As Samuel Johnson said: 'The second George was never an Augustus to learning or genius.'[75] Johnson's friend Oliver Goldsmith nostalgically wrote in mid-century: 'When the great Somers was at the helm, patronage was fashionable among our nobility.'[76] The author of *Letters concerning the Present State of England. Particularly Respecting the Politics, Arts, Manners and Literature of the times (1772)* stated that Lord Somers 'never neglected any opportunity of promoting and rewarding writers of merit.' Although the accession of George III led to the patronizing of Hume, Johnson, and others, royal and aristocratic patronage had waned since the time of Somers and the Earl of Oxford: 'Was an author, of twice the wit and parts of Swift, now to give himself the airs of that famous poet, with the ministers of state of these days, he would be turned out of doors; but the Oxford ministry, with all their faults, paid an attention to literature, which would be sufficient to cover a multitude of sins.'[77] During the reign of George II, the English republic of letters turned into a commercial marketplace, which could more cheaply import, rather than produce, ideas.

The decline of plebeian patronage is evident in the English universities. Lawrence Stone writes that, 'by 1750, fellowships were "rarely given to scholars of low condition, whatever be their merit," for they had become part of the expanding patronage system for younger sons of the squirearchy.'[78] Guy Fitch Lytle, in 'Patronage Patterns and Oxford Colleges,' calls patronage the system 'from the feudal era to the time of Jane Austen and beyond ... by which men, if they could, advanced. On the one hand, it was the working out in practice of the principles and rewards of hierarchy; on the other hand, it was the only counterbalance to hierarchical privilege for those whose ambition exceeded their birth.' Lytle adds that, 'the potential student and graduate needed a patron to select him for education, to pay for his way in the schools, to present him with his first job, and to guide him through his subsequent promotions.'[79] We might note that Stone and Lytle use patronage to mean patron-client relationships until the eighteenth century, while 'the expanding patronage system' of the eighteenth century refers to upper-class cronyism. When Bacon and Hobbes went to university, a majority of undergraduates from Oxford and Cambridge came from plebeian backgrounds (socially lower than Hobbes, who was the son of a poor parson) but, by 1810, less than 1 per cent of undergraduates did so.[80] Until the late seventeenth century, poor boys received an education from scholarships, living in halls, accepting the status of a 'battler' or servitor, or obtaining private patronage. To quote Stone again: 'Wealthy bishops, noblemen, and knights often paid for the able son of a poor tenant, partly to act as servant/companion for their own son in college, and partly with an eye to later use in administrative positions in the management of the household and estate.'[81] However, the conservative reaction to the English Civil War and the alleged role of over-educated and underemployed university graduates in fanning flames of discontent replaced patron-client relations with cronyism and eliminated the recruitment of plebeians into the political culture of eighteenth-century England.[82] Trenchard and Gordon maintained: 'There are few instances in which the Public has suffered more, than in breeding up Beggars to be what are called Scholars, from the Grave Pedant to the solemn Doctor, down to the humble Writer and Caster of Accounts.'[83] Universities were not sites of Enlightenment in England or in France. France had its aristocratic salons and royal academies through which *roturiers* enlightened French society.

The Royal Society of London was founded in 1662 to advance scientific knowledge, and it made a specific decision not 'to meddle with Divinity, Metaphysics, Moralls, Politics, Grammar, Rhetoric or Logic,'[84] that is, the subjects of interest to the French and Scottish Enlightenments. However, the English Royal Society differed from the French royal academies not just in its refusal to consider metaphysics, morals, and politics but also in its mode of recruiting members. Roger Hahn notes that: 'Colbert did not hesitate to exclude men of high social standing whose interest in science was superficial or tied to ends other than the advancement of knowledge.'[85] By contrast, the presidents of the English Royal Society, Sir Hans Sloane and Sir Joseph Banks, were held to be snobs, since most fellows of the Society were aristocrats.[86] Voltaire, an admirer of English manners, deprecated the English Royal Society because it was the preserve of wealthy amateurs, whereas 'in France, to be a member and pensioner of the Academy, it is not enough to be an amateur; one must be a scholar and contest the seat with rivals.'[87]

Patronage, in the sense of patron-client relations or the duties the rich owe to the talented poor, was defended by egalitarians, such as Rousseau, as the best way to mitigate social inequality.[88] Fierce opponents of patronage, such as Gordon Wood, admit that 'this system of personal influence did not necessarily scorn merit or discourage social mobility.' Wood cites the example of Benjamin Franklin's 'meteoric rise,' claiming that it was 'not simply his hard work, brilliance and character that moved him upward; most important was the ability to attract the attention of an influential patron,' such as governors Sir William Keith and William Burnet (son of the celebrated Whig bishop, Gilbert Burnet) in America and later the leading patron of the radical Enlightenment, Lord Shelburne. Generalizing on Franklin's life, Wood asserts that 'patronage was the basic means of social mobility in the eighteenth century ...'[89]

Adam Smith said that, 'before the invention of the art of printing,' scholars were beggars.[90] In the next chapter, we shall examine Smith's contention that print culture creates a democratic marketplace of ideas that removes the vulnerability of scholars and supplants the need for patronage. Was Smith more forward-looking than Rousseau, whose savage attack on civilized inequality contains a shameless pitch for patronage? Rousseau called out for a ten-year-funded research project: are there not, Rousseau asks, 'to be found two closely united men – rich, one in money and the other in genius, both loving glory and aspiring to immortality – one of whom would sacrifice twenty thousand pounds of his wealth and the other ten years of his life to a celebrated voyage around the world' to discover human nature?[91] Genius and money, Rousseau thought, rarely co-exist within a single individual. Plato notwithstanding, Rousseau believed that genius, that fire in the belly of the soul, is uncommon among the comfortably situated, particularly hereditary aristocrats. This study is located between Smith's historical claim that the art of printing makes patronage outdated and Rousseau's transhistorical claim that philosophers need patrons for the leisure to think.

2 Enlightenment and Print Culture

In writing that 'before the invention of the art of printing, a scholar and a beggar seem to have been terms very nearly synonymous,'[1] Adam Smith implied that a democratic print culture superseded the need for aristocratic and royal patronage and that scholars could thrive in a commercial marketplace of ideas. To be sure, Smith's *Theory of Moral Sentiments* and his *Wealth of Nations* sold very well, much better than the philosophical works of his friend, David Hume. However, the careers of both men relied heavily on aristocratic patronage. Smith's university position depended on the favour of the 3rd Duke of Argyll (who made 151 university appointments between 1724 and 1763, almost half of the appointments in Scottish universities in this period).[2] He supplemented his income as a professor by boarding and tutoring the brother of Lord Shelburne (who was also the patron of Franklin, Price, Priestley, and Bentham), and he left the university to take up a patronage position as commissioner of customs provided by the Duke of Buccleugh.

Smith often visited Voltaire while the patriarch of Ferney was writing and amassing wealth. Voltaire seemed to suggest that his enormous wealth flowed from his fluent pen, writing his banker, Jean Robert Tronchin, on 21 January 1761: 'I was born poor, I have devoted my life to a beggar's trade, that of scribbling on paper, that of Jean-Jacques Rousseau, and yet there I am with two castles, two pretty houses, 70,000 pounds annual income, 200,000 pounds of ready cash, and some oak leaves of royal bounty that I do not care to count.'[3] Yet, as we shall see, the bounty Voltaire received from royal and aristocratic patrons was more than honorific (oak leaves); his income owed far more to such bounty, and to his shrewd and unscrupulous investments, than to his scribbling like Jean-Jacques Rousseau. Following Smith's view that the age of print allows independence of patronage, Ernest Mossner argues: 'Hume was the first distinguished man of letters in Britain to make a modest fortune from literature alone.'[4] Since Voltaire made his fortune more from his investments and royal patronage than from his writing,[5] Mossner's claim, if true, should not be limited to Britain. But, in fact, Hume became wealthy and respectable from accepting a position as secretary to Lord Hertford and tutor to his son, Lord Beauchamp.[6] He indicated the reason for his acceptance of Hertford's offer in a letter to Smith of 9 August 1763: 'It wou'd be easy to prevent my acceptance from having the least Appearance of Dependence.' Hume did not elaborate in his letter on the appearance and the reality of dependence, or how he could keep up the appearance of independence. An invariable feature of all members of the Enlightenment is the desire to avoid the appearance of dependence. I shall return to the careers of Hume and Smith subsequently, but here I simply wish to make the point that men of the Enlightenment tended to see the free, commercial press as the means to a dignified, independent existence.

Lord Shelburne, the great patron of the radical Enlightenment in Britain, associated liberalism with freedom of the press and illiberalism with repression of press freedom. He extolled the 'new principles which have been making a slow but certain progress ever since the democracy of the press. Cardinal Wolsey, upon the first discovery of printing, told the clergy to be on their guard, for if they did not destroy the press the press would destroy them.'[7] Here Shelburne provided a clear statement of Enlightenment goals, namely, to clear away clerical obstacles to freedom of thought, and also a manifesto of the more progressive strand of the Enlightenment – the democratic mission of the free press.

Smith's and Shelburne's hypothesis that, prior to the invention of printing, men of letters had to depend on royal courts or aristocratic houses to earn a living is supported by many contemporary scholars. John Lough, in referring to medieval *jongleurs* and troubadours, asserts that before 'the invention of printing, the writer had to depend on the generosity of patrons.'[8] Bardic poets and minstrels were 'peddlers of glory' promising fame or immortality to their patrons.[9] Thorarin the Flatterer angered King Canute by writing too short an encomium on him, and Canute threatened to cut off his head unless he produced richer praise by next dinner. Thorarin rose to the challenge with the *Stretch-Song* on King Canute and was handsomely rewarded as a result.[10] Karl Julius Holzknecht writes that, before the age of print, the choice for 'a man of intellect or genius' was to find a billet within the church or to be a 'retained entertainer' at court.[11] Christine de Pisan earned a living from her pen by dedicating her poems and prose in flattering terms to the royalty and aristocracy of Europe.[12] Hermits or anchorites enjoyed high social prestige in their solitary confinement in praying for the souls of their medieval patrons.[13] Astrologers were a common feature of royal courts in the Middle Ages until the fifteenth century, when the printing press brought astrology to a larger audience and so enabled it to emerge from the universities and courts of medieval Europe.[14]

David Zaret elaborates on Shelburne's idea of a democratic print culture: 'Central to print culture is an alliance between commerce and controversy, forged by the interest of authors and stationers in producing texts for which public demand exists.'[15] Print proliferated in the Reformation and Counter-Reformation. Translation of the Bible into the vernacular stimulated readership and created a bull market in theology. Lucien Fevre and Henri-Jean Martin note that 'all Germany caught fire. Pamphlets filled with the thunder of violent prose came out on all sides.' While Luther's adversaries sold poorly, 'Luther, on the other hand, made the fortune of his printers.'[16] John Foxe, whose *Book of Martyrs* was a best-seller from the sixteenth to the nineteenth century, wrote: 'How many presses there be in the world, so many blockhouses there be against the high castle of St Angelo, so that either the pope must abolish knowledge and printing, or printing must at length root him out.'[17] Elizabeth Eisenstein ties together the Reformation with the Enlightenment: 'Condorcet agreed with Luther that Gutenberg's invention inaugurated a new epoch that ended the Dark Ages and Papal rule.' She adds:

New careers in printing shops were opened to sixteenth-century students and clerks who had previously found patronage in the church. Obscure young men such as Erasmus and Rabelais could rise in the world without staying in clerical orders. As a friendless young canon from Rotterdam, Erasmus avoided having to defer to his clerical superiors by taking advantage of the new forms of patronage extended after print. Hundreds of complementary copies given him by his printers were used by the clever author to fool hundreds of patrons into thinking of themselves as dedicatees and thus providing hundreds of pensions and favors in return. Erasmus thus showed how men of letters could be emancipated from client status – well before an author's copyright or royalties existed. By garnering favors and pensions from many different lords and ladies, he freed himself from being dependent on any single one and could use his considerable powers of persuasion to win support for causes that he himself held dear. Similar strategies were adopted by the philosophes. When their work came off the presses, Voltaire and Rousseau often made a point of having dozens of copies specially printed on fine 'papier de Holland' and sent to powerful personages who would assure them of their support and protection. 'Few people have made themselves so dependent in order to become independent' – the remark was not made about Erasmus but, by Goethe, about Voltaire.[18]

While Eisenstein refers to the survival of patronage, albeit modified by the rise of print culture, Peter Burke seems to think that democratic print culture superseded the age of clerical, royal, and aristocratic patronage: 'Erasmus ... was successful enough with his books to free himself from dependence on patrons.'[19] Burke's assessment is odd. For example, Erasmus's *The Education of a Christian Prince* is dedicated to the future Hapsburg emperor, Charles V, and includes the encomium, 'But you, noble Charles, are more blessed than Alexander, and will, we hope, surpass him equally in wisdom too.'[20] Had Erasmus's hopes been realized, he would have proved himself a better tutor than Aristotle. Erasmus counselled princes to avoid flatterers and reject adjectives such as 'the invincible,' but in his *Panegyric for Archduke Philip of Austria* he referred to Philip as an 'invincible prince,' a gesture for which he was well rewarded. He also sent the *Panegyric* through the bishop of Arras 'because you give wholly disinterested support for letters, and always act as a kind of Maecenas or father to all learned men.'[21] Erasmus's most faithful patron was William Warham, the archbishop of Canterbury, whom Erasmus called 'Primate of all England, and deservedly of the whole universe, if men were to be judged by their virtues' and 'my incomparable Maecenas.'[22] Erasmus did not enjoy a reputation as an independent man of letters among the men of the Enlightenment. Edward Gibbon referred to him as 'a parasite of all the great men of his time, he was neither ashamed to magnify their characters, by the lowest adulation, nor debase his own by the most impudent solicitations to obtain presents which very often he did not want.'[23] Gibbon thought that the age of independent authors arose only in his time; but, in his self-assessment as an independent man of letters, subsisting by his pen, he ignored the patronage of lords North and Sheffield. William Robertson, in the work that received the largest advance from booksellers in the eighteenth century and was dedicated to George III, 'a Monarch who is no less a judge than a patron of literary merit,' blamed Erasmus's failure to support the Protestant Reformation in part on 'his excessive deference for persons in high stations; his dread of losing the pensions and emoluments which their liberality had conferred upon him.'[24] In fact, however, print culture co-existed with patronage for centuries. Perhaps one might question Hume's and Smith's view that the free marketplace of ideas, stimulated by the invention of print technologies and facilitated by a commercial press, are the necessary and sufficient conditions for the development of scholarship and thought. Perhaps lives of scholarship and philosophy require, at all times and places, patronage of one form or another. In short, print culture did not supersede, but rather modified, authorial dependence upon patrons.

At the rosy dawn of Enlightenment, Francis Bacon explained the reason for patronage and the aversion of authors to acknowledging patrons. Flattery, Bacon asserted in *The Advancement of Learning*, a work dedicated to James I and generous in its praise of the king's intellectual virtues and writings, abases 'the price and estimation of Learning. Neither is the moderne dedications of Bookes and Writings, as to Patrons to be Commended: for that Bookes (such as are worthy of the name of Bookes) ought to have no Patrons, but Truth and Reason.'[25] However, most men of learning lack an independent income; they 'usually begin with little' and cannot enrich themselves quickly as others do since 'they convert not their labours chiefly to lucre and increase.' Hence, they must court and submit themselves to the rich and powerful. Such submission is not cowardice but prudence, or 'submissions to the occasion, and not to the person.' Thinking requires leisure, which for the most part can only be supplied by the rich and powerful.[26] Bacon thought the invention of printing was somewhat democratic because it 'communicateth Bookes to men of all fortunes'. But, if printing is democratic in the distribution of knowledge, it is patronal in its production; most scholars and scientists are not independently wealthy. Bacon's contemporary, Galileo, in the hope of devoting more of his time to research and less to teaching, obtained the patronage of the Medici family by dedicating *Sidereus nuncius* (1610) to Grand Duke Cosimo di Medici and offering to name some stars after the Medici family.[27]

The invention of printing altered the lives of writers by providing a wider readership for books but did not dissolve patron-client relationships in the republic of letters. Most books in the sixteenth century were theological or classical in content, and too expensive to be bought other than by the wealthy. Poems were printed in England from the 1550s but 'patronage was a social and financial necessity' for writers arranging to have their work printed. In accepting dedications, patrons not only rewarded writers directly but also conferred on them legitimacy and prestige, improving their marketability with purchasers at the bookstalls.[28] Martin Butler writes: 'Patronage might have been a desirable alternative to the compromises that had to be made in the literary market-place, but it was not free from dilemmas of its own. In order to maintain goodwill, the poet as client would have to make his social and political priorities acceptable to his patron, and thus he might well be involved in marginalizing any doubt he had about that which he was expected to praise.'[29] Similarly, John Lough asserts that a French poet of the sixteenth and seventeenth centuries acted 'as publicity manager for his patron, to avenge any insults to him by other writers and to attack his enemies.'[30] George Chapman suggested that he was giving good value as publicity agent to the Earl of Somerset for accepting patronage of *Batrochomyomachia*:

> This *Dedication* calls no Greatnes then,
> To patrone this Greatnes-creating Penn.

Shakespeare's career combined capitalist enterprise with royal and aristocratic patronage. Until Shakespeare established the Globe Theatre with his fellow actor and friend, Richard Burbage, and obtained a share in the profits, most theatre troops were patronized by Queen Elizabeth and leading aristocrats, such as the Earl of Leicester. Shakespeare earned about ten times as much as an actor than as a playwright (roughly £180 compared to £17) but also received about 130 pounds yearly from the sale of his poems. In the absence of copyright, he depended upon friendship with his printer, John Field, and the patronage of the Earl of Southampton, to whom Shakespeare dedicated his poems. James I proved an even more generous patron than Elizabeth, granting a royal licence to Shakespeare's troop and even supporting the actors when the Globe was closed because of the plague.[31] In like manner, Ben Jonson received a pension from James and was generously supported by various aristocrats, including the Duke of Newcastle.[32] While, in a sense, commerce had begun to replace aristocratic patronage in the theatre, with the major patrons being the paying audience (especially the upper-class patrons with the expensive seats), the commercial model does not explain how individuals secured patents, organized companies, and produced plays. During the Stuart period, Deborah C. Payne points out, the dramatic marketplace was 'an ascriptive-hierarchical system' from court to lord chamberlain to master of the revels to theatre managers; before the Civil War, aristocrats secured sporadic patronage for clients, and, afterwards, the patronage of Charles II and James II constituted the very infrastructure of the theatrical system.[33] William Godwin attributed the closing of theatres in 1642 not so much to Puritan assessments of their ungodliness – classical drama was acceptable since it was written for republicans – as to the monarchical and aristocratic doctrines presented in the Stuart theatre.[34]

In sixteenth-century France, according to François de La Croix du Maine, of the 3,000 learned men in the country, 'the greater part are employed in the service of your Majesty.'[35] Since the Concordat of 1516, the crown had at its disposal ecclesiastical patronage. In the seventeenth century, playwrights and poets were often rewarded with ecclesiastical positions, or sinecures and pensions from church revenues. Boileau and Racine were granted ecclesiastical positions, while Corneille received handsome rewards for 'grovelling' dedications to the rich and powerful, such as Cardinal Richelieu. The success of Molière's *Comédie Française* depended on his skills as a courtier soliciting royal favour and that of aristocratic patrons and hosts for his travelling troop of actors.[36] The market for books in France lagged behind that of England; Montaigne, in the sixteenth century, accepted the money offered him by the publisher of *Essais*, but he did not need payment or patronage; the professional writer in France did not emerge until two centuries later.[37] Voltaire's father told him early in the eighteenth century: 'Literature is the profession of a man who wishes to be useless to society, a burden to his relatives, and to die of hunger.'[38] Only in nineteenth-century France were the rights of the author protected by law from publishers and theatre managers and writers could make money from the productions of their pens.[39]

In England, it was only in the 1640s that print – primarily, pamphlets, ballads, and handbills – reached large numbers of readers. During the Restoration, unlicensed publications were curtailed, but they mushroomed during the Exclusion crisis. While royal patronage was limited after the Glorious Revolution, Whig magnates, through an expanding civil list and patronage positions in the civil service, provided livings for an increasing number of men of letters.[40] But perhaps the most important element of the transition from aristocratic to bourgeois patronage was publication by prior subscription, a means for the bookseller-printers to share financial responsibility and to assess consumer demand. In England, from 1617, publication by subscribers 'was one aspect of the general transformation from individual patronage by the few into more general public support.'[41] To be sure, aristocrats were widely sought after to head the masthead of subscribers. Aristocratic subscribers bought 653 copies of Pope's translation of Homer's *Iliad* at six guineas a set and, a decade later, 847 copies of Pope's translation of Homer's *Odyssey*, gaining Pope the enormous sum of 9,000 guineas and indicating to non-aristocratic customers that Pope was quality.[42] Samuel Johnson lacked his usual acuity when he said, 'How foolish was it in Pope to give all his friendship to Lords.'[43] For his part, Alexander Pope thought himself to be the first writer to live independently of patronage. He wrote Lord Carteret on 16 February 1723: 'I take my self to be the only Scribler of my Time, of any degree of distinction, who never receiv'd any places from the Establishment, any Pension from a Court, or any Presents from a Ministry.'[44] Pope's subscription lists, however, suggest that he replaced individual with collective patronage by the aristocracy. Similarly, Voltaire's *La Henriade* appeared in 1728 with 343 subscribers; almost half of the number who purchased multiple copies were English peers. Steele's *Tatler* and Addison and Steele's *Spectator* had a high percentage of aristocratic and genteel subscribers. As brokers of Whig patronage, Addison and Steele promoted the popularity of Locke in particular and English experimental philosophy in general.[45] The powerful subscribers to Diderot's and D'Alembert's *Encyclopédie* prevented the government from banning its publication. The central factor in the resumption of publication of the Enlightenment's defining work was not authorial rights to freedom of expression but rather the property rights of aristocratic and opulent subscribers who had paid for a complete set of volumes.[46] Robert Dodsley, who published Johnson's *Dictionary* by subscription, was very disappointed by Johnson's refusal of Lord Chesterfield's belated offer of patronage because a dedication to Lord Chesterfield would, Dodsley thought, greatly increase sales. Subscription, John Brewer maintains, was a crucial tactic of the bourgeoisie, or middling sort, to liberate men from patron-client relationships: 'The author who wanted money to publish a book and the builder who sought capital for constructing houses no longer needed to go cap in hand to a patron or sponsor, but could launch a public subscription through the newspaper.'[47] However, in the first half of the eighteenth century, W.A. Speck notes, 'far from demonstrating the rise of a middle-class readership ... subscriptions to books document that a substantial section of the book trade was dominated by the upper classes of Augustan Britain.'[48]

Nevertheless, the market for books expanded throughout the eighteenth century, partly because booksellers sold expensive books in portions to attract the custom of less wealthy readers.[49] George Colman, writing in the *Connoisseur* of 14 February 1754, celebrated the progress of knowledge brought about by the commercial press: 'We can [not] suppose, that the history of *Thucydides* was retailed weekly in six-penny numbers; that *Seneca* dealt out his morality every Saturday; or that *Tulley* wrote speeches and philosophic disquisitions, whilst *Virgil* and Horace clubbed together to furnish the poetry for a Roman Magazine.'[50] Circulating libraries arose in the 1740s and mushroomed in London in the second half of the century.[51]

Newspapers and journals provided another source of income for men of letters. In 1777 Paris acquired its first newspaper, *Le Journal de Paris*, seventy-five years after the *London Evening Post*.[52] Its editor, Jean-Baptiste-Antoine Suard, later edited other journals, such as the *Gazette de France*, was elected to the Académie Française, and ultimately garnered an annual income of 20,000 livres. Robert Darnton stresses the difference between English and French newspapers: 'The missing element [in French journals] was the market: Suard lived on sinecures and pensions, not on sales of books. In fact, he wrote little and had little to say – nothing, it need hardly be added, that would offend the regime. He toed the party line of the *philosophes* and collected his reward.'[53] Darnton does not point out that, on the other side of the channel, there was a literary marketplace but no *philosophes* (except in the Celtic fringes). In addition to providing income for journalists, the English press allowed scholars to advertise their need and talent to a larger number of potential patrons. For example, Arthur Murphy, in *Gray's-Inn Journal* no. 61, of 15 December 1753, advertised his forthcoming 'critical enquiry into the poetic merits of the celebrated *Voltaire*' and promised his English readers that he would prove the superiority of Shakespeare and other English poets, whose works Voltaire had plagiarized. Murphy, in the subsequent number of 22 December 1753, lamented the absence of an English Maecenas, like Baron Somers, the patron of Locke and Addison. 'The Circumstance, which in my Opinion, reflects the greatest lustre upon the character of Lord *Sommers*, is the Encouragement he afforded to such a Genius as Mr.

Addison, who might have remained in a less conspicuous Point of View without the Assistance of such a Patron.' Murphy suggested that his inconspicuous station was attributable not to the fact that he was a lesser genius than Addison but to his want of patronage: '... the kindly protection of the Lord *Sommers* hindered him [Addison] from sinking into Obscurity, and from being compelled by Necessity to sully that fair Fame, which is now the Reward of his Excellent Performances.'[54] Rather than scholars ceasing to be beggars, the press afforded them new ways of begging.

An advertisement on the front page of the *Morning Chronicle and London Advertiser* of 26 December 1762 is addressed 'To the OPULENT and the GREAT.' The first two sentences of the ad read: 'LUXURY is probably at its height, and Letters certainly upon their decline. However, a person, who has pretensions to them, hopes by this means to find, that there is still a MAECENAS or a POLLIO left, who will afford him a retreat in some country seat, the more remote the more eligible, there to finish a work in which he was engaged, and which, in spite of all the efforts he can make, he shall never be able to do, without some aid from patronage and protection.' We do not know who sent the letter and what, if any, was the response of the opulent and the great. It was probably not written by Hume, who might have heard from his *amie intime,* the Comtesse de Boufflers, the mistress of Rousseau's patron, the Prince de Conti, that France could no longer provide hospitality for the author of *The Social Contract* and *Émile* (published in 1762), and that the celebrated author would need a country retreat in England. There were many other men of letters besides Rousseau in need of 'patronage and protection,' if I may repeat the redundancy of the individual who paid for the advertisement.

While most of the eighteenth-century press was commercial in character, political and religious propaganda, such as the literature advocating the abolition of slavery, was free in the sense of having no cost to readers.[55] Oxford and Cambridge provided free-of-charge poems of praise to royal, noble, and politically powerful benefactors, written in Greek, Latin, Hebrew, Anglo-Saxon, Coptic, Arabic, Turkish, Persian, Syraic, and Syriaco-Palymrean.[56] One wonders why Adam Smith, Samuel Taylor Coleridge, and John Henry Newman thought Oxford and Cambridge intellectually bankrupt during the eighteenth century.[57] Yet, despite these lofty exceptions, print culture was largely commercial in character. The press was a commercial trade.

Daniel Defoe understood that the printing business employs a host of men of letters, besides scholars, and employs them in an entirely capitalist manner: 'Writing ... is become a very considerable Branch of the English Commerce; Composing, Inventing, Translating, Versifying, &c., are the several Manufactures which supply this Commerce. The Booksellers are the ... Employers. The several Writers, Authors, Copyers, Sub-Writers, and all other Operators with Pen and Ink, are the Workmen employed by the said Master Manufacturers, in the forming, dressing, and furnishing the said Manufactures ...'[58] Defoe could be said to be a professional writer or even a literary proletarian. He proudly asserted that 'the God that gave me brains will give me bread.' But, after he was imprisoned for debt and seditious libel, he sought and received the patronage of Robert Harley as well as of powerful Whigs such as lords Somers and Halifax, not only writing tracts for the government but also spying on his fellow dissenters.[59] The dissenting individualist and author of *Robinson Crusoe* was compelled by fortune, or his lack thereof, to be a hired pen. Using the talents of impoverished men was a weapon of the powerful. As Charles Montagu, 3rd Earl of Halifax, wrote to Defoe's patron, Sarah Churchill, Duchess of Marlborough: 'A little money can not be better placed by those who are in Power, than in obliging and engaging those who have Wit, and Storys, that may be turned on them or the Enemy.'[60]

Isaac D'Israeli, a notable man of letters at the end of the eighteenth century and the father of the Victorian prime minister, cited the example of Defoe to show the vulnerability of the professional writer. D'Israeli defined a professional author as one 'with no other means of subsistence, than such as are extracted from the quill.' Professional authors were at the mercy of capitalist booksellers. 'The following facts will shew the value of *Literary Property*; immense profits and cheap purchases! The manuscript of ROBINSON CRUSOE ran through the whole trade, and no one would print it; the bookseller, who, it is said, was not remarkable for his discernment, but for a speculative turn, bought the work, and got a thousand guineas for it.' D'Israeli thought Johnson's view that booksellers are the modern patrons of literature to be misleading: 'A trader can never be a patron, for it would be romantic to purchase what is not saleable; but where no favour is conferred, there is no patronage.'[61] Whereas the crown and nobility patronized for fame, booksellers supported writers solely for profit.[62]

The commercialization of the press was simultaneously the professionalization of letters. Charles Lamb was pleased not to be a professional writer: 'Slavery, worse than all slavery, to be a bookseller's dependent, to drudge your brains for pots of ale and breasts of mutton, to change your free thoughts and voluntary members for ungracious task work.'[63] Henry Fielding, in *The Author's Farce*, penned the lines: 'How unhappy the fate / To live by one's pate / And to be forced to write hackney for bread! / An author's a joke / To all manner of folk / Whenever he pops up his head, his head / Whenever he pops up his head.'[64]

A professional, whether a writer, an artisan, or an athlete, connotes not only someone who works for money – not an amateur – but also someone who has a specialized skill rather than being a dilettante, a jack of all trades, or a Renaissance man. He is proud of that skill and participates in the determination of the standards of his craft. A professional does not just look to her boss or employer but to her fellow professionals to assess whether or not she has done her job satisfactorily. But there are various kinds of professionals. A lawyer takes on a case of those with money to pay her, and advocates a cause, regardless of truth or justice, advancing a series of arguments that do not have to be internally consistent in the hope that one of the arguments will cause reasonable doubt in a juror or that some set of arguments will make a judge think that the balance of probabilities favours the lawyer's cause. Truth or justice is expected to emerge from the adversarial contest between lawyers for the prosecution and the defence. Are professional writers like lawyers, advocates of a particular interest or partisan cause, who command a high fee for their reputation for victory? Henry Fielding wrote that 'a Writer, whose only Livelihood is his Pen,' must, like 'every other Advocate,' be allowed to sell his services to those who will pay for them.[65] Are professional writers more like architects (by definition subject to a patron) or sculptors (who may or may not be patronized)? Frank Jenkins, an historian of architecture, writes: 'If it were possible for an architect to manifest his creative instincts and talents, unrestricted by a real or imaginary client, the result would be sculpture but it would not be architecture.'[66] Samuel Johnson likened himself to an architect – not, as most writers would do, to a sculptor – when the government, whose pensioner he was, cut the best lines from his 'Taxation No Tyranny'; he thought this no more untoward than if he had designed a five-storey building and his patron decided that three storeys would do.[67] Or is the professional writer like an accountant who provides different accounts for his employer and the tax men? Or a professional athlete who balances his team's victory with a personal display of prowess, one who wins but also thrills and entertains? Or does his love of truth and passion for justice outweigh his display of professional skill?

Rousseau consistently maintained that he was not a professional writer. When he turned down Malesherbes's offer of an official position on the *Journal des Savants* (a job that would involve one week's work a month, the writing of two articles a month), he wrote Malesherbes: 'They imagined that I could write as a trade (*métier*) as all the other literary people did, instead of which I could never write except out of passion.' Rousseau elaborated his position in his *Confessions*: 'I felt that writing in order to have bread might soon stifle my genius and kill my talent which was less in my pen than in my heart, and had been born solely out of an elevated and proud way of thinking which alone could nourish it. Nothing vigorous, nothing great can come from an entirely venal pen.' Authors, in this view, are great only to the extent that they do not see their task as a *métier*. 'In order to be able, in order to say great truths one must not be dependent on success.'[68] Raymond Birn draws our attention to the paradox that Rousseau both maintained an aristocratic disdain for the commercial marketplace in books and also was the first to claim an author's inalienable property in his literary productions, that is, an author's work is not something sold once and for all time to publishers.[69] Geoffrey Turnovsky argues that Rousseau was able to maintain generally amicable relations with his publisher, Marc-Michel Rey, because his main concern was not to make money from his writings but to establish an intimate relationship with his readers. 'Rousseau's real stake in the book trade actually lay, like Voltaire's, in the diffusion of his works than in their sale or ownership. In contrast to Voltaire, however, who was concerned mostly with the extent and quantity of his readership, Rousseau focused on its quality.'[70]

The eighteenth century gave birth to the consecration of the author. Writers in the age of print are the tribunes of the people; in the republic of letters, they are what the orators were in classical republics. Chrétien-Guillaume de Malesherbes, the protector of the Encylopedists, in his inaugural address to the Académie Française, asserted: 'A tribunal independent of all the powers of the earth and respected by all was raised up, giving every talent its due and pronouncing on every sort of merit; and, in an enlightened age, an age where every citizen can speak to the entire nation by the printed word, the *gens de lettres* are, in short, amongst a dispersed public what the orators of Rome and of

Athens were amidst their assembled peoples.'[71] Malesherbes was prescribing what the freedom of the press should be, not describing what the duties of the director of publications in fact were. The *philosophes* both led and followed public opinion, but 'the powers of the earth' were not entirely defenceless against it; they had the repressive power of censorship and the productive power of patronage.[72]

Writers were torn between dependence on aristocratic patrons and the demands of the commercial market. Thomas Odell's *The Patron* (1729) and Samuel Foote's *The Patron* (1774) were plays performed for the London stage depicting foolish or sham patrons but, in their dedications to the Earl of Sutherland and Earl Gower, Odell and Foote explain that the character of these sham patrons reveals the qualities of real patrons.[73] While Johnson insisted that booksellers were the modern patrons of letters, his bookseller-publisher, Robert Dodsley, wrote that '*none rise but by favour.*'[74] David Hume, lamenting the commercial failure of his philosophy, wrote to his kinsman, Henry Home, on 13 February 1739: 'Tis so rare to meet with one, that will take Pains on a Book, that does not come recommended by some great name or Authority.' And to Michael Ramsay, he wrote nine days later: 'Such Performances make their way very heavily at first, when they are not recommended by some great Name or Authority.' The champion of commercial publishing was henceforth to send first copies of his works, and those of his friend, Adam Smith, to the patron of Scotland, the 3rd Duke of Argyll. Samuel Johnson, also no friend to aristocratic patronage, intimated the need for patrons in *Adventurer, 138*: 'Whoever has remarked the fate of books must have found it governed by other causes than general consent arising from general conviction. If a new performance happens not to fall in the hands of some, who have the courage to tell and authority to propagate their opinion, it often remains long in obscurity, and perhaps perishes unknown and unexamined.'[75] Oliver Goldsmith's caricature of a commercial bookseller, Mr Fudge asserts: 'Others may pretend to direct the vulgar but that is not my way: I always let the vulgar direct me; wherever popular clamour arises, I always echo the million.'[76] Jeremy Black indicates that Goldsmith accurately captured the attitude of the commercial press, which tended to be uncritical because it accommodated itself to the views of readers and advertisers.[77] Writers of the eighteenth century aspired to enlighten the public and at the same time were responsive to market demand. The success story of the commercial marketplace was, of course, the novel, but dictionaries, encyclopedias, histories, and cookbooks did well too. While copyrights on dictionaries were most valuable to booksellers, the histories of Hume, Smollett, Goldsmith, Catherine Macaulay, Robertson, and Gibbon also sold well. Robert Dodsley gave Edmund Burke £300 for *An Essay for the Abridgement of the English History* (1757), compared with six guineas for *A Vindication of Natural Society* (1756) and twenty guineas for *A Philosophical Enquiry into the Origin of our Ideas of the Sublime and the Beautiful* (1757).[78] Hume led the way in obtaining a share of profits, rather than just receiving lump-sum payments from the booksellers, so that historians shared in the success of later editions of their works.[79] In the marketplace of ideas, David Hume the historian, assisted by David Hume the economist, was a hotter commodity than David Hume the philosopher.

Roger Chartier writes that 'thought of (and thinking of himself or herself) as a demiurge, the writer none the less creates in a state of dependence. Dependence upon the rules (of patronage, subsidy and the market) that define the writer's condition.'[80] Another scholar, Jean Guéhenno, states that eighteenth-century 'authors earned little or nothing, practically all the profits going to the publishers. If a writer was not well enough off to be independent, like Montesquieu, Voltaire or Buffon, he had to seek the favor of the great and only lived comfortably at their tables or in their castles.'[81] Still another observer, Dustin Griffin, insists that all major British writers of the eighteenth century were dependent upon patronage; 'there was no rapid or complete changeover during the century from an aristocratic culture to a commercial culture, no sudden change from a patronage economy to a literary marketplace.' Griffin maintains that it is completely unhistorical 'to assume that authors can be divided into the servants of art and the servants of political paymasters.'[82] Commerce, patronage, and the consecration of the author were interrelated variables in the eighteenth-century republic of letters.

While all *philosophes* prided themselves on their independence, one of the foremost patrons of Enlightenment, Malesherbes, in the course of an argument about why writers should not be judges or censors of literature, provided an intelligent account of why *gens de lettres* were anything but independent-minded:

In France, *gens de lettres* are a very dependent class of citizens, because it is certainly not a profession useful in itself. The greater part of those who have embraced letters have been determined by a dominating attraction, have sacrificed hopes of fortune to their own satisfaction and desire for glory. However, since one cannot live on glory, it is by the favours of the court, or the patronage positions which the court names, that they have hoped to subsist in their old age, at an age when assistance has become a necessity.

A man of letters is thus a man dependent on many powerful persons, and one must definitely not expose oneself to their displeasure by the approval of a book.[83]

Malesherbes's observations on men of letters are relevant not only to their disqualifications as censors of literature but also, in the absence of a welfare state and tenured positions, to their need for patrons.

The status of writers rose in the last half of the eighteenth century partly through denial; writers denied their professionalization within a commercial press culture and also denied their dependence on royal and aristocratic patrons. Samuel Johnson's letter to Lord Chesterfield and Jean D'Alembert's *Essai sur la société des gens de lettres et des grands*, both written at mid-century, are widely hailed as manifestos of the modern author who has kissed patronage goodbye.[84] But the facts are otherwise. Though Johnson's pension from George III was perhaps less impressive than D'Alembert's five pensions, his friend, Oliver Goldsmith, favourably compared the numerous small pensions French writers received with the larger English pension which slowed Johnson's literary productivity.[85] Johnson, who has been taken as the prototype of a modern professional author, pronounced, in his preface to *A Dictionary of the English Language*, that authors were the chief source of national glory. Yet, at the same time, he declared himself a professional writer and said that only blockheads wrote for reasons higher than money. This emphatic assertion might have served to distance him from Lord Camden's sentiment, expressed in an address on literary property to the House of Lords in 1774: 'Glory is the Reward of Science, and those who deserve it, scorn all meaner Views. I speak not of the Scribblers for bread, who teize the Press with their wretched Productions ... It was not for Gain that *Bacon, Newton, Milton, Locke* instructed and delighted the World: it would be unworthy of such Men to traffic with a dirty Bookseller for so much as a Sheet of Letter-press.'[86]

While Johnson insisted that booksellers are the modern patrons of literature, he raised the status of authors by his altercation with his employer, the bookseller Osborne, who rudely insisted that Johnson abandon scholarship and get on with writing. William Shaw wrote of Johnson's decisive battle with Osborne: 'No body of men are more uniform and eager in taking advantage of such necessities, who, like Johnson, are reduced to dependence on their favour. Osborne was base enough to make Johnson feel his situation, by a brutal sarcasm, which he blurted in his face, on finding him reading with great coolness, while the quantum of copy promised by this time, was not yet begun. Johnson, surprised into a passion, by the bookseller's rage and ferocity, started from his seat, without uttering a word, and, with the book in his hand, instantly knocked him down.'[87] One might expect booksellers to be more concerned with literary productivity than scholarly quality, but competitors of Osborne admired Johnson's silent statement that he was a scholar and not a literary proletarian, and treated him with the dignity that Johnson thought he merited. Booksellers did in fact become important patrons of literature; Joseph Johnson provided Mary Wollstonecraft with free board and lodging before she had written anything, and Joseph Cottle published Coleridge, Southey, Wordsworth, and Lamb and was recognized by them as their benefactor. Coleridge wrote to Pottle: 'Had it not been for you none, perhaps, of them [his poems] would have been published, and some not written.'[88]

Johnson's fight with Lord Chesterfield is well known, and the leading man of letters in England then is now known as 'not the Lord of Wits but merely a Wit amongst Lords' and someone 'with the manners of a dancing master and the morals of a whore.' Johnson's victory in class struggle provides a self-interested reason for *noblesse oblige*; if aristocrats do not honour talent, they may be held up to contempt. However, the manner in which he fought with Osborne and Chesterfield is significant: it is unthinkable that Johnson, an adherent of the grand principle of subordination who would not bow to the great, would punch out Lord Chesterfield, as he did Osborne. Johnson's modern patrons of literature are precisely those to whom he did not have to bow down. I shall return to the life of Johnson but wish here to point out that the contradiction between Johnson's pride in his independence and his acceptance of royal patronage was characteristic of his time.

The ideal of independent thought was fabricated in conditions of royal or aristocratic patronage. Indeed, important patrons, such as Lord Bute, instructed reliable clients to write with greater appearance of independence; their use as government pensioners would be diminished if they were seen as such.[89] Voltaire's entry on *gens de lettres* in the *Encyclopédie* asserts that writers are more independent-minded than other men and need royal patronage 'to strengthen this independence in them' or else they will have to abase themselves to aristocrats. Yet this statement did not fully accord with Voltaire's view in *Le Siècle de Louis XIV* that Cardinal Richelieu patronized writers 'who are usually men of a cringing spirit' since 'true genius ... rarely stoops to dependence.'[90] Writers of the eighteenth century doffed their caps to the ideal of democratic print culture but simultaneously held out their caps to potential patrons.

Enlightenment and Freedom of the Press

Whereas Lord Shelburne associated Enlightenment with freedom of the press, and darkness with censorship and the Roman Catholic Church, we have reason to doubt these equations. Elizabeth Eisenstein states that 'the *Index Librorum Prohibitorum* acted more as a stimulus than as an antidote, providing free publicity for expurgated passages and forbidden titles.'[91] The thinkers of the French Enlightenment agreed with both Shelburne's opinion and Eisenstein's. Pierre Bayle, in *Nouvelles de la république des lettres,* and Diderot, in his entry 'Censeurs' in the *Encyclopédie,* quoted Virgil's *Aeneid* – 'Craving the far shore the suppliant band,/ Seeking the first passage, each with outstretched hand;/ But the sad sailor takes now these, now those,/ The rest repels, abandoned, as he goes' – and hence likened authors to the souls of the dead awaiting the privilege of Charon rowing them across the Styx.[92] If thinkers in the French Enlightenment thought censorship irrational and ignominious, they also thought of it as a challenging barrier to overstep. D'Alembert wrote that 'the fear of a burning [*fagots*] is very refreshing.'[93] Voltaire asserted: 'Burning [*la brûlure*] for a book was what the title of academician was for a man of letters.'[94] Diderot, in his *Lettre sur le commerce de la librairie,* wrote: 'The more severe the proscription, the more it raised the price of the proscribed work, the more it stimulated curiosity to read it, the more it was bought, the more it was read.'[95] Daniel Roche claims that 'police activity under Louis XIV, Louis XV, and Louis XVI did not prevent the circulation of forbidden books or the distribution of pirated editions; indeed, for some of them, it served as the best possible advertisement.'[96] Diderot advocated a policed book trade, albeit with more enlightened censors paid for by the booksellers, to prevent pirated editions and to maintain the quality and price of editions, so that authors could negotiate a better price for their work. Robert Shackleton concludes: 'It is wrong to think of the censors and the whole apparatus of censorship as basically and unanimously opposed to new ways of thought, or even as essentially repressive.'[97] Since forbidden books, whether libels, pornography, or philosophy, were sold clandestinely as 'oeuvres philosophiques', forbidden fruit were more delicious and marketable in France than on the other side of the channel, where, with less state censorship, works of philosophy might fall deadborn from the press or fail to find a publisher at all. Those of us raised on Mill's *On Liberty* may have to rethink the proposition that freedom is the necessary and sufficient condition for the development of thought; England had less press censorship than in France, and less government intervention in universities than in Scotland, but philosophy did not flourish in England, as it did in France and Scotland, or it flourished more within the Church of England (bishops Berkeley and Butler) than without. Perhaps patronage is more essential to thought than freedom, and the political conditions of France and Scotland required protectors for intellectuals more than in England.[98]

Jeremy Black has argued that the free, commercial press of England did not, like *les philosophes*, attempt to lead public opinion but rather followed the opinions of the advertisers and readers they sought to attract. Black characterizes the eighteenth-century British press as merging moral righteousness and religious conviction to bring about reforms congenial to readers and advertisers. He writes: 'Preceptive rather than persuasive, instructive items were directed not at rival views requiring intellectual challenge but at like-minded readers. The general thrust of the articles was on the need for action by those holding similar views.' Black believes that the British press appealed to the religious sensibilities of its readers and advertisers and thus 'newspapers tended to be hierarchical and conservative in their assumptions.'[99] Samuel Johnson was able to find a more congenial home in the English commercial press than enlightened secularists could.

Certainly, *the philosophes* did not write for the people in the way that English writers did. Voltaire declared:

Never will philosophers set up a religious sect. Why? Because they do not write for the people, and because they are without enthusiasm.

Divide the human race into twenty parts. Nineteen of those are composed of those who work with their hands, and will never know if there is a Locke in the world or not. In the remaining twentieth part how few men do we find who read! And among those who do read there are twenty who read novels for every one who studies philosophy. The number of those who think is exceedingly small, and they are not intending to disturb the world.[100]

French thinkers, while looking to England in many ways, were not notable in championing England's free commercial press. Diderot and Rousseau, though completely opposed with respect to the merits of royal patronage, agreed that the policed press gave writers more security than the English system, which was without officially licensed printers and state censors with the power to authorize or forbid publication. Diderot wrote of the English system: 'If the work by its daring draws onto itself public condemnation, the magistrate confronts the printer who either is silent or names the author: if he remains silent, a process is served against him; if he names the author, one proceeds against the author.'[101] The reciprocity of interest between bookseller and author on which the health of the book trade depends, Diderot thought, is undermined without prior authorization to publish without fear of prosecution. Rousseau also held France to be the country most conducive to speaking the truth; if one gets state permission to publish, then 'I did not owe to any one anywhere else on account of my maxims and their publication.'[102] One might find it peculiar that the lines above were written in England, where Rousseau sought asylum from persecution in France and Switzerland, or that Diderot, who had been imprisoned in France for his writing and whose great venture, the *Encyclopédie*, was temporarily closed down by the state, would prefer French policed publication to English commercial freedom. Indeed, both men may have been partly ingratiating in their praise of French censors, but one must consider that Hume was afraid to publish his boldest works on religion and morals during his life and entrusted the chore of getting them published to his apprehensive friend, Adam Smith.

In 1695 the English licensing system for the press expired and that year could be said to mark a new era of freedom of the press, though that freedom continued to be limited by laws of libel, sedition, treason, and blasphemy. Thomas Aikenhead was burned in Edinburgh for impugning the Trinity in 1697, providing a lesson of caution for John Locke and particularly for John Toland.[103] Just as the printer John Twyer was hanged, drawn, and quartered in 1664 for refusing to divulge the name of the author of *A Treatise for the Execution of Justice*, and just as William Anderton was hanged in 1694 for refusing to name the authors of several Jacobite tracts, so John Matthews was declared guilty of high treason and executed for printing *Vox Populi, Vox Dei* in 1719 and John Shebbeare was fined, pilloried, and imprisoned in 1759 for declaring the Hanovers usurpers.[104] Morover, numerous Grub Street journalists and publishers were imprisoned in the first half of the eighteenth century; prosecutions waned only as the Jacobite threat receded after the failure of Bonnie Prince Charlie's venture in 1745. John Tutchin was arrested for writing the *Observator* and died in prison, and Nathaniel Mist and twenty-two others were imprisoned for publishing *Mist's Weekly Journal* in 1721. Robert Nixon, Richard Franklin, Henry Haines, and Nicolas Amherst were arrested for seditious libel in 1737; Johnson's publisher, Robert Dodsley, was imprisoned for publishing Paul Whitehead's poem, *Manners*, in 1739; and Richard Nutt was pilloried and imprisoned in 1754 for sedition.[105] John Wilkes vigorously resisted his prosecution for seditious libel in 1763 and fought for the practice that a jury, rather than a judge, would determine whether printed material was deemed libelous, a practice made into law by Fox's Libel Act of 1792.[106] Peter Brown writes that the Glorious Revolution did not ensure freedom to 'comment on the established practices of politics and religion ... to anyone lacking the protection of great wealth or distinguished patronage.'[107] The English names punished for printing offences are perhaps less illustrious than those imprisoned in France – Voltaire, Jean-François Marmontel, Diderot, Morellet, and Linguet – but they indicate that the English press was not entirely free from government repression, and that the decision of the Paris parlement of 1757 to punish with death those whose books disturbed public order might be compared with the punishment of Shebbeare two years later in England. Further, some of Britain's leading authors did have brushes with the law. Jonathan Swift's *The Public Spirit of the Whigs* was censored by the House of Lords but, despite a £300 reward for discovery of the author, the government could not bring Swift to trial or even prosecute his printer. Governmental power turned two of the most powerful anti-government writers, Daniel Defoe and Henry Fielding, into a government spy and a magistrate upholding law and order. Defoe, who was imprisoned for debt and for seditious libel, was freed from both prison and penury by spying on his fellow dissenters for the Tory minister Robert Harley. The satirical voice of Henry Fielding had to be muzzled by an act of parliament, the Theatrical Licensing Act of 1737.

Protesting against the Theatrical Licensing Act, Fielding's patron, Lord Chesterfield, declared in the House of Lords (and proved that he was at least a wit among lords): 'This Bill is not only an encroachment on liberty, but it is likewise an encroachment on property. Wit, my Lords, is a sort of Property: the property of those who have it, and too often the only property they have to depend on. It is indeed a precarious dependence.'[108]

Yet, real property outweighed wit, and Fielding was forced to turn to the law for his subsistence. Until then, he had made a comfortable subsistence by threatening to satirize important persons on stage if he was not patronized, taking money to suppress his own work, and presenting successful comedies at the Haymarket and Drury Lane. But he neglected the counsel of Baldesar Castiglione, who wrote: 'One must also take great care not to make fun of those who are universally favored and loved by all and who are powerful, because in doing so a man can sometimes call down dangerous enormities upon himself.'[109] When Fielding satirized Robert Walpole after accepting his patronage, Walpole undermined his livelihood by passing the Theatrical Licensing Act. Fielding succeeded, with the patronage of lords Chesterfield and Lyttleton, in reaching the giving rather than the receiving end of the law, and, as a magistrate, came to think that liberty of the press should be curtailed by seditious libel laws.[110] In 1748 he wrote in *The Jacobite's Journal* that, without patronage, impoverished writers will be compelled to slander the great: 'In a country where there is no public Provision for Men of Genius, and in an Age when no Literary Productions are encouraged, or indeed read, but such as are season'd with Scandal against the Great ... and if the Public will feed a hungry Man for a little Calumny, he must be a very honest Person indeed, who will rather starve than write it.'[111] In giving a semi-apology for his theatrical comedies (which George Bernard Shaw thought the equal of Shakespeare and inferior only to his own),[112] Fielding provided a striking example of the dilemma facing professional writers, a justification for patronage, and an intimation that men of genius can be bought.[113]

On both sides of the English channel, scandalous libels were bestsellers, however much governments attempted to repress them.[114] James Bramston, in *Man of Taste* (1753), wrote:

Can statutes keep the British Press in awe
When that sells best, that's most against the law.[115]

Government repression was both an incentive and disincentive to publication; the wider sweep of French censorship made philosophy, as well as obscenity and scandal, forbidden fruit. Meanwhile, Diderot's and Malesherbes' desire for secure copyright laws to facilitate authors getting a better price for their wares was shared by many British authors. The Copyright Act of 1710 conferred ownership of all copies on the bookseller for twenty-one years. Pirated editions of works appeared in Ireland, Scotland, and America, particularly after the War of Independence. British authors were generally as keen as Diderot to have unauthorized editions of their works suppressed. Some booksellers wanted a perpetual copyright; the heirs of Jacob Tonson, who had bought *Paradise Lost* for £5 in 1667, obtained an injunction to restrain other booksellers from printing Milton's epic poem. In 1774 the House of Lords found against Andrew Millar's claim of perpetual copyright of Thomson's *Seasons*.[116] The Scottish booksellers at the Chapter Coffee House, whom Johnson praised for having raised the price of literature, negotiated contracts with Hume, Robertson, and Gibbon that enabled the authors to profit from multiple editions of their works and excited the envy of their French contemporaries.

The British government had other weapons besides prosecution to control the press after the expiration of the Licensing Act. The Stamp Act of 1712 provided government revenues and raised the price of print; five English newspapers went under and four survived the introduction of the Stamp Act.[117] Yet, despite this act and legislation to tax advertisements, the press and its readers proliferated throughout the eighteenth century. Subsidies were provided for journals and pensions for writers friendly to government on both sides of the channel. In England, subsidies and pensions for literary figures became a common feature of the reigns of Queen Anne and George I, with Defoe, Swift, Addison, Steele, Fielding, Smollett, and Johnson writing political propaganda. Baron Somers patronized Locke, Toland, and Tindall[118] and, together with the Whig grandees lords Halifax and Newcastle, provided posthumous patronage for John Milton. (We might consider whether writers might be neglected without patronage after, if not during, their lifetime.) In his commissioned *Life of John Milton* (1698), John Toland began the rehabilitation of Milton, who had been ignored from the Restoration to the Glorious Revolution. Milton, Toland wrote, was 'a person of the best accomplishments, the happiest genius, and the vastest learning which this nation, so renown'd for producing excellent writers, could ever yet show.' Toland also bowed down to John Locke, who 'must be confest to be the greatest philosopher after CICERO in the universe.'[119]

Subsequent Whig publicists eliminated Cicero in their praise of Locke, the greatest of all philosophers, with Somers's 'loyal henchman,' Joseph Addison, providing posthumous patronage. John Valdemir Price has written: 'Addison doubtless did much to encourage the popularity of Locke: no philosopher has ever had a better publicity agent, and

Addison himself had the professed intention of bringing "Philosophy out of the Closets and Libraries, Schools and Colleges, to dwell in Clubs and Assemblies, at Tea Tables, and in Coffee Houses" (*Spectator* 20). Almost overnight, Addison made Locke in particular and philosophy in general not only respectable but fashionable.' While Addison succeeded in making Lockeian, empirical philosophy popular, and giving England a reputation as the philosophic nation throughout the eighteenth century, the irony is that after Locke and his student, the 3rd Earl of Shaftesbury, most of eighteenth-century British philosophy was produced on the Celtic fringes. Price continues: 'Except for Joseph Priestley and Richard Price, who, for all their merits, cannot be termed major philosophic writers, there was hardly an Englishman in sight. Indeed, except for Locke and Shaftesbury, the names that one associates with the triumph of British empiricist philosophy are Irish or Scottish: Berkeley, Burke, Hume, Hutcheson, Adam Smith, Lord Kames, etc.'[120]

Whig magnates wielded the carrot as well as the stick after the Glorious Revolution, and then, with the Hanover succession and the ascent of Robert Walpole, the British government controlled the press not by the French system of licensing and censorship but by the common law on treason, seditious, and blasphemous libel, by taxation or the Stamp Act, and by government patronage of writers. Governmental patronage of writers was most pronounced in Scotland, which, with the elimination of Tories and Jacobites from the universities in the early eighteenth century, a subject that I will examine in detail in chapter 6, became the birthplace of the idea of a free marketplace of ideas. England, with relatively greater freedom of thought – or less governmental regulation of the press and the universities – than in France and Scotland, produced less (philosophic) thought than Scotland and France. Scotland, patronized and purged, and France, with its state regulation of authors and publishers fell far short of Smith's ideal of a self-sustaining marketplace of ideas, but it was these two countries that produced the remarkable thinkers who constituted the Scottish and French Enlightenments.

3 Seneca in the Age of Frederick and Catherine

Seneca's *De Beneficiis* was frequently translated into English and French in the seventeenth and eighteenth centuries, including two French translations in 1776 and a new translation in 1778 when Baron D'Holbach published Seneca's collected works. Since Rousseau shared Hume's admiration for Seneca, Hume concluded his account of Rousseau's ingratitude for Hume's patronage, *Exposé succinct de la contestation que s'est élevée entre M. Hume et M. Rousseau,* with a quotation from Seneca's *De Beneficiis.*[1] G.M. Ross notes the curious fact that Seneca was widely respected by philosophers of the eighteenth century but not by philosophers before or since.[2]

A century before D'Holbach's and Diderot's work on Seneca, in 1678, Sir Roger L'Estrange, the chief apologist for the Stuart court, published an abstract of Seneca's *Of Benefits* that went through four editions and two re-issues before the Glorious Revolution and another twenty editions in the eighteenth century. After the American Revolution, at least sixteen different editions and printings of Lestrange's abridgement of Seneca were published in the next seventy years. Though it seems fitting that Seneca's classical work on patronage should be translated and abridged by the leading publicist for the Stuarts (who, Whig opponents claimed, aspired to Bourbon absolutism), the boom in the patronage business after the Glorious and American revolutions may appear paradoxical. However, patronage may be said to supply social cement when patterns of authority are disrupted, as they were with the decline of the Roman republic or with the revolutions of the seventeenth and eighteenth centuries. L'Estrange's Seneca was an alternative not only to Hobbes's *Leviathan* but also to Filmer's *Patriarcha.* Patronage supplies an alternative to

social-contract and divine-right doctrines, or to conceptions of authority derived from the people or from God.

L'Estrange's Seneca offered a secular supplement to Anglican or
Tory notions of authority to bind superiors and inferiors in Hanover
England and republican America, as well as Stuart England and
Bourbon France. L'Estrange's Seneca declared: 'The Benefits of Princes,
and Great Men, are Honours, Offices, Moneys, Profitable Commissions
and Protection: The Poor Man has nothing to present but Good-Will,
Good Advice, Faith, Industry, the Service and Hazard of his Person, an
early Apple peradventure, or some other cheap Curiousity ...'[3] Hobbe-
sians might not find the hazard of one's person to be a cheap curiosity
but more cavalier individuals might chance their life in the service of
a bountiful patron. However, the point here is that patronage binds
rich and poor together, arises as an alternative to civil war, and is
especially significant when habits of authority are questioned, as was
the case in the Roman Principate or in the revolutions of the seventeenth and eighteenth centuries, when legitimate rule was challenged
and when neither election nor hereditary succession was the established norm of constitutional authority. Royal patronage in France was
modest compared to that of great aristocrats until the Fronde; after
the aristocratic rebels were suppressed, Colbert prevailed upon Louis
XIV to become a major patron of letters.[4] Roger Hahn writes that
'Colbert wanted to be remembered as the *Mecenas des gens de lettres,* and
to that end he had already initiated a talent search for men of letters,
artists, and scientists who would welcome government subsidy.'[5]
Voltaire's entry on 'Gens de lettres' in the *Encyclopédie* asserts that the
foundations and academies established by Louis XIV enabled men of
letters, born without fortune, to live a life of intellectual and spiritual
independence; they no longer had to depend on base dedications
flattering aristocratic vanity.[6] Voltaire's view seems paradoxical but it
was essentially the same view as that held by Samuel Johnson, who
accepted a royal pension but refused the support of the well-born and
opulent. As we shall see, Voltaire sometimes wrote that royal patronage
undermined the independence of writers, and he certainly did not scorn
support and protection from his aristocratic friends; however, his view
that royal patronage is the only alternative to the detestable flattering
of aristocrats is consistent with his resentment of the flogging he
received from the servants of the Chevalier de Rohan, his failure to get
the support of the Duc de Sully (at whose house the outrage occurred),
and his exile to England, where he wrote the anti-aristocratic *Lettres*

philosophiques. Voltaire asked rhetorically: 'And isn't it a good thing for the human race that the authority of those little brigands was stamped out in France by the legitimate power of our kings, and in England by the legitimate power of the kings and people?'[7] The Enlightenment was divided not so much on the question of patronage but on the question of whether royal or aristocratic patrons better secured independence of the writer. Seneca served both royal and aristocratic patrons.

Julien Offray de la Mettrie's *Anti-Sénèque* described Seneca as 'the most illustrious of the Stoics, or rather of the Eclectics (for he was Epicurean and Stoic at the same time, and he chose and took what he found best in each sect),' who combined the Epicurean goal of pleasure with the Stoic goal of virtue and emphasized above all the knowledge of truth.[8] La Mettrie held that Seneca's Stoicism impeded his happiness. A Stoic is 'a sort of leper well armed against the pleasures of life' and, 'although he was a tutor to a prince, laden with literary honours and very rich for a man of learning,' he was not happy and 'wrote about happiness as one writes for a lost dog.'[9] La Mettrie suggested that his profession, as a physician, was worthier than that of a moral philosopher since opium provides 'more happiness to us than the treatises of all the philosophers.'[10]

La Mettrie's *Anti-Sénèque* drew strong fire from his fellow materialist, Diderot, who called him 'dissolute, shameless, buffoon, flatterer, [someone who] was made for the life of courts and the favour of the great. He died, as he had to die, a victim of his own intemperance and madness.'[11] To be sure, La Mettrie praised his patron, Frederick the Great, and the practice of patronage; he wrote: 'To appreciate worth is worthy and to reward it is divine. Kings: imitate the hero of the North and be the heroes of humanity, as you are its leaders. When you lower yourselves to become patrons, you raise yourselves.'[12] Indeed, Frederick himself eulogized La Mettrie, after the latter's death. Frederick declared that, after the Battle of Fontenoy,[13] when La Mettrie lost his patron, the Duc de Grammont, and then wrote up his experiences of the effects of war wounds on the mind, the medical philosopher's 'only protection was his merit.' Frederick concluded: 'The title of philosopher and the reputation of being unfortunate were enough to procure for La Mettrie a refuge in Prussia from *the king*.'[14] Frederick did not include the story Voltaire told of how La Mettrie's gluttony led to his food poisoning, on which Diderot drew.[15] Diderot's description of La Mettrie as 'made for the life of courts and the favour of the great' might be thought to be a bit much since Diderot's lives of Seneca justified his acceptance of Catherine the Great's patronage. As Voltaire wrote to Frederick, individuals always quarrel about 'fame, position, women, and above all the favours of you masters of the earth.'[16] Eighteenth-century thinkers looked upon Roman history as a mirror of their own times, and Diderot's accounts of the life and times of Seneca – *Essai sur la vie de Sénèque le philosophe, sur ses écrits, et sur les règnes de Claude et de Néron* and *Essai sur les règnes de Claude et de Néron, et sur les moeurs et les écrits de Sénèque, pour servir d'introduction à la lecture de ce philosophe* –[17] was his apology for his own life and for the necessity of patronage in the life of philosophy.

Seneca on Patronage

Seneca's *De Benefiis* is the *locus classicus* of patronage. The title is now often translated as *Of Favours* but I shall generally follow the practice of the seventeenth and eighteenth centuries and call the work *Of Benefits* or *Des Bienfaits*. I do so even though *favours* captures the personal, particularistic, and discretionary character of the gifts given, received, and requited in *De Benefiis* better than the current use of the word 'benefits'. Seneca emphasized the supererogatory character of benefits: 'A benefit is something that is given by a stranger (a stranger is one who, without incurring censure, might have done nothing) ...'[18] A benefit or a favour is thus conceptually distinct from a duty or *officium*. A benefit is not bestowed on friends or kin. Patronage is thus conceptually distinct from nepotism and cronyism.

Cicero's *Offices* distinguished ordinary from perfect duties, beneficence from justice (or what others have the right to expect of us).[19] Seneca's *Benefits* emphasize the former at the expense of the latter. The century spanning the republican Stoicism of Cicero's *Offices* and the monarchical Stoicism of Seneca's *Benefits* reflected the transformation of patrician patron-client relationships into imperial bestowal of public office. As G.E.M. De Ste Croix writes: 'With the collapse of the Republic and the virtual elimination of the democratic features of the constitution in the last half-century B.C., patronage and clientship became as it were the mainspring of Roman public life.'[20] Imperial appointment replaced election to public office. To be sure, the staggered voting of the centurial committees provided for election by wealth not numbers, and it was hardly more democratic than the voting in the aristocratic senate. However, De Ste Croix draws our attention to the distinction between patronage posts and elected office.

For Seneca, patronage, or the discretionary bestowing of benefits, is particular not general. One who benefits everyone benefits no one (Ben, 1.14.1; 6.18.1). For example, the Hobbesian sovereign who protects everyone by imposing a universal code of law equitably on all subjects is not a patron who confers benefits on all his subjects. When Hobbes (*Lev.* chapter 11) insisted that benefits oblige, and obligations are thraldom, he used the word 'benefits' in the sense of specific gifts that are conferred by patronage, not the great public good of security which the sovereign provides to all subjects and to which all subjects are obliged. A universal protector is not a particular patron. Although Burke called God, as we have seen, 'the universal Patron, who in all things eminently favours and protects the race of man,'[21] he was straining earthly usage; patronage and universality are mutually exclusive, as Burke himself intimated when he asserted that humans are pre-eminently favoured (presumably over non-humans) by God.

Indeed, the Hobbesian-Rousseauan-Kantian-Rawlsian formula of justice as fairness, impartiality, or equal subordination of all citizens to universally binding rules is the standing antithesis to the ethics of patronage. However, it is perhaps by means of this antithesis between impartiality and patronage that the latter becomes visible. Without the ideal of *res publica* or norms of impartiality, particularist distribution systems would not be recognized as patronage; kinship or feudal systems of distribution, if they could wear 'a clear public face,' would not be understood as patronage.[22] Ronald Weissman compares Roman and early-modern European patronage: 'Like Roman patronage, and unlike feudalism, Renaissance patronage often contravened society's official political ethic, if not necessarily its laws. While a cult of honour and loyalty openly and proudly characterized the feudal ethic, in neither Renaissance Italy nor ancient Rome did the partiality, implicit in patronage, serve as society's openly and officially sanctioned political morality.'[23] Patronage does not appear as patronage in clan-based societies, where the duties of kinship are so pervasive that no alternative is conceivable, and in feudal societies, where the hierarchical relationships, and attendant obligations, are well defined or clearly specified. If patronage is everywhere, it makes a notable appearance nowhere.

After the violent class struggle and civil wars of the late Roman republic, patronage offered a form of class collaboration and an alternative to armed conflict. For Seneca, 'obedience is to be won by benefits rather than by arms.'[24] Seneca's advice to princes is the opposite of chapter 16 of Machiavelli's *Prince*, where he recommended arms not benefits to Lorenzo di Medici, a member of a family that had ruled Florence for a century by means of patronage. And Seneca's *De Clementia*, written to encourage Nero to rule with clemency rather than severity, is the antithesis of chapter 17 of *The Prince*, where Machiavelli recommended cruelty rather than clemency, arguing that it is safer for a prince to be feared than loved. Seneca's patronage is an alternative not only to Hobbesian justice but also to sovereign rule by the sword. Montesquieu's Usbek, in letter 104 of *Lettres Persanes*, wrote that, for Europeans, 'there is only one tie that can bind men, which is that of gratitude.'[25] Patronage is an alternative to despotic rule by fear. Thus, just as J.G.A. Pocock has characterized seventeenth- and eighteenth-century republican thought as 'the Machiavellian moment', so an alternative 'Senecan moment'[26] might characterize those thinkers participating in royal or aristocratic patronage systems.

In the previous chapter, we assessed critically Adam Smith's view that a commercial marketplace of ideas replaced patronage in the republic of letters. Diderot's *Encyclopédie* was perhaps the most successful commercial enterprise of the eighteenth century but more so for his publisher, Le Breton, than for Diderot himself. Diderot lived in relative poverty until delivered from that condition by Catherine the Great. Diderot's patronage forms the antithesis to the Smithian view of booksellers as the modern patrons of literature. As Peter France notes: 'Nor is the bookseller a better task-master than the patron, as Diderot found out with Le Breton.'[27] Here, I will use Smith's name to represent an element of eighteenth-century thought that might be called liberal constitutionalism or, following C.B. Macpherson, possessive individualism, while I will employ J.G.A. Pocock's typology of a Machiavellian moment, consisting of republicanism or civic humanism, as conceptual alternatives to what I have called the Senecan moment in eighteenth-century thought. These moments are not mutually exclusive; they are ideal types, which co-existed, in greater or lesser degrees, in different individuals. Liberalism, republicanism, and enlightened despotism co-existed in the Enlightenment, and within individual thinkers of the time as well. Liberal constitutionalists, such as Locke or Smith, participated in patronage systems, as did republicans, such as Montesquieu and Rousseau, and Senecans, such as Voltaire, Diderot, and Kant (who not only accepted patronage but justified it in their writings), had elements of liberalism and republicanism in their political thought. What I wish to indicate is the internal coherence of the following systems of ideas, which are presented, as distinct from languages of politeness and civility, in dynamic tension with one another.

Smithian Moment	Machiavellian Moment Language of Legitimation	Senecan Moment
rights	virtue	grace (gracious giving, grateful receiving)
equality of right	equality of citizens	inequality of patron-clients
universal rules	citizens /non-citizens	particular favours
Society understood as		
mercantile bargain	military fraternity	reciprocal dependence
contract of self-interested independent individuals	patriotic solidarity	hierarchical cooperation
Economic characteristics		
commerce	agriculture	government service
property as an end	property means to citizenship	property means to social harmony
wealth as goal	wealth for power	wealth for influence
equal opportunity for unequal wealth	property for farmer-soldier	patrician wealth for talented or useful plebeians
commercial and competitive marketplace of ideas	support for useful sciences	maximal support for arts and sciences
Mode of government		
representative government	direct participation	benevolent despotism
professional army (right of self-preservation)	citizens' militia (equal duty to bear arms)	professional army (clients' duty to patron)

Chief virtue

justice (respect for property)	courage	generosity
(severity to propertyless)	(severity to non-citizens)	clemency

Chief vice

| infringing property right | corruption (selfishness and cowardice) | ingratitude |

No individual is a walking ideal type but Rousseau represents to me the closest approximation to the archetypical republican, both in his critique of liberal constitutionalism or possessive individualism and in his repudiation of royal patronage. However, it could easily be objected that my archetypes are unreal because virtually everyone, with the exception of Rousseau, Hamann, and Herder, favoured commerce as the vehicle of enlightened progress, and thus associating commerce with the Smithian moment unjustifiably separates commerce from commercial republics and empires (and my archetypes of Machiavellian and Senecan moments). But, again, let me repeat my view that all eighteenth-century thinkers were a mixture of Smithian, Machiavellian, and Senecan moments; distinctions are to be made on the basis of the proportions of the ingredients in each thinker. My purpose is merely to give the Senecan moment more time than it has previously enjoyed – not to displace useful typologies such as possessive individualism or civic humanism.

In his argument against representative government, Rousseau decried (*Social Contract*, III.15) the lack of citizens' involvement in military and civic affairs; we pay our taxes to have others do our fighting and thinking for us. However, until the American Revolution, when a citizen's army bested a professional army, 'the Machiavellian moment' was a minority voice among eighteenth-century thinkers.[28] Although the Highlander, Adam Ferguson, attempted to muster support for a Scots militia at Edinburgh's Poker Club, most of his Lowland compatriots thought professional armies superior to citizen's militias. William Robertson, in *The History of the Reign of the Emperor Charles V*, the book that received the highest advance from a publisher and was the envy of all European writers in the late eighteenth century, wrote that only when Christians adopted standing armies were they able to defeat the Turks militarily.[29] The success of the American and then the French armies countered the expectations of most Enlightenment thinkers; as Goethe's Faust has it, 'In the beginning was the deed.' Republican ideas came to have wide currency after, not before, the republican revolutions.

Rousseau also stood out from his contemporaries in thinking that individual differences did not justify large inequalities in property holdings. He thought (*Social Contract*, II.11) that 'no citizen should be rich enough to be able to buy another, and none poor enough to be forced to sell himself.' Echoing Mandeville, Voltaire responded: 'The human race, such as it is, cannot subsist unless there is an infinity of useful men who possess nothing at all; for it is certain that a man who is well off will not leave his own land to come to till yours, and if you have need of a pair of shoes, it is not the Secretary to the Privy Council who will make them for you.'[30] While most enlightened thinkers were less candid than Mandeville and Voltaire, most thinkers in the eighteenth century, on both sides of the English channel and the Atlantic Ocean, thought that inequality inheres in private property and that the prime function of government is to secure the rights of private property.

The Senecan moment in eighteenth-century thought was based on the recognition of inequality as the basic fact of social life. Distinct from a contract of equal individuals, or friendship as a bond between equals, patronage was a personal relationship between unequals or 'a lop-sided friendship.' Voltaire put it this way: 'In our unhappy world it is impossible for men living in society not to be divided into two classes, the one the rich who command, the other the poor who serve.'[31] Voltaire added a political dimension to his assessment of the inevitability of a division between rich and poor in a letter to Frederick the Great on 28 October 1773: 'When I begged you to be the restorer of the *beaux arts* of Greece, my prayer did not go so far as to implore you to re-establish Athenian Democracy. I very much dislike government by the rabble.'[32] Given the impractibilty of democratic equality, egalitarians, such as Rousseau and Paine, justified patronage on the grounds that it provided desirable opportunities for the talented poor, being even 'a masterpiece of justice and humanity' (*Social Contract*, IV.3). Advocates of hierarchy, such as Burke, supported the rights and duties of patrons as essential to civilization.

At mid-century, Johnson's letter to Lord Chesterfield and D'Alembert's *Essai sur la société des gens de lettres et des grands* proclaimed patronage obsolete, and many thinkers agreed with them, although they, like D'Alembert and Johnson, accepted royal or aristocratic patronage. Diderot was the only thinker of the eighteenth century to provide an extensive, although indirect, justification of patronage, and thus was the only member of the Enlightenment to lay out the conditions for living a philosophic life.

Diderot's Seneca

Diderot's lives of Seneca contain in their titles the words *sur les règnes de Claude et de Néron*; they are concerned with the despotic and unstable times in which Seneca and Diderot lived. Accordingly, both essays are about patronage writ large. Ostensibly addressing Seneca's relationship to Nero, they in fact constituted Diderot's apology for his relationship to Catherine the Great. Seneca's and Diderot's services to their patrons, Nero and Catherine, are to be understood with respect to the uncertain succession to the thrones of Rome and Russia. In Russia, Peter the Great had abolished hereditary succession and Catherine's predecessor, Empress Elizabeth, had supplanted Ivan VI, who was killed in prison during Catherine's reign. Catherine came to the throne after her husband had been killed by Catherine's lover, Count Orlov, and his brothers. Diderot and Voltaire arranged the suppression of the French ambassador's hostile account of Catherine's *coup d'état*, Claude Carloman de Rulhière's *Histoire ou anecdotes sur La Révolution de Russie en L'année 1762*.[33] Catherine's rise to power by the murder of her husband and rival to the throne follows the pattern set by Seneca's patron, Agrippina, the mother of Nero. Just as Seneca served as 'spin doctor' after the deaths of Claudius, Nero's rival Britannicus, and finally Agrippina herself, so Diderot and a host of other *lumières* performed as public-relations officers to improve Catherine's image in the west.

Agrippina rescued Seneca from banishment in Corsica after she had supplanted the previous wives of Emperor Claudius, established her son, Nero, as successor to the throne, gave Seneca the post of tutor to Nero, and then had Claudius and his son, Britannicus, killed. Agrippina was later killed by her son once he was secure on the throne. The parallel between Agrippina, the patron of Seneca, and Diderot's own patron, Catherine, could not have escaped the philosopher's attention. Agrippina's responsibility for the death of her husband, Claudius, and Catherine's responsibility for the death of her husband, Tsar Peter, gave employment to philosophers in the task of legitimizing rule. Catherine utilized D'Alembert, Voltaire, Diderot, Grimm, and Samuel and Jeremy Bentham to present a benign image to Europe. D'Alembert declined Catherine's offer of enormous wealth in exchange for being the tutor of her son, Paul, although he did accept a pension from her. Since Catherine had claimed that her murdered husband died from a severe colic brought on by a hemorrhoidal hemorrhage – doubtless, from Catherine's point of view, a suitably ignoble death – D'Alembert remarked to Voltaire that he dare not go to Russia because he was prone to hemorrhoids and apparently this condition was a mortal illness in Russia.[34]

Diderot, in his *Essai sur les règnes de Claude et de Néron*, recommends that the tutors of princes be elected by the people (an idea that was in contrast to the position of Rousseau, who believed that *princes* should be elected).[35] Tutors in eighteenth-century France tended to be aristocratic clerics; Louis XV's tutor, Cardinal Fleury, governed France under Louis XV from 1726 to the cardinal's death in 1743. Diderot's suggestion that tutors be elected intimated that philosophers replace clerics as the educators of princes. His reflections on Seneca's life as tutor to Nero illustrate the proper relationship of *les philosophes* to the great.

While Diderot admired Seneca as a man and thinker, he was disconcerted by the results of his education of Nero. On the same page where Diderot recommends that tutors of princes be elected, he asserts that Nero 'was born bad' but then goes on to claim that the effects of Seneca's education were beneficial, that the first five years of Nero's twelve-year reign were good, and that Seneca limited Nero's propensity to evil. Diderot, like the other *philosophes*, strongly held the view that virtue could be taught, and he himself saw philosophers as the educators of the human race: 'Two great philosophers were two great educators: Aristotle raised Alexander; Seneca raised Nero' (*ERCN*, 518). Yet Diderot did not think an unenlightened people had the wisdom to select wise tutors; his recommendation that 'the choice of a prince's tutor should be the privilege of the entire nation that the prince governs' was designed only to highlight the importance of philosophic tutors. Enlightenment, he believed, was the result of princes implementing reforms proposed by philosophers: 'The common man [*l'homme peuple*] is the stupidest and wickedest of men; to take the commonness from man [*se dépopulariser*] or to make him better, is the same thing. The voice of the philosopher that counters that of the people, is the voice of reason. The voice of the sovereign that counters that of the people, is the voice of madness' (*ERCN*, 506; *EVS*, 506).

Despite Diderot's suggestion that tutors of princes be elected by the people, he did not consider illegitimate his appointment by Catherine or Voltaire's by Frederick. Diderot is clear that the honours Frederick and Catherine bestowed on Voltaire and himself as royal tutors were well deserved (*ERCN*, 616, 620). The fact that neither Catherine nor Frederick heeded Diderot's and Voltaire's counsel, any more than Alexander followed Aristotle's or Nero followed Seneca's, did not impede Enlightened thinkers from paying court to the great. If all philosophers tend to hope that their teaching will have practical effect, thinkers of the eighteenth century were particularly prone to viewing powerful princes as the means of bringing about enlightened reforms.

For example, Catherine and Frederick generously supported Voltaire's campaign on behalf of the Calas family.[36] Voltaire and *les lumières*, who fought to rehabilitate Calas's reputation and discredit the intolerant state that unjustly punished him, refused to intercede on behalf of the Huguenot minister Rochette and the Hugenot laymen in the Grenier family (who tried to free Calas from prison) because they feared a popular insurrection; justice, to the enlightened, must be handed down from on high, rather than demanded from below.[37]

Powerful princes nurtured the Enlightenment's desire to be effective, as when Frederick the Great wrote Christian von Wolff in 1740 that 'philosophers must be the preceptors of the universe and the master of princes: what the philosophers thought and discovered, monarchs would put into practice.'[38] He also wrote Voltaire that 'authors are the legislators of the human race' and he wished 'that you might be the tutor of princes.' Indeed, Frederick added: 'The Newtons and the Wolffs, the Lockes and the Voltaires, the men who think best, should be the masters of the world.'[39] Voltaire's *Mémoires* declared: 'Ordinarily, we men of letters flatter kings; this one praised me from head to toe.'[40] According to Nancy Mitford, 'Frederick had always courted the intellectuals, and from a small outlay, consisting mostly of flattery, he now reaped rich rewards. The *philosophes* were on his side, to them he represented freedom of thought as opposed to the bigotry and obscurantism of their own king.'[41]

If Frederick and Catherine provided generous patronage to philosophers, and perhaps warranted Kant's characterization of Enlightenment as the age of Frederick, the Roman principate was one of the high water marks of patronage. Voltaire's *Le siècle de Louis XIV* designates four great ages when the arts have flourished; the age of Alexander, the age of Augustus, the age of the Medicis, and, finally, the age of Louis XIV. This classification exhibits an anti-republican bias or a predisposition to monarchical patronage. Voltaire's Louis XIV was a king whose prestige derived from honouring the arts, and especially the writers who provided him with his renown as the sun king.[42] Voltaire added an anti-Christian twist to Senecan doctrine on patronage, writing to Frederick the Great in March 1737: 'We Catholics have a kind of Sacrament which we call Confirmation; we choose a saint to be our patron in Heaven, a sort of tutelary God; I should like to know why I should be permitted to choose a little god rather than a king. You are made to be my king, much more assuredly than Saint Francis of Assisi or Saint Dominic are made to be my saints.'[43] Voltaire's arch-enemy, Joseph de Maistre, agreed with Voltaire that the arts flourish best under monarchies: 'Alexander, Augustus, Leo X, the Medici, Francis I, Louis XIV, and Queen Ann, sought out, employed, and rewarded more great men of all kinds than all the republics in the world together. It is always one man who has given his name to his century, and it is only by the choice of men that he was able to merit this honour.' De Maistre omitted the great patrons of the Enlightenment: 'D'Alembert (and Voltaire) were close to Frederick, and Diderot was close to Catherine; and Russia remains peopled with barbarians, and Prussia remains peopled with slaves.'[44]

The Roman principate, like eighteenth-century France, was a period in which *novi homines* (new men, or men from a non-senatorial background), as well as mistresses of kings or emperors, had unprecedented opportunities to acquire power and wealth. The old aristocracy in the Roman principate was either killed (when senators opposed the emperor) or bought off by gifts and grants (as in eighteenth-century France), while new men and provincials filled the senatorial ranks. It was in this context that *beneficia*, or material interests, replaced *fides*, faithful or loyal service, as the principle of the Roman empire,[45] and perhaps also of Bourbon France. Montesquieu was more the exception than the rule of *les lumières* in favouring a role for hereditary aristocrats in government. Seneca's neglect of the senatorial classes was followed in the political theories of Voltaire, Diderot, and Linguet, even more than Rousseau.

The Roman principate could even be imagined to embody the Enlightenment demand of careers open to talents. Voltaire's *Essai sur les moeurs* championed China as a meritocracy ruled by the lettered.[46] In Rome, by the end of the first century of the Christian era, 'ability and loyalty rather than nobility earned promotion and privileges.'[47] Agrippa and Maecenas (whose name has become proverbial for patronage, since he passed on Augustus's favour to poets, such as Virgil, Horace,

Ovid, and Propertius) were favourites of Augustus. Seneca, who, like Burke and Hume, was a well-born but not aristocratic provincial, became the wealthiest man of his time and certainly the richest philosopher of all time, a patron of Juvenal and Martial and a thinker who surpassed all others 'in singing the praises of poverty.'[48] J.P. Sullivan writes that 'the connection between literature, patronage and politics and between art, economics and political advancement' was 'nowhere more clearly seen than in the Neronian period.'[49] Seneca was not the only philosopher who thought that monarchy was the regime most hospitable to philosophy but who came to a bad end at the hands of Nero.[50] It was the best of times and the worst of times for philosophers; as Ronald Syme says, the monarchical court was filled with 'doctors and magicians, philosophers and buffoons.'[51]

Seneca's monarchic doctrine was presented in *De Clementia* and *De Beneficiis*. Emperors are to rule with humanity and mercy, rather than severe justice, and by means of the liberal bestowing of benefits. These generous ideals could well be considered as anti-republican, for, as Miriam Griffin points out, liberality and clemency 'presuppose the inferior position of those they benefit.'[52] However, patronage provides a social glue for hierarchical societies and thus Seneca's teaching was read with attention by republicans as well as monarchists in the eighteenth century. The longest of Seneca's moral essays is concerned with *beneficia*, the reciprocal exchange of services, a custom 'which more than any other binds together human society.'[53]

Seneca's *De Beneficiis* elaborates the art of patronage, or of securing grateful obedience. The three graces – the art of gracious giving, grateful receiving, and graceful requiting, all captured in Botticelli's images of holding hands and dancing around in a circle – make the world go around (*Ben.* 1.3.2.6). Only wise men really know how to bestow benefits and repay favours.[54] Seneca asserted (*Ben.* 2.22.1): 'The man who receives a benefit with gratitude repays the first installment on his debt.' Indeed (*Ben.* 2.30.2), 'he who receives a benefit gladly has already returned it.' Seneca counselled against enacting legislation against ingratitude – for the art of graceful giving will minimize base ingratitude – but the *ingratus homo* was for Seneca, as for Cicero, 'the lowest form of social life.'[55] As Joseph Amato writes, gratitude is a conservative emotion; it 'serves the authorities of established tradition' and 'affirms the worth of maintaining present relations.'[56]

Seneca accepted Aristotle's view (*Nichomachean Ethics*, IX.vii) that the love of benefactors for those benefited may be stronger than vice versa, because conferring favours is active and honourable, while receiving them is passive and dishonourable. But Seneca's treatise on patronage does not encompass the psychology of ingratitude, or help to explain Seneca's ingratitude to his patron, Agrippina, or his probable complicity in the Pisonian conspiracy against Nero.[57] Whatever Seneca's practice, his teaching on *Benefits* (2.20.2) was that tyrannicide is fruitless and that Brutus was wrong to kill his benefactor.

Within the patronage system, ingratitude is the worst of vices. In Dante's *Inferno* (canto 34, 60–6), the ninth circle, the darkest part of hell, is reserved for those, such as Judas and Brutus, who have betrayed benefactors. Edward Hyde, Earl of Clarendon, would have consigned Thomas Hobbes to hell as a Leveller who exhibited 'extreme malignity to the Nobility, by whose bread he hath bin alwaies sustained ...'[58] After the Restoration, the Earl of Clarendon was first minister to Charles II, who was well disposed to Hobbes. However, many of Charles's ministers and heads of colleges may have shared Clarendon's antipathy to ungrateful plebeians and denied them access to an education endangering hierarchy in church and state. Post-Restoration England purchased political stability at the expense of thought. Eighteenth-century Oxford and Cambridge became moribund when talented plebeians no longer could gain entry to the universities, which functioned largely to prepare the upper classes for the clerical profession, particularly after the crisis of non-juring clerics after the Glorious Revolution.

John Locke did not make the mistake of appearing ungrateful to his superiors. In his dedicatory epistle to the Earl of Pembroke, offering *An Essay concerning Humane Understanding* to the earl's protection, Locke wrote: 'Worthless Things receive a Value, when they are made the Offerings of Respect, Esteem, and Gratitude ...' In an earlier letter to the Earl of Pembroke, Locke protested too much that he was not ungrateful to his former patron, Lord Shaftesbury, whom he had served so faithfully. He declared: 'Some of my friends, when they considerd, how small an advancement of my fortune I had made, in soe long an attendance, have thought, that I had noe great reason to brag of the effects of that Kindenesse. I say not this, my lord, to complain of my dead master, it will be noe way decent in me, But in this extremity, I cannot but complain of it as an hard case, that haveing reaped soe litle advantage from my service to him whilst liveing, I should suffer soe much on that account now he is dead.'[59] While soliciting Pembroke's patronage, Locke knew that he should not appear ungrateful to his former patron.

Diderot's *Encyclopedia* entry on Locke indicates that he knew, as Locke did, the grammar of patronage: 'You can acquire a man of merit such as *Locke*, but you cannot *buy* him. This is a fact that wealthy people, who use money as the measure of everything, overlook, except perhaps in England. An English lord has rarely complained of the ingratitude of a scholar. We wish to be loved ...'[60] Diderot provided an Enlightenment ideal in his description of Locke; he was not a hired hand but a man of merit who deserved love and recognition, as well as money, from the great. By contrast, Rousseau, as Diderot well knew, presented himself as outside the patronage system. In letters to his 'ami protecteur' Malesherbes, Rousseau wrote that he hated the rich and asserted: 'I have always been unable to stand benefits. For every benefit demands gratitude: and I feel my heart to be ungrateful from the very fact alone that gratitude is a duty.'[61] Rousseau seemed to have felt the truth of the Inuit adage: 'Gifts make slaves just as whips make dogs.'[62] It seems, then, that egalitarians, such as Hobbes, Rousseau, Priestley, and Paine were more uncomfortable within the patronage system than enlightened liberals, such as Locke, Voltaire, Hume, Smith, Diderot, Franklin, and Kant. As Burke thundered: 'Ingratitude to benefactors is the first of revolutionary virtues.'[63]

Kant repaid Frederick's patronage with both praise and gratitude when he equated 'the age of enlightenment' with 'the century of Frederick': 'He deserves to be praised by a grateful present and posterity as the man who first liberated mankind from immaturity (as far as government is concerned), and who left all men free to use their own reason in all matters of conscience.'[64] Although Rousseau and Kant are often coupled as the teachers of moral autonomy – that humans are morally bound only by rules of their own making – Rousseau shunned royal patrons and Kant did not. Diderot frequently cited Rousseau's letter to Malesherbes in his apology for the life of Seneca. Diderot's biography of Seneca was his counter to Rousseau's *Confessions*, in which Rousseau presented his account of their broken friendship over the issue of patronage. Rousseau thought that Diderot had pressed him rather too warmly to accept a royal pension for *Le devin du village* in order to support his family, and he defended what Diderot saw as Rousseau's ingratitude to his *patronne*, Mme d'Épinay. While Rousseau wrote that Mme d'Épinay's venereal disease was the reason he was unable to accede to her request that he accompany her to Geneva, Diderot expressed his gratitude to Mme Geoffrin for refurnishing his apartment (with, among other objects, paintings by Rubens and

Vernet) by writing *Regrets sur ma vieille robe de chambre* for her.[65] The editors of Diderot's *Oeuvres Complètes* have appended Diderot's *Note sur la désunion de Diderot et de J.-J. Rousseau* to his *Essai sur les règnes de Claude et de Néron*, indicating the difference between the two thinkers with respect to the proper gratitude to be shown to patrons.

To return to Seneca's views on the ingratitude of Brutus to Caesar, we must consider Seneca's view that the assassination of Caesar was wrong and fruitless in the context of the amount of dissimulation necessary to survive in the courts of Caligula, Claudius, and Nero. However, Seneca's statement about the folly of Brutus trying to resurrect a republic and his view that 'a state reaches its best condition under the rule of a just king' (*Ben.*2.20.2) are consistent with Stoic doctrine.[66] To the extent that the contemplative life is superior to the active life, or the life of philosophy is preferable to that of the statesman and citizen-soldier, monarchy may be preferable to republics. Contemplatives, Seneca stressed, need the leisure provided by monarchs. In letter 73 to Lucilius, which his translators have entitled 'On Philosophers and Kings,' Seneca wrote: 'It seems to me erroneous to believe that those who have loyally dedicated themselves to philosophy are stubborn and rebellious, scorners of magistrates or kings or of those who control the administration of public affairs. For, on the contrary, no class of men is so popular with the philosopher as the ruler is; and rightly so, because rulers bestow upon no men a greater privilege than upon those who are allowed to enjoy peace and leisure.' If kings and philosophers are naturally linked in patron-client relationships, philosophers are ready to acknowledge their debt to rulers by obedience and loyal service: 'This is what philosophy teaches us most of all – honourably to avow the debt of services received, and honourably to pay them; sometimes, however, the acknowledgement itself constitutes payment. Our philosopher will therefore acknowledge that he owes a larger debt to the ruler who makes it possible, by his management and foresight, for him to enjoy rich leisure, control of his own time, and a tranquillity uninterrupted by public employments.'[67]

Diderot, too, wholeheartedly espoused the reciprocal relationship between philosophers and kings. Seneca had proved 'that the philosopher is anything but a seditious rebel or bad citizen' (*ERCN*, 492). Philosophers respect law and order and teach magistrates, generals, priests, sovereigns, and subjects their duties. Diderot recommended that philosophers be awarded a civic crown of oak leaves for saving citizens from priestly superstition and educating them in civic duties

(*ERCN*, 539). It is priests, not philosophers, who preach sedition and revolution against monarchies. Religion inculcates millenial expectations in the masses, whereas philosophy preaches Stoicism them. 'Man is exposed to misfortune and pain; the philosopher teaches man how to suffer' (*ERCN*, 492). As distinct from the priest, 'it is the philosopher who feels a benefit, it is he who is prompt in recognizing it and requiting it by his acknowledgement' (493).

Diderot was certainly not alone amongst the *philosophes* in opposing the altar more vigorously than the throne; Voltaire and D'Alembert also did not want to offend the state as well as the church, and they criticized both Rousseau and D'Holbach's *Essai sur les préjugés* for their imprudent criticism of state and church alike.[68] As Robert Darnton indicates: 'The *Encyclopédie* treated the state with more respect than the church, and it did not contest the supremacy of the privileged orders.'[69]

Kant also seemed to support Seneca's view of the natural bond between philosophers and kings: he wrote that 'a high degree of civil freedom seems advantageous to a people's *intellectual* freedom, yet it also sets up insuperable barriers to it. Conversely, a lesser degree of civil freedom gives intellectual freedom enough room to expand to its fullest extent.'[70] While Moses Mendelssohn agreed with Kant that intellectual freedom flourished in Frederick's Prussia, Gotthold Lessing wrote: 'Do not talk to me of your liberty of thought and the press. It reduces itself to the permission to let off as many squibs against religion as one likes. Let someone raise his voice for the rights of subjects or against exploitation and despotism, and you will soon see which is the most slavish land in Europe.'[71] Rousseau tested Frederick's reputation for tolerance when he refused Frederick's offer of patronage during the time he was on the run from France and Geneva, and he told Frederick to save his benefactions for those who had lost limbs in his service.[72]

While Diderot accepted Seneca's view that the pacific vocation of philosophy ties it to monarchy, he could not espouse Seneca's counsel of reclusion in the face of tyranny. In letter 14, to Lucilius, Seneca wrote: 'So the wise man will never provoke the anger of those in power; nay, he will even turn his course, precisely as he would turn from a storm if he were steering a ship.'[73] Diderot loftily commented that Seneca's advice here is cowardly, counselling us to suppress the truth and deny the philosopher's vocation. 'What then is the use of philosophy, if it remains silent? Either speak or renounce the title of the educator of the human race. You will be persecuted, that's your destiny;

one will see you drink hemlock' (*ERCN*, 513–14; *EVS*, 672) as Socrates and Seneca did (but, we might add, Diderot did not – he was anything but stoical when incarcerated in Vincennes). Philosophers, Diderot airily asserted, prefer a virtuous attachment to truth to life itself and look forward to future princes to put into practice philosophic truths, even if present princes take their lives (*ERCN*, 455). Diderot praised Seneca's father for pointing out the barriers to a philosophic life; the interests of truth counter those of 'the priests who sell the lie, magistrates who protect it, and sovereigns who detest philosophy' (*ERCN*, 293). Less loftily, Diderot espoused 'a great and useful idea' found in D'Alembert's *Éloge de l'abbé de Saint-Pierre*, namely, that men of letters leave a will where they can freely write what their conscience dictates, unrestrained by the fear or circumspection required in despotic regimes; in their last will and testament, writers would be able 'to ask the pardon of their century for only having a posthumous sincerity' (*ERCN*, 464). Prudently, Diderot withheld his critical observations on Catherine's legal code until after his death. Catherine, for her part, when offering patronage to Diderot, wrote to Diderot's friend and Catherine's client, Friedrich Melchior Grimm, commanding: 'Acquire for me all the works of Diderot. *Of course they will not get out of my hands and will not harm anyone.* Send them together with the library.'[74] Catherine did not want her subjects to be corrupted by the writings of those she patronized, such as Voltaire and Diderot.

Free speech, coupled to obedience to authority, seemed to have been the definitive slogan of the Enlightenment. Jeremy Bentham's dictum to speak freely and obey punctually[75] was espoused by Kant and Diderot. Graciously deferring to his royal patron, as Diderot did to Catherine, Kant wrote: 'But only a ruler who is himself enlightened and has no fear of phantoms, yet who likewise has at hand a well-disciplined and numerous army to guarantee public security, may say what no republic would dare to say: *Argue as much as you like and about whatever you like, but obey!*' Kant gave the Enlightenment its motto: *Sapere aude!* Joseph Amato's commentary on this motto overstates the case: 'Dare to know!, even if this led him into direct confrontation with public authorities, even if it meant risking his immortal soul.'[76] Given Kant's joining of obedience and freedom of thought, a more accurate transcription of Kant's injunction than Amato's might be: Have the courage to use your own understanding but not to act on it. As Diderot put it in his *Supplément au voyage de Bougainville*: 'We must speak out against senseless laws until they're reformed and, in the meantime, abide by them.'[77]

Diderot and Seneca were at one on the need to express themselves with circumspection in tyrannical regimes; however, paradoxically enough, Diderot also sang the praises of free speech. Seneca reported that Augustus lamented that his favourites, Agrippa and Maecenas, were no longer alive to tell him the shortcomings of his daughter, Julia. Seneca commented (*Ben.* 6.32.3–4): 'There is no reason for us to suppose that Agrippa and Maecenas were in the habit of speaking the truth to him; they would have been amongst the dissemblers if they lived.' This observation poses problems for Seneca's doctrine of patronage. Favours are supposed to be freely given, and gratefully received, but apparently Agrippa and Maecenas were not free to give Augustus good advice. Nor is one free to refuse gifts from men of poor character who are in power; if the powerful threaten duress, the wise man does well to comply (*Ben.* 2.18.7; 5.6.7).

Seneca reported that Socrates refused the invitation to attend the court of King Archelaus, saying that he would not be able to repay benefits bestowed on him. Yet, while Socrates was morally free to refuse, he could have benefited King Archelaus with his wisdom. Seneca (*Ben.* 5.6.2–7) construed Socrates' refusal to mean 'that the man whose freedom of speech even a free state could not endure declined to enter into voluntary servitude.' Thus, despite Seneca's praise of patronage as the basis of social bonds, he suggested that Socrates' acceptance of royal patronage would have been 'voluntary servitude' and perhaps his own service to Nero was involuntary, particularly in the closing years of Seneca's life. Seneca's praise of royal patronage might be said to be situational, rather than principled.

Diderot disagreed with Seneca's view that philosophers must accept the favours of a tyrant. He wrote (*ERCN*, 345): 'The philosopher must refuse the gifts of a tyrant. The more the gifts are illegitimate, the more the refusal must be stubborn; there is no overpowering force against probity.' However, the pension Diderot received from Catherine was not from a tyrant but from 'a great sovereign' (*ERCN*, 616).

Diderot believed Seneca's *De Beneficiis* to be a 'sublime treatise' (*ERCN*, 474), full of 'divine precepts' and 'celestial sentiments' (*EVS*, 690) and surpassing all of Seneca's other writings in its fecundity (*ERCN*, 545; *EVS*, 696). It provides a model of how philosophers should respond to the benefactions of the powerful. Diderot's justification of patronage in his lives of Seneca is an essential complement to Adam Smith's self-interested market exchanges of goods and services. Patronage and self-interested market exchange are not mutually exclusive.

Indeed, as we shall see in chapter 6, Smith was a strong supporter of the Senecan moment, or the exchange of favours and gratitude; the laws of gratitude, next to the laws of justice (respecting property rights and observing contracts), are the clearest and most vital aspect of moral philosophy. Diderot, like Smith and many eighteenth-century thinkers, merged Bernard Mandeville's egoism with Lord Shaftesbury's sociability or benevolence.[78] He answered the great question he posed: 'What is the object of philosophy? It is to tie men together by a commerce of ideas, and by the exercise of mutual beneficence' (*ERCN*, 456–7). Eighteenth-century civil society, that is, a marketplace of goods, services, and ideas, complemented by the shadow market of patron-client relations, supplants the mighty Leviathan – the state – in holding together asocial individuals. Patronage and market exchange, rather than state force, were held to be the social bonds of the eighteenth century.

Despite occasional criticisms of Seneca's cowardice and toadying, especially with respect to his *Consolation to Polybius*, Diderot's *Essai sur la vie de Sénèque* and his *Essai sur les règnes de Claude et de Néron* constitute a spirited defence of Seneca as well as an apology for his own 'living,' or the importance of patronage to the philosophic way of life. In contrast to John Millar, who thought that Seneca, although the best of the Romans, accumulated wealth by despoiling Britons and thus contaminated his philosophy by an unseemly love of money,[79] Diderot denounced as aristocratic prejudice those who criticized the philosopher for amassing enormous wealth from Nero's patronage; no one comments adversely on the patricians who profited under the principate because 'they are only the Great, and Seneca was a sage!' (*ERCN*, 407). Men of letters – Voltaire and Hélvetius come to mind – as well as hereditary aristocrats, have a right to amass great wealth. Moreover, Seneca, with his great fortune, was a generous benefactor to other men of letters: 'Seneca wrote, lived and died as a sage' (*ERCN*, 329). Indeed, for purity of word and deed in corrupt times, Diderot was tempted to call his teacher on patronage '*Sancte Seneca*' (*EVSP*, 676; *ERCN*, 518). Following his acknowledgment of Catherine as his sole patron after long travails earning his living and enriching merchants of the *Encyclopédie*, which inhibited him from following his bent as a philosopher and writer (*ERCN*, 620), Diderot concluded that Seneca was 'a great thinker, a virtuous educator and a great minister' (*ERCN*, 621).

Diderot and Voltaire praised Catherine for enlightening her people, just as Kant's essay 'What is Enlightenment?' praised his patron,

Frederick the Great, for enlightening his people. They remained silent on Catherine's dismemberment of the rebel, Pugachev, although Voltaire wrote D'Alembert at the time that Catherine's regime was 'the most despotic on earth,' a judgment he had earlier made about Frederick's Prussia.[80] Catherine's patronage of Diderot relieved him of the bitter poverty that he described in his alter ego, Rameau's nephew; helped him and Voltaire with Enlightenment causes in France, such as obtaining redress for the Calas family; and provided him with the illusion of bringing civilization or reform to Russia by means of Catherine's enlightened despotism. Daniel Brewer asserts that 'the Enlightenment as a whole can be summed up as the conjuncture of knowledge and power.'[81] In this sense, the relationship of Diderot and Catherine was the Enlightenment writ large; as Jean Starobinski notes, the classical asymmetry of patron to client is 'more pronounced when the person flattered is not merely a wealthy individual but a tyrant or prince.'[82] Seneca was not only the tutor of Nero but the preceptor of the Enlightenment.

Almost all writers in the eighteenth century lived from patronage, even though the ideal of intellectual independence was then at its apogee. Most writers deprecated patronage as outdated and servile while living from government pensions or patronage posts. Rousseau and Paine, who fared relatively poorly from patronage, wrote positively of the practice. Indeed, the latter's panegyric to patronage celebrates Catherine the Great. While it may seem paradoxical that a republican praises the effects of royal patronage – Condorcet's pensions from the academies of Berlin and St Petersburg were withdrawn after his profession of republican sympathies in the French Revolution – Paine lacked an independent income. In a letter of 16 February 1784 to General Lewis Morris, a wealthy New York landed gentleman who signed the Declaration of Independence, Paine wrote:

> The countries the most famous and the most respected of antiquity are those which distinguished themselves by promoting and patronizing science, and on the contrary those which neglected or discouraged it are universally denominated rude and barbarous. The patronage which Britain has shown to Arts, Science and Literature has given her a better established and lasting rank in the world than she ever acquired by her arms. And Russia is a modern instance of the effect which the encouragement of those things produces both as to the internal improvement of a country and the character it raises abroad. The reign of

Louis the fourteenth is more distinguished by being the Era of science and literature in France than by any other circumstance of those days.[83]

Voltaire, who was patronized by Frederick the Great and Catherine the Great, indicated, in his *Siècle de Louis XIV*, that all great ages are monarchical; Paine, the great republican, did not go quite that far but gave due praise to the greatest patron of Enlightenment, Catherine, thus showing the extent of the 'Senecan moment' in the age of reason. Those who wrote most strongly against patronage, such as D'Alembert in *Essai sur la société des gens de lettres et des grands* or Johnson in his letter to Lord Chesterfield, did rather better than Paine: D'Alembert received five modest pensions and Johnson a moderate government pension. Diderot's *Essai sur la vie de Sénèque* and *Essai sur les règnes de Claude et de Néron* are indirect arguments for the patronage of philosophy.

We might conclude, then, that intellectual patronage existed in a condition of denial. For example, Edward Gibbon voiced the refrain of David Hume and Samuel Johnson in his *Memoirs*: 'I cannot boast of the friendship and favour of princes; the patronage of English literature has long since been devolved on our booksellers, and the measure of their liberality is the least ambiguous test of our common success.'[84] Gibbon apparently did not consider the patronage appointment to the Board of Trade for £750 per annum (two and a half times greater than Johnson's pension), which Lord North procured for him from George III, to be princely favour. Also, on the page previous to his declaration of authorial independence, Gibbon says that Lord Sheffield made him rich after his sinecure with the Board of Trade expired in 1782: 'My friend Lord Sheffield has kindly relieved me from the cares to which my tastes and temper are most adverse.'[85]

Enlightenment thinkers espoused the ideal of a Smithian self-sustaining marketplace of ideas, denying all patronage but the funds accruing from booksellers in their role as 'modern patrons of literature,' even as they enjoyed the patronage they declared obsolete. Diderot's lives of Seneca expressed the real world of Enlightenment, as distinct from the ideal world of a life free of patronage. His justification of patronage represented an element in eighteenth-century thought that was distinct both from the liberal idea of a press culture producing a democratic republic of letters and from Rousseauan republicanism and rejection of royal patronage.

4 Patronage and the Modes of Liberal Tolerance: Bayle, Care, and Locke

Pierre Bayle and John Locke were two heroes of the Enlightenment. Voltaire praised 'the wise Locke' and 'the immortal Bayle, the glory of human nature,'[1] while Edward Gibbon wrote of Bayle: 'Without a country, or a patron, or a prejudice, he claimed the liberty and subsisted by the labours of his pen.'[2] Locke was not without a country or religious prejudice and, because he was patronized, did not subsist by the labours of his pen. A third figure of the period, the popular journalist Henry Care, like Bayle, did subsist by the labours of his pen and, like Locke, was a leading Whig thinker who attempted to exclude the Catholic James, the brother of Charles II, from succession to the throne during the Exclusion Crisis in 1679–81. But when James ascended to the throne in 1685, the year that Louis XIV revoked the Edict of Nantes (which a century before had extended toleration to Huguenots in France), Care and Bayle supported James II's comprehensive toleration, while Locke (and the Protestant landowners who patronized him) thought that Catholicism would jeopardize liberty and property and thus excluded Catholics from his proposals for religious toleration. Léo Pierre Courtines writes: 'In comparison with Bayle's more carefully reasoned theories, Locke's ideas today seemed anything but tolerant.'[3] In this chapter, I intend to examine the relationship between forms of patronage and the variants of liberal doctrine on religious toleration.

The Unpatronized and Unprejudiced Pierre Bayle

Bayle almost lived up to the Enlightenment ideal of an independent man of letters. He had a patron in Rotterdam, Adrien Paets, who offered him a modest pension of 500 florins to teach philosophy at L'École Illustre, established by Paets for Bayle and his former mentor, and later adversary, Pierre Jurieu, after both men had been hounded by the French government in 1681 from the Protestant Academy in Sedan as part of the suppression of Huguenots in the years leading up to the Revocation of the Edict of Nantes. Bayle's relationship to his republican patron was to spoil possible relationships to William of Orange, the monarch whose claims Jurieu supported in the Netherlands and in Britain. Paets's wife bequeathed 2,000 florins to Bayle to buy books. He received no salary for editing *Nouvelles de la République des Lettres* from 1684 to 1687, but the position allowed him to get books postage free through his publisher, Jacques Desborbes.[4] Bayle came closest to Adam Smith's ideal scholar, who is, thanks to the invention of print, no longer a beggar. His bachelorhood, or freedom from domestic responsibilities, facilitated his independence.

Bayle was also the Enlightenment ideal of a truly tolerant man. Voltaire saw Bayle in his own image, a man whose tolerance derived from his scepticism, as distinct from a Protestant with the inner certainty that conscience should be immune from government regulation.[5] Gibbon saw Bayle in his own image, as a convert and then apostate from Catholicism. Had Bayle stayed within the Catholic Church, Gibbon wrote, he would have enjoyed 'the comforts of a benefice, or the dignity of a mitre' whereas, at Rotterdam, he lived 'in a private state of exile, indigence, and freedom.' Gibbon quoted Bayle with a hearty slap on the back: 'I am most truly a Protestant; for I protest indifferently against all systems and all sects.'[6]

As an apostate from Catholicism, Bayle had better grounds to fear persecution from the Catholic Church than Locke, Care, or his colleague Pierre Jurieu. When Bayle was exiled in Rotterdam, the French government responded by billeting soldiers in his parents' house, beggaring his family, and preventing them from sleeping by blowing horns at night. His father died in 1685, the year of the Revocation of the Edict of Nantes, and then his brother, Jacob, after being imprisoned and tortured, died in jail, leaving Pierre racked with guilt since he knew that he, rather than his father and brother, was the real target of the punishment.[7] Bayle had drawn the ire of the court of Louis XIV by his criticism of Louis Maimbourg's *Histoire du Calvinisme*. He was particularly disgusted with Maimbourg's attack on Calvinism because Maimbourg, when a Jesuit, had been persecuted by the Roman hierarchy, but when provided with 'a fat pension' and with 'his title of

Historiographer especially protected by the greatest Prince of the World' he attacked ultramontane Catholics and Huguenots at the behest of his royal protector. Monseigneur Maimbourg had to renounce 'the prejudices of his order' and change his views on the position of the pope in his religion in order to bow to Louis the Great and 'to become a Court Jesuit, and Jesuit Pensioner.'[8]

Bayle prided himself on his independence of thought and expressed particular contempt for those who, like Maimbourg, had traded their principles for patronage. The longest entry in Bayle's *Dictionnaire historique et critique* is on Spinoza, whom Bayle praised for his independence and for living in accordance with his principles, however misguided. Bayle thought Spinoza's *Tractatus Theologico-Politicus* to be atheistic and 'a Pernicious and Execrable Book' but the author was nonetheless 'a Sociable, Affable, Honest, Officious, and a good Moral Man.' Spinoza was poor and 'would not have had the wherewithal to live, if one of his Friends had not left him by his Will, wherewithal to maintain himself.' His heretical views made him lose his pension and led to his excommunication from his Amsterdam synagogue, forcing him to retire to the country where he lived by making microscopes and telescopes and devoted his life to the pursuit of truth undistracted by friendships and urban amusements. 'The *Palentine* Court offered him a Professorship of Philosophy at *Heidelberg*, but he refused it, being an Employment little consistent with his great Desire of inquiring into Truth, without any Interruption.'[9] Spinoza was a model of an independent man of letters. While Bayle disagreed with Spinoza's atheism, he thought it important to show that an atheist could be an upright man in order to undermine views that morality depended upon religion and thus the state has a duty to maintain orthodoxy or the dominant religion by all means including force. Commenting on Matthias Knuzen, the leader of a professedly atheist sect called the Conscienciaries, Bayle claimed 'that the notions of natural religion, the Ideas of the *honestum*, the impressions of reason, in a word the inward light of conscience, may continue in the mind of a man, even when the notion of the being of God, and the belief of another world are intirely rooted out.'[10] In this respect, Bayle differed from Locke, who thought that atheists could not be moral agents and hence could not be tolerated in any society.

Bayle criticized the vanity of Spinoza's apparently histrionic death and seemed to approve of Hobbes's calmness as he approached his own end. After reporting that Spinoza told his landlady not to allow any ministers to visit him on his deathbed, Bayle asked: 'Can there be a more Ridiculous and Extravagant Vanity, a more Foolish Passion for a Wrong Notion of Constancy?' He elaborated that Spinoza 'was extremely desirous to Immortalize his Name, and wou'd have willingly Sacrificed his Life to that Glory, tho' in order to obtain it, he had been torn in Pieces by the Mob.'[11] Bayle appeared to think that, while the Christian may endure martyrdom for his immortal soul, atheists may be equally steadfast in the face of violent death for the sake of immortalizing one's name. Thus, the republic of letters may be governed by the desire for glory, since fear governs visible despotisms and conscience rules the invisible City of God.

Bayle shared the fear of Catholicism exhibited by his Huguenot compatriot Pierre Jurieu and by English Protestants. He wrote, in *Commentaire philosophique sur les paroles de Jésus-Christ, Contrain-les d'entrer* (1686): 'There is no doubt that the goal of the pope and his henchmen is to subjugate the whole world. They are prompted to this by the interest in dominating and amassing riches.'[12] In the same connection, Bayle thought that Louis XIV's revocation of the Edict of Nantes was a breach of his duty to enforce his royal authority; it was the action of a bigot under the thumb of a confessor, not an autonomous regal decision.[13] Yet, despite his fear of the Catholic threat to freedom of conscience, Bayle advocated comprehensive toleration for Catholics, as well as for Protestants, Jews, Muslims, pagans, and atheists, insisting that no state, no matter whether the dominant religion is Catholic or Protestant, has any right to interfere with the God-given right to freedom of conscience. 'Since God hath assumed to Himself the power and the dominion of the conscience, who alone can rightly instruct and govern it, therefore it is not lawful for anyone whatsoever, by virtue of any authority or principality they bear in the government of this world, to force the conscience of others.'[14] Jurieu believed that Bayle's teaching amounted to religious indifference and would impede Protestant states from combating papal imperialism; Bayle's arguments for the rights of erroneous conscience, Jurieu indignantly charged, would prevent Protestant princes, like William of Orange, from establishing true religion.[15] Jurieu used William of Orange's influence to deprive Bayle of his position teaching philosophy at L'École Illustre in Rotterdam. Yet, Bayle refused the patronage of various English aristocrats after the Glorious Revolution, including Baron Somers, the patron of Locke, Toland, and Tindal. Robert Adams wrote that 'Bayle ... declined the pension that Somers tried to arrange for him. Touchy as Doctor

Johnson with Lord Chesterfield, he worked on in his independent refuge at Rotterdam ...'[16] Perhaps because of an Augustinean pessimism about human nature, Bayle seemed to take as his motto the old aphorism 'Beware of Greeks [or Englishmen] bearing gifts.'[17]

Bayle had numerous English contacts in Holland, including John Locke and Gilbert Burnet, whom Bayle met at the house of the Quaker Benjamin Furly. He also met Anthony Ashley Cooper, 3rd Earl of Shaftesbury, who introduced him to Pierre Des Maizeaux, Bayle's English translator and biographer, and Des Maizeaux in turn advised Bayle that the English liked bulky works of scientific scholarship.[18] Since he was dismissed from his teaching position in 1692, Bayle used his enforced leisure, and the enormous number of notes he had amassed as editor of *Nouvelles de la République des Lettres*, to write the first work to be published under his own name, the *Dictionnaire historique et critique* (1697), commissioned by his publisher Reinier Leers. Bayle rejected the advice of his friends to dedicate the work to Sir William Trumball, secretary of state to William of Orange. He also turned down the offer of 1,200 guineas from the Duke of Shrewsbury if Bayle would dedicate the *Dictionnaire* to him, and rejected the patronage of the Duke of Buckingham and the earls of Albemarle and Halifax.[19] Bayle thought that there was as much 'grovelling and making oneself agreeable to the parties in power' in England as there was in France. Only by 'the free gift' of scholarship could the man of letters earn 'a good title to nobility in the republic of sciences.' However, Bayle modestly portrayed himself as a member of the 'third estate in the Republic of Letters,' a description he thought suitable for those who catalogue writers not particularly famous or illustrious.[20]

Bayle believed that patronage would compromise his independence in the republic of letters, and particularly his position favouring equitable treatment of Catholic and Protestant minorities. He supported the Duke of York during the Exclusion Crisis, when Locke and Care were vigorously attempting to exclude him from the crown, and when James came to the throne in the year that Louis XIV had revoked the Edict of Nantes, Bayle supported James's Declaration of Toleration to Catholics and Protestant Dissenters (Care, now patronized by the Stuart court, supported the measure as well, but Locke, who supported the intolerance of a Church of England under threat by a Catholic king, opposed it). Bayle thought that the Catholics of England and Scotland (roughly 2 to 5 per cent of the population) were so few in number that they could not unite under a Catholic king to oppress

Protestants. Also, Bayle's experience in Holland showed him that Catholics could be tolerated without undermining civil order. His conflict with Pierre Jurieu, who wanted William of Orange to be the white knight leading a crusade against the Catholic foe, made him vividly aware that intolerance was not a Catholic monopoly and made him fear an even greater oppression of Huguenots in his native France. Bayle approved of the English system of subjecting ecclesiastical to civil power but disapproved of religious uniformity in Protestant as well as Catholic forms. He insisted on 'that eternal law which shows us ... that religion is an affair of conscience not subject to control'[21] but thought that the cause of toleration was perhaps best secured by Hobbesian Erastianism – 'better Leviathan than Torquemada.'[22] However, he worried about Protestant Torquemadas; the burning of Servetus at the hands of Calvin for denying the Trinity was 'a hideous blot upon the early days of the Reformation.'[23] Bayle seemed more concerned that Protestants avoid inflicting evil than that they be protected from suffering it. The forcing of conscience is iniquitous not because, as Locke had it, it is impossible; Locke's view was that 'no man can, if he would, conform his faith to the dictates of another.'[24] Bayle knew such a view to be false; the rape of the soul, like the violation of women's bodies, however morally impermissible, is all too possible. French Catholics in the past century had effectively converted Huguenots back into the Catholic Church by state force. Locke maintained that 'confiscation of estate, imprisonment, torments, nothing of that nature can have any such efficacy as to make men change the inward judgment that they have framed of things.'[25] Bayle, on the other hand, recognized that 'there are few who in the extremity of suffering will not betray conscience.'[26] Since religious persecution is an act of rape not of love,[27] supporters of William of Orange tended to exhibit the opposite of Christian love. Bayle wrote: 'God preserve us from Protestant inquisition, which within five or six years would be so terrible as to make us long for the Roman one, as for a good thing.'[28] Bayle's fears seemed and seem extravagant to most Scots and English, but perhaps not so to the Irish, although the bloodshed there could not properly be called an Inquisition. From Bayle's perspective, to accept the patronage of the great lords who had profited by the expropriation of the English monasteries might compromise a disinterested stance in the grand cause of comprehensive toleration, not just the toleration for Protestants that Locke and Jurieu wanted.

Bayle's ideal was fraternal cooperation and mutual respect and civility in the republic of letters. Yet Bayle's goal of disinterestedness and complete impartiality was always fatally compromised by patronage and the practice of dedicating books to great men. Bayle was aware of the dilemma facing poor men without patrons. He strongly criticized the philosopher Bion, who responded to the poet Theognis's verse 'One cannot say, nor do, if poor he be ... His Tongue is bound to th' Peace, as well as he' by asking: 'How comes it to pass then ... that thyself being so poor, pratest and gratest our ears in such a manner.' Bayle declared: 'The insolent and insulting spirit of that Philosopher appears here; a poor poet, who complains that Poverty tyes his Tongue, ought not to be treated in that manner: for though Experience shews very often, that want of Bread and Clothes make one very talkative; yet it is certain, that there are many things a Man ill-clothed dares not say.'[29] Poor men, like Theognis and, as we shall see, Henry Care, may be caught between dependence on a patron or remaining silent and starving to death.

Since the norm of scholarly cooperation befits the republic of letters, Bayle favoured non-violent competition among rival faiths to provide the public with examples of piety and good works and rational accounts of faith. If Gibbon and Voltaire underestimated the Protestant faith underlying Bayle's championship of freedom of conscience, they were right to cherish his independence and impartial toleration.

Henry Care: Toleration for Hire?

Whereas Gibbon praised Bayle for living by his pen, Henry Care, another supporter of James II's Declaration of Indulgence, was deprecated by his contemporaries, and posterity, for living by his pen, that is, for being a professional writer who prostituted his pen for his patrons. In its entry on Care, the *Dictionary of National Biography* cites Anthony Wood's judgment that Care was 'a poor snivelling fellow' who wrote 'not for Religion or Conscience sake, which he before did pretend, but meerly for Interest.' Care's support for the Declaration of Indulgence was not a matter of principle; rather, he was 'made a Tool to print matters for the abolishing of the *Test* and Penal Laws.' Care had been 'deeply engaged by the fanatical party, after the popish plot broke out in 1678, to write against the church of England.' Care, Wood asserted, 'whose breeding was in the nature of a petty fogger, a little despicable wretch ... after K. James II came to the crown, [was] drawn over so far by the R. Cath. Party for bread and money sake, and nothing else, to write on their behalf, and to vindicate their proceedings against the men of the church of England.'[30] Similarly, Care has recently been described derisively as 'the hardestworking [sic] horse' in 'the king's journalistic stable.'[31] Neither Wood nor posterity seems able to credit Care's support for James II's Whiggish policy of religious toleration, or his opposition to the monopoly position of the Church of England, as principled, just as modern scholars appear unable to see Locke's opposition to the Declaration of Indulgence or support for the established church as unprincipled.

In her recent fine biography of Henry Care, Lois Schwoerer attributes the neglect of Henry Care to the impression that he was a 'loser,' a plebeian on the losing side of the Exclusion Crisis and then the Glorious Revolution.[32] Unlike Locke, Care was unable to secure aristocratic patrons, and so he first wrote anti-Catholic Whig tracts for urban plebeians before, in the year preceding the Glorious Revolution, writing strongly in favour of comprehensive toleration. We might ask, given the different reputations of Care and Locke, whether accepting royal patronage is inherently illiberal but accepting aristocratic patronage is more liberal or at least less servile. Judging him simply by his doctrines would make Care, like Bayle, an advocate of comprehensive toleration, more liberal than Locke, whose *Letters concerning Toleration* exclude Catholics and atheists and whose *Reasonableness of Christianity* excludes toleration for Catholics, atheists, Jews, and Muslims. Lois Schwoerer calls for a contextual reading of Care, who 'changed sides in printed tracts as the market, the persecutory policies of the government required.'[33]

Care seemed to follow the career path of the leading journalist of the English Civil War, Marchamont Nedham, who supported parliament from 1642 to 1646, supported King Charles I in 1648, betrayed him in 1649–50, supported the Rump Parliament from 1650–3, sided with Cromwell on that parliament's dissolution in 1653, and then remained an adherent of Cromwell until he lauded the restoration of Charles II. Blair Worden writes: 'His nimble pen ... turned to the winning side in order to stay out of jail or save his skin. Invariably short of cash, he was invariably willing to write for it.'[34] If Care's and Nedham's penurious career as journalists required them to change course, Care was on the losing side while Nedham was on the winning side.

Care came from a lower-middle-class background. Little is known of his education, but, since he had French, Latin, Greek, and a little Hebrew, Schwoerer speculates that he probably had some grammar-school education that facilitated his self-education in bookshops and lending libraries.[35] Working as a law clerk who wrote thoughtful pamphlets extolling the role of juries in protecting English liberties, Care entered the republic of letters by writing pamphlets on women in the 1670s to exploit the growing female market for literature; he dedicated *Female Pre-Eminence* to Queen Caroline but she took no notice of it. Another of his works, *The Grandeur and Glory of France* (1673), was dedicated to James, Duke of Monmouth, and Care may have attempted to secure the protection of Locke's patron, Lord Shaftesbury.[36] His failure to secure a patron led him to look to those of 'middle or meaner Rank' for readers of his anti-papal journals, the *Weekly Pacquet of Advice from Rome* and the *Popish Courant*, from 1678 to 1683, fuelling and responding to the bigotry of the Popish Plot during the Exclusion Crisis. Care's anti-popery also took aim at the established church for not doing enough to combat the Catholic threat. In the *Weekly Pacquet* of 24 December 1681 Care wrote: 'If such a pitiful lay ignorant fellow [like me] can say so much against Popery, what might an Hero in Cap and Gown, circled with Postiles and Polyantheas, and all the Ammunition of Pocket-Learning; or a man of Parts and Leisure, a Reverend Divine, with ten Cartloads of Books, and three Spiritual Preferments, the helps of Conversation and bountiful Patrons, the assistance of the Bodlean [sic] Library, and the prospect of promotion, to spur a flagging Industry, what, I say, might such an one have wrote upon the subject?' Care did not write from 1683 to 1687 but took up his pen to defend James's Declaration of Indulgence to Catholics and Dissenters, and in this regard he even surpassed the leading Stuart apologist, Sir Roger L'Estrange, whose support for James's policy of toleration was muted by his attachment to the established church.[37] James II set free 1,200 imprisoned Quakers in the first year of his reign and gradually extended toleration to Baptists and other dissenters. Locke thought that, since Quakers refused to swear oaths to the civil authorities, their promises of loyalty, like those of atheists and Catholics, were unreliable – a not insignificant matter because it was on such promises that the social contract was based. For his part, Care claimed that his support for James's Declaration of Indulgence was principled; it was deference to his God, not simply to his king: 'Every man (on Peril of his Soul) must endeavor to satisfie his Conscience, and stand or fall in the great day of Trial, to his own Master; who alone is the Judge thereof.'[38]

Was it Protestant principle or royal patronage that prompted Care to support James's policy of religious toleration? J.R. Jones claims that: 'Henry Care boldly took the bull by the horns in using the Revocation [of the Edict of Nantes] as an argument for trusting James.'[39] Care thought that James would never jeopardize England's prosperity and tranquillity, as Louis XIV had done with his Revocation of the Edict of Nantes. James's Declaration of Indulgence was aimed at those who supported Whig principles in the Exclusion Crisis but, as Jones writes, 'Protestant landowners began to fear a reversal of the Restoration land settlement.'[40] Powerful Whigs saw James's Declaration of Indulgence as a subtle means of reintroducing Catholicism into England and thereby undermining security of property and religious liberty. In contrast, Care did not think the Church of England a model of enlightened tolerance and staked his ground on a matter of fundamental principle: 'Ever since I was capable of understanding any thing of Religion, I have thought Liberty of Conscience to be the Birth right of Mankind by a Charter Divine.'[41] He believed that his support of James's Declaration of Indulgence was consistent with basic Whig principles, even though he had attempted to exclude James from the throne a decade earlier. In short, Care was consistently a proponent of Whig doctrine, but his reputation, unlike that of the most renowned Whig, as an intellectual prostitute, serving those who bring him money, will probably endure.

The Judicious Locke

John Locke's judgment that a Catholic king could overturn the Protestant religion in Britain, or ruin the country in the oppressive attempt to do so, has generally been accepted by posterity. Locke justified the Glorious Revolution by the threat posed by the Catholic James to liberty and property, a threat sufficient to warrant armed resistance to government. An assessment of the validity of Locke's position that Catholic kings were intolerable in Protestant Britain, relative to Bayle's and Care's view that James could not overthrow the Protestant religion and would not jeopardize England's commercial supremacy in the attempt to do so, requires historical knowledge well beyond my competence. My concern here is limited to the relationship between patronage and Whig doctrine, and thus I intend to judge Locke's teaching on toleration with the same criteria of significance as have been used to judge Care's ideas.

In *The Career of Toleration: John Locke, Jonas Proast and After*, Richard Vernon refers to Proast's 'distinguished High Church Anglican patronage' but never mentions Locke's patrons.[42] To be sure, Locke worked out the main arguments for his theory of tolerating Protestant dissenters (but not Catholics and atheists) in his capacity, as Maurice Cranston writes, of 'domestic philosopher to the Whig leader, the first earl of Shaftesbury.'[43] Before entering the household of Anthony Ashley Cooper, the 1st Earl of Shaftesbury, Locke called upon the state to impose religious uniformity.[44] After doing so, he accommodated his views to those of his patron. W.M. Spellman states that 'Shaftesbury was a strong opponent of arbitrary and absolutist government, and he always associated Roman Catholicism with this form of temporal rule. Together with his career-long call for toleration for Protestant Dissenters and in support of the rights of Parliament, Locke's tenure as a political confidant and adviser in Shaftesbury's service was to prove a rich and productive one.'[45] Shaftesbury's ministry was selected by Charles II because of the royal interest in toleration but, because the king wanted toleration for Catholics while Shaftesbury wanted toleration for Protestant dissenters but not for Catholics, the two men had become foes by the mid-1670s. Shaftesbury's liberal views on toleration preceded those of Locke but, as Maurice Cranston notes, 'Ashley's very zeal for toleration was indeed but an aspect of his interest in trade.'[46] K.H.D. Haley also sees 'the relatively liberal ideas of Locke and Ashley on freedom of conscience for Protestants link with their interest in matters of trade and colonization.'[47] Locke probably helped Shaftesbury draft *A Letter from a Person of Quality to his Friend in the Country*, which advocated limiting toleration exclusively to Protestants in order to benefit England's trade.[48] While *An Essay Concerning Toleration*, written for Shaftesbury in 1667, emphasized the practical consequences of pursuing a policy of religious toleration, the later and better known *Letters concerning Toleration* made only passing reference to Britain's economic interest in toleration and chastised Jonas Proast as being 'very uncharitable' in supposing that Locke's prime interest was 'the advancement of trade and commerce.'[49]

Certainly, Locke shared Shaftesbury's interest in the advancement of trade and commerce. Locke's writings justified the common Whig goal of fusing landed and commercial interests (or investing rents in land on commercial ventures) and provided an especial justification of Shaftesbury's interest in colonial expansion, the slave trade, and plantations in America. Locke's political writings, from *The Fundamental Constitutions for the Government of Carolina* to *Two Treatises of Government*, consistently defended slavery. In 1678 he gathered secret information in France for Shaftesbury with respect to the cultivation of silk, olives, and wines for use in the Carolinas. Chapter 4 of *The Second Treatise of*

Government is devoted to slavery, and the next chapter, on property, justifies private property on the basis of the labour contained within it and refers to the production of tobacco, sugar, wine, and silk – crops not notably cultivated in England's green and pleasant land by free-born Englishmen.[50]

Jeremy Waldron asserts that Locke could not 'possibly have believed in the moral legitimacy of African slavery as an institution in the English colonies in America.' Although Locke profited by the Royal Africa Company, and 'played a large role in drafting' *The Fundamental Constitution of Carolina*, Waldron reminds us that Locke did not have 'academic tenure' or 'a certain amount of prestige, safety and independent prosperity' and thus his justification of slavery should be understood in light of Locke's role as secretary to Shaftesbury, the chief of the lords proprietors of the Carolinas. Locke, Waldron concludes, 'was not the sort of man one would expect to disassociate himself fastidiously from power and patronage in order to vindicate his *own* views.'[51] In other words, Waldron attributes the views he finds abhorrent in Locke to the fact that he was a client of Shaftesbury, but, for the views he approves of, he attributes these to Locke's independence from his 'patron, Anthony Ashley Cooper and his political cronies.'[52] Therefore, works in Locke's hand, such as *The Fundamental Constitution for the Government of Carolina* and *Letter from a Person of Quality to His Friend in the Country*, are held to be Locke's only in his capacity of secretary, insofar as these works do not support interpretations of Locke as an egalitarian liberal.

Locke has never been described, however, merely as a hired hand to Shaftesbury. The work *Some Considerations on the Lowering of Interest and Raising the Value of Money*, although dedicated to Sir John Somers, was written at Shaftesbury's request, as was *An Essay Concerning Toleration*. Yet, Locke's place, as Haley asserts, 'was not in any way that of a paid employee.' Rather, 'he was a friend, with other sources of income, who had been invited to live in Ashley's household.'[53] Ashley had sold Locke an annuity on a Dorset farm on favourable terms, advised him to invest in the Royal Africa Company, and rewarded him with two patronage posts as secretary of presentations (vetting ecclesiastical livings or ensuring that other 'friends' of Shaftesbury obtained them) and as secretary to the Council of Trade and Foreign Plantations (to which he submitted his chilling *Report to the Board of Trade*, which at least proves that he did not confine forced labour to Africans). As a result of Shaftesbury's patronage, Locke lived a 'comfortable life unrestricted by any financial anxiety.'[54] But he did not see himself, nor was he seen, as an intellectual mercenary; he was in some sense a friend of Shaftesbury, although contemporaries said that Locke 'belonged to the late Earl of Shaftesbury' and the dean of Locke's Oxford college, Christ Church, referred to Shaftesbury as Locke's 'master'.[55] Diderot, as we saw, stated that Shaftesbury *acquired* Locke but did not *buy* him. Essentially, Locke was and was not a friend and a servant of Lord Shaftesbury. A patron-client relationship has the personal dimension of friendship but without the equality; it has the subordination of servants or wage labourers but without the legal compulsion of hired labour. The client gratefully and gracefully requites the benefits conferred by the patron.

Since Shaftesbury was too occupied in public affairs to have the leisure for scholarship and thought, his 'friendship' with Locke was not based on a meeting of minds any more than on an equality of wealth and power. Nevertheless, Pierre Coste indicated that Shaftesbury's patronage of Locke was not purely economic in character: 'Nothing ever gave him [Locke] a more sensible pleasure than the esteem, which the Earl conceived for him, almost the first moment he saw him, and which he afterwards preserved as long as he lived. And indeed, nothing set Mr. LOCKE's merit in a better light, than the constant esteem of my Lord SHAFTESBURY, the greatest Genius of his age.'[56] After Shaftesbury's disgrace following the Exclusion Crisis and the fabricated Popish Plot, and later his death, Locke looked to Lord Pembroke for political protection (to prevent extradition for alleged participation in the Rye House Plot and Monmouth Rebellion) and for patronage of his philosophy. Locke dedicated his *Essay concerning Human Understanding* to Pembroke to stimulate demand for the book: Cranston notes that his dedication 'was virtually a certificate of noble interest.'[57] This dedication emphasizes the important role of patronage. Locke wrote: 'Truth scarce ever yet carried it by Vote any where, at its first appearance: New Opinions are always suspected, and usually opposed, without any other Reason, but because they are not already common.' But Locke claimed that his *Essay* has 'grown up under your Lordship's Eye, and has ventured into the World by your Order, does now, by a natural kind of Right, come to your Lordship for ... Protection ...' Locke's *Essay* has been apparently vouchsafed by Pembroke: although it advances new opinions, these should not be treated with suspicion, for, while not common, they have noble favour.

Locke received £29 from his publisher, Thomas Bassett, for the *Essay*, but that was a negligible proportion of the author's income. Locke, unlike Bayle and Care, did not depend upon his pen for his subsistence. He accepted a patronage appointment as commissioner of appeals, pressed Whig governments for compensation for past services as secretary to the Council of Trade or non-payment of his salary of £600 yearly from the 1660s to 1680s as secretary to the Council of Trade and Plantations. Locke was not, as Bayle was, an independent man of letters.

Locke's *Essay* is thought to provide a philosophic basis for or an 'epistemology' of toleration.[58] However, it is far from clear whether Locke, in the manner of Voltaire, provided an epistemology for sceptical toleration or for a warranted certainty in individual judgments based on the authority of one's own sense experience and one's reflections on it. Voltaire wrote: 'What is toleration? It is an appendage to humanity. We are all composed of weaknesses and errors; let us forgive each other for our stupidities; this is the first law of nature.'[59] In this sceptical tradition of Montaigne, Hobbes, Voltaire, Hume, and Diderot, philosophers favoured the state deciding religious matters that would otherwise remain contestable. Locke, for his part, was not an Erastian after he entered the service of Lord Shaftesbury; he came to urge a separation of church and state, or at least an immunity for Protestants from imposed religious uniformity. His epistemology seems both to justify and to undermine confidence in conscience or individual judgment of right and wrong. Montaigne, Hobbes, Voltaire, Hume, and Diderot could not accept Locke's certitude that 'the principal and chief care of every one ought to be his own soul first, and, in the next place, of the public peace ...'[60] On the other hand, Bayle and Care, who, with Locke, argued for the disestablishment of religion, could not accept Locke's opposition to innate ideas, and particularly to conscience as an innate practical principle. In this matter, Locke was Hobbesian in his philosophy and anti-Hobbesian in his politics; in his philosophic *Essay* (I.lll.8–10), Locke followed Hobbes in declaring that conscience is merely uncertain opinion, contingent upon one's environment and upbringing, but, in his *Second Treatise of Government*, conscience or the sanctity of individual judgment is the basis of armed resistance to government, a position inimical to that of Montaigne, Hobbes, Voltaire, Hume, Diderot, and Locke's fellow Protestant, Bayle.

Whereas Bayle and Care favoured comprehensive toleration, Locke, as we have seen, limited toleration to Protestants, excluding Catholics, Quakers, and atheists. While these exclusions do not appear consistent with Locke's view that governments cannot compel belief, Locke

thought that Catholics do not keep their promises and civil commitments because they owe an allegiance to a foreign prince (or pope),
Quakers will not swear oaths, and atheists have no ground to do so; the
social contract depends upon people being bound by their word. Locke
did not credit, as Bayle, Care, Penn, and many of Locke's fellow Whigs
did,[61] James II's promise to safeguard liberty of conscience and the
titles of Protestant landowners to the former property of religious
orders and of Irish Catholic gentry.[62] Lawrence Stone writes that James
frightened 'the propertied classes, most of whom now owned some land
which had belonged to the pre-Reformation Church, about the security
of their estates ...'[63] James II's Declaration of Indulgence sounded a
Whiggish note when it committed the king to the 'two things men value
most,' the free exercise of their religion and 'the perfect enjoyment of
their property.' James wrote that, while he heartily wished his subjects
to embrace the Catholic Church, he wished them to do so voluntarily
and thought that the policy of comprehensive toleration would promote 'the increase of trade and encouragement of strangers.'[64] James
Tyrrell may have been inaccurate when he wrote Locke on 6 May 1687
that there was general satisfaction with James's Declaration of Indulgence 'so that I find few but the High Church men highly displeased.'[65]
This claim underestimated popular and clerical dissatisfaction with
James's policy of comprehensive toleration, but, even so, James had
support not only from the two thousand Quakers released from prison
but also from numerous Whigs besides Care. Locke, and powerful
Whigs such as the Marquis of Halifax, did not trust the Catholic king
and supported the intolerant Church of England, believing it to be a
lesser threat to liberty and property than the Catholic Church. Care's
view that James would not upset Britain's commercial interests by
persecuting Protestants did not seem cogent to Locke: Locke kept his
interest in the promotion of trade and commerce apart from his
support for the church establishment from 1685 to 1688, and he made
no mention of it in his *Letters concerning Toleration*. Nor did Locke
address himself to Bayle's view that a Catholic king could not overturn
the religion of an overwhelming Protestant country, other than to
assert that ''tis eternally true that the dull herds of followers are always
bought and sold.'[66] Louis XIV's Revocation of the Edict of Nantes in
1685, and the possibility that James could follow Louis's practice of
billeting Catholic soldiers from Ireland on Protestant landowners,
coupled with the fear that Catholic claims to property forfeited in the
Civil War and confirmed in the Restoration might unsettle the estab-

lished order of property, were arguments enough for the Glorious Revolution. Locke thought that 'our delivery from popery and slavery' began with the arrival of William of Orange, and, if James should be restored, 'Jesuits must govern and France must be our master.' The Glorious Revolution was a bulwark against 'popish rage and revenge' for those 'who have any regard to their country, their religion, their consciences, and their estates'; an English gentleman, if subjected to papal conversion, would become 'a miserable French peasant.' Locke would 'desire every Protestant, every Englishman to lay his hand upon his heart and consider' whether supporters of James could be tolerated. Indeed, after James withdrew to Ireland, an Englishman was in danger of seeing 'his children stripped and his wife ravished' by 'those of a contrary religion.'[67]

Locke chose the winning side, and his Whig doctrine has been recognized as the most influential philosophy of the English-speaking world. He received the patronage of Whig magnates during his lifetime but also posthumously, through Joseph Addison, a broker for the patronage of Whig grandees. Not until the French Revolution had defanged the Catholic Church did Whig doctrine espouse Bayle's and Care's comprehensive toleration. Even Voltaire agreed with Locke that James's efforts to abolish laws against nonconformists were designed 'so as quietly under cover of liberty, to bring Roman Catholicism in.'[68] Yet, one wonders why Voltaire would have written the invasion manifesto for James's grandson, Bonnie Prince Charlie, if he thought Catholicism a mortal threat to liberty.

Is the fact that Care had a royal patron and Locke had aristocratic patrons of peripheral historical interest but of no theoretical interest in assessing the validity of their ideas about religious toleration? Bayle boasted: 'I am not in the service of the emperor or the king of France, I am in the service of truth.'[69] However, perhaps serving a patron and the truth are not mutually exclusive. The truth or falsity of Locke's ideas, one might argue, is independent of the conditions of their production, and his legacy depends on the widespread recognition of their truth, not on posthumous patronage. I would not wish to argue that Locke's ideas are only of historical interest and that questions of their enduring validity is misplaced.[70] Yet the central question, which differentiated Locke from Bayle and Care – whether James II's Declaration of Indulgence was an attempt to impose papal despotism on Britain in the guise of comprehensive toleration – cannot be settled. Perhaps Bayle was right to think that the religion of 98 per cent of the British population could not be overturned by zealous Stuart kings, but perhaps, too, Locke was right to think that the charters of cities, the authority of parliament, and the liberties and properties of Englishmen were threatened by projected Stuart absolutism. And, perhaps James II's and Locke's shared interest in trade was not, as Care thought, sufficient to overbalance James's zeal for his religion. That is, the validity of Locke's doctrine of limited toleration or Bayle's and Care's doctrines of comprehensive toleration is not so much a matter of fact as it is of interpretation of James II's intentions.

If truth in political theory is not verifiable with reference to the facts, or in terms of a correspondence theory of truth, can it be assessed in terms of logical consistency? Locke's teaching may be less internally coherent than either Bayle's or Care's teaching, but the theoretical inconsistencies may reflect the complexities of practical judgment on an indeterminate future. However, if truth depends on the extent of its recognition, or its universal 'intersubjectivity' (as Hegel argued), patronage provides recognition to thinkers and is an important factor in the circulation as well as the production of ideas. One of the prime functions of patrons is to provide thinkers with recognition, as Locke indicated with respect to Shaftesbury and Pembroke, and which Addison provided for Locke posthumously.

To conclude this reflection on patronage, independence, and toleration, may I appeal to fairness or procedural justice? If Care's ideas, or those of Locke's antagonist, Jonas Proast, are judged by the source of their patronage, then Locke's ideas should be similarly assessed; or, if Locke's ideas are assessed independently of his patrons, then Care's and Proast's ideas should be similarly judged. Care's ideas should be no more dismissed because he accepted royal patronage than Locke's ideas should be dismissed because he enjoyed aristocratic Whig patronage. Voltaire, as we have seen, thought royal patronage essential to avoid demeaning dependence upon aristocrats.

5 Voltaire and His Female Protectors

Émilie, Marquise du Châtelet, *née* Gabrielle Émilie Le Tonnelier de Breteuil, was the translator of Mandeville's *Fable of the Bees* and Newton's *Principia*; she also wrote *Institutions de Physique* and *Discours sur le bonheur*. She was clearly remarkable in her own right, but here I propose to examine her role as *protectrice* of Voltaire. In the conclusion to her preface to Mandeville's *Fable of the Bees*, she questioned why no great work of art or thought has come from women and attributed this deficiency to their inadequate education.[1] I wish to supplement her response to this question by examining the role of patronage in the French Enlightenment and the gendered asymmetry in patron-client relationships in eighteenth-century France.

All major writers of the eighteenth century depended upon royal or aristocratic patrons.[2] It was quite respectable, even honourable, for a man to be patronized or subject to the protection of a woman but women who received fur coats, as Voltaire did from Empresses Elizabeth and Catherine for services to the throne of Russia,[3] would be less than fully respectable.

Olympe de Gouges may have been the exception to the rule that eighteenth-century writers depended upon patrons. Perhaps the closest person to a 'self-made man' in eighteenth-century France, the plebeian Marie Gouze was married at sixteen, widowed with a son at seventeen, refused advantageous marriage proposals because 'marriage is the tomb of trust and love,' went to Paris with a rich protector, and there began a transformation from a barely literate, provincial wife to feminist theorist, actress, playwright, and revolutionary orator. She assumed the name Olympe de Gouges because it had a celestial ring to it as well as an aristocratic title; she claimed to be an illegitimate daughter of an academician, the Marquis Le Franc de Pompignon. Her noble title and bearing bestowed on her the right to enter Parisian salons, where she became friends with Condorcet and Mercier. In *La Déclaration des droits de la femme* (1791), de Gouges brought nationality and natality together in a vivid definition of the nation as the coming together of men and women. In addition, de Gouges advocated that women should have not only the same rights but also the same duties and punishments as men. She was guillotined for defending Marie Antoinette, a fitting end, many men thought, for a pushy female.[4]

There are other examples of eighteenth-century women who achieved intellectual distinction. Laura Bassi, who taught Newtonian physics at the University of Bologna, was patronized by Cardinal Prospero Lambertini, whose respectability and perhaps also his homosexuality allowed him to be the protector of an enlightened woman.[5] Mary Wollstonecraft was patronized by the radical publisher, Joseph Johnson, who may have seen a market for women's and children's literature in an aspiring writer. Speculating on his possible homosexuality or at least his lack of sexual feelings for women, Claire Tomalin writes: 'Johnson shrugged off any misinterpretations there may have been about setting up a young woman in a rent-free house.'[6] Although Wollstonecraft had exhibited little talent as a writer in 1787, in five years – after the publication of her *Vindication of the Rights of Men* and particularly her *Vindication of the Rights of Woman* – Johnson's patronage bore fruit.

But the patronage available to eighteenth-century women was certainly less impressive than that available to men. As we have seen, Jean D'Alembert explained 'the patronage of the great' by noting that they 'are quite happy to be learned on condition that they can become so without trouble, and so wish to be able to judge a work of intelligence without hard study, in exchange for the benefits they promise to the author or for the friendship with which they think they honor him.'[7] D'Alembert's reason for the support given to savants by the great who want a cheap education particularly applied to the *grandes dames*, such as Mme de Lambert, Mme de Tencin, Mme du Deffand, and Mme de Boufflers, who held court for the *philosophes* partly because they had no chance of an education otherwise.[8] Similarly, Daniel Gordon asserts that salons 'gave women such as Geoffrin the opportunity to acquire a level of education that they could not attain in regular society.'[9] This view does accord with the situation of *les salonnières*, who had no other opportunity for an education than by conducting salons for *les lumières*.

But it did not correspond to the life of Madame du Châtelet whose life exhibited no repugnance to 'hard study.' She wrote that the love of study is an essential human need,[10] as necessary to a woman's life as romantic love.

D'Alembert also implied that nobility and learning are mutually incompatible. While this claim is certainly not universally valid – one only has to consider the scholarly and noble families of Montaigne and Montesquieu – Condorcet's and Vauvenargues's family thought that their careers as savants would derogate from their standing as nobles.[11] Émilie du Châtelet dedicated her *Institutions de Physique* to her son, vowing 'to keep you from the ignorance which is still only too common amongst persons of your rank.'[12] Du Châtelet did not mean to imply that opportunities for aristocratic boys were no better than for girls; there was no female equivalent of Louis le Grand, where Voltaire was educated with his aristocratic school friends. But aristocratic youth were often well but narrowly educated for a career in the army, diplomatic service, or law. Diderot and D'Alembert's colleague on the *Encylopédie*, Chevalier de Jaucourt, was unusually broadly educated for a member of an aristocracy.

Although Émilie de Breteuil had no opportunity to enter Louis le Grand, she was relatively well educated for an aristocratic girl at the beginning of the eighteenth century, but her education ceased at the age of nineteen, when she married Florent Claude, the Marquis du Chastellet-Lomont (Voltaire changed Chastellet to Châtelet, which he found classier), and bore him legitimate heirs, before beginning a series of love affairs with the Comte de Guebriant and the Duc de Richelieu. Du Châtelet then combined her intellectual and sexual passions in relationships with philosophers, scientists, and poets, such as Pierre Louis Moreau de Maupertuis, Voltaire, Alexis-Claude Clairaut, Julien Offray de La Mettrie, and Jean-François de Saint-Lambert. Although du Châtelet tended to combine her scholarly and erotic passions, not all her lovers were her tutors and not all her tutors were lovers. Du Châtelet was also educated in mathematics and physics by Francesco Algarotti, Daniel Bernoulli, Charles-Marie La Condamine, and Johann Samuel König.

Du Châtelet was generally more attached to her lovers than they were to her; she wrote, with respect both to Voltaire and to Saint-Lambert, that she 'had to love for two.'[13] Judith Zinsser says that Maupertuis and Clairaut 'had their own projects and careers that took precedence over sojourns at Cirey or an evening tutorial at her house in Paris.'[14] The exception to the rule that men were no match for her overwhelming ardour may have been La Mettrie, whose *La Volupté* (1747) was dedicated to 'Madame la Marquise de ***' and celebrated their sexual enjoyment: 'Blessed are those whom nature has endowed with vigorous organs! For them, every day rises serene and voluptuous; for them, delight is a true need endlessly renewing itself, and the need is father to the pleasure.'[15] La Mettrie lacked the idealism of Immanuel Kant, who thought intellectual women unattractive: 'A woman ... like the Marquise de Châtelet, might even have a beard; for perhaps that would express more obviously the mien of profundity for which she strives.'[16] It would appear that Émilie du Châtelet was more than a patron or protector of La Mettrie, as of Voltaire, but, after La Mettrie's *Histoire naturelle de l'âme* (1745) had been shredded and burned by order of the parlement, he printed another addition, prefaced by a 'Critical letter to Mme du Châtelet.'[17] We know little about the relationship of La Mettrie and du Châtelet from sources other than La Mettrie's writings. Perhaps we might speculate that La Mettrie was hoping du Châtelet could do for him what she had done for Voltaire, namely, restore him in favour with the court at Versailles. As well as providing Voltaire with political protection, Mme du Châtelet helped to secure Diderot's release from prison.[18]

When Voltaire and Émilie were staying with the Duchesse de Richelieu, they heard that Voltaire's *Lettres philosophiques* had been burned by the parlement and that *une lettre de cachet* leading to imprisonment at Auxerre had been issued. Voltaire fled to the property of the Marquis du Châtelet at Cirey, 'a ruined castle on the borders of Champagne and Lorraine.'[19] Du Châtelet's protégé, having already been jailed in France, and later to be arrested while fleeing Prussia, liked to live close to borders; he always seemed ready to flee whatever jurisdiction he had offended. After du Châtelet's death and his own flight from Prussia, Voltaire settled in Geneva, close to the border with France, and then in Ferney, close to the border with Switzerland. He was banished from Paris after the death of du Châtelet and returned only after Louis XV died. On her deathbed, the pious Queen Marie Leczinska asked her husband to punish Voltaire's impiety. Louis XV responded: 'What can I do, madame? If he were in Paris, I should exile him to Ferney.'[20]

Cirey proved an excellent site for Voltaire and du Châtelet to work, and they offered hospitality to a large number of notable mathematicians and scientists on their way to Switzerland or Germany. Voltaire lent money to the marquis to repair and refurbish the château. Voltaire was very wealthy, and so his relationship to du Châtelet was the opposite of that of Diderot and Mme Geoffrin, who repaired and furnished the philosopher's apartment. Voltaire recorded in his *Mémoires*: 'Most [men of letters] are poor and poverty saps courage; and every philosopher at court becomes as slavish as the first official of the crown.' He went on to add: 'I have seen so many men of letters poor and scorned that I concluded for a long time that I would not add to their number.'[21] Following the lead of 'le sage Locke,' who had made his money in the slave trade, Voltaire invested money in the Companie des Indes that he obtained from royal gifts and aristocratic subscribers to the English edition of his *Henriade*, and then made a fortune from a fund-raising lottery in Paris when Voltaire noticed that the controller general had miscalculated the terms of the monthly draw.[22] He later made money by supplying armies and finally by producing luxury goods (watches, lacework, and silk) and selling them to his royal and aristocratic friends. Voltaire's loan to the Marquis du Châtelet for the repair of his château was different from the loans he made to other aristocratic friends who repaid with interest. Only after the death of his wife, which concluded Voltaire's stay at Cirey, did the marquis repay Voltaire about one-fifth of the cost of the repairs to the château. Voltaire's dependence on Mme du Châtelet was not financial; indeed, he provided scientific equipment and defrayed some of the costs of publishing her works.[23] Their relationship could be understood as based on an exchange of financial support for political protection.

Cirey was advantageously situated close to Lunéville, the court of King Stanislas Leczinski (who was the father of Louis XV's wife and godfather of the daughter of du Châtelet and Saint-Lambert). Émilie and Voltaire went there for court entertainments or, when Voltaire encountered the disfavour of Queen Marie Leczinski, for sanctuary. For example, Voltaire and Émilie prudently retired to Lunéville after Voltaire accused the queen's aristocratic friends of cheating at cards (Émilie was losing heavily at the time), when he wrote a poem celebrating the twin conquests of Louis XV and Madame de Pompadour, and when du Châtelet precipitously entered a carriage reserved for the queen's ladies in waiting.[24] Mme du Châtelet remained on good terms with the pious Queen Marie Leczinski, who detested Voltaire. Also, her noble background gave her access to court circles in Versailles and Lunéville. As René Pomeau explains Émilie's protection of Voltaire: 'Mme du Châtelet, née Le Tonnelier de Breteuil, was necessary to assist him in his relations with the court.'[25] In this respect, Émilie was following in a family tradition; her father, the Baron de Breteuil, had earlier interceded with the regent, Philippe d'Orléans, who had placed Voltaire in the Bastille.[26] De Breteuil was successful in liberating Voltaire from imprisonment.

Once ensconced at Cirey, Mme du Châtelet began a campaign to have the *lettre de cachet* against Voltaire revoked to allow him to return to Paris. She wrote to Mme du Deffand to rally her friends to defend Voltaire against Louis XV's minister, Jean-Frédéric Phélypeaux, Comte de Maurepas; to the Duchesse d'Aiguillon, another friend, to speak to the *garde de sceaux* (guardian of the royal seal), Germain Louis Chauvelin; and to still another, the Duchesse de Richelieu, to intercede with the procurator general, Guillaume-François Joly de Fleury, and Chauvelin to revoke the *lettre de cachet.*[27] Their efforts succeeded, Voltaire being allowed to return to Paris in the spring of 1735. Through patient and skilful diplomacy, Mme du Châtelet got Voltaire back in the good graces of Louis XV's chief minister, Cardinal Fleury and cultivated the Comte de Maurepas. Thanks to du Châtelet and Maurepas, Voltaire was not banished for his tragedy, *Mahomet*, which many understood to be a criticism of Christianity.[28]

After having facilitated Voltaire's return to Paris and securing him political protection, du Châtelet was jealous of the emerging patronage of Voltaire by Crown Prince Frederick, soon to be Frederick the Great. The praise Frederick and Voltaire heaped on one another, replete with homoerotic overtones,[29] was certainly extravagant. Voltaire explained: 'He treated me as godlike; I treated him as Solomon. These epithets cost us nothing.'[30] However attractive du Châtelet was as a protector, Frederick 'had wit, graces, and, what is more, he was a king, which is always a grand seduction, considering human weakness.'[31] Louis XV rebuffed Voltaire, while Frederick embraced him; Frederick became his king. Voltaire was more jealous of rivals to Frederick's favour than of other lovers of his *amie-protectrice.*[32] Nevertheless, one might note that the poet's breach with Frederick, after du Châtelet's death, arose over Voltaire's fights with two of Frederick's favourites, La Mettrie and Maupertuis, who were also Émilie's former lovers. Possibly the ghost of du Châtelet impaired the stability of Frederick's patronage of Voltaire.

Voltaire's visit to the Netherlands and Prussia, although partly concerned with the legal affairs of the du Châtelet family, was much more protracted than Émilie would have liked. Voltaire found an 'Émilie germanique' in the Countess of Bentinck, and he enjoyed being fêted in various German courts, and particularly by the most enlightened of all princes, Frederick. Nevertheless, Paris was the center of Voltaire's world, and the prospects of royal favour and admission into the Académie Française were enhanced in the 1740s with the rise of his schoolmates, the Marquis d'Argenson and his brother, the Comte d'Argenson, to important government ministries, and the emergence of Mme de Pompadour as the royal favourite. When Voltaire left Frederick for the first time to return to France, the enlightened king tried to put du Châtelet in her proper place, midway between a cook and himself, by bidding adieu to 'the lover of Valori's cook, Madame du Châtelet and my sister.'[33]

Once Voltaire returned to Paris, du Châtelet had an increased inducement to ingratiate Voltaire to the court; she did not want him to prefer the company of Frederick's court, from which she was excluded, to that of Versailles, Fontainbleau, or Lunéville, where she was welcome. Émilie persuaded Voltaire to write a paean to Cardinal Fleury extolling his wisdom and power – Voltaire wrote that the 'order' in the cardinal's soul flowed into the world and pacified it – and she cultivated Mme de Tencin and the Comte de Maurepas on Voltaire's behalf. Through the efforts of du Châtelet (together with his friends the Duc de Richelieu and the Marquis d'Argenson) and the powerful support of his new protector, Mme de Pompadour, Voltaire was appointed to the offices of gentleman in ordinary to the king's chamber, royal historiographer, and then, in 1746, he was made a member of the Académie Française. In the same year, du Châtelet was elected to the Bologna Institute for her achievements in science, three years before she died bearing the child of Saint Lambert.

After du Châtelet's death, Voltaire had other powerful protectors and patrons, royal and aristocratic, male and female, in England, France, Prussia, Russia, Austria, Denmark, Poland, Sweden, and Lorraine. As he wrote Mme du Deffand: 'It is always necessary to have some crowned head up one's sleeve.'[34] But even Frederick the Great and Catherine the Great, coupled to the domestic protection of Mme de Pompadour and, through her, of the Duc de Choiseul, were not enough to rescind Voltaire's exile from Paris. With Mme du Châtelet no longer serving as Voltaire's ambassador to Versailles, he was not permitted to return to Paris during the reign of Louis XV. Voltaire had more powerful protectors than Émilie du Châtelet but none more devoted or effective; only she was able to get Voltaire back to the centre of his world.

Women of the Enlightenment

Patronage, as we have seen Burke define it, is 'the tribute which opulence owes to genius.' Jean-Jacques Rousseau held similar views; his first Parisian *patronne* was Mme de Beuzewal, who, he wrote, 'was a good but limited woman since, too full of her illustrious Polish nobility, she has little idea of the consideration [*des égards*] owed to talents.'[35] Rousseau insisted that only 'minds without cultivation and without enlightenment, who know no other object for their esteem but influence, power, and money, are very far from suspecting that some regard is owed to talents and that it is dishonorable to insult them.'[36] Burke and Rousseau, however different their politics, did not think that genius was usually found among the opulent, particularly hereditary aristocrats. The ideas of genius and taste (or producers and discriminating consumers of ideas) are inventions of the eighteenth century. Taste, Voltaire asserted, 'belongs to a very small number of privileged souls ... It is unknown in bourgeois families, where one is constantly occupied with the care of one's fortune.'[37] Taste (and thus the patronage of genius) belongs to a leisured aristocracy. As John Lough writes: 'Though the philosophes were for the most part *roturiers*, they lived in a society in which, outwardly at least, the possession of blue blood still retained its traditional importance.'[38] The taste-genius dichotomy maps roughly onto the patron-client relationship, and specifically to aristocratic female protectors and bourgeois male protégés. Aristocratic French women paid ample tribute to the genius of *les lumières*.

The French intellectual world of the salons was heterosocial, as distinct from the largely homosocial Bluestocking circles of England, where Elizabeth Montague patronized Hannah More, Fanny Burney, and other women[39] and from the masculine clubs of Samuel Johnson and David Hume in England and Scotland. Also, the heterosocial salons stood in sharp contrast to the French royal academies, the nineteenth-century French *cercles*,[40] and the Café Gradot, where Émilie du Châtelet had to dress as a man to be admitted to conversations with fellow scientists and mathematicians. The heterosocial environment of the eighteenth-century salons gave the French Enlightenment its distinctive character. André Morellet thought Lord Shelburne's masculine salon at Bowood almost as brilliant as those in Paris, but civilization, the abbé thought, depends upon 'the free commerce of the two sexes.'[41] Similarly, Abbé Galiani believed that Italy was like England with respect to the social segregation of the sexes and wrote nostalgically to Mme d'Épinay about the salon culture of Paris: 'There is no way to make Naples resemble Paris if we cannot find a woman to guide us, to govern us, to "Geoffrinize" us.'[42] Both Morellet and Galiani thought that there were minds in Italy and England as good as those in Paris but that intellectual society there lacked the civilized sparkle of the Parisian salons.

French women constituted roughly 3 per cent of the authors in the eighteenth century, but that percentage did not do justice to women's contribution to the French Enlightenment.[43] For such women, writing was an avocation, a form of self-expression, but not a livelihood; women usually wrote when widowed or when separated from their husbands.[44] Their prime calling was to preside over salons. While many of the *salonnières* were married – Mme Helvétius, Mme d'Holbach, Mme Suard, and Mme Necker served as hostesses to follow the interests of their husbands and advance their careers – many of the most notable *salonnières* were unmarried, like Claudine-Alexandrine Guerin, Mme de Tencin (who made a great deal of money through her friendship with the Scottish financier John Law), and Julie de L'Espinasse, or were widows, like Anne-Thérèse de Marquenat-de Courcelles, Marquise de Lambert (who opened her salon after the Marquis de Lambert died), and Marie-Thérèse Rodet Geoffrin (whose salon flourished only after her old, rich, and grumbling husband died). Many of the leading *patronnes* were separated from their husbands, like Louise Tardieu d'Esclavelle de la Live, Mme d'Épinay, and Marie de Vichy-Chamrond, Marquise du Deffand. Since by law, women's property, except that inherited or set aside by the marital contract, was at the disposition of the husband, the career of a *salonnière* was best suited to women who lived apart from a husband.[45] Émilie du Châtelet's wealth was in the hands of her husband,[46] and so her relationship to Voltaire was quite unlike the relationship of Mme Geoffrin to Diderot, D'Alembert, Morellet, and Thomas, all of whom were assisted economically by the wealthy *salonnière*. When her wealthy old husband was alive, Mme Geoffrin had to fight him for money to conduct her Monday and Wednesday salons for artists and men of letters, since he held the expenses lavished upon such parasites to be a frivolous waste of his resources.[47] Whereas Diderot and other *philosophes* obtained financial support from Mme Geoffrin, du Châtelet depended on Voltaire financially and gave him political protection in return.

A successful career as a *salonnière* depended upon learned skills and graces. Mme de Tencin attended the salon of Mme de Lambert and

Mme Geoffrin attended Mme de Tencin's. In addition to providing a congenial table, the salons afforded a venue for intelligent conversation, for creating a sense of group solidarity and common purpose, and for launching a literary career and sheltering authors from the insecurities of their way of life.

Parisians salons were the defining institution of the French Enlightenment,[48] as the universities were for the Scottish and German Enlightenments and the free press was for the English Enlightenment (if England can be said to have had one). In this respect, Diderot exemplifies the French Enlightenment (just as Smith and Kant serve as exemplars of academic Enlightenments, and Samuel Johnson, with one foot in the Church of England and the other in the commercial press, represents the English free press). Diderot, Morellet, and others dined at Mme Geoffrin's each Monday and Wednesday, Tuesday at Mme Helvétius's, Thursday and Saturday at Baron d'Holbach's, and Fridays at Mme Necker's; besides these fixed engagements, Morellet made frequent appearances in the salons of Mme de Boufflers, Mlle de Riaucourt, Mlle de L'Espinasse and Mme Suard.[49] When his *patronne* and former lover, Mme de Tencin, died, the ninety-two-year-old Fontenelle was reported to have said: 'Oh well, I will go to dinner on Tuesdays at Mme Geoffrin's.'[50] Parisian salons were different from Samuel Johnson's London clubs and David Hume's and Adam Smith's Edinburgh clubs in that the British thinkers paid for their own meals and the French thinkers did not. Further, like Smith's and Kant's universities, Hume's and Johnson's clubs were homosocial, whereas the Parisian salons were heterosocial, as distinct from the nineteenth-century Parisian *cercles*. The distinctive character of the French Enlightenment derived from this heterosocial environment. Women are the leaven of the staff of life, making the French variety lighter and more palatable than the oatcakes and pumpernickel produced in the Scottish and German universities.

The Parisian salons were the chief alternative to royal patronage in the academies centred in Versailles or dispersed in the provinces; they served, in a sense, as the loyal opposition to royal government.[51] The academies honoured writers who were already recognized or well connected, whereas salons were the means for aspiring writers to come to public notice. As Robert Darnton writes: 'For impecunious writers salon life was above all a matter of fortune hunting.'[52] Voltaire and Rousseau were the only *philosophes* not be regular habitués of the salons, although both began their careers in Parisian salons. Voltaire and

Rousseau thought that attendance at salons interfered with the task of writing, and Voltaire was rich enough to dispense with the financial support the *salonnières* provided. Moreover, Mme du Châtelet did not appear at her best in salons, as she did in court circles and intimate intellectual gatherings. Madame Newton-Pompom-du-Châtelet, as Voltaire called her, was happier flaunting her diamonds and pompoms at court than in conversing in salons; Mme Geoffrin and Mme Du Deffand did not think Émilie added to the harmony and intellectual festivity at their salons.[53]

In tandem with Mme du Châtelet, Voltaire associated his career path more with the royal courts and academies than with the aristocratic salons. In his entry 'Gens de lettres' in the *Encyclopédie*, Voltaire wrote that royal patronage strengthens the independence of men of letters because it obviates the need for obsequious dependence on aristocrats. The opposite position was espoused by André Morellet, who wrote that Cardinal Richelieu founded the Académie Française 'in order to have a permanent corps of accomplices.'[54] Daniel Roche says of the royal academies: 'They gave government support in exchange for independence. Their salaries and pensions – rather modest – alienated less than they liberated.'[55]

After being educated by his patroness and lover, Mme de Warens, Rousseau arrived in Paris to embark upon his musical and literary career. Père Louis Castel advised him to visit the *salonnières*, noting, 'One does nothing in Paris except by women.'[56] Similarly, Leopold Mozart was later to advise his son that women 'do everything in Paris.'[57] Edmond and Jules de Goncourt write that women were 'the commanding voice of the eighteenth century.' They assert that 'the woman of the eighteenth century was the patron of letters. Through the attention she bestowed upon them, through the entertainment she sought in them, through the protection she granted them, she attached them to her person and attracted them to her sex, she directed and governed them.' Female taste complemented male genius; women inspired, counselled, and judged men of letters. 'Without her patronage, without the recommendation of her enthusiasm, no one could get plays played, applauded or even read. Every mode of literature, every sort of writer, every pamphlet, every volume, even a masterpiece, required that she sign its passport and open it a way to publicity.'[58] David Hume said that, in Britain, the 'Fair Sex' are 'the Sovereigns of the Empire of Conversation' but, in France, 'the Ladies are, in a Manner, the Sovereigns of the *learned* World, as well as of the *conversible*; and no polite Writer pretends to venture upon the Public, without the Approbation of some cele-brated Judges of that Sex.'[59]

A more recent and powerful argument has been put forth by Dena Goodman, who states that the *salonnières* were a major factor in the French Enlightenment because they created the conditions for polite conversation, in part by repressing male aggression, duels of wit, and struggles for pre-eminence.[60] Women were, in the metaphor of Eliza-beth Montague, the scabbard for the rapier wit of men. Montague declared: 'Wit in women is apt to have bad consequences; like a sword without a scabbard, it wounds the wearer and provokes assailants. I am sorry to say that the women who have excelled in wit have failed in chastity.'[61] The witty head of the Bluestockings, whom no one suspected of such a failure, patronized Hannah More and Fanny Burney in the largely homosocial British intellectual world. Lord Shelburne, the patron of Price, Priestley, and Bentham, was favourably impressed by the salons of Mme Helvétius, Mme Geoffrin, and Mme du Deffand but was astonished that Mme de Boufflers and Mlle de L'Espinasse partici-pated in philosophic conversations.[62] Mary Wollstonecraft attributed the greater diffusion of knowledge in France than in other parts of Europe 'to the social intercourse which has long subsisted between the sexes.'[63]

The Parisian salons were a counterweight to the royal offices and academic status granted at Versailles. Indeed, Voltaire had a markedly ungallant view of the *salonnières*: 'There are a great number of small societies in Paris always presided over by some woman who, in the waning of her beauty, lets shine forth the dawning of her wit.'[64] Vol-taire's description probably referred to Mme de Tencin, but it could have described Mme du Deffand, who had almost as racy a past during the Regency as Mme de Tencin and who also conducted salons to rectify a neglected education and to restore lost respectability. Despite Voltaire's seeming contempt for the *salonnières*, he knew that good relations with Mme du Deffand would enhance his career and per-suaded du Châtelet to cultivate a friendship with Mme de Tencin, who had previously opposed Voltaire's election to the Académie Française.[65] As Thomas Hankins writes of the *salonnières*: 'Not only could they ruin a reputation by turning away from their *salons* any person unfortunate enough to earn their displeasure, but they also controlled elections at the academies and influenced the granting of pensions by the court.'[66] When D'Alembert was elected to the Académie Française, Parisians understood that the Marquise du Deffand had triumphed over her rival, Mme de Chaulnes, whose candidate was bested in the horse race by du Deffand's D'Alembert.[67] In addition, the *salonnières* purchased numerous copies of the books of their protégés – whether or not they had obtained official permission to be published in France – distributed them to their friends, 'puffed' them, and discussed them at their salons. In short, the *salonnières* functioned, in contemporary terms, as unpaid lobbyists and literary and publicity agents.

Mme de Tencin was perhaps the first *salonnière* to dissolve social hierarchy in her salon in favour of talent; 'by virtue of Madame de Tencin's magic wand, as it were, everyone turned into a philosopher.'[68] When Mme de Tencin began her career as a *salonnière* in the 1720s, men of letters tended to be either men of learning or of science, but by the 1750s men of letters were not necessarily either scientific or erudite.[69] Charles Duclos characterized mid-century Paris in terms of a closer liaison between wealth and learning than ever before; both sides had profited by the relationship. '*Les gens du monde* have cultivated their wit, formed their taste, and acquired new pleasures,' while *les gens de lettres* have become less bookish and erudite – they 'have found recognition and support [*considération*], perfected their taste, polished their wit, softened their manners ...'[70] The complementarity Duclos found between wealth and learning was particularly pronounced between wealthy women and men of letters because aristocratic men had military and political occupations and thus lacked the leisure or gentle inclinations of aristocratic women.

This glittering, feminized world of the salons had critics then as now. Salon culture favoured 'grace, wit lightness and elegance' over scholarly rigour and philosophic depth; it supported 'the *littérateurs*, not the *érudits*.'[71] Helvétius wrote: 'In order to please in the world, one mustn't plumb the depths on any matter, but to glide incessantly from subject to subject; one must have very varied, and, from that, very superficial, knowledge; to know everything without wasting one's time in knowing one thing perfectly, and thus to give more of the surface than the depth.'[72] If attendance at the salons depreciated learning, depth, and systematic philosophy, it helped to prepare writers for the royal academies and for the general reading public. The *salonnières* protected men of letters, discussed and promoted new literary works, provided a milieu for the distribution of prohibited books, and tipped writers off when there would be a police raid on sources of illegal publications.[73]

Mme de Tencin assisted in the election of Pierre Carlet de Chamblain de Marivaux to the Académie Française, just as Charles de

Secondat, Baron de Montesquieu, had earlier owed his election to that august body to Mme de Lambert.[74] Mme de Tencin addressed Montesquieu as 'mon petit Romain,' affectionately putting him in his social place, and assisted in the publication of his *L'Esprit des lois* and also paid for the errata in its first edition.[75] By means of Mme de Tencin, and her brother Cardinal Tencin, Voltaire established a correspondence with Pope Benedict XIV. Voltaire sent him his jingoistic poem *La Bataille de Fontenoy* and received papal praise for it. Voltaire forged an addition, asserting that the pope had praised his tragedy, *Mahomet*, execrated by Voltaire's opponents among *les dévôts*. By this daring and unscrupulous manoeuvre, Voltaire managed, with the neutrality of Mme de Tencin, to scupper the opposition to his admission to the Académie Française.[76]

Mme de Pompadour

Voltaire grossly underrated the efforts of Mme du Châtelet, himself, and their aristocratic friends when he credited his election to the academy to Mme de Pompadour: 'I concluded that, in order to make the smallest fortune, it would be worth more to speak four words to the mistress of a king than to write a hundred volumes.'[77] Yet, however inaccurate this claim was, it balanced Diderot's ungrateful turning on the earliest and strongest supporter of the *Encyclopédie* once she had died.[78] Mme de Pompadour was a great *patronne* of *les lumières*; she provided income to Rousseau, Marmontel, Duclos, and other writers, as well as offering political protection to Voltaire, Montesquieu, Helvétius, Quesnay, and the *Encyclopédie*. Jean-François Marmontel was a poor, unknown writer until Mme de Pompadour read him, gave him lodging and a sinecure, freed him from financial worries, and lionized him; she got him elected to the Académie Française despite the powerful opposition of the Duc de Praslin.[79] Mme de Pompadour also provided Charles Duclos with a large pension, got Voltaire his post as royal historiographer, and intervened with Cardinal Tencin and Pope Benedict XIV to secure Voltaire membership in the Académie Française.[80] Since writers needed official permission to publish, they tended to think that criticism of their work had government backing. Thus, the great champions of liberal freedom of thought, Voltaire and Montesquieu, turned to Mme de Pompadour to have criticisms of their work suppressed.[81] Montesquieu, admittedly, prefaced his *Lettres Persanes* with the proud boast that the merits of his work would stand on their own and hence he did not 'seek protection for this book.'[82] However, experience was to show that, however more favourably situated the aristocratic Montesquieu was than most other *philosophes*, he needed political protection, as well as financial support, from Mme de Lambert, Mme de Tencin, and Mme de Pompadour. Voltaire was wealthier than Montesquieu but had greater need of political protection; he 'often besieged the authorities with requests to suppress parodies and libels written against him or against the philosophic group.'[83] Following a heated exchange with Rousseau, Voltaire even recommended that Rousseau be subject to capital punishment for blasphemy and sedition.[84] Besides Chrétien-Guillaume de Lamoignan de Malesherbes, few luminaries of Enlightenment thought that freedom of the press extended to their enemies as well as themselves. In this poisonous, perilous atmosphere, Voltaire, Marmontel, Diderot, Morellet, and Linguet were imprisoned, as indeed were forty-five writers, or 10 per cent of those writers on file with Joseph d'Hémery, a police inspector surveying French writers at mid-century.[85] One of these writers, Helvétius, was fortunate to have Mme de Pompadour as an ally; she helped to stay the prosecution against him after the publication of *De l'Esprit* (1758).

Madame de Pompadour would not have been able to help the *philosophes* had not she, in an earlier incarnation, been given respectability by *les salonnières*. Jeanne-Antoinette (later La Pompadour), the daughter of the scandalous Poissons, was raised by her mother's protector, the farmer-general Le Normaut de Tourneheim, who married her to his nephew. Jeanne-Antoinette Poisson became Mme d'Etoiles but achieved social respectability only by being accepted into the salons of Mme de Tencin and Mme Geoffrin.[86]

Catherine the Great

Voltaire ungallantly explained the importance of women in the French Enlightenment, as we have seen, in terms of their needing to shine once their beauty had faded. One of those he may have had in mind was Mme du Deffand, who, after a racy youth as mistress of the regent, Philippe d'Orléans, 'with her moral reputation in shreds ... began to value herself for her mind and intelligence.' Aristocratic women, such as Mme du Deffand, felt undereducated and useless and were painfully aware that their intelligence had not had an opportunity to develop.[87] Mme de Tencin (who left her son by Chevalier Destouches – D'Alembert – on the porch of Saint-Jean-le-Rond church) also began her illustrious career as a *salonnière* in 1726 to repair her reputation after a lover killed himself at midday outside her house, an event that led to her incarceration because her suicidal lover had left a note incriminating her in John Law's Mississippi scheme.[88] Thus, Mme de Tencin and Mme du Deffand not only patronized letters to cultivate their minds but also to obtain respectability, which they had lost during the Regency. As just noted, the desire for respectability was also an important motive for the greatest protector of French letters, Mme de Pompadour, who needed acceptance in the salons before being acceptable as the royal favourite. Yet another example of the same phenomenon was Catherine the Great, who began to patronize *les lumières* after having her husband, Peter, and also her rival to the Russian throne, Ivan, killed.

Once she had dispatched both Peter and Ivan, Catherine patronized Voltaire, D'Alembert, Grimm, Marmontel, Diderot, Galiani, Condorcet, Bentham, and other thinkers to present an Enlightened exterior to Europe. Vittorio Alfieri, the aristocratic opponent of patronage, called Catherine the 'philosophizing Clytemnestra.'[89] Together with Diderot, as we have seen, Voltaire arranged the suppression of the French ambassador's hostile account of Catherine's *coup d'état*, Claude Carloman de Rulhière's *Histoire ou anecdotes sur La Révolution de Russie en L'année 1762*,[90] and he dismissed the murder of Ivan as the merest trifle.[91] The anonymous champion of patronage in *Letters concerning the Present State of England* (1772) wrote: 'This patronizing quality amongst princes, has even had the effect of charity, to cover a multitude of sins: no white-washer equals ... a poet or historian.'[92]

Friedrich Melchior Grimm described the heavenly proximity of Catherine: 'Spending my life with her, every day, one day like another, seeing only her, often from morning to night, going only to the court, dining with her in public or privately, chatting, talking for hours on end – freely, with complete confidence: doesn't that sound like a dream?'[93] The *salonnières* disapproved of Voltaire, D'Alembert, and Diderot for deserting them for someone who murdered her husband. The anti-philosophic Whig gossip, Horace Walpole, wrote that the Duchess of Choiseul had assured him that Catherine had killed her predecessor, Empress Elizabeth, as well as her husband Peter and rival Ivan, and then was selected by the French literati 'as the patroness of philosophy and toleration! She had been artfully generous to a few of them; and a poet and an author will go as far in whitewashing a magnificent tyrant, as a Cossack or Calmuck in fighting for those who pay him. From Augustus to Catherine the Second, no liberal usurper has ever wanted an ode or a panegyrist.'[94] Walpole was wrong to think that money was the main reason for the services of the *philosophes.* Recognition and fame moved Grimm and Voltaire more than money; the possibility of using Catherine's power to implement enlightened reforms was an incentive for Voltaire, D'Alembert, and Diderot. And the sexual dimension of being close to a powerful and glamorous despot – Voltaire confided to D'Alembert on 26 June 1773 that Catherine's regime was 'the most despotic power on earth'[95] – gave Catherine an advantage over the other great patron of Enlightenment, Frederick. Diderot wrote that the tsarina combined 'the soul of Caesar with all the seductiveness of Cleopatra.'[96] More prosaically, Bentham said of Catherine: 'In a female body she had a masculine mind.'[97]

Voltaire was a master of the art of flattery; it was for him, Jean Sareil wrote, less a matter of toadying than skilful application of the form of the time.[98] Yet Voltaire's flattery did not succeed with Louis XV, and it was only afterwards that he concentrated more successfully on royal mistresses – as well as Frederick the Great.[99] He prefaced his reflections to Frederick the Great on the immortality of the soul with the declaration: 'Monseigneur, the royal family of Prussia has excellent reasons for not wishing the annihilation of the soul. It has more right than anyone to immortality.'[100] Voltaire flattered powerful men besides Frederick, such as Maupeou, D'Argenson, and Choiseul,[101] but he seemed to shine best at this genre with women. Voltaire wrote to Catherine on 22 December 1767, signing himself 'The priest of your temple': 'Your writings are a monument to your fame; there are three of us, Diderot, D'Alembert and myself, who raise altars to you; you are making a pagan of me: madam, I fall at your majesty's feet not merely with profound respect, but in idolatry.'[102] Jean Starobinski argues that flattery is an asymmetrical exchange between client and patron – 'the exchange of *words* for favors.' Whereas the aristocratic salon afforded a fine venue for flattering patrons, no one could match a tyrant or prince as an object of words of praise.[103]

Sexual inequality or gender complementarity not only allowed Voltaire's considerable talent at flattery to flower but also facilitated patron-client connections by stabilizing the relationship between power and genius. Equals compete, and rivalry is destructive of patronage. Voltaire's most stable patron, besides Mme de Pompadour and Catherine, was 'Mme Newton-Pompom-du Châtelet,' as Voltaire affectionately called her. She had, he thought with pride, the best female mind for science in Europe, but her pompoms and diamonds were perhaps even more attractive. Judith Zinsser writes that Voltaire often wished his beloved Émilie 'were less learned and her mind less sharp.'[104] In the same vein, Hume observed of Voltaire's other great patron, Frederick, that he 'is too much a rival to be a very constant patron.'[105] And so John Gray can assert: 'Voltaire and Frederick had a good deal – indeed, too much – in common.'[106] Voltaire burned with resentment when a rival, Laurent Angliviel La Beaumelle, wrote that Voltaire obtained unprecedented reward for a man of letters (21,000 *livres* annually) and asserted that Frederick conferred benefits on him 'for the same reason that a prince of Germany commits himself to heaping benefits on a clown or a dwarf.'[107] Frederick broke with Voltaire over his rivalry with La Mettrie and Maupertuis; he took it upon himself in a high-handed manner to side with Maupertuis in an academic dispute, and Voltaire left Prussia. Frederick had him arrested as he fled Prussia with some papers and possessions of the king's.

The much publicized rift between Hume and Rousseau provides another example of equals as competitors. In March 1765 Rousseau referred to Hume as 'mon très cher Patron' and three times later in the month as 'mon cher Patron,' but relations cooled when the prickly and sensitive Rousseau perceived himself to be held as the proud possession of Hume. Rousseau would not accept a pension from George III until Hume was eliminated as broker of royal patronage.

The instability of patronage relationships was minimized if the client respected his patron as a social superior. Alternatively expressed, the *amour propre* of plebeians who considered themselves geniuses – and rightly, if one credits this eighteenth-century linguistic or conceptual invention – was less threatened by those who were social superiors but not intellectual competitors. One competes or cooperates with equals, but respectfully defers to superiors; Hobbes accurately described the natural condition of independent, equal, vainglorious men. The relationships of Hume and the Earl of Hertford, Rousseau and the Prince de Conti, were complementary, not competitive, but the relationship of Hume and Rousseau, like that of Frederick and Voltaire, were competitive. Gender difference facilitated hierarchical complementarity that did not degenerate into competition or rivalry. Catherine was the greatest patron of Enlightenment.

Frederick the Great thought that the *philosophes* provided greater service to Catherine than whitewashing her role in the murders of her rivals to the throne of Russia: they promoted her foreign policy.

Frederick wrote to Voltaire on 24 May 1770: 'The Empress of Russia ... has paid Diderot in hard cash for a dispensation to allow the Russians to fight the Turks.'[108] Frederick certainly was not singling out Diderot for blame. In Voltaire's case, he presented Catherine's imperialism against Poland and the Ottoman Empire as serving the cause of liberalism; in a curiously contemporary note, he wrote to Catherine on 15 November 1768: 'Clearly, people who neglect the fine arts and who lock up women, deserve to be exterminated.'[109] While Voltaire's *Candide* has endowed the author with a reputation for pacifism, his letters to Catherine are bloodthirsty: on 30 October 1768 he wrote: 'Madam, your imperial Majesty restores me to life by killing Turks.'[110] Voltaire justified Catherine's partition of Poland as championing the cause of religious toleration among members of the Catholic and Eastern Orthodox churches. He repeatedly tried to persuade the Poles that their true enemy was Rome, not Russia, and supported the partition of Poland in letters to both Catherine and Frederick.[111]

Voltaire praised Catherine's *Nakaz* (*Instruction on Legislation*) to the skies. He wrote her in 1770 that 'your Code ... is finer than Justinian's.' In the next year, he asserted that 'I regard this work as the finest monument of the age' and at the same time sent her a consignment of watches made on his estate for which he was munificently rewarded.[112] In his *Philosophical Dictionary*, Voltaire wrote that 'an empress has just given to that vast state [Russia] laws which would honor Minos, Numa and Solon, if they had been intelligent enough to invent them.'[113] Catherine thought Voltaire's and Grimm's praise of her *Nakaz* much more perspicacious than Diderot's mixture of praise and criticism, which was sent to her after his death.[114] Voltaire ensured that he was repaid for his praise by enrolling Catherine as patron of his cause of justice for the Calas and Sirven families, as well as a customer for his watches. In addition to being an enlightened sponsor of Voltaire, Catherine was an enlightened role model by having herself inoculated for smallpox in 1768, thereby distinguishing himself from the unenlightened Louis XV, who died of the disease.[115]

Voltaire tended to be jealous of Catherine's patronage of other thinkers. When Helvétius dedicated his *De l'homme* to Catherine, Voltaire wrote her: 'I by no means share his [Helvétius's] opinion regarding the basic theme of his book. He claims that all men are born equal.' To support his view of human inequality, Voltaire asserted that 'Mustapha,' the tsarina's Turkish enemy, was by no means the equal of Catherine,[116] – he also alerted her to the danger of 'the mad Jean-

Jacques Rousseau, who has thought fit to make himself sovereign judge of all the monarchs from the height of his attic.'[117] (Rousseau did not support the partitioning of Poland as Voltaire did.) Similarly, Voltaire again showed his prickly side when D'Alembert attempted unsuccessfully to get his patron, Catherine, to intercede on behalf of French volunteers who had been captured in Poland and were now held prisoner in Russia. Voltaire praised Catherine for rebuffing D'Alembert, saying that such intercession was not the philosopher's business, and Catherine responded by deprecating D'Alembert's limited sympathies: 'Should one show humanity only for one's compatriots?'[118] Voltaire did not seem pleased to share Catherine's patronage with his Enlightenment comrades-in-arms.

Although Frederick and Horace Walpole saw the *philosophes* as intellectual mercenaries, they did not view themselves as such. Nevertheless, with respect to his apologia for Catherine's war with Turkey, Voltaire wrote: 'I glory in being a scribe of her powerful genius.'[119] Voltaire recognized that a court-appointed historian has to dress up the naked truth with *bienséance*.[120] Thus, in his *Philosophical Dictionary*, under 'Historiographer,' he asserted: 'It is rare that a historiographer dares speak the truth.' As J.H. Brunfitt writes, Voltaire, as royal historiographer, 'sought to write history which would be agreeable to the King; which would magnify the achievements of the monarchy or at any rate discreetly ignore details which the monarch (or "les grands") would prefer to remain unmentioned.'[121] When criticized for the errors in his commissioned history of Peter the Great, Voltaire replied: 'My dear fellow, they gave me excellent fur cloaks and I am a very chilly mortal.'[122] We typically think of women receiving fur coats for favours received. But Voltaire, thanks to the generous support he received from women, was the greatest name in the Enlightenment, and he saw a statue raised, during his lifetime, to his honour.

6 Scottish Universities and Their Patrons: Argyll, Bute, and Dundas

If universities in England and France were not agents of Enlightenment, as universities were in Scotland, Holland, Germany, and Scandinavia, Adam Smith provided an economic explanation, namely, that clerical patronage in England and the Catholic countries drew the best minds of those societies into the churches. Smith thought that the Patronage Act of 1712, which allowed lay patrons to select clergy but forbade multiple benefices, provided Scots with the best of all worlds: frugal clergymen who owed their livings to their social betters – not their congregations, as had been promised in the 1707 Act of Union – while bright and ambitious young men were drawn to a more prosperous career in the universities.[1] In contrast, the English universities of the eighteenth century, Smith believed, had lost their intellectual vitality and become mere training grounds for a career in the clergy, a path that had grown sufficiently comfortable to suit those of gentle birth.

Certainly, Enlightenment figures in France and England had a low opinion of the universities in their countries. Diderot's entry on 'université' in the *Encyclopédie*, Voltaire's *Dictionnaire philosophique*, and Gibbon's *Memoirs* described French and English universities as barbarous and feudal, held back by clerical obscurantism and scholasticism.[2] Universities had a small part to play in England's scientific revolution and more generally in the intellectual life of French society, where *salons* and *salonnières* were centres of enlightened discussion.[3] Newtonian physics was taught at Edinburgh but not in Cambridge; attempting to purge its reputation for radicalism in the Interregnum, Restoration Cambridge was, Newton's biographer writes, 'fast approaching the status of an intellectual wasteland.'[4]

The decline of English universities in the eighteenth century arose from the English Civil War. Many dons were purged from universities with the imposition of the covenant – a declaration to support an anti-episcopal church order in 1644–5 – and others were purged with the Restoration of Charles II in 1660.[5] More important, as we have seen, there was a drastic decline in the number of plebeian youth entering Oxford and Cambridge during the eighteenth century. University education became increasingly expensive from the Restoration through the eighteenth century; an education at the universities of Edinburgh and Glasgow could be had for about one-fifth of the cost of an Oxford and Cambridge education. And so, in addition to the superior education provided in Scotland, the less wealthy, as well as those who could not subscribe to the articles of the Church of England, were drawn to the Scottish universities.[6] The superior and cheaper education in Scotland produced a backlash of anti-Scottish sentiment in England in the 1760s, much like the anti-Semitism of later, directed at the better-educated, ambitious, and ungentlemanly outsiders prospering in business and acquiring posts in the West Indies, the Hudson's Bay Company, and the East India Company. David Hume encountered anti-Scottish prejudice from English gentlemen, and most of the luminaries of the Scottish Enlightenment emerged from a lower social station than Hume, who came from the lesser gentry.

The Act of Union of 1707 and the Patronage Act of 1712 gave increased scope to Whig patronage in Scotland. Indeed, highly desired positions in taxation and revenue, such as Adam Smith's post as commissioner of customs, were acquired through patrons, and promotion through the military was difficult without patronage.[7] Smith himself emphasized the positive effects of the Patronage Act but did not mention the fact that Tories and Jacobites were purged from the Scottish universities, which created positions for ambitious young men of the right political and religious views. The institutional forms of aristocratic Whig patronage in Scotland were the church and the universities. Charles Camic asserts: 'For each of Scotland's established professional positions – each clerical benefice, each appointive legal office, each university chair – there was a patron, an individual or corporate body legally empowered to choose a successor for the position upon the death or resignation of its previous occupant.' He concludes: 'It was impossible for an eighteenth-century Scot to make it in the Church, the university, or the middle and upper levels of the law alone and by his own devices. To break in or get ahead, he needed at least the official backing of the illustrious patron of the office he was seeking ...'[8]

In this chapter, I wish to doff my bonnet to the 3rd Duke of Argyll, who appointed Smith as well as half the professoriat of Scottish universities in the 1740s and 1750s.[9] Argyll was the general of a formidable anti-Jacobite intellectual army committed to union with England, the Hanover succession, moderation of religious zeal, an orientation to a progressive future, the improvement of Scottish manners and speech, and deprecation of ancient virtue as feudal violence and barbarism.[10] Richard Sher writes: 'In no other country were the principles of the Enlightenment so deeply rooted in the universities or so openly and enthusiastically espoused by leaders of the established church.'[11] Sher makes clear that patronage and Enlightenment were inseparable; the more devout and doctrinaire were hostile to the law of patronage, less tolerant of religious and social differences, and less conservative in politics; the 'Moderates,' the beneficiaries of patronage, were liberal on questions of religious tolerance, intellectual freedom, and enlightenment but maintained a 'staunchly conservative stance on most questions of social, political and ecclesiastical law and order.'[12] Stephen Shapin asserts that merchants rarely were patrons of art or science; the Scottish Enlightenment was largely the product of a conjunction of the landed elite and the professoriat, with the professors benefiting from the patronage and approval of their social superiors, and the gentry, who came to Edinburgh to supervise the education of their sons, basking in the glory of the 'Athens of the North.'[13]

Jacobites were purged from the universities of Edinburgh and Glasgow in 1690, and from all Scottish universities in 1717; acts of the Scottish parliament in 1690 proclaimed that professors should be 'well affected to their Majesties and the Established government of Church and State' and that universities should 'purge out and remove' those not satisfied with the Glorious Revolution.[14] However, unlike the purging of the English universities during the Restoration, which diminished both intellectual vitality and the number of plebeian undergraduates, the purging of Scottish universities had positive effects. With the elimination of Tories from the universities, Locke and Newton became staple features of Scottish curricula, whereas they were not taught in Oxford or Cambridge.[15] Nicolas Phillipson notes that the university replaced the old Scots parliament as the intellectual centre of Scotland, creating a new elite to replace the greater nobility who left Edinburgh for London.[16] The economic benefits for Scotland of union with England were not immediate; the Scottish economy picked up only three decades after union. In this context, according to Michael Fry, Scottish loyalty to the union was purchased by patronage.[17] The Scottish Enlightenment was the result. Sir James Steuart was the only thinker of the Scottish Enlightenment to support Charles Edward Stuart in 1745. If the Scottish Enlightenment was the dying breath of Scottish independence, it was a noble death.

David Allan argues that the Scottish Enlightenment was not a bolt from the blue and refers to a grand tradition of literature and scholarship in Scotland, citing the sixteenth-century historians Hector Boece and George Buchanan, but such men of letters were starved of patronage and recognition. Allan concludes that 'Scotland required, but lacked, its Maecenas.'[18] Eighteenth-century Scotland received its Maecenas first in the group of nobles known as the Squadrone, then the 3rd Duke of Argyll, then Lord Bute, and, finally, Henry Dundas, who used London patronage to bind Scotland into the union. In the Athens of the North, Hegel's owl of Minerva spread its wings in the twilight of Scottish independence. Hume wrote to Gilbert Elliot in July 1757: 'Is it not strange that, at a time when we have lost our Princes, our Parliaments, our independent Government, even the Presence of our chief Nobility, are unhappy, in our Accent & Pronunciation, speak a very corrupt Dialect of the Tongue which we make use of; is it not strange, I say, that, in these Circumstances, we shou'd really be the People most distinguish'd for Literature in Europe.'[19] The anglicization of the Scots tongue was a feature of the Scottish Enlightenment, with Hugh Blair and Adam Ferguson teaching eloquence and Thomas Sheridan being imported to teach elocution or an Irish imitation of the proper English accent. English replaced Latin as the language of the Scottish universities. Thus, Lord Monboddo claimed that Hume died confessing not his sins but his Scotticisms.[20]

The Patronage Act of 1712 betrayed the principles of the Act of Union of 1707. The Scots were promised their own kirk, more democratic than episcopal churches in that local congregations, or the elders and principal men within them, would select a minister suitable to his parishioners. However, the Patronage Act also foisted Church of England practices on Scotland, subordinating church to the state and established order; that is, lay patrons from the gentry and aristocracy selected about two-thirds of the ministers of the church and provided their livings, another quarter of the livings were presented by the crown, and the town councils were responsible for the remaining 10 per cent.[21] This reversal of the Act of Union was a political hot potato for over a century; many Presbyterians thought that the Patronage Act brought Anglo-Catholic hierarchy and servility to Scotland. Archibald Bruce wrote: 'A Patron is a Protestant Pope' and 'a modern clergyman's chief end, is to serve the *Patron*.'[22] However, few members of the Scottish Enlightenment, like the clergy patronized from above, supported the popular Presbyterian cause. Francis Hutcheson, in *Considerations on Patronages Addressed to the Gentlemen of Scotland*, claimed that disbursing church benefices through lay patrons led to the 'servile compliance [of ministers] with the humor of ... great [Lords] whether that humor be virtuous or vitious.'[23] But his voice was unusual among the luminaries of the Scottish Enlightenment. Thomas Gordon thought that the opposition to lay patrons arose from the spiritual pride of clergy who wanted to subordinate civil to clerical authority. Gordon wrote: 'From this Root of spiritual Pride proceeds the too common Ingratitude of Clergymen to their Patrons for very good Livings. They think it Usurpation in Laymen to have Church Benefices in their Gift.' [24] Adam Ferguson, William Robertson, John Jardine, Alexander Carlyle, Hugh Blair, and John Home were enlightened ministers whose careers were furthered by lay patrons. Indeed, Adam Ferguson's career began in 1745 when the Duchess of Atholl requested that the general assembly of the Church of Scotland allow Ferguson to take his examinations early so that he could qualify as chaplain in her son's regiment, the Black Watch, and later his patroness requested that Ferguson's sermon of repentance for the rising of 1745 be translated from Gaelic into English and published in London. As the only Highlander amongst the Scottish Enlightenment, Ferguson proved that even warlike Highlanders could see the benefits of the union and the Hanoverian succession.[25]

Hume and Smith supported lay patrons as a welcome means of reducing religious enthusiasm, which was also the goal of the great patron of the Scottish Enlightenment, the 3rd Duke of Argyll. Completely in accordance with his principles, as secretary to General Henry Seymour Conway, the brother of Lord Hertford, Hume (as distinct from Locke, who held the same position under Shaftesbury, despite his views on the separation of religion and politics) 'took pride and found amusement in assuming the role of patron to the Scottish church.' He 'used his influence with General Conway to steer Scottish church patronage into the proper channels, that is to say, to the Moderate Party.'[26] The Scottish Enlightenment espoused religious moderation imposed from above; the professoriat was an integral part of the Whig patronage that purchased loyalty to the union of Great Britain.

David Hume

David Hume failed to obtain the university positions at Edinburgh and Glasgow that he desired. He wrote, in *My Own Life*, that 'the Whig party were in possession of bestowing all places, both in the State and in Literature.'[27] His complaint that he was deprived of all patronage does not seem to accord with his view that there is no point in patronizing the arts and sciences because effective demand for authors will not ensure quality in their supply – patrons cannot make geniuses or talented authors.[28] Indeed, Hume's argument for no government support for the arts and sciences ran counter to the course of the Scottish Enlightenment and to the course of his own life. When Hume wrote Gibbon that he was too good a writer to be English and that 'it is Lamentable to consider how much that Nation [England] has declined in Literature during our time,'[29] he did not consider that England did not have an Argyll, Bute, or Dundas to coordinate and sponsor the arts and sciences in England. As we have seen, Sir Robert Peel, as prime minister in the 1840s, complained, that he had no means 'to reward achievements in science and scholarship except clerical preferment.'[30] Smith's observation of the effects of the Church of England's monopoly on patronage was much more acute than Hume's attribution of English factiousness to explain Scottish superiority over England in philosophy, scholarship, and letters in the mid-eighteenth century.

Hume's *Treatise of Human Nature* was a commercial failure because, he thought, he did not have a patron. In February 1739 he wrote to Henry Home that few would take care to read a book which 'does not come recommended by some great name or authority.' Shortly after, he wrote to Michael Ramsay that 'such Performances make their way very heavily at first, when they are not recommended by some great name or authority.' In an attempt to obtain the recommendation of Bishop Butler, and avoid offending him, Hume declared that 'I am at present castrating my work, that is, cutting off its noblest parts.'[31] Hume was always attentive to the problem of balancing expectations of readers and patrons to maximize literary fame. He wrote his bookseller, Andrew Millar, that he spiced his *History* with his irreligious views to augment sales, and was irritated that Millar passed on Hume's view, incorrect as it proved to be, that spicy impiety would augment sales of the work.[32] In addition to general readers, Hume had to attend to the great among his readers. He wrote to Charles Erskine, Lord Tinwald, 'I have established it as a Maxim never to pay court to my Superiors by

any of my Writings; but tis needless to offend them,' and he asked
Tinwald to send on a copy of his *Essays Moral and Political* to the 3rd
Duke of Argyll, who is 'oblig'd to me, that I have not dedicated them to
him, & put him out of Countenance, by the usual Fawning and Flattery
of Authors.' Indeed, Hume asked Tinwald to give his book 'not to the
Duke of Argyle [sic], but to Archibald Campbell [Argyll's family name],
who is undoubtedly a Man of Sense & Learning.'[33] Doubtless, Hume
was not intending to offend Argyll when he portrayed his grandfather,
the 9th Earl of Argyll, as one of the great heroes of his *History of
England*, a loyal Briton who was forced to stand up for liberty and turn
against his Catholic king and who was executed bravely (in contrast to
the Duke of Monmouth, whom he supported).[34] Hume clearly wanted
to have it both ways when he wrote to the Earl of Balcarres that his
History 'is in general rather more agreeable to ... Tories; and, I believe,
chiefly for this reason, that, having no places to bestow, they are
naturally more moderate in their expectations of a writer. A Whig, who
can give hundreds a year, will not be contented with small sacrifices of
truth; and most writers are willing to purchase favour at so reasonable a
price.'[35] Hume's equation of historical truth with impartiality, rather
than exhaustive research,[36] accords with his desire to attract both Whig
and Tory patrons.

While Hume's patrons, Generals Conway and St Clair, and the Earl
of Hertford, were Whigs or apolitical, Smith's greatest patron, the Duke
of Buccleugh, was a Tory, and Henry Dundas was also a Tory. But the
Whig Argyll was the man who orchestrated the Scottish Enlightenment.
Boswell was to complain, 'Why always an agent, a salesman for us like
cattle? Archibald Duke of Argyll drove us like bullocks for an age,' but
in fact the great Scots drover of cattle[37] tamed wild Highland beasts or
drove them into the forefront of the republic of letters, while all
Boswell did was to create the greatest Englishman of his time.[38] The 3rd
Duke of Argyll was the Maecenas who made his country the brain of the
British body politic or, to use a Humean metaphor, the slavish reason
in the British soul. The Scottish Enlightenment was an enlightenment
from above, not from below, and even opposed to the Popular Party
(the parishes that wished to defy the Patronage Act) below.

Hume wanted university positions at Edinburgh and Glasgow and
thought that they were in Argyll's power to grant, despite widespread
Presbyterian opposition to university posts for the notorious heretic
and atheist. Although scholars have blamed Smith for not standing up
for his friend and the greatest British thinker of the eighteenth cen-

tury, Hume put the blame directly on Argyll. He wrote to John Clephane that his friends would have succeeded in obtaining him a university position 'in spite of the violent and solemn remonstances of the clergy, if the Duke of Argyle [sic] had had courage to give me the least countenance,' but he did allow that Argyll supported his position as librarian to the Faculty of Advocates, despite the strength of the opposition to his appointment.[39] Later, Hume wrote to Smith that Argyll could arrange Smith's appointment at Edinburgh and Ferguson's appointment at Smith's vacated chair in Glasgow, whatever the opposition, since his agent 'Lord Milton can with his Finger stop the foul Mouths of all the Roarers against Heresy.'[40] Hume was less successful than his friend Smith in obtaining Argyll's favour. Smith was introduced to the duke by Neil Campbell, principal of Glasgow College, and shortly after, he asked Argyll's help in securing a post in the custom's office for a friend.[41] Hume wrote Smith that Argyll was the first one to receive Smith's *Theory of Moral Sentiments*, and he later reported to Smith that the Duke was 'decisive ... in its favour.'[42] Smith was not alone among the luminaries of Scotland to receive Argyll's favour; the duke's recommendation enabled William Robertson to obtain a good price for his *History of Scotland* and facilitated his obtaining the position of principal of Edinburgh University.[43] Besides Smith, Ferguson, and Robertson, Argyll appointed Francis Hutcheson, John Millar, and Thomas Reid to their university posts.[44] Hume might well have felt aggrieved since the duke had promoted the careers of the other remarkable minds of the Scottish Enlightenment, leaving him as the sole figure to develop a literary career outside the Scottish universities.

As a result, Hume's literary supply was responsive to market demand and the expectations of patrons. His philosophy sold poorly; the *Treatise of Human Nature* 'fell *dead-born from the Press*,' his *Enquiry concerning Human Understanding*, which was written with the leisure provided by a patronage appointment with General St Clair, was 'little more successful' than the *Treatise*, and the *Essay concerning the Principles of Morals*, which Hume thought 'incomparably the best' of his writing, 'came unnoticed and unobserved into the World.'[45] But because 'it has been my Misfortune to write in the Language of the most stupid and factious Barbarians in the World,'[46] Hume turned to history, thinking it 'the most popular kind of writing of any';[47] in fact, the leading British philosopher of the Enlightenment is recorded in British libraries as 'David Hume, the historian.' However, the first edition of his *History of England* sold only forty-five copies.[48] Hume then toned down his criticisms of religion in the second volume of his *History* and deleted his attack on religious sectarians in his second edition of the first volume, with the result of much improved sales. Hume's contemporary, the cleric John Brown, wrote that Hume 'knew the *Godly* were not to be his *Buyers*' of the *Essays* and so spiced them with impious sentiments, but 'when he finds that his History must *sell* among the *Godly*, or *not sell* at all; *then ... Gain* produceth *Godliness*.'[49]

Hume's *Essays Moral and Political* sold well and earned him almost £200, or roughly half what he earned a year as companion to the mad Marquess of Annandale and less than he earned as secretary to General St Clair, General Conway, and the Earl of Hertford. In 'Of Essay Writing,' Hume described himself as an ambassador between the *learned* and the *conversible*, between those who toil in scholarship or the 'more difficult Operations of the Mind' and the leisured patrons of learning who are inclined 'to the easier and more gentle Exercises of the Understanding.' The 'Fair Sex' were 'the Sovereigns of the Empire of Conversation' to whom Hume, as an 'Ambassador from the Dominions of Learning,' paid court. In France, as distinct from Britain, as we saw in the previous chapter, it was said that 'the Ladies are, in a Manner, the Sovereigns of the *learned* World, as well as of the *conversible*: and no polite Writer pretends to venture upon the Public, without the Approbation of some celebrated Judges of that Sex.'[50] Hume, for his part, presented the same message as Cesar Chesneau Dumarsais's entry 'Philosophe' in the *Encyclopédie* and Charles Duclos's *Considérations sur les moeurs de ce siècle* (1750) – namely, the mutually beneficial relationship between learning and polite society whereby the former are polished and the latter enlightened – but he added the dimension of gender. In 'Of the Study of History,' Hume wrote that history is particularly suited to female readers, despite their apparent preference for novels,[51] and was determined to cast his net widely. He sold the bookseller Andrew Millar two volumes of his *History of England* for 800 guineas; the text was now adjusted to suit the religious sensibilities of readers and balanced between the Whig and Tory propensities of both readers and potential patrons.

While Hume began to earn a frugal competence from his *Essays* and *History*, he became quite wealthy from his positions as secretary to General Conway, General St Clair, and the Earl of Hertford, none of which were too arduous to keep him from writing. Hume spent about five hours a day in the office but he had little to do but read books, write books and letters, and talk to friends.[52] He accepted the patron-

age of Lord Hertford, as he wrote to Smith in 1763, because 'it wou'd
be easy to prevent my Acceptance from having the least Appearance of
Dependence.' Hume did not explain why he would not appear dependent, but perhaps the offer of employment from an English lord
would not strike his compatriots as involving the same degree of
dependence as Scottish patronage networks. Two years later, Hume
wrote Smith that Hertford 'procured me a Pension of 400 a Year for
Life. Nothing coud be more to my Mind: I have now Opulence and
Liberty.'[53] Or, as he phrased it in *My Own Life*, he enjoyed 'a much
larger Income by means of Lord Hertford's friendship' than he had
before. However, Hume received more than money from the patronage
of a pious noble courtier; he received respectability. Hume chortled in
self-satisfaction: 'So that in spite of Atheism and Deism, of Whiggery &
Toryism, of Scoticism & Philosophy, I am now possessed of an Office of
Credit, and of 1200 Pounds a Year; without Dedication or Application,
from the Favour alone of a Person, whom I can perfectly love and
respect.'[54] Hume wrote to Sir Gilbert Elliot (Elliot, James Oswald,
William Mure, and John Home were Hume's most regular correspon-
dents and also Scottish agents of London patronage) that Lord Bute's
patronage had done him no good, since Bute was a hated Scotsman
like himself, but 'since I have Lord Hertford's Friendship: Nobody,
henceforth, need be afraid to patronise me, either as a Scotsman or a
Deist.'[55]

We might note here the common usage, both by patrons and clients,
of a language of friendship to describe the relationship, and also the
eighteenth-century usage that 'patronize' meant dignify, as distinct
from current meaning of the word as an action that undermines
dignity. Hume's respectability and social credit increased through his
relationship to Hertford, although Hume irritated the pious with his
frequent boast that Lord Hertford would make him a bishop if he were
asked.[56] As Hume wrote to James Oswald, 'it seems to me almost
incomprehensible how it should happen, that I, a philosopher, a man
of letters, nowise a courtier, of the most independent spirit, who has
given offence to every sect, and every party, that I, I say, such as I have
described myself, should obtain an employment of dignity, and a
thousand a year.'[57] Given Oswald's efforts to secure patronage for
Hume, one can imagine the sour smile on Oswald's face as he read this
letter.

We might analyse the stability of Hume's relationship to Hertford,
given Hume's professions of independence, which he shared with his

peers in the republic of letters. Hume truly respected the pious courtier; his respect for nobility, which, despite bearish growls, Rousseau
shared, facilitated a relationship with someone who was in no sense
Hume's, or indeed Argyll's, intellectual peer. Indeed, the very asymmetry of the infidel commoner and the pious nobleman bonded the
patron-client relationship. Hume, as we have seen, thought Voltaire
and Frederick to be too much in rivalry for Frederick to be a reliable
patron.[58] Hume and Rousseau were also social equals and too much in
intellectual competition for there to be stability in Hume's patronage
of Rousseau, or for Hume to be a broker in George III's patronage of
Rousseau.

At the outset of their relationship, Hume wrote Rousseau that he
revered him over all other writers in Europe, and they were soulmates
in their 'love of philosophical Retreat ... Neglect of Vulgar Prejudices,
and ... Disdain of all Dependance.'[59] But deference and egalitarian
friendship were incompatible, and, as already noted, Rousseau came to
feel that Hume wanted to have him as a proud possession. Hume
published his account of Rousseau's ingratitude, contrary to Smith's
advice and his view that it takes two to tangle – 'I am thoroughly
convinced that Rousseau is as great a Rascal as you.'[60] Smith's jocularity
of tone did not belie his conviction that Hume's decision to publish his
account of the rift with Rousseau was a serious error and an act of
weakness on his part. Hume feared the power of Rousseau's pen and
wanted to write his own account first, for posterity's sake.

Hume prided himself on his independent status in the republic of
letters and suggested that men of letters could support themselves in a
non-subsidized marketplace of ideas. Indeed, while a recipient and
donor of government patronage, Hume was responsive to market
demand, as well as patronal expectations, in his writings. Still, had the
Duke of Argyll secured for Hume the university positions he desired,
the leading British philosopher of the eighteenth century would be
listed in British libraries not as David Hume the historian but as David
Hume the philosopher.

Adam Smith

It is ironic that the man who saw print technology as rendering patronage obsolete and commercial liberalization or free trade as the way to
the wealth of nations should have been born the son of a customs
official, and died a customs officer, a post provided for him by Tory

patrons, the Duke of Buccleugh and Henry Dundas, later Viscount
Melville. The former lured Smith from the academy by the offer of a
lucrative post as his tutor and travelling companion. Smith's academic
career began with the patronage of Archibald Campbell, 3rd Duke of
Argyll, obtained for him by William Cullen, professor of chemistry at
Glasgow. Smith repaid his debt to Cullen by arranging a pension for
Cullen's daughters with 'our present Minister for Scotland,' Henry
Dundas, or 'Harry the Ninth' as he was popularly known. Dundas
congratulated himself in 1801 with the thought: 'Every professor in the
universities of St. Andrews and Edinburgh has been appointed for
more than 20 years past either actually by myself or upon my recommendation, and I take the satisfaction to reflect that in not one instance have I been mistaken.'[61] Henry Cockburn wrote that Dundas was
'the Pharos [lighthouse of Alexandria] of Scotland. He who steered
upon him was safe; who disregarded his light was wrecked.'[62] For
example, William Smellie, who later took up the editorship of the
Encylopedia Britannica, wanted the chair of natural history at Edinburgh
but wrongly chose the Earl of Buchan as patron, rather than Dundas,
and did not get the post he coveted.[63] Smith was more judicious in his
choice of patrons. He wrote the Duke of Buccleugh, 'I took the first
opportunity in my power of speaking to Mr. Dundas about Dr. Cullens
[sic] Daughters,' adding that, although 'ministers seldom gain much
credit by granting of Pensions,' in the case of the Cullens, Dundas's
patronage would be an exception.[64] The visible hand of patronage
complemented the invisible hand of the market in the life of Smith and
his associates. Indeed, the co-existence of patronage and the market
could well be illustrated in the pragmatic friendship of the political
manager of Scotland, 'Harry the Ninth,' and the commercial publisher
William Creech.[65]

Although Smith's *Wealth of Nations* suggests that the age of patronage
of letters has passed, his *Theory of Moral Sentiments* indicates the com-
patibility of patron-client and market relations. Indeed, Smith saw 'the
laws of gratitude,' next to the laws of justice (respecting property rights
of others and observing contracts), as the most precise and important
aspects of moral philosophy. When you owe someone £5, you must pay
it back at the appointed time; however, if someone has given you a gift
or has done you a good deed, you must requite it but also exercise
discretion with respect to the value of what is returned, depending on
the age, status, and situation of the benefactor. The two moral sentiments animating our moral judgments are resentment for injuries done

to us (and, by sympathy, those done to others) and gratitude for what benefits us (and, by sympathy, what benefits others). Smith seemed to have the cause-effect relationship inverted when he wrote: 'The sentiment which most immediately prompts us to reward, is gratitude.' We would normally think that reward creates gratitude, rather than vice versa. While Smith was keen to keep the cynicism of Bernard Mandeville – author of *The Fable of the Bees* and popularly known as the 'man-devil' – at bay, he suggested that our beneficence is bought by gratitude, or is animated by what Smith called 'the importunities of gratitude.'[66] Smith is clear that an honourable man follows the laws of gratitude regardless of what he happens to feel. Even if one does not feel grateful to a patron, one 'will endeavour to pay all those regards and attentions to his patron which the liveliest gratitude could suggest.' The person who acts gratefully without feeling so 'may do all this too without any hypocrisy or blameable dissimulation, without any selfish intention of obtaining new favours, and without any design of imposing either upon his benefactor or the public.'[67] In fact, Smith provided a powerful account of the psychological, as distinct from the material, benefit of patronage, quite separate from the approbation of the impartial spectator that regulates the rest of our moral conduct. Smith explained:

> What most charms us in our benefactor, is the concord between his sentiments and our own, with regard to what interests us so nearly as the worth of our own character, and the esteem that is due to us. We are delighted to find a person who values us as we value ourselves, and distinguishes us from the rest of mankind, with an attention not unlike that which we distinguish ourselves. To maintain in him those agreeable and flattering sentiments, is one of the chief ends proposed by the returns we are disposed to make to him. A generous mind often disdains the interested thought of extorting new favours from its benefactor, by what may be called the importunities of its gratitude. But to preserve and to increase his esteem, is an interest which the greatest mind does not think unworthy of its attention.[68]

Smith, no more than Hume, thought it unworthy of his attention to court patrons.

Smith wrote his best-sellers, the *Theory of Moral Sentiments* and *The Wealth of Nations*, while a professor in Glasgow and Edinburgh. Hume, who would have given his eye teeth to have sold his philosophy in comparable numbers to Smith, twitted the author of the *Theory of Moral*

Sentiments, which had distinguished between what is praiseworthy and what is praised, with the reflection that 'nothing, indeed, can be a stronger presumption of falsehood than the approbation of the multitude.' Thus, Hume, who desired fame and equated virtue with what receives social approbation, teased Smith, who equated virtue with conscience (either God within the human breast or internalized social approval), with the counsel to 'think on the emptiness, and rashness, and futility of the common judgments of men,' for 'a wise man's kingdom is in the breast; or, if he ever looks further, it will only be to the judgment of a select few, who are free from prejudices, and capable of examining his own work.'[69] While Hume was parading his friendship and admiration as mock disapproval and envy, he raised the question of whether all works of thought and scholarship can be supported by market demand. If quality is not merely what is praised and bought but what is praiseworthy or praised by tasteful patrons, such as the Duke of Argyll, the quality of the work is not equivalent to the quantity of market demand. Smith's *Moral Sentiments* is more the exception than the rule that profound philosophy can be a best-seller; it presented Enlightenment social psychology in a manner more acceptable to Presbyterian and Anglican readers than the more uncompromising secularism of Hume or of French atheists.

Smith, as noted above, saw the greater production of intelligence in Scotland than England to be the result of the Patronage Act, which enabled lay patrons to bestow moderate or virtuous livings on the Scottish clergy but nothing sufficiently grand to deflect ambitious young men from a more prosperous life in the universities. He deprecated the fixed salaries of Oxford dons and recommended the Scottish (and German) practice of professors charging fees for their lectures to reward them for excellence in teaching. Ian Ross elaborates: 'Scottish professors at this period earned an appreciable part of their income from student fees payable to them directly, and therefore had an incentive to teach well, maintain distinction in their disciplines and attract students.'[70] Smith seemed to think that the provision of university courses, like the provision of exotic vegetables in shops, should depend upon market demand; he found 1753 a lean year and wanted to cancel classes at Glasgow because of the few students enrolled in his courses.[71] In addition to student fees, professors could enrich themselves by boarding aristocratic youth. On Sir Gilbert Elliot's recommendation, for £400 yearly, Smith boarded Lord Fitzmaurice, the brother of Lord Shelburne, the patron of Price, Priestley, Bentham, and others.

Shelburne expected Smith to act as tutor and guardian to Fitzmaurice, writing Smith that Glasgow was not like English universities: 'The great fault I find with Oxford and Cambridge, is that Boys sent thither instead of being the Governed, become the Governors of the Colleges, and that Birth and Fortune are more respected than Literary Merit.'[72] Hugh Blair, William Robertson, and Adam Ferguson also made substantial sums from boarding the sons of English peers and gentlemen, roughly twice the amount of their salaries.[73]

In addition to his salary, fees, and the money earned from boarding aristocrats, Smith tutored the 3rd Duke of Buccleugh from 1764 to 1766, a task for which he received an annuity of £300 a year, and this attention was to be rewarded when Buccleugh offered him the post of commissioner of customs the year after *The Wealth of Nations* was published. Smith wrote Buccleugh that he renounced his annuity as tutor since 'by the interest of the Duke of Buccleugh, I was appointed' commissioner of customs by Dundas, but 'his Grace sent me word by his Cashier, to whom I had offered to deliver up his bond, that though I had considered what was fit for my own honour, I had not consider'd what was fit for his; and he never would suffer it to be suspected that he had procured an office for his friend, in order to relieve himself from the burden of such an annuity.'[74] The transaction evinced a mutually beneficial exchange of bourgeois profit and aristocratic honour.

Roger Emerson notes that Glasgow professors tended to have less genteel backgrounds than the professors of other Scottish universities but 'served the gentry more than those elsewhere'; 32 per cent of Glasgow's professors, twice the percentage of other Scottish universities, 'tutored or taught aristocratic boys.'[75] Alexander Carlyle, from his own experience, observed that the career of tutor engendered 'a certain obsequiousness or *bassese* [sic].'[76] Adam Ferguson gave up teaching moral philosophy to act as a travelling tutor to Lord Chesterfield's godson, who succeeded him as 5th earl in 1773, at a salary of £400 yearly and a pension of £200 for life, but he later returned to the university because he felt that the pension was inadequate to his needs. Ferguson was also a tutor to Lord Bute's children and supplemented his educational income as a paid writer for Lord North.[77] John Millar entered the household of Lord Kames as tutor to his son before entering Edinburgh's Faculty of Advocates and then was appointed by Lord Bute as Regius chair of civil and Scots law at Glasgow. As already noted, Bute also appointed William Robertson, the most successful academic in the Scottish Enlightenment, as principal of Edinburgh.

Robertson began his career as a tutor and then worked as a clergyman for a decade before entering the university, and, through the patronage of Bute and Dundas, he achieved ascendancy in the Church of Scotland, promoting the interests of the Moderates and penalizing the Popular Party.[78] Robertson, who had profited from the patronage of Argyll, Bute, and Dundas, made a large sum from booksellers for his *History of Scotland* and an unprecedented sum, the envy of all European men of letters, for his *History of Charles V.* However, as Richard Sher observes, 'the combined annual income of nearly £700 from his pension and his offices as principal, parish minister, and historiographer royal of Scotland would have made Robertson one of the wealthiest Scottish ministers up to this time even if he had never earned a single pound from his histories.'[79] Whether Robertson was a counter-example to Smith's contention that ambitious young men can do better in the university than in the church is questionable since Robertson did well in both church and university.

The Scottish Enlightenment was the product of governmental patronage that served to integrate Scotland into the union with England. However, Hume and Smith, the two most notable thinkers of this remarkable Enlightenment, advocated a free marketplace of ideas, with no government support for the arts and sciences and scholars and thinkers no longer dependent upon patrons but earning an independent existence through the sales of their books. Their life experience, and those of their colleagues, such as Ferguson, Millar, and Robertson, only partially accorded with their professions of independence. In reality, the 3rd Duke of Argyll presided over the early evening, and Henry Dundas over the late evening, of this most glorious sunset in Scottish history.

7 Independence in Theory and Practice: D'Alembert and Rousseau

Patronage is indeed, as Julian Pitt-Rivers calls it, 'lop-sided friendship,' a combination of friendship and social inequality, and patron-client relationships are most stable when both parties do not see the other as equal enough to be a competitor or rival. As Sharon Kettering writes, in her study of patronage in seventeenth-century France, 'the nearer a client was to his patron in rank and power, the less likely the relationship was to be durable ...'[1] Rousseau resented the patronage of his peer Hume and of *nouveaux riches*, such as Mme d'Épinay and Baron d'Holbach, but accepted it from the Duc de Luxembourg or the Prince de Conti, the largest landowners in France with the bluest of blood. What Rousseau said in *Julie, ou la nouvelle Héloise* of her caste-proud father, M. d'Etange, whose snobbery prevented the love of Julie and Saint-Proux and forever destroyed the happiness of his daughter, was also applicable to the author himself: namely, that he could not 'bear the idea of being indebted to someone who is not of noble birth.'[2]

Rousseau's career began when he found solace in the arms of 'ma chère patronne,' Mme de Warens. Rousseau's greatest debt was to Mme de Warens, who received pensions from the King of Sardinia and two clerics, Michel-Gabriel Bernix, bishop of Annecy, and François-Hyacinthe de Valperque, bishop of Maurienne, and the French ambassador to Constantinople, Jean Louis d'Ussan, Marquis de Bonac. She had fled her husband, a Protestant Swiss landowner, converted to Catholicism, and apparently received pensions for missionary activity. Claude Anet, her twenty-year-old servant, fled with her, converted to Catholicism, and shared her bed until Rousseau, who also converted to Catholicism, reached the age of twenty and replaced Anet as Warens's lover, whereupon Anet committed suicide. Rousseau, in turn, was replaced five years later by the twenty-year-old Jean-Samuel-Rodolph Wintzenried, but the romantic Rousseau did not follow Anet's example. One wonders whether the church knew about, and approved of, the missionary position adopted by Mme de Warens, as Rousseau claimed it did. Mme de Warens educated Rousseau and obtained positions for him first as a clerk and then as a music teacher to the daughters of the aristocracy. Later, Warens got Rousseau a post as tutor to the sons of the Seigneur de Mably, a brother of the enlightened abbés de Mably and de Condillac. Rousseau proved to be a failure as a tutor but thereby obtained an entrée into the French Enlightenment.

As already recounted, when Rousseau arrived in Paris, Father Castel advised him to visit the *salonnières* as the indispensable condition of success in Paris.[3] Later, during his attempt to have his opera *Les muses galantes* performed, Rousseau declared that 'no one who can make it in Paris who lives in isolation.' He failed to interest Jean-Philippe Rameau and then thought of asking Alexandre-Jean-Joseph La Riche de la Poplinière, a tax collector, to produce his work since 'M. de la Poplinière was Rameau's Maecenas.'[4] Though Rousseau found his first *patronne*, Mme de Beuzewal, insufficiently aware of the 'consideration' owed to men of talent,[5] it was at her salon that he met his future 'ami-protecteur', Lamoignon de Malesherbes, and also his next employer, Comte de Montaigu, the French ambassador to Venice. Rousseau served under Montaigu in Venice, but, since the comte also did not have sufficient regard for the talented plebeian, they fought and Rousseau returned to Paris. There, Rousseau worked as a secretary and then treasurer to the Dupin de Franceuil family, earning 800 *livres* annually from 1746 to 1748, and he then had his salary raised twice, to 1,200 livres, in 1750, when he began his lifetime liaison with Thérèse Levasseur. As a paid employee of the Dupins, Rousseau helped them write a Hobbesian defence of monarchy as the best means of averting a natural condition of universal warfare; and this tract also included a justification of slavery.[6] Rousseau met Frederick the Great at the Dupin home. While Rousseau was to become known as an egalitarian republican, he also acquired a reputation as a misogynist, though, in the employ of Mme Dupin, he wrote voluminously on the rights of women.[7]

Rousseau's friendship with Diderot developed while he was employed by the Dupins. Rousseau claimed that it was Diderot's 'fault' that Rousseau was 'thrown into his own profession.' Professional misfortune befell Diderot first: he was jailed for slighting Mme du Pré de Saint Maur, the lover of Marc-Pierre de Voyer, the Comte d'Argenson.

Diderot was miffed that the physician René Antoine Ferchault de Réaumur had preferred rank (Mme du Pré de Saint Maur) to genius (Diderot and his peers) in allowing Mme du Pré de Saint Maur to be the first witness of his operation to relieve blindness. Diderot wrote that Réaumur 'has not wished to let the veil fall except in the presence of some eyes of no importance.'[8] Unfortunately, those eyes of no importance had gazed into eyes of some importance, namely, the Comte d'Argenson, secretary of war and director of publications, who had Diderot imprisoned. Later, Diderot was humiliated when the *Encyclopédie* was prefaced with a lavish dedication to the man who had had him jailed.

If the Comte d'Argenson was powerful enough to have Diderot imprisoned and then extort a dedication in Diderot's life work, he was also influential enough to keep Rousseau from the Bastille for his outrageous pamphlet proving the preferability of Italian to French music. However, d'Argenson did not respond to Rousseau's request for more money for his charming opera, *Le devin du village*, prompting the author to write: 'The silence of that unjust man remained in my heart, and did not contribute to increasing the very mediocre esteem that I always had for his character and his talents.'[9] Rousseau's sense of injustice about d'Argenson seems odd in that Rousseau said that he got more money from the six weeks of labour in writing *Le devin du village* than he received for *Émile*, 'which cost me twenty years of meditation and three years of labor.'[10] And, curiously, he did not hold the same grievance against publishers who profited from his literary productions as he did against d'Argenson for his failure to improve his remuneration for *Le devin du village*,[11] despite the fact that the opera was to prove the most stable source of his life earnings.[12] Rousseau praised to the skies the comte's brother, the Marquis d'Argenson, in *The Social Contract* (IV.viii). Diderot's friend and collaborator, D'Alembert, also praised the Marquis d'Argenson as well as his patron, the Comte d'Argenson, in his celebrated attack on patronage, *Essai sur la société des gens de lettres et des grands, sur la réputation, sur les Mécènes, et sur les récompenses littéraires.*[13]

While Rousseau was prudent in praising the Marquis d'Argenson in *Du Contrat social,* he was insufficiently clear in his praise of the powerful Duc de Choiseul in the same work, and even less prudent in refusing the advice of his *ami protecteur*, Malesherbes, to excise the sentence in the *Nouvelle Héloise* declaring that the wife of a charcoal-burner is worthier of respect than the mistress of a prince. (He had originally said 'king' rather than 'prince', but here he had accepted Malesherbes advice to use the latter word, since not only Mme de Pompadour, the mistress of the king, but also Mme de Boufflers, the mistress of Rousseau's protector, the Prince de Conti, and perhaps the prince himself would find Rousseau's sentiment not to their taste.[14]) Rousseau was alert to the need for political protectors, despite his refusal to accept royal patronage.

D'Alembert's Theoretical and Rousseau's Practical Rejection of Patronage

On the way to visit Diderot in the prison of Vincennes (or, according to Diderot, after a conversation with him), Rousseau had his celebrated epiphany about the bounty of nature and the corruption of civilization. The result of this epiphany was Rousseau's *Discours sur les arts et les sciences*, where, despite his apparent assault on the republic of letters, he concluded with a plea for patronage: 'Therefore may Kings not disdain to allow into their councils the men most capable of advising them well; may they renounce the old prejudice, invented by the pride of the great, that the art of leading people is more difficult than that of enlightening them ... May learned men of the first rank find honorable asylum in their courts.'[15] However, with the success of his assault on the civilizing effects of the arts and sciences, Rousseau assumed the role of uncorrupt judge of civilized hierarchy, renounced his post as treasurer to de Franceuil, and resolved to earn his living as a music copyist. His triple vow of poverty, liberty, and truth, as the Marquis d'Argenson noted in his journal entry of 16 April 1753, was an intolerable threat to government policy and 'have indisposed the government against him.' Even when Rousseau's *Le devin du village* was such a success at court, earning him 100 *Louis* (almost 3,000 *livres*) from Louis XV and 50 *Louis* from Mme de Pompadour (as well as an equivalent sum from the Opera and his printer, Pissot), Louis XV proposed either to give Rousseau a pension or to have him incarcerated with the mad at Bicêtre.[16] Diderot told his friend to accept the pension for the sake of Thérèse and her mother, precipitating the first friction between Diderot and Rousseau. Rousseau wrote that Diderot 'spoke to me about the pension with a warmth that I would not have expected from a philosopher on such a subject.'[17]

Bernard Williams has written that Rousseau and Diderot fell out primarily 'over two different conceptions of what it takes to be a truthful person.' According to Williams, Rousseau's conception of truthfulness as sincerity leads to self-absorbed solitude, whereas Diderot's authentic human being is responsive to the desires of others.[18] But Williams does not mention Rousseau's and Diderot's differences with respect to the acceptance and obligations of patronage, or the difficulty in telling the truth when one is a recipient of patronage. Burke deprecated Rousseau's refusal of patronage, calling it vain and an attempt at 'unsocial independence.'[19] I wish to bring Williams's and Burke's criticisms of Rousseau together; that is, the impossibility of sincerity or transparency was connected to the impracticality of Rousseau's extricating himself from royal protection. Whereas Voltaire thought that a royal pension was public rather than private patronage, Rousseau, according to Benoît Mély, was not wrong in thinking a royal pension to be a form of personal dependence, whereby the man of letters is entirely subject to the whim of the monarch.[20] On the other hand, Rousseau would have had good grounds for thinking, in his twilight years, that there was something in Voltaire's view that a man of letters should have a few crowned heads up his sleeve. Jean Guéhenno writes that Rousseau's 'greatness [like that of Diderot], if not that of a servant, was that of a plebeian in need of protectors.'[21] Diderot was less disposed to deny his dependency than his former friend.

Rousseau wished to walk alone, proud of his savage independence. However, when he began to live with Thérèse Levasseur, he claimed that his expenses more than doubled. He heard talk in the alehouses and restaurants that 'the one who best peopled the foundling hospital was always the best applauded. That won me over ... since it is the practice of the country, when one lives there one can follow it ...'[22] The man who rejected the other-orientedness of social expectations for the inner-directedness of heart and conscience was moved by bar-room banter and refused to take responsibility for the abandonment and probable deaths of his children.

Cynical contemporaries thought that Rousseau's stance of independence of patrons was a profitable pose, boosting his status with the aristocracy and helping his books to sell,[23] but D'Alembert's *Essai sur la société des gens de lettres et des grands* persuaded others that Rousseau's independent stance was more than canny posturing.[24] D'Alembert's *Essai* irked men of letters other than Rousseau in that it proposed to deprive them of patronage, just as it irritated some of the great aristocrats who believed that D'Alembert wished to deprive them of their titles.[25] D'Alembert asserted that, in place of the Roman imperial call for bread and circuses, 'it would be highly desirable that all men of letters would have the courage to say *bread and liberty*!' 'LIBERTY, TRUTH and POVERTY (for when one fears the last, one removes oneself far from the other two), there are three words that men of letters must always have before their eyes, as sovereigns must have POSTERITY.'[26]

Benoît Mély acutely observes that Rousseau, in vowing to earn his living as a music copyist, intended to 'reform' his life in the sense of reverting to his Calvinist origins, as befitted his aspirations to become a citizen of Geneva, and renouncing the decadence of Catholic and hierarchical Paris.[27] Another scholar, Daniel Roche, writes that Rousseau 'proposed to live according to a charter of material independence, as a pledge of intellectual independence.'[28] But Rousseau protested that living as a music copyist was not at all an affectation of independence, it was a necessity. 'I sell the work of my hands, but the products of my soul are not for sale.' His noble amateurism co-existed with relative poverty as he asserted his place in the republic of letters. John Stuart Mill was later to advise writers to take a job so that they could, as Rousseau wished, avoid the pressure of writing for money.[29] Rousseau thought that if he did not copy music, 'he would have to plot, rush from house to house ... pay court to the Nobles, to the rich, to women, to artists, to all those he would be allowed to approach.'[30]

Yet Rousseau's profession as a music copyist, according to Benoît Mély, made him the recipient of collective aristocratic patronage, rather than being dependent on individual patrons.[31] Indeed, Jean Guéhenno indicates that Rousseau's household depended as much on gifts that Thérèse and her mother received from aristocrats as on the pay Rousseau received as a music copyist.[32] Rousseau's income from his part-time employment as a music copyist, and as a writer and musician, was insufficient to support his dependents. As is well known, Rousseau stated that he abandoned his five children in an orphanage to their probable deaths, although he maintained throughout his life that they would have fared better in the orphanage than they would have being raised by Thérèse and her mother, or by Rousseau's aristocratic friends. If Mme d'Épinay or the Duchesse de Luxembourg had raised them, he said, they would have grown up hating their parents, but, 'by abandoning my children to public education for lack of power to bring them up myself; by destining them to become workers and peasants rather than adventurers and fortune hunters; I believed I was performing an action of a citizen and father, and I looked at myself as a member of Plato's Republic.'[33]

Rousseau wrote to Mme de Franceuil on 20 April 1751 that, if he had not abandoned his children, he would either have had to write for money or depend upon patronage; 'it would be necessary to have recourse to protection, to intrigue, to tricks, to court some low employment,' and he concluded that 'it is the social station of the rich ... that steals my children's bread from mine.'[34] However, Rousseau allowed aristocratic friends to place Therèse's father in a hospital and to provide her mother with a pension so that he could maintain his independence in the republic of letters. Thus, he still felt himself able to make the proud declaration: 'I felt that writing in order to have bread might stifle my genius and kill my talent which was less in my pen than in my heart, and had been born solely out of an elevated and proud way of thinking which could alone nourish it. Nothing vigorous, nothing great can come from an entirely venal pen.' The plebeian with the aristocratic outlook insisted that, if he wrote for money, he would have to write what is untrue to 'please the multitude.' Authors are only great when writing is not a trade (*métier*) but flows from a burning passion. 'In order to be able, in order to say great truths one must not be dependent on success.'[35] Yet Raymond Birn draws our attention to the paradox that Rousseau both maintained an aristocratic disdain for the commercial marketplace in books and sought to establish an author's private property in his literary productions.[36] In fact, Rousseau acquired a reputation as an Arab or a Jew for his skill in bargaining with the booksellers.[37]

Thanks to Mély and Birn, we know how much money Rousseau made from his writings – 600 *livres* from Claude Pissot for his *Discourse on Inequality*; 2,160 *livres* from Marc-Michel Rey, 1,000 *livres* from Étienne-Vincent Robin and Jean-Augustin Grangé, and 1,200 *livres* from Nicholas-Bonaventure Duchesne for *Nouvelle Héloise*, and 6,000 *livres* from Duchesne for *Émile*. After *Émile* and *The Social Contract* were condemned, Rousseau's books were less marketable, although there was an enormous demand for underground and pirated editions of them. Birn estimates that Rousseau, in his productive years between 1754 and 1764, received from Rey 60 per cent of his living expenses.[38] Yet, in the end, all this data takes us only so far. We have no idea whether Rousseau's royalties constituted 10 or 40 per cent of his lifetime's income, whether the music copying at 6 sols a page until 1770 and then 10 sols a page – Rousseau estimated that he copied between 6,000 and 9,000 pages between 1770 and 1777[39] – earned him 5 or 15 per cent of his income, and whether aristocratic patronage made up most or just a large part of his income. Rousseau constantly claimed to be poor, but we have no way of knowing whether David Hume's suspicion that Rousseau was not as poor as he professed to be was well founded. Certainly, the expenses of moving from Geneva to France, back to Geneva, to Neuchâtel, to England, and back to various places in France would have depleted much of his savings. Also, the costs of sending proofs to his publishers were high, sometimes amounting to 500 *livres* per year.[40]

What is peculiar is that the populist writer, who sold more books than any of his contemporaries, and who, in *The Social Contract* (II.ii), equated telling truth with paying 'court only to the people,' maintained, in *Confessions* and *Rousseau Judge of Jean Jacques*, a Platonic contempt for catering to the vulgar populace. 'Writing books to make a living would have made me dependent on the public. From then on, the issue would have been not to teach and instruct, but to please and succeed.' Indeed, when Rousseau said that the products of his hands but not of his soul were for sale, he was emphatically declaring himself *not* to be a professional writer – unlike, for example, Samuel Johnson. In this regard, too, he explicitly contrasted himself with his former friend, 'the illustrious Diderot, who does not soil his hands with paid work and disdains small profits'; while Diderot's contemporaries considered him more honourable than Rousseau, the clear implication of Rousseau's comparison is that the products of Diderot's soul were for sale.[41] Rousseau thought that most of his contemporaries had sold their souls, receiving payment from others to preach duty to the weak and justify the rights of the strong.[42] Books lie, he wrote to Charles Beaumont, because authors are 'quick to decry leaders who do not treat them as they want to be, and even more prompt to exalt the iniquity of those who pay them.' His family was sacrificed to this desire for independence coupled with a contempt for professional writers.

D'Alembert's *Essai sur la société des gens de lettres et des grands* evinced the same desire for the independence of men of letters. As distinct from Voltaire's entry 'gens de lettres' in the *Encyclopédie*, which claimed that royal patronage strengthened the independent-mindedness of men of letters, D'Alembert thought that royal patronage strengthened the throne. In his view, men of letters sought out the great not only for fortune but also for recognition, 'to procure for oneself the kind of glory that is based on talent.' However, D'Alembert argued, authors are the best judges of their own works; he loftily asserted that 'the value of a work is intrinsic and independent of opinion.'[43] Patrons are unnecessary because the worth of a work is independent of its reception or recognition. D'Alembert admitted that geometricians are freer of popular estimation than poets are and that the desire for recognition is natural, but philosophers must scorn what Montaigne called 'toutes les allures de l'amour-propre.' What men of letters primarily search for among the great are impartial judges, less severe than their rivals, to confirm the worth of their work. The approbation of the great will generate the approval of less notable groups whose applause would not in itself be satisfying but, when combined with the plaudits of the great, is highly gratifying.[44] It is a prejudice to think the great are 'more enlightened connoisseurs' or more tasteful judges of genius or talent than those without birth and fortune. D'Alembert seemed to advocate professional critics within the ranks of men of letters to replace the great as judges of literary merit. These 'aristarchs' should be obliged to make their judgments of literature in writing so that their own taste could be judged; foot soldiers should judge the worth of generals in the republic of letters.[45] D'Alembert's suggestion anticipated the practice of contemporary granting agencies where fellow scholars judge the merits of those soliciting funds for scholarship and thought.

D'Alembert's suggestion to have professional critics replace grand patrons is the only practical recommendation in his *Essai.* He proffered inspiring maxims, such as 'one could say to all men of letters, write as if you loved glory; comport yourself as if you were indifferent to it,' and he advised writers to remember that renown is 'a kind of spectre composed of mouths and ears without eyes.'[46] Further, he stated that humans are different in terms of talent, birth, and wealth; the first is most important but tends to be the least regarded by men. 'The sage above all does not forget that, if it is an exterior respect that talents owe to titles, it is another, more real respect that titles owe to talents.'[47] D'Alembert seemed to want to have his cake and eat it too; he wanted patronage, or what the titled owe to the talented, but did not think that the titled were entitled to dispense patronage.

D'Alembert thought that the artificial style in dedications to great men degraded the French language. But, in his call to honour men of talent rather than the titled and opulent, he honoured the great men who had recognized talent, namely, the Marquis d'Argenson and, especially, Frederick the Great, who rewarded only merit.[48] Thus, while there was room for class collaboration in the republic of letters between writers and the great, D'Alembert urged his fellow writers to unite, gird their loins, avoid flattering the great to obtain money and fame, and set the tone on matters of taste and philosophy for the French nation and for humanity. He did not suggest how writers were to support themselves but rather enjoined them to know their own worth. He insisted that writers espouse, or at least not fear, poverty but at the same time claimed that poverty was the result of aristocratic patronage. 'The Maecenases of whom I speak have for their maxim that men of letters must be poor. The reason they give is that necessity sharpens genius, and that opulence numbs and enfeebles its exercise; but their true motive is by this means to have a more numerous court and more mouths to flatter them.'[49] It is unclear whether D'Alembert would have favoured Hume's and Smith's professions of reliance on a free market of ideas, or whether he would have favoured government support for the arts and sciences; he both denied that incentives can elicit great talent or genius, which seemed to be a random 'impulsion of nature,' and also showered praise on Frederick the Great for supporting the arts and sciences.[50]

The inconclusiveness of D'Alembert's attack on patronage, and his failure to provide practical alternatives, helps to explain both Rousseau's reluctance to accept patronage in practice and his justification of it in theory. We have seen how Rousseau concluded his attack on the corrupting effects of the arts and sciences with a plea for court patronage of the wise and learned. In his *Discourse on Inequality*, Rousseau seemed to demand from some rich man sufficient funds for a ten-year, worldwide anthropological study.[51] Similarly, in his *Social Contract* (IV.iv), Rousseau praised Roman patron-client relationships as 'a masterpiece of politics and humanity,' essential to the stability of the patriciate, 'which never lead to any abuse, but which has never yet been followed.' Martin Thom thinks that client relationships 'ought logically to have been anathema to Rousseau. One cannot help but be puzzled as to why a philosopher so committed to the principle of independence should have lauded so complete a dependence.'[52] In his *Considérations sur le Gouvernement de Pologne*, Rousseau advocated patronage of the poor by the great as a means to mitigate inequalities of wealth in Poland.[53] And in his *Reveries of a Solitary Walker*, in response to charges of ingratitude towards benefactors, Rousseau asserted that 'the holiest of all' contracts is that 'between the benefactor and the beneficiary. They form a sort of society with each other, more restricted than the one which unites men in general. And if the beneficiary tacitly pledges himself to gratitude, the benefactor likewise pledges himself to preserve for the other, as long as he does not make himself unworthy of it, the same good will he has just shown him and to renew its acts for him whenever he is able to and whenever it is required.' Perhaps remembering his profession of ingratitude to Malesherbes, and Diderot's charge that he had been ungrateful to Mme D'Épinay, Rousseau added that the beneficiary's pledge of gratitude is conditional on the justice of the patron. A benefactor may justly refuse a favour the first time it is asked. However, when the patronage is habitual, the client has a right to expect it without repeated requests: 'He who, in a similar case, refuses the same person the kindness he hitherto accorded him, frustrates a hope he has authorized him to conceive. He deceives and belies an expectation he has engendered.'[54] The breach in patron-client relations, in Rousseau's interpretation, derives not so much from the ingratitude of clients as from the injustice of patrons. Rousseau expanded on this point in *Émile*: 'Ingratitude would be rarer if kindness were less often the investment of a usurer. We love those who have done us a kindness; what a natural feeling! Ingratitude is not to be found in the heart of man, but self-interest is there; those who are ungrateful for benefits received are fewer than those who do a kindness for their own ends. If you sell me your gifts, I will haggle over the price; but if you pretend to give, in order to sell later on at your own price, you are guilty of fraud; it is the free gift which is beyond price. The heart is a law to itself; if you try to bind it, you lose it; give it its liberty, and you make it your own.'[55] Rousseau pointed out the contradiction in patronage; it is supposed to be a free gift but there is always interest to be repaid. Patronage can never have the transparency, sincerity, the heart-to-heart relationship Rousseau vainly sought in friendship. Rousseau wrote that, if he were opulent, he would provide benefactions at a distance; 'I should want companions about me, not courtiers, friends not protégés; I should wish my friends to regard me as their host, not their patron.'[56] Rousseau perhaps justified patron-client relationships in *The Social Contract* and elsewhere because he thought that social equality was unattainable and patronage mitigated inevitable inequality. However, Rousseau could never feel as comfortable with patronage as many of his contemporaries did.

The austere citizen of Geneva was caught in a role strain. As a plebeian in the republic of letters, he needed patrons, but as a republican, imbued with an ethos of civic virtue, he was uncomfortable about accepting royal patronage. Condorcet was later (in 1792) to lose the patronage of the Prussian and Russian courts for his avowed republicanism. Rousseau did not accept the pension that Louis XV wished to bestow on him for *Le devin du village*, and later, when on the run from France and Geneva, he accepted the political protection of Frederick the Great but refused to accept Frederick's gift of wine, wheat, and wood, declaring that such gifts would be better given to his subjects who had lost limbs in his wars and would be readily available to all subjects if Frederick would renounce his policy of military conquest.[57] Jean Guéhenno writes that Rousseau's response to Frederick's generosity was 'the most pedantic, arrogant and fatuous letter possible,'[58] and Rousseau himself acknowledged that his 'good scolding' was written with 'the rusticity of a peasant.' However, compared to Voltaire's letters to his royal patrons egging them on to martial glory, Rousseau's peasant arrogance has elements of nobility in it, even if, as T.C.W. Blanning points out, 'between 1740 and 1786, Prussia was at war for a shorter period of time than any other major power.' Blanning adds: 'Frederick's Prussia was the most tolerant state in Europe – bar none.'[59]

Yet, although Rousseau deprecated Frederick's policy of pursuing military glory at the expense of popular welfare, he later admitted: 'I regarded Frederick as my benefactor and protector, and I attached myself so sincerely to him that from that time I took as much interest in his glory, as I had found injustice in his successes until then.'[60] Rousseau was inclined to judge the world in terms of whether or not he was accorded respect. He obtained a pension from Frederick's Marshall, Lord Keith, throughout his life. When he was chased from Neuchâtel despite Frederick's protection, he sought refuge in England, where he wrote Frederick: 'Permit your kindness, Sire, to follow me with gratitude and may I always have the honour of being your *protégé*, as I will always be the most faithful of your subjects.'[61]

Hume had written Rousseau that he would find not only refuge but also independence in England since English booksellers gave a better price for literary works than French booksellers and one could live there frugally from the fruit of literary labours.[62] Hume also indicated that King George III wished to give Rousseau a pension for his literary talent. Rousseau ultimately accepted the pension, but he refused to accept it through the mediation of Hume, who, he suspected, wanted to possess him and to whom Rousseau did not want to feel obliged. James Boswell wrote to Rousseau's friend, Alexandre Deleyre, on 15 October 1766: 'I have an idea that M. Rousseau would have been willing to accept a pension. But he wished to have it on a footing that no man can even have a pension on. He has ideas of independence that are completely visionary and which are unsuitable for a man in his position.'[63] Boswell anticipated Burke's view that Rousseau did not know his proper place and disrupted the mutually advantageous relationship between opulence and genius, patrons and clients. Independence, Boswell thought, was impossible for a man in Rousseau's position – by which he meant a man without an independent income. Without such, he who pays the piper calls the tune.

Rousseau was hard on Hugo Grotius and Jean Barbeyrac as royal pensioners in *The Social Contract* (II.ii):

> Grotius, a refugee in France, discontent with his own country and wishing to pay court to Louis XIII to whom his book is dedicated, spares no pains to deprive the peoples of all their rights and bestow them upon kings in the most artful way possible. This would also have much to the liking of Barbeyrac, who dedicated his translation to the king of England, George I. But, unfortunately, the expulsion of James II, which he calls abdication, forced him to be on his guard, to equivocate, to be evasive, in order to avoid making William appear to be a usurper. If these two writers had adopted true principles, all those difficulties would have been removed, and they would have remained consistent, but they would have told the sad truth and paid court only to the people. Indeed, truth does not lead to success, and the people confers neither embassies, professorial chairs, nor pensions.

Rousseau even made it a general maxim that one should distrust all authors who are 'quick to descry leaders who do not treat them as they want to be, and even more prompt the iniquity of those who pay them.'[64] The aristocratic Rousseauan, Vittorio Alfieri, in *The Prince and Letters*, expanded Rousseau's view that royal patronage is fatal to men of letters: 'Men of letters are generally recompensed by the prince by some pecuniary subsidy which shuts their mouths upon the clear strong expression of every enlightening truth that might make its way into the dull intelligence of the ignorant servile mob.' Alfieri found fault with his fellow aristocrat, Montesquieu, in that he did not have an income sufficient to his wants and had to court the government in order to live a life of scholarship and philosophy: 'Who can doubt for instance that if Montesquieu and Corneille had not been recompensed and honoured by princes, and if they had a completely independent income, they would not have gone much farther in their principles, developing and illuminating with their powerful pens many important subjects concerning human happiness which are now veiled and scarcely hinted at in their timid pages.'[65] Voltaire agreed with Alfieri that an independent income is the condition of independent thought and became rich from investments in speculative, shady, and morally questionable spheres,[66] from interest on loans to capitalist enterprise at Ferney. For his part, Montesquieu lived above his income as a feudal proprietor, but he increased this income by marrying a wealthy Huguenot who became an efficient manager of his estates and by selling the presidency of the Bordeaux parlement that he had inherited; his income after selling his presidency was about 60,000 *livres* per year, relatively modest for a landowner and only about 30 per cent of Voltaire's income but about fifty times Diderot's salary as editor of the *Encyclopédie*.[67] Alfieri, however, overestimated the economic dimension of Montesquieu's and Voltaire's search for royal patrons, which was motivated by a desire more for political protection than for economic patronage. He also underestimated the difficulties that poor writers, such as Rousseau and Diderot, had without patrons.

Aside from his problems with accepting royal patronage, Rousseau was uncomfortable with receiving patronage from the wealthy, although it was easier if it came from those with noble lineage, such as the Duc and Duchesse de Luxembourg or the Prince de Conti, rather than rich parvenus, such as Mme d'Épinay or Baron d'Holbach. Benoît Mély locates Rousseau's distinction between Jean-Jacques, the friend of aristocrats, and Rousseau, the anonymous music copyist, in the author's reluctance to accept aristocratic beneficence; as he told Mme de Créqui, 'indebtedness and friendship are incompatible in my heart,' and he wanted to remain Jean-Jacques to her and to support himself as Rousseau the copyist.[68] Rousseau wrote to his *ami-protecteur*, Lamoignon de Malesherbes, that 'I have a violent aversion for the social stations that dominate the others.' He cannot hide his feelings even from someone of such illustrious blood as Malesherbes. 'Son of the chancellor of France, and First President of a Sovereign Court: yes Sir to you who have done a thousand good things for me without knowing me and to whom in spite of my natural ingratitude, it does not pain me at all to be obliged. I hate the rich, I hate their status, their harshness, their prejudices, their pettiness, and all their vices, and I would hate them even more if I despised them less.' Rousseau strongly resented feeling obliged to benefactors; he wrote to Malesherbes that, owing to his love of independence, 'I have always been unable to stand benefits. For every benefit demands gratitude; and I feel my heart to be ungrateful from the very fact alone that gratitude is a duty.' Yet Rousseau exempted Malesherbes and the Duc and Duchesse de Luxembourg from his hatred of the rich and the concomitant pain of feeling obliged to them. He turned down the patronage appointment at the *Journal des Savants* (which would have provided him with a living for one week's work a month, turning out two articles) but not because he did not want to feel obliged to Malesherbes; rather, he explained, he did not take on the post because he did not write for money. Nor did he resent or feel painfully obliged to the Duc de Luxembourg: 'Ah, M. the Maréchal, I hated the Grandees before I knew you, and I hate them even more, since you make me feel how easy it would be to make themselves adored.'[69] Rousseau accepted aristocratic patronage insofar as he was regarded, or considered himself, as the equal of the great. Indeed, it was particularly agreeable to Rousseau that the great paid court to him. When patronized by the Duc de Luxembourg, Rousseau noted with complacency, 'I was perhaps the best and most agreeably lodged private man in Europe' and received 'M. And Mme Luxembourg, M. the Duke of Villeroy, M. the Prince de Tingry, M. the Marquis d'Armentières, Mme the Duchesse de Montmorency, Mme the Duchesse de Boufflers, Mme the Comtesse de Valentinois, Mme the Comtesse de Boufflers, and [many] other people of that rank who did not disdain to make the pilgrimage from the chateau at Mont Louis by means of a very tiring climb.' Rousseau assured his readers that the pilgrimage of the great tò worship at his shrine did not go to his head and that he enjoyed the company of peasants every bit as much as he did that of the cream of the French aristocracy. Aristocrats, like the Marquis d'Argenson, thought that Rousseau's critique of the power of wealth, and the corruption of luxury, was directed against parvenus; as Mély notes, Rousseau was to rely on the support of the feudal aristocracy throughout his life.[70]

Rousseau displayed proper pride to Baron d'Holbach, 'the son of a parvenu,' and told him, when Rousseau refused to attend his salon: 'You are too rich.' D'Holbach gave Rousseau the profits from the baron's book on chemistry 'and this act of charity no doubt accounted for the largest part of his income' during a productive but not income-producing stay at the Hermitage, arranged by Mme d'Épinay in 1756–7. Rousseau acknowledged that d'Holbach had done him a service and placed him under an obligation. But, Rousseau thought, he was under no obligation to requite that obligation or 'to repay to others, out of my essential resources, what he gave to me out of his superfluity.'[71] D'Holbach may well have had Rousseau in mind when he wrote, in *La*

Politique naturelle (1773): 'A being independent of others necessarily sinks into indifference or malice: it is the feeling we have of our dependence with respect to others that inclines us to kindness itself.'[72] Nor was Rousseau inclined to feel any obligation to Mme d'Épinay, the wealthy wife of a tax collector. After Rousseau told her that the Hermitage would be a perfect refuge for him to work, Mme d'Épinay 'had this work done in silence and at very little expense, by separating some materials and workmen from the Chateau.' Rousseau's ingratitude to his chatelaine led to his rupture with his friends Diderot and Grimm, who, with d'Épinay, provided living expenses to Thérèse and her mother. For Rousseau, friendship and gratitude were incompatible. Jean Guéhenno writes: 'For him to accept favors, it had to be clearly understood that he owed nothing in return.'[73] Rousseau added strains to his relationships with d'Épinay, Diderot, and Grimm when he fell in love with Sophie d'Houdetot, lover of Rousseau's friend Saint-Lambert, who had cuckolded Voltaire with his lover, Émilie du Châtelet.[74] Rousseau had refused a pension from Mme d'Épinay because accepting the pension would 'make a valet of a friend.' The breach with Mme d'Épinay occurred when she asked him to accompany her to Geneva and he refused to go. Rousseau indicated that he was reluctant to go to a city where Voltaire had assumed command – he was shortly to air his differences with Voltaire in his *Lettre à D'Alembert*, attacking the theatres for encouraging civilized dissimulation and discouraging civic virtue. He was also reluctant to impair his own virtue by participating in a cure for Mme d'Épinay's venereal disease. Diderot charged him with ingratitude, depicted his solitary independence and reliance on conscience as nurturing evil, and broke off their friendship, the closest Rousseau had ever enjoyed. Voltaire also became Rousseau's implacable enemy for his refusal to gratify his *patronne*, and this before their public differences on the theatre, on equality, and on Voltaire's project of de-Christianizing the ruling class. Benoît Mély ably argues that Rousseau's break with his fellow *lumières* arose over the issue of patronage and the proper conduct governing *protectrice* and *protégé*, accompanying Mme d'Épinay to Geneva would have meant public acknowledgment that he was a protégé – or, in his eyes a valet – attached through benefits to a patron.[75]

After his break with Mme d'Épinay and his friends among the *philosophes*, Rousseau said that he restored his finances with the proceeds from his *Lettre à D'Alembert* and *Nouvelle Héloise*. All the while, he relied on his patrons, the Prince de Conti and the Duc de Luxembourg, to avoid the costly expense of postage to and from his publishers in Holland. Raymond Birn points out the paradox that the unprofessional genius, whose earnings from his pen were secondary to the burning expressions of his heart, was the first in a pre-copyright age to assert 'his authorial uniqueness by challenging the claims of legitimate publishers and book pirates alike to ownership of his printed texts.'[76] Rousseau's literary career exhibited both the ancient pattern of aristocratic patronage and the modern contractual relationships with bookseller-publishers. From 1762, Rousseau's publisher, Marc-Michel Rey, provided Thérèse Levasseur with a pension, relieving Rousseau's wealthy friends of the charge.

But 1762 was a fateful year for Rousseau, when both *Émile* and *The Social Contract* were published and prosecuted. Christopher Kelly asserts that Rousseau shunned protectors in order to consecrate his life to the truth[77] but in fact he misjudged the power of his protectors, Malesherbes, Luxembourg, and Conti, to prevent prosecution. Rousseau thought 'that I had Mme de Luxembourg and M. de Malesherbes as a breast-plate,' and, even though he feared that his writings 'might appear too bold for the century and the country in which I was writing,' he regarded France as the country most suitable to publishing bold new truths; if one gets state permission to publish, then 'I did not owe to anyone anywhere else an account of my maxims and their publication.'[78] But, after the Paris parlement ordered the arrest of Rousseau on 9 June 1762, the Petit Conseil of Geneva followed suit, and the Estates General of Holland and the Vatican were not far behind. With the assistance of the Luxembourgs, Rousseau escaped France only to be arrested in Berne in July. He consistently blamed his misfortunes on the Duc of Choiseul, who had failed to detect Rousseau's covert praise of him. Rousseau's praise of the powerful government minister, the Duc de Choiseul, in *The Social Contract* (III.vi) was not as clear as that of the Marquis d'Argenson in the same work (IV.viii). After a fierce attack on monarchy in III.vi, Rousseau qualified his attack as follows: 'The people makes a mistake in its choice much less often than the prince, and a man of real merit is nearly as rare in a ministry as a fool at the head of a republican government. So it is that when, by some lucky chance, one of those men who are born to govern takes control of public affairs in a monarchy that has almost been wrecked by this bunch of fine managers, people are amazed at the resources he finds, and it is epoch-making for the whole country.' Rousseau believed that, if he had been better at the arts of courtly flattery, the duke would have realized that he was being praised and would have stopped prosecution of *The Social Contract*. Certainly, Rousseau's flattery was less direct than that of Voltaire, who referred to Choiseul as his 'hero and protector.'[79] Jean Ghéhenno concludes: 'Had Choiseul recognized the eulogy for what it was, great benefits would have ensued both for Jean-Jacques and his native country. But Choiseul had misread the text or had been misled.'[80] On the advice of the Prince de Conti, Rousseau wrote an obsequious letter to Choiseul, laying out his praise in clearer terms, but did not get a response. Throughout his life, Rousseau remained convinced that Choiseul was 'the hidden author of all the persecutions I experienced in Switzerland' and elsewhere.[81] However, Rousseau's view that Choiseul's misunderstanding was responsible for his being hounded from pillar to post and Guéhenno's claim that the misunderstanding could have been avoided are inconsistent with Rousseau's profession of the revolutionary boldness of his writing, or his conviction that the wealthy and powerful could never 'love my principles and their author.'[82] Unlike Voltaire, who believed that the content of his writings could be delivered to a public behind the veil of anonymity, Rousseau wanted his readers to love the author as well as his principles. Geoffrey Turnovsky writes that, for Rousseau, 'the book was conceived as a medium whose primary purpose and value lay in its capacity to project an image of its author before a reader.'[83]

As well as refusing to hide behind the veil of anonymity, Rousseau proudly proclaimed that, of 'his patrons and protectors, there is not a single one who has not been wounded to the quick by' his criticisms of wealth and nobility.[84] He may have thought that his churlish behaviour to patrons would manifest the singularity of his genius; he wrote that 'above all great ladies absolutely want to be amused,' and thus he thought that 'it would be better to offend them than to bore them.'[85] But Hume had a different view. Rousseau, he said, 'has not had the precaution to throw any veil over his sentiments; and as he scorns to dissemble his contempt for established opinions, he could not wonder that all the zealots were in arms against him. The liberty of the press is not so secured in any country, scarce even this, as not to render such an open attack of popular prejudices somewhat dangerous.'[86]

Rousseau's attempt to live a life of spiritual independence as a man of letters, a life free of paying court to patrons, was a failure. He accepted the patronage of Frederick the Great, through his agent Lord Keith, and later he accepted a pension from George III on condition that the agent not be David Hume, 'the patron, zealous protector, and most excessive benefactor of J.J.,' the man who lured him to England and had Allan Ramsay paint his portrait as a wild man.[87] His fight with Hume on the question of accepting royal patronage earned him the reputation of a lunatic across Europe. He continued to write but never came close to receiving what he obtained for *Émile*. Moreover, his expenses increased, with costly moves and postal costs eating up one-quarter of his income.[88] He returned to France under the protection of the Prince de Conti but soon began to chafe under the prince's care and surveillance, and kept on the move around France. As Robert Wokler states: Rousseau's 'meanderings [were] made all the more furtive by his principal patron of the time, the Prince de Conti – who really *was* a warder masquerading as a protector.'[89] Hunted and haunted, Rousseau found refuge with the Marquis de Girardin at Ermenonville, where he studied botany and died. After his death, his wife, Thérèse, applied for assistance to Catherine the Great but received no response.[90]

Although D'Alembert's *Essai sur la société des gens de lettres et des grands* supported Rousseau's attempt to live independently of patronage in theory, Rousseau stood almost alone in the Enlightenment – or, for that reason, outside the Enlightenment – in entertaining apparently conflicting positions, namely, that patronage jeopardized freedom of thought and that patronage mitigates inequalities of condition and opportunity. The man who celebrated patron-client relationships as 'a masterpiece of politics and humanity' knew how fragile and demeaning such relationships could be. Whereas Voltaire thought that 'it is not inequality which is the real evil, it is dependence,'[91] Rousseau believed that independence, the Enlightenment ideal, was impossible without equality.

8 Samuel Johnson and the Question of Enlightenment in England

I have indicated that the issue of whether England had an Enlightenment has been much debated. The most forceful claim for England's Enlightenment has been made by Roy Porter in *The Creation of the Modern Mind: The Untold Story of the British Enlightenment*,[1] where, as we have seen, Samuel Johnson features prominently. My concern in this chapter is to clarify Johnson's relationship to England's questionable Enlightenment, and specifically to the role of the press in diffusing Enlightenment. Franco Venturi contrasts Edward Gibbon, 'the English giant of the Enlightenment,' 'an isolated figure in his own country, a solitary figure' and Samuel Johnson, 'a native English god.' Lester Crocker expands Venturi's position by stating that 'Samuel Johnson was perhaps the major influence of the age in the English-speaking world. It is not necessary to deny an Enlightenment in Great Britain or to make him part of such an Enlightenment ...'[2] The fact that Johnson is well loved within the English-speaking world, and has been virtually ignored by scholars without, is worthy of consideration.[3] But the question here is Johnson's relationship to Enlightenment. J.G.A. Pocock asserts that Johnson was not a member of his country's conservative Enlightenment, built on the twin pillars of William Warburton's *The Divine Legation of Moses* (1738) and Edward Gibbon's *The Decline and Fall of the Roman Empire* (1776): Johnson as 'a concerned and evangelical Christian ... could never have been a *philosophe*.'[4] Pocock's characterization seems just, but the grounds of it are unclear. Burke was a member of Pocock's conservative Enlightenment because Burke's Christianity was political, a judgment Brian Young contests.[5] Pocock does not say whether Warburton's Christianity was less sincere than Johnson's – for how could we know that? – or whether the difference between Johnson and Warburton was more social than religious. Since Pocock thinks that the English Enlightenment was an instrument of aristocratic and clerical ruling groups,[6] Warburton was part of the aristocratic patronage system and Johnson was not.

Stephen Miller, on the other hand, argues that 'Johnson was a man of Enlightenment insofar as he always defended progress, including scientific and technological progress.'[7] Yes, but so did many eighteenth-century thinkers, including the prophetic and evangelical Presbyterians of the Popular Party – those opposed to the Scottish Enlightenment.[8] If Johnson, the Scots of the Popular Party, and those who believed in commercial, scientific, and technological progress are to be considered Enlightenment figures, 'Enlightenment' is in danger of becoming synonymous (as a noun and adjective) with 'eighteenth century' and losing any distinctive intellectual features. Miller continues: 'Johnson also strongly argued in favor of educating the poor – both men and women; and he vehemently opposed slavery ... He also attacked imprisonment for debt, criticized capital punishment for theft, and deplored British and French imperial policy in the new world.'[9] If Miller is arguing that Johnson was admirable, I would agree, but he falsely assumes that the Enlightenment favoured educating the poor, opposed slavery, deplored imperial policy in the new world, and was uniformly humane with respect to imprisonment for debt and capital punishment. With respect to the education of the working classes, Enlightenment figures, such as Locke, Mandeville, Voltaire, and others, tended to oppose primary education of peasants and labourers, while Protestant and Catholic churches were inclined to favour the elimination of illiteracy.[10] As Voltaire wrote to D'Alembert on 2 September 1768, 'We have never pretended to en-lighten shoemakers and servants; that is the job of the apostles.'[11] Locke, Voltaire, Hume, Mirabeau, and Kant supported slavery, while Montes-quieu, Buffon, Ferguson, Helvétius, Raynal, Condorcet, Rousseau, and von Herder (if one considers the latter two Enlightenment figures) opposed it, if not with the force of the Quakers, Methodists, and Chris-tian abolitionists such as William Wilberforce, Granville Sharp, James Ramsay, and Thomas Clarkson.[12] Harvey Chisick contrasts Hume's enlightened conservatism with Johnson's Christian conservatism:

> Traditional conservatism recognised the religious obligation of charity and the secular obligation of paternalism. Hume, it seems, recognised neither. There is a fine expression of traditional conservatism in Samuel Johnson, who, while agreeing with Hume on the importance of rank,

order and subordination, and disagreeing with him on much else, is
reported to have said that 'a decent provision for the poor is the true test
of civilization.' Hume, I think, would have regarded the terms in which
Johnson expressed himself as outmoded, for he recognised no obligation
on the part of society or of any individual to provide for another.[13]

The point is that Johnson is not an adherent of Enlightenment by the
standards of Hume. If we were to revert to the *Oxford English Dictionary*'s
1897 definition of Enlightenment as 'shallow and pretentious intellectualism, unreasonable contempt for tradition or authority,' we would
have the benefit of not having nationalist prejudices construct an
English Enlightenment comparable to the Scottish, French, and
German Enlightenments. Or, if we were to appeal to nationalist
prejudice and to aversion to 'intellectualism,' we might say that England did not have an Enlightenment but it did have Samuel Johnson
and he is worth all the *philosophes* and Scottish professors combined.

Johnson and Press Culture

The strongest argument for considering Johnson an Enlightenment
figure, it seems to me, is that his career was tied to England's relatively
free and commercial press. Alvin Kernan describes Johnson's letter to
Lord Chesterfield, rejecting his patronage, as 'the Magna Carta of the
modern author.' Johnson was at the centre of a transformation from
the older amateur, aristocratic, and patronal republic of letters to a new
profession of letters, 'a print-based, market-centered, democratic
literary system.' Johnson's books, Kernan argues, bear the impress of a
print logic: a printed catalogue of books, a set of poets' biographies
designed to introduce the poets' works, a dictionary, an authoritative
edition of Shakespeare. Indeed, in Kernan's felicitous metaphor,
Johnson's life was like a printed broadsheet, a life in bold letters,
outsized, emphatic in expression.[14] Thomas Carlyle wrote that Johnson's letter to Lord Chesterfield was 'that far-famed Blast of Doom,
proclaiming into the ear of Lord Chesterfield, and, through him, of the
listening world, that patronage should be no more.'[15] Fine, dramatic
stuff, and fully in accord with Adam Smith's myth that the age of print
rendered patronage obsolete. Johnson's view that booksellers are the
modern patrons of literature was repeated by Edward Gibbon when he
falsely claimed that 'the patronage of English literature has long since
been devolved on our booksellers.'[16] Yet, if Johnson was the embodi-

ment of press culture, as Kernan argues, he specifically represented the older, polite periodical press, as distinct from the popular daily newspapers whose style and politics Johnson deprecated but which made him a national icon in the 1770s.

Johnson believed that the press diffuses light among the reading public. In *The False Alarm,* Johnson wrote: 'One of the chief advantages derived by the present generation from the improvement and diffusion of Philosophy, is deliverance from unnecessary terrours, and exemption from false alarms.' He thought that the readers of the polite periodical press, from the *Spectator* to the *Idler* and *Rambler,* were enlightened to be capable of thoughtful political judgment, as distinct from 'the people' swayed by Wilkite demagogic journalism. Readers of periodicals were too enlightened to fall for vain hopes and unreasonable fears. 'Causeless discontent and seditious violence will grow less frequent, and less formidable, as the science of Government is better ascertained by a diligent study of the theory of Man.'[17] The sentences above, with different prose styles, might be found in the works of Voltaire, Hume, or Diderot, and they would subscribe to Johnson's counsel, 'Let us not begin by turning all reason out of Doors,' though not to its corollary that 'religion ... is the highest Exercise of Reason.'[18] As Jeremy Black indicates, the English press of the eighteenth century appealed to the religious and moral convictions of their readers and advertisers and tended to be hierarchical and conservative in its politics.[19] Black overlooks Wilkes and the radical press in this assessment, but he captures an aspect of the commercial press in which Johnson could find a home. If the free, commercial press was the chief vehicle of enlightenment in England, it was also the means by which Johnson became a national cultural hero.

The man who thought that the chief glory of a nation derives from its authors characterized the eighteenth century as the age of authors, in which 'the itch of literary praise' was greater than ever before. Johnson declared in *The Idler*: 'The present age ... might be stiled with great propriety The Age of Authors; for, perhaps, there was never a time, in which men of all degrees of ability, of every kind of education, of every profession and employment are posting with ardour so general to the press. The province of writing was formerly left to those, who by study, or appearance of study, were supposed to have gained knowledge unattainable by the busy part of mankind; but in these enlightened days, every man is qualified to instruct every other man ...'[20]

Johnson's career in the press, and his view that booksellers are the modern patrons of literature, must be understood in the context of the fact that his father, a Litchfield bookseller, was too poor to have Samuel properly educated. Born deaf in one ear, blind in one eye and short-sighted in the other, large and ungainly, with what we would now call Tourette's syndrome, Johnson was teased as a schoolboy and indeed for the rest of his life. When Alexander, Earl of Eglintoune, regretted that Johnson had not been educated with more refinement and had not acquired the manners of a gentleman, Johnson's friend, Guiseppe Baretti, said that no matter how cultivated an education Johnson had received, he would have remained a bear. 'True, (answered the Earl with a smile,) but he would have been a *dancing* bear.'[21] Johnson learned to take care of himself in the schoolyard when teased, which stood him in good stead in later life. When the actor/dramatist Samuel Foote threatened to lampoon Johnson's mannerisms on stage, Johnson told Foote that he would be sitting in the front row armed with a cudgel. Foote did not go ahead with his sure-fire hit and he and Johnson remained friends.[22] When Paul Fussell calls Johnson a 'male Cinderella,'[23] emphasizing his rags-to-riches success story, he forgets that Cinderella had recourse to a fairy godmother; when Voltaire or Montesquieu were threatened with satire, they turned to Mme de Pompadour. Johnson was a stout Englishman who relied on his good right arm for his aid.

Adam Smith said that 'Johnson knew more books than any man alive.'[24] Yet the most bookish of men could afford only one year at Oxford; his patron, 'a gentleman of Shropshire,' withdrew promised support. Eighteenth-century Oxford was an expensive boarding school for the gentry and provided vocational training for 'squarsons'; scholar-ships were granted on the basis of gentle connections, not merit.[25] When Boswell asked the 'Great Cham' why he had taken to the repub-lic of letters, Johnson replied: 'Because, Sir, I had not money to study law.'[26] With respect to his time at Oxford, Johnson said: 'I was miserably poor, and I thought to fight my way by my literature and my wit; so I disregarded all power and all authority.'[27] Johnson exhibited insuffi-cient deference for the dons he could not respect, and also proud independence. When someone, seeing that Johnson's shoes were entirely worn out, left a new pair of shoes at his door, Johnson threw them away with indignation.

When he left Oxford, he prayed 'that the powers of my mind may not be debilitated by poverty, and that indigence do not force me into any criminal act.'[28] Johnson taught school but, as Paul Fussell notes, 'this was an unhappy situation, for the job required him to be civil to the main patron of the school, to live in his nearby stately home and to serve there as sort of a lay chaplain. Sir Wolstan's ignorance and brutality made him an insupportable patron, and Johnson only lasted six months.'[29] Johnson then married the forty-six-year-old Elizabeth ('Tetty') Porter, who brought Johnson £800, enough for him to set up a boarding school. He taught the actor David Garrick, whose imitations of his teacher indicated that Johnson was passionate about his beloved Tetty, despite the differences in their ages. He was not a success as a teacher and set out to London to earn his way in the republic of letters. He was employed by booksellers as a Grub Street hack until Robert Dodsley offered ten £10 for his poem *London*, which numerous booksellers had previously rejected. Alexander Pope admired *London* and wrote to Earl Gower, a friend of Dean Jonathan Swift, who asked Swift to confer on Johnson an MA degree from Trinity College in Dublin so that he would be qualified to be the master of a charity school with a regular salary, rather '*than be starved to death in translating for booksellers.*'[30] Pope's plea failed, as did Johnson's application to the bar.

Johnson, as we have seen, raised the status of Grub Street authors to a more genteel level by punching out his bookseller, Thomas Osborne, who demanded greater productivity and less scholarship from Johnson. Other booksellers respected Johnson self-estimation that he was not a literary proletarian. Johnson's fortunes improved somewhat; he obtained £200 yearly from the Earl of Oxford as literary secretary from 1738 to 1741 and then received another £200 a year as a reporter of parliamentary debates.[31] Afterward, Johnson was commissioned by Robert Dodsley to write the famous *Dictionary* and came afoul of 'the Maecenas of the age,' Lord Chesterfield, who not only provided personal patronage to Pope, Fielding, Smollett, and other writers but also, as secretary of state, had the gift of public patronage at his disposal, providing sinecures for writers. Paul Korshin states that the reason for the breach between Johnson and Chesterfield was that Johnson wanted public not private patronage.[32] Korshin's interpretation is consistent with Voltaire's entry on 'Gens de lettres' in the *Encyclopédie*, which argued that royal patronage strengthens the independence of authors who would otherwise be dependent on the favour of some aristocrat. It is also consistent with Johnson's response to Dr. Richard Brocklesby, who offered Johnson a pension of £100 annually for life. Johnson replied: 'God bless you through Jesus Christ, but I will take no money but from my sovereign.' After Johnson declined Brocklesby's gift, Burke accepted a similar offer, saying that 'I shall never be ashamed to have it known, that I am obliged to one who can never be capable of converting his kindness into a burden.'[33] Johnson and Burke shared the grand principle of subordination, but in practice Johnson seemed to side with Rousseau on poverty and independence while Burke consistently favoured wealth and civilized interdependence. To patronize and to condescend meant, in the eighteenth century, to pay proper respect to the lower orders; Johnson's attitude to patronage and the condescension seem modern and do not accord with his grand principle of subordination.

However, there were other factors, besides the fact that Chesterfield no longer had the sinecures of the secretary of state to bestow, that could account for the famous row between the greatest patron of the time and the plebeian writer. In his fictionalized account of his fight with Chesterfield (Aurantius), Johnson wrote: 'Aurantius from the moment in which he discovered my poverty, considered me as fully in his power.'[34] According to Boswell, Johnson thought that Chesterfield had kept him waiting while the lord was conversing with Johnson's rival, Colley Cibber. Also, Johnson liked to be the centre of attention and of conversation, and he knew that 'great lords and ladies don't love to have their mouths stopped.' As Hester Thrale observes: 'Johnson's conversation was by much too strong for a person accustomed to obsequiousness and flattery; it was *mustard in a young child's mouth!*' In addition to Johnson's lack of deference and politeness in conversation, Johnson's table manners – he ate like a pig – may have offended Lord Chesterfield. Johnson said that he never dined with Chesterfield and thus could not have been the model for the tasteful lord's 'respectable Hottentot,' a violent man who 'throws his meat any where but down his throat.' When Johnson referred to Chesterfield as having 'the morals of a whore, and the manners of a dancing master,' he implied that the lord's good manners did not mitigate his bad morals.

However well Johnson demonstrated the benefits of aristocrats patronizing talented plebeians, or the costs of not doing so, his hostility to the great, which Hume and Burke at times shared, did not accord with his Tory respect for hierarchy. As I have said, Johnson's letter to Lord Chesterfield has been widely taken to sound the death knell of patronage, despite the facts that Johnson received a small sum (£10) from Chesterfield, that Chesterfield twice 'puffed' Johnson's *Dictionary* in *The World*, and that Johnson's publisher, Robert Dodsley, strongly desired Chesterfield's patronage of the *Dictionary* to boost sales. Johnson's letter asked: 'Is not a Patron, my Lord, one who looks with unconcern on a man struggling for life in the water, and, once he has reached ground, encumbers him with help? The notice which you have been pleased to take of my labours, had it been early, had been kind; but it has been delayed till I am indifferent, and cannot enjoy it; till I am solitary, and cannot impart it; till I am known, and do not want it. I hope it is no cynical asperity not to confess obligations where no benefit has been received, or to be unwilling that the Publick should consider me as owing to a Patron, which Providence has enabled me to do for myself.'[35]

Note that Johnson did not reject patronage outright; on the contrary, he strongly suggested that he would have welcomed Chesterfield's patronage while his beloved Tetty was alive. Indeed, when Boswell asked Johnson why he did not court great men, Johnson replied: 'Why, sir, I never was near enough to great men, to court them. You may be prudently attached to great men and yet be independent. You are not to do what you think wrong; and, Sir, you are to calculate, and not pay too dear for what you get. You must not give a shilling's worth of court for six-pence worth of good. But if you can get a shilling's worth of good for six-pence worth of court, you are a fool if you do not pay court.'[36]

Johnson's attempt to lay bare the patronage economy inevitably failed because patronage must remain shrouded in mist; the patron cannot be seen as a buyer and the client cannot be seen as a seller. Patronage is part of a gift economy where reciprocity is expected but the price tags of the gifts cannot be visible. Nevertheless, Johnson's metaphor of monetary exchange comes closer to the truth of the author's condition than any of his (or our) contemporaries. Although Johnson became known for declaring booksellers the modern patrons of literature, 42 of the 208 essays he wrote in *Rambler* are devoted to the subject of patronage.[37] *Rambler no. 91* concluded: 'The Sciences, after a thousand indignities, retired from the palace of Patronage, and having long wandered over the world in grief and distress, were led at last to the cottage of Independence, the daughter of Fortitude; where they were taught by Prudence and Parsimony to support themselves in dignity and quiet.'[38]

Johnson shared Hume's self-image as an independent thinker; 'no man,' Johnson declared, 'who ever lived by literature, has ever lived more independently than I have done.' He also completely espoused Smith's view that the art of printing had rendered patronage obsolete. Learning, Johnson thought, had become a trade. 'A man goes to a bookseller, and gets what he can. We have done with patronage. In the infancy of learning, we find some great men praised for it. This diffused it among others. When it becomes general, an authour [*sic*] leaves the great, and applies to the multitude.' When Boswell interjected that it was a pity authors were not better patronized, Johnson replied: 'No Sir. With patronage, what flattery! What falsehood! While a man is in equilibrio, he throws truth among the multitude, and lets them take it as they please: in patronage, he must say what pleases his patron, and it is an equal chance whether that be truth or falsehood.' To Professor Robert Watson's questions: 'But is not the case now, that, instead of flattering one person, we flatter the age?' Johnson replied, 'No Sir. The world always lets a man tell what he thinks, his own way.'[39] Johnson's view that the reading public are competent judges of literature was the antithesis of David Hume's position: 'As to the Approbation or Esteem of those Blockheads who call themselves the Public, & whom a Bookseller, a Lord, a Priest, or a Party can guide, I do most heartily despise it.'[40] Johnson's position that writers should rely on the public rather than patrons reveals his delight with victory in debate as much as a love of truth; it is not fully consistent with his view in *Adventurer 138* that, without some authority to praise a book, 'it often remains long in obscurity, and perhaps perishes unknown and unexamined.'[41]

Despite his ambiguity on the subject of the necessity of patrons for the arts and sciences, Johnson became known as a clear opponent of patronage. He prefaced his *Dictionary* with the claim that it was written with 'little assistance of the learned, and without any patronage of the great; not in the soft obscurities of retirement, or under the shelter of academic bowers, but amidst inconvenience and distraction, in sickness and in sorrow.' Shortly after Johnson's death, John Courtney wrote as part of a long panegyric:

> By grateful bards his name be ever sung,
> Whose sterling touch has fix'd the English tongue!
> Fortune's dire weight, the patron's cold disdain,
> 'Shook off, like dew-drops from the lion's mane;'
> Unknown, unaided, in a friendless state,
> Without one smile of favour from the great;
> The bulky tome his curious care refines,
> Till the great work in full perfection shines:

Fourteen pages of praise, spiced with minor foibles, later, Courtney added:

Who firmly scorn'd, when in a lowly state,
To flatter vice, or court the vain and great.[42]

Courtney provided a footnote to the last couplet: 'It is observable that Dr. Johnson did not prefix a dedication to any one of his various works.' In this regard, Paul Fussell writes that Johnson 'never did dedicate one of his own works to nobility ... but ... he obliged countless frailer friends by writing theirs for them, and writing them with both accuracy and *brio*.' Boswell noted: 'In that courtly species of composition no man excelled Dr. Johnson.'[43] For example, Johnson wrote dedications to the earls of Orrery and Middlesex in order to get Charlotte Lennox's novel, *The Female Quixote*, into print.[44] Yet Johnson and Hume were at one on the moral degradation of dedicating books to nobles. As a counter-example to his usual preference for modern over ancient civilization, Hume wrote: 'It was the practice of the antients to address their compositions only to friends and equals, and to render their dedications monuments of regard and affection, not of servility and flattery. In those days of ingenuous and candid liberty, a dedication did honour to the person to whom it was addressed, without degrading the author. If any partiality appeared toward the patron, it was at least the partiality of friendship and affection.'[45] Johnson, the adherent of the grand principle of subordination, wrote of the degradation of John Dryden's acceptance of patronage: 'Of this kind of meanness he never seems to decline the practice, or lament the necessity: he considers the great as entitled to encomiastick homage, and brings praise rather as a tribute than a gift, more delighted with the fertility of his invention than mortified by *the prostitution of his judgment*. It is indeed not certain, that on these occasions his judgment much rebelled against his interest. There are minds which readily sink into submission, that look on grandeur with undistinguishing reverence, and discover no defect where there is elevation of rank and affluence of riches.'[46]

Johnson did not enjoy aristocratic patronage as Hume did, and his financial worries did not end with the success of his *Dictionary*. He was arrested for debt in March 1756 and he had to write his way out of prison. Johnson's *Dictionary* had provided an uncompromising definition of pension as 'pay given to a state hireling for treason to his country,' and it was thus with considerable embarrassment that he accepted a pension of £300 yearly, on the grounds that it was not a 'political bribe' but 'solely as the reward of his literary merit.'[47] From this time, Johnson's productivity as a writer dropped, particularly in the years immediately following receipt of his pension. As we have seen, Johnson claimed that only blockheads write for reasons other than money, and thus, no longer pressed by financial exigency, he could now indulge his bouts of depression and laziness. His friend Oliver Goldsmith compared the situation of English to French men of letters. In *The Present State of Polite Learning*, Goldsmith stated: 'The French nobility have certainly a most pleasing way of satisfying the vanity of an author without indulging his avarice. A man of literary merit is sure of being caressed by the great, though seldom enriched. His pension from the crown just supplies half a competence, and the sale of his labours makes some small addition to his circumstances; thus the author leads a life of splendid poverty,' and unlike Johnson, 'seldom becomes wealthy or indolent enough' to cease literary labour.[48]

Johnson's pension was attacked by radicals, such as Jack Wilkes, who used Johnson's definition of a pension to bring discredit on the government of George III and Lord Bute.[49] Johnson laughed off the criticisms: 'Why, Sir ... it is a mighty foolish noise that they make. I have accepted of a pension as a reward which has been thought due to my literary merit; and now that I have this pension, I am the same man in every respect that I have been; I retain the same principles. It is true, that I cannot now curse (smiling) the House of Hanover; not would it be decent for me to drink King James's health in the wine King George gives me money to pay for. But, Sir, I think the pleasure of cursing the House of Hanover, and drinking King James's health, are amply overbalanced by three hundred pounds a year.'[50] Johnson was more straightforward about the duties of accepting patronage than most of his contemporaries, and so, like Rousseau, was reluctant to accept patronage; at the same time, however, like Voltaire, he thought royal patronage less demeaning than aristocratic patronage. Johnson wrote tracts for the government insofar as they were consistent with his principles. The government excised from his brilliant pamphlet *Taxation No Tyranny* the following sentences, which to my mind capture the essence of the conflict between the English and the Americans: 'That the Colonists could with no solidity argue from their not having been taxed while in their infancy, that they should not now be taxed. We do not put a calf to the plow; we wait till he is an ox.' Johnson said that it was the government's business to cut what it wanted. 'If an architect says, I will build five stories, and the man who employs him says, I will have only three, the employee is to decide.'[51] For a proud man like Johnson, it was difficult to accept the duties of clientship but, unlike Rousseau, he saw himself as a professional writer, not a genius entitled to authorial autonomy. For his services to the government, Johnson received an honorary doctorate from Lord North and became known to posterity as Dr Johnson.

Johnson accepted the duties of clientship because he espoused, as Rousseau rejected, the grand principle of subordination, reverence for hereditary ranks, and respect for wealth. He accepted as much as Rousseau did that human beings are naturally equal but, unlike Rousseau, he also adhered to the doctrine of original sin. Johnson took the Hobbesian view that humans are equally vain, and, if intrinsic merit were the only criterion of social distinction, the result would be a war of all against all, with physical force emerging as the sole criterion of the superiority after which all strive. Thus 'subordination is very necessary for society, and contentions for superiority very dangerous.' Moreover, hierarchy allows for civilized mental pleasures, whereas social equality would promote common sensual pleasures: 'Subordination tends greatly to human happiness.'[52] Johnson's Toryism meant that he did not want 'to give more real power to Government' but 'more reverence.' He thought that 'in republics there is not a respect for authority but a fear of power.' Johnson asserted: 'Government has the distribution of offices, that it may be enabled to maintain its authority.'[53] Johnson told Boswell that it is only opinion, or respect for authority, that 'prevents us, who are the rabble, from rising up and pulling down you who are gentlemen from your places.'[54] The poor will always resent the oppression of the rich; they have little to lose and are apt to rise in rebellion unless they respect the authority of government. 'Liberty is, to the lowest rank of every nation, little more than the choice of working or starving.'[55]

Johnson's Toryism was markedly similar to Burke's Whiggery, despite Johnson's suspicion that party politics erodes principle and Burke's support for the principle of partisan politics. Subordination is necessary because modern civilization rests on private property and the essence of such property is its unequal distribution. Government is to secure property rights, and good government balances political power with ownership of property. Johnson discussed the function of parliament with less cant than Burke's subsequent celebration of the blessing of parliamentary government: 'Parliament is a larger council to the King; and the advantage of such a council is, having a great number of men of property concerned in the legislature, who, for their own interest, will not consent to bad laws.'[56] (To be sure, Johnson's view here ignored the power of government to control parliaments through patronage and placemen, something that he wrote about elsewhere.) Johnson's and Burke's view that good legislation derived from the dominance of the landed interest was questioned in his day, as in ours. But Johnson and Burke thought that to secure property and ensure its transmission from generation to generation is the main function of government. Johnson's Tory vision of an ordered society encompassed the virtue of female chastity, which, Johnson thought, was 'of the utmost importance, as all property depends on it.' In this respect, Johnson is well known for his harsh response to Boswell's question as to whether Lady Diana Beauclerc was justified in her adultery because of her husband's prior adultery and brutality: 'The woman's a whore, and there's an end on't.' But he so frequently praised Lady Diana to Hester Thrale that she mentioned Beauclerc's bad character. 'Oh yes said he I know she is a Strumpet; had she not been so, she would have sate in Heaven next Jesus Christ.'[57]

Twenty-eight years before Burke's *Reflections on the Revolution in France*, Johnson expressed the core of Burke's fear of Enlightenment theories: 'Human experience, which is constantly contradicting theory, is the great test of truth. A system, which is built on the discoveries of a great many minds, is always of more strength, than what is produced by the mere workings of any one mind, which, of itself, can do little. There is not so poor a book in the world that would not be a prodigious effort were it wrought out entirely by a single mind, without the aid of prior investigators. The French writers are superficial; because they are not scholars, and so proceed upon the mere power of their own minds; and we see how little real power they have.'[58] Enlightenment philosophy, claimed the very English non-philosopher, is dangerous because it is cut off from a tradition of scholarship, or the collective experience of peoples. It is philosophic arrogance to think that one can construct a world according to the theories untested by experience. Johnson, like Burke, was in principle against theoretical principles and thought that the experience of estate management or state government is the condition for acquiring political skill or art. He recommended that 'the towering head of speculation' should 'bow down unwillingly to groveling experience' on political matters.[59]

Like Burke too, Johnson knew that the constitution they loved was not a meritocracy but a hierarchy based on property. Johnson thought that 'in such a country as ours, no man is appointed to an office because he is the fittest for it ... because there are so many connections and dependencies to be studied.' Only a despotic prince, such as Frederick the Great, could realize the Enlightenment ideal of careers open to talents.[60]

Johnson was patronized by Henry and Hester Thrale, a wealthy brewer and his lettered wife, who provided Johnson with room, board, and a library in return for entertaining their guests. When Hester Thrale gave Johnson a gold pen, he requited the gift with verses suggesting that the pen could be accepted as symbolic of her mental gifts. Verses 2 and 3 read:

> If bounteous Thrale could thus transfer
> Her Learning Sense and Wit;
> Who would not wish a Gift from her,
> Who – not to beg – submit?
>
> Paupers from Grubstreet at her Gate
> Would crowd both young and old;
> Who day and Night would supplicate
> For Thoughts – not Pens of Gold.

After Henry Thrale died, Johnson hoped that Mrs Thrale would continue to care for him and was devastated when she married Gabriel Piozzi, an Italian musician. William Shaw wrote that no event, other than the death of his wife, caused Johnson more grief than the remarriage of Hester Thrale.[61]

Mrs Thrale provided, next to Boswell's *Life*, the most readable and revealing account of Johnson. Hester Thrale, who was more than a patron to Johnson, evaluated various of her acquaintances, including Johnson, Garrick, Boswell, Thrale, and Burke, on a scale of qualities. (We might consider which qualities are cherished in husbands, in friends, and in those one patronized.) Male and female qualities were assessed differently; the only overlapping qualities were 'Person, Mien and Manner' and 'Good Humour,' in which she modestly rated herself 10 out of 20. Men were rated according to Religion (R), Morality (Mo), Scholarship (S), General Knowledge (GK), Person & Voice (PV), Manner (Ma), Wit (W), Humour (H), and Good Humour (GH). (Piozzi, unfortunately, was not ranked but one suspects that he would have had ratings closer to Boswell than to Johnson, Thrale, or Burke.)

Johnson – R 20, Mo 20, S 19, GK 20, PV 0,   Ma 0,   W 15, H 16, GH 0.
Garrick – R 10, Mo 15, S 3,   GK 16, PV 18, Ma 17, W 19, H 19, GH 0.
Boswell – R 5,   Mo 5, S 5,   GK 10, PV 10, Ma 17, W 7,   H 3, GH 19.
Thrale –   R 18, Mo 17, S 9,   GK 9, PV 18, Ma 17, W 0,   H 0, GH 5.
Burke –   R 16, Mo 10, S 14, GK 19, PV 12, Ma 14, W 0,   H 0, GH O.[62]

Johnson's relationship to the Thrales was a complex mixture of patron-age, friendship, and love. Johnson could not by patronized by the great, Mrs Thrale thought, because he bullied people into philosophic conversations; 'he loved to talk better than to hear, & to dispute better than to please.'[63] His disputation was more agonistic than philosophic; it aimed more for victory than truth. He used low blows for victory; as his friend Oliver Goldsmith said, when Johnson's wit misfires, he clubs you over the head with his pistol butts. If his conversational style was not to the taste of the aristocracy, it was sufficiently entertaining for the guests of the Thrales. Henry Thrale used Johnson to impress visitors and advance his political career as a Tory member of parliament. Sir John Hawkins wrote that Thrale imposed on Johnson the role of trained seal to bark on cue for his food (plus lodging and library), rather as Diderot portrayed Rameau's nephew's manner of living. Johnson was obliged to provide dinner-time conversation displaying religion, wit, eloquence, and learning. Hawkins, balancing malice and ponderousness, wrote: 'This, it must be confessed, was a burdensome task to one who, like others, must be supposed to have had his som-brous intervals, and, in the hours of repation, to wish for the indul-gence of being silent, or, at least, of talking like other men. To be continually uttering apophthegms, or speeches worthy of remem-brance, was more than could have been expected of Socrates.'[64] Given what we know about Johnson's gargantuan appetites, Hawkins may well have been right that Johnson paid dearly at the Thrale's table by conversing wittily instead of wolfing down food. However, there were benefits as well as costs to someone of Johnson's sombrous disposition; Mrs Thrale cared for him in his depressions and, by her account, would tie him up and whip him when Johnson thought he was going mad.[65]

Hester Thrale Piozzi indicated that, despite his Christianity or perhaps because of his fear of punishment for sinners, Johnson was afraid of death. (Johnson and Burke famously thought Hume's stoicism in face of impending death was an act aimed at the applause of specta-tors.) Johnson loved life – heaven was unlikely to provide him the pleasures he experienced on earth, conversing in a tavern. Hume wrote

My Own Life for posterity. Johnson did not write his autobiography but, after his death, an unprecedented number of biographies flooded the press, resurrecting the dead man, warts and all, and establishing the Christian truth of the irreplaceability of individual life, the invaluable irreducibility of individuality, and the questionableness of Johnson's view that 'the best part of an author will always be found in his writings.'[66] England may not have had an Enlightenment, but, because of the prohibitive cost of Oxbridge and the monopoly of patronage in the hands of the Church of England, its commercial press produced Samuel Johnson, a man for whom intellectual independence was more than a slogan.

9 Irish Antagonists: Burke and Shelburne

If we accept Burke's definition of patronage as the tribute that opulence owes to genius, Lord Shelburne was the greatest patron of Enlightenment in England. However, the opulence of Shelburne and the genius of Burke did not join forces; in fact, the compatriots were life-long antagonists. Shelburne was a link between the British, French, and American Enlightenments; he patronized Smith, Blackstone, Franklin, Price, Priestley, and Bentham, and, through his patronage of André Morellet, was connected to Helvétius, d'Holbach, Turgot, and other *philosophes*. He attended the salons of Mme du Deffand, Mme de Boufflers, and Mme Geoffrin, but, while he admired the role of women in the French republic of letters, his own salon at Bowood, which was partly modelled on Parisian salons, were British in their homosociality. Joseph Priestley perceived a common feature of Parisian salons and Bowood; most people Priestley met in Paris and Bowood were both ignorant of, and unbelievers in, Christianity.[1] Shelburne arranged for Bentham to be translated into French and Condorcet into English, and Talleyrand asked Shelburne to write to Washington on his behalf. Shelburne also secured a judgeship in India for the Orientalist and poet, William Jones. Indeed, if England had an Enlightenment, Shelburne could be said to be its chief patron. David O. Thomas writes: 'Shelburne delighted in surrounding himself with prominent intellectuals, and boasted that in his willingness to seek the advice of men like Dunning and Price he was superior to his leader Chatham.'[2]

Shelburne would seem to have been a walking archetype of Enlightenment; he declared his two cardinal principles to be: '*The first is, to be bound to no man*' and 'The second essential rule is, *to see with your own eyes.*'[3] Although Shelburne has been described as 'an original political thinker in a conservative age,'[4] D'Alembert's hypothesis that patrons surround themselves by intellectuals because they want a cheap education is applicable to Shelburne. Bentham, who believed Shelburne to be a celestial presence, also wrote that he 'had a most wretched education.'[5] Samuel Johnson thought Shelburne quite able for an aristocrat: 'His parts, Sir, are pretty well for a Lord; but would not be distinguished in a man who had nothing else but his parts.'[6] Because of his American and French connections, Shelburne was chosen by George III to be his chief minister in negotiating peace with both the Americans and the French at the end of the American War of Independence. For his attempt to extricate Britain from a war with two nations with conflicting interests, Shelburne confirmed a reputation he had earlier acquired as untrustworthy, or even treasonous, his nicknames being 'Malagrida' or 'the Jesuit of Berkeley Square.' (Gabriel Malagrida was an Italian Jesuit unjustly accused of, and cruelly executed for, being a co-conspirator in an attempt on the life of the Portuguese King Joseph in 1758.) When Shelburne's and Burke's compatriot, Oliver Goldsmith, dined with the lord, he said with clumsy benevolence: 'What can make People call your Lordship *Malagrida*? For by what ever I have heard Malagrida was a very *good sort of Man*.'[7]

While Burke's *Reflections* exhibit his disposition for a politics of prudence and practical know-how, and against theoretical principle, he thought that Shelburne 'wants what I call principles, not in the vulgar sense of a deficiency of honour, or conscience – but he totally wants a uniform rule and scheme of life.'[8] Yet Burke shared the views of Lord Shelburne on important matters such as the repudiation of taxation on absentee Irish landlords, the despotic character of the Quebec Act of 1774, conciliation with America, and the desirability of free trade. Adam Smith wrote to Burke on 1 July 1782 calling on him and Fox to join Shelburne's peace ministry,[9] but the Whigs preferred party politics and opposed Shelburne in a Fox-North government, a coalition of the 'friends' and 'enemies' of American independence. Subsequently, at the end of his short government, Shelburne was able to secure legislative independence for Ireland.

Conor Cruise O'Brien attributes Burke's 'obsessive' loathing of Shelburne to Burke's secret Catholicism and his irrational detestation of Protestant Irishmen, such as Henry Grattan and Shelburne.[10] He states that the charge of Jesuitism 'was far wide of the mark for Shelburne,' but presumably his compatriot Burke, also characterized as a Jesuit by the English, was a more accurate shot. The enthusiastic anti-

Celt, John Wilkes, more celebrated for his anti-Scots bigotry, said that Burke's oratory 'stank of whiskey and potatoes.'[11] The Irish, like the Scots, encountered bigotry at the imperial centre. What David Hartley, the son of the philosopher, said of Shelburne could have equally been said of Burke: 'Shelburne is an Irishman and has all the impudence of his nation. He is a palaverer beyond all description. He palavers everyone and has no sincerity.'[12] Irishmen of whatever background, for the English, tended to be Jesuitical, dishonest wordsmiths. For his part, Burke's *Letter to a Noble Lord* deprecated 'the dull English understanding,' nurtured on roast beef and beer and 'wholly unproductive to speculation.'[13]

If O'Brien's attribution of the antagonism between Burke and Shelburne to Catholic-Protestant hatred is accurate, Burke's opposition to the Quebec Act, which provided political rights to Catholics for the first time in the British Empire, needs explanation. Shelburne's opposition to the Quebec Act was consistent with the anti-Catholicism of English radicals and 'friends' of America. As for Burke, if his Catholic sympathies were as pronounced as O'Brien claims, one has to wonder why his duty as agent to New York merchants took primacy over his support of Catholics. Further, although Shelburne considered Catholicism politically dangerous until the French Revolution, he supported the Catholic Relief Act of 1778 and had little sympathy with the Gordon rioters, who opposed the Quebec Act and feared the extension of its principles to the British Isles.[14] Burke, however, may have thought Shelburne sympathetic to the Gordon rioters. There were other differences between the two men. Shelburne, unlike Burke, supported the French Revolution and subsequently came to advocate comprehensive toleration, or the complete emancipation of Catholics from any civil or political disabilities placed upon them.[15] While Shelburne and Burke took similar positions (although their personal differences kept them from forming a common government) with respect to the American Revolution, they adopted antithetical positions on Warren Hastings, control over patronage in India, and, most emphatically, the French Revolution. Shelburne supported the French Revolution because it eliminated Catholicism as a threat to liberty and property and enabled him henceforth to support a policy of universal toleration; Burke opposed the French Revolution because its anti-clericalism threatened the social order on which liberty and property depend. He openly delighted that a Birmingham mob, partly sparked by Burke's attack on Price and Priestley in *Reflections*, burned down the house of Priestley, the radical pensioner of Shelburne, although wiser men, such as Henry Dundas, thought that the mob could easily swing from pro-government to anti-government views.[16]

Burke's opposition to the French Revolution was sparked by Richard Price's paean of praise to the dawning New Jerusalem. Price was Shelburne's protégé and Burke took aim, through Price, at Shelburne. In *Reflections on the Revolution in France*, Burke attacked Shelburne's circle at Bowood when he assaulted Price for his connections 'with literary caballers, and intriguing philosophers; with political theologians, and theological politicians, both at home and abroad.'[17] Burke may have been alluding to Shelburne's pensioner, the chemist and radical Joseph Priestley, when he characterized the revolutionary spirit of freedom as 'the wild *gas*, the fixed air is plainly broke loose.'[18] As he wrote to Philip Francis, while composing his *Reflections*: 'I intend no controversy with Dr. Price or Lord Shelburne or any other of their set. I mean to set in a full View the danger from their wicked principles and their black hearts ...'[19] Shelburne is not mentioned in Burke's *Reflections* or in his *Letter to a Noble Lord*, written in response to the Whig peers who attacked Burke's acceptance of a pension for his *Reflections*, but it is clear that Burke had a visceral hatred of landed aristocrats who would not stand up for the interests of their class and also relied on commoners, like Burke, to maintain the proper balance of property. No Jacobin had the rage of Edmund Burke when he wrote that 'I have strained every nerve to keep the Duke of Bedford in that situation, which alone makes him my superior.'[20] Burke thought, as David Thomas writes, that 'Shelburne was something of a rogue aristocrat: one who was not prepared to act as an aristocrat should to defend the powers and privileges of his class but who was ready to further his own ambitions by calling into being forces which would eventually weaken if not destroy the aristocracy.'[21] Samuel Johnson thought Shelburne was 'one who was for sinking us all into the mob.'[22]

Burke as an Unprincipled Agent of Principals

William Cobbett thought that Burke had 'no notions, no principles, no opinions of his own ... He was a poor, needy dependent of a Borough-monger, to serve whom, and please whom, he wrote; and for no other purpose whatever ...'[23] Cobbett's contemporary, Thomas Love Peacock, similarly wrote that Burke 'had prostituted his own soul, and betrayed his country and mankind, for £1,200 a year.'[24] Karl Marx also thought that Burke's political philosophy was for sale; he was, Marx opined, a sycophant and a hireling. As an agent for New York merchants, he was a liberal at the time of the American War of Independence but, 'in the pay of the English oligarchy,' became a romantic reactionary at the time of the French Revolution. Burke's great talents, which Marx recognized, served whoever provided his income.[25] Cobbett, Peacock, and Marx oversimplified not so much because Burke did not think of himself as a hireling or a lackey but because Burke's ideas did not change as markedly as Marx thought from the American to French revolutions. Burke wrote: 'I was not made for a minion or a tool' and did not cultivate 'one of the arts, that recommend men to the favour and protection of the great.'[26] To be sure, as O'Brien writes of Burke: 'We all deceive ourselves at times and a great man may have greater powers of self-deception than the rest of us. And perhaps that is the way acculturation occurs.'[27] Indeed, the culture of patron-client relations requires genteel self-deception on the part of both the patron and the client.

Burke was a paid agent of New York merchants and referred to them (not his Bristol constituents) in parliament as 'my principals.'[28] His famous *Letter to the Electors of Bristol,* where he asserted that the duty of a representative is to exercise his independent judgment as to the interests of the entire nation, and not just follow the parochial wishes of his constituents, reflected the fact that the interests of American merchants, whose agent Burke was, and his constituents, the Bristol merchants, conflicted.[29] When the Bristol electorate concluded that Burke was more attentive to the interests of New York than to those of Bristol merchants, he was not re-elected; however, he was immediately appointed to represent a pocket borough or constituency possessed by the Marquess of Rockingham. The safety net of Rockingham's patronage was essential to Burke's lofty independence of judgment from his constituents' will. Burke received large sums of money from Lord Rockingham and his son Fitzwilliam – in his will, Rockingham cancelled debts of £30,000 Burke incurred at his estate in Beaconsfield, a colossal amount, five times as much as the debt Lord Verney, Burke's patron before Lord Rockingham, sued Burke for in chancery.[30] Thomas Paine agreed with Marx that Burke's liberal politics had been transformed by his aristocratic connections. Inverting conservative charges that egalitarians bit the hand that fed them, Paine wrote that Burke's change of principles arose from 'praising the aristocratic hand that hath purloined him from himself.'[31] Similarly, Thomas Jefferson wrote that the 'Revolution in France does not astonish me so much as the revolution of Mr. Burke.'[32] But, as Ian Crowe writes, the charges of Burke's contemporaries and Marx that Burke sold his principles for money 'have simply not been proven.'[33] Indeed, as O'Brien indicates, if Burke had been a lackey of Lord Fitzwilliam, he would have kept quiet about the French Revolution, which Fitzwilliam, at the outset, supported.[34] Further, it is true that Burke, who had been celebrated for his attacks on royal patronage and his attempts to trim the king's civil list, accepted a royal pension for his *Reflections on the Revolution in France*. But his acceptance of the pension did not fully contradict his earlier position since, in the course of a robust critique of royal placemen and pensioners, Burke had asserted: 'I would therefore leave to the crown the possibility of conferring some favours, which, whilst they are received as a reward, do not operate as corruption.'[35] In any event, he regarded his pension as a due reward for a lifetime of service to his country, not as a selling out of his principles to the crown.

Sir Lewis Namier, the strongest supporter of eighteenth-century political patronage, agreed with Marx and Paine that Burke's principles were sufficiently flexible to accommodate himself to whatever interest he served. Statesmen entering parliament were of a higher quality, Namier believed, when their talents were recognized by a few powerful patrons than when they appealed to a larger constituency of voters. Talented commoners, such as William Pitt, or, in America, Alexander Hamilton and Benjamin Franklin, could quickly rise through patronage. Burke, however, though a talented commoner, did not rise to the heights of Lord Shelburne or Burke's aristocratic friend Charles James Fox (who succeeded Rockingham as leader of the Whigs), because he had the manner of a lackey.[36] According to Namier: '... if Burke was in a way looked down upon by his associates, this was not due so much to the contempt which the nobly born felt for his origin as to the admiration which he had for theirs; clearly no one can treat as an equal a man so full of respect and admiration.'[37] Burke seemed to glory in the humility of his party principles: 'Low as I am ... I am connected; I glory in such connection ... When I find good men, I will cling to them, follow them in and out, wash the very feet and be subservient, not from interest, but from principle: it shall be my glory.'[38] Yet, while Burke gloried in his connections to aristocratic Whigs, he could not help but resent 'waiting three hours in the lobby of the House of Lords, among their Lordship's footmen.'[39] He served as errand boy for Rockingham, Devonshire, and Portland, giving John Wilkes, who spoke so disparagingly of Burke, money to stay out of England.[40]

Doubtless, Namier's assessment of Burke as a liveried servant of the aristocracy is biased by his distaste for Burke's heated oratory, coloured with anti-Semitic symbolism,[41] which was antithetical to Namier's admiration for the genteel, dispassionate politics of balancing interests. However, Namier is correct when he notes that patrons desire service without the appearance of servility. Samuel Johnson admired the character of the gentleman, sent on an errand for the 5th Duke of Argyll, who left the room whistling 'to shew his independency.'[42] Jeremy Bentham reported that, when Lord Shelburne asked Bentham what services he could perform for his patron, Bentham proudly responded that he was like the prophet Balaam who could speak only 'the word that God putteth in my mouth.' Bentham asserted that Shelburne understood his statement to be 'a declaration of independence' and that the services he performed for Shelburne were 'in the pursuit of the *greatest happiness* principle.' His refusal to serve Shelburne, Bentham said, served 'to endear me to him.'[43]

Conor Cruise O'Brien writes that the fact that Burke received money from the New York Assembly, then from Rockingham, Fitzwilliam, and finally from the crown, did not affect his views or cloud his judgment on political positions.[44] O'Brien admires Burke's pride and independence of character, the antithesis of Shelburne, 'a courtier to his fingertips, [who] did his best to comply with his royal master's wish.'[45] Furthermore, O'Brien's hypothesis that Burke was a secret Catholic serves to solve Charles James Fox's problem with Burke, namely, how he could support American independence and oppose the independence of (Protestant) Ireland. If O'Brien's hypothesis is valid, and Burke was really an Irish Jacobite, his frequent speeches and writings in support of the Glorious Revolution, and specifically how it had beneficial effects on Ireland, were dishonest, or as O'Brien puts it, came from 'a persona that does not fit his inner being,'[46] as was his opposition to the Quebec Act.

If O'Brien's claim that Burke's principles remained fundamentally consistent is questionable, the antithetical view of Marx that Burke's views were entirely conditioned by the source of his income is also open to objection. For patronage is part of a gift economy; a client is not simply a paid employee or an agent of a principal. Burke's claims of independence were a common refrain throughout the eighteenth century, and were a correct if one-sided response to patron-client relationships. A gift, unlike a wage or fee, cannot be closely or tightly tied to services performed. Burke did acknowledge in his conditions of acceptance of a pension from his first patron, William Gerard Hamilton, that 'when I have taken it, I ought no longer to consider myself as possessed of my former freedom and independence.' However, he later resented that Hamilton wanted a '*slave*... and he refused to have a faithful *friend*.'[47] With Rockingham, Burke acquired a patron that he could consider a friend. Colonel Isaac Barré, who was 'hired by Shelburne as a mouthpiece in the House of Commons,' and Burke were held by contemporaries to be comparable as dependents of Shelburne and Rockingham. 'The financial position of Barré and Burke set them apart from the independent members.' Shelburne and Rockingham assured Barré and Burke of their independence, and both Barré and Burke thought of themselves as such, but such professions were generally taken with a grain of salt.[48]

Burke felt less burdened by receiving patronage than Samuel Johnson. When Dr Brocklesby offered Johnson an annuity of £100 to assist him in his impoverished old age, Johnson offered his thanks and declined, but, afterwards, the much more comfortably situated Burke accepted a pension on the condition that it was unconditional.[49] Psychological dispositions, as well as the fact of receiving a fee or a pension, distinguish the status of friend, client, and employee.

Patrons as Employers or Friends

Do patron-client relationships depend on monetary exchange? Whereas Burke and Priestley were paid by Rockingham and Shelburne, Bentham and Price probably did not receive any money from Shelburne but nonetheless considered him to be their patron, and were considered both by contemporaries and historians to be protégés or clients of Shelburne. A client may be viewed as someone between a friend and an employee, with clients tending to consider themselves more friends than employees of their patrons, and patrons seeing clients more as employees, however much they called them friends. In his fine biography of Richard Price, David Thomas writes: 'Although Shelburne became Price's patron, Price was never dependent upon him financially, and, as far as I am able to ascertain, did not receive any monetary assistance from him. In this respect the relationship was quite different from that between Shelburne and Priestley, or between Rockingham and Burke. Price was very sensitive, as indeed was Priestley, on the question of dependence, and strove to avoid anything that would limit his freedom of action.'[50] Bentham was independently wealthy, and he and Price sought Shelburne's patronage to advance their own political projects – relief of dissenters, fiscal reform, and support for the revolutions in America and France in the case of Price, and legal reform and support for the Panoptikon in the case of Bentham. Just as Voltaire, Diderot, and Kant looked to Frederick the Great and Catherine the Great to advance their enlightened causes, and Burke in 1791 solicited Catherine's aid in his counter-revolutionary endeavours, Price and Bentham saw in Shelburne a potent means of putting their theories into effect. Still, Shelburne is more properly called the patron, rather than the friend or political ally, of Price and Bentham, because of the asymmetry of hospitality; Price and Bentham received board and lodging at Bowood but did not reciprocate at their more humble abodes.

The patronage of intellectuals at Shelburne's Wiltshire estate in Bowood is conceptually distinct from the London clubs of Samuel Johnson and Edmund Burke, the Edinburgh clubs of Hume, Smith, and Ferguson, or the Lunar Society of Birmingham, which bonded scientific entrepreneurs such as Erasmus Darwin, Matthew Boulton, Josiah Wedgwood, James Watt, and Joseph Priestley. As distinct from aristocratic salons, clubs are composed of social equals and are self-supporting. Jenny Uglow, in writing of the Lunar Society, characterizes eighteenth-century sociability as follows: 'In the eighteenth century clubs are everywhere: clubs for singing, clubs for drinking, clubs for farting; clubs of poets and pudding-makers and politicians.'[51] Lord Shelburne was present at the periphery of the Lunar Society, providing Wedgwood and Boulton with vases and candlesticks to reproduce commercially, and introduced Boulton to the architects James and Robert Adam, but his function as patron began when he detached Priestley from the group and provided him with a well-paid position and an opportunity to pursue research in chemistry.[52] Peter Brown writes that 'millionaire foundations are the only modern parallel to the arrangement Priestley had entered.'[53]

In *The History and Present State of Electricity with Original Experiments*, Priestly seems to precede Burke in defining patronage as the tribute opulence owes to genius when he makes an especial pitch for the wealthy to patronize natural sciences, rather than history or philosophy, which apparently does not require patrons. Although Priestley advocated that science be disconnected from war and tied to commerce, he called for patrons, rather than investors, and dedicated the work to James Earl of Morton. He wrote:

Natural philosophy is a science which more especially requires the aid of wealth. Many others require nothing but what a man's own reflection may furnish him with. They who cultivate them find within themselves everything that they want. But experimental philosophy is not so independent. Nature will not be put out of her way, and suffer her materials to be thrown into all that variety of situations which philosophy requires, in order to discover her wonderful powers, without trouble and expence. Hence the patronage of the great is essential to the flowering of this science. Others may project great improvements, but they only have the power to carry them into execution.

Priestley went on to indicate that science promotes piety, as well as providing comfort and luxury to the wealthy. 'From the great and opulent, therefore, these sciences have a natural claim for protection; and it is evidently their interest not to suffer promising inquiries to be suspended for want of the means of prosecuting them.'[54] Five years after Priestley wrote the above, Shelburne responded to the 'natural claim' of the scientist.

Shelburne offered to double the salary Priestley earned as a dissenting minister and provide him with a lifetime pension to continue his scientific research if he would become his librarian, companion, and researcher. Yet the noble patron was, according to Robert Schofield, 'extraordinarily sensitive to Priestley's amour-propre, not overpowering him with financial arguments, but assuring him that the position entailed necessary and useful work for which he was particularly qualified.'[55] Priestley did not immediately accept Shelburne's offer, causing some anxiety among Priestley's friends, Price and Franklin. When he did accept, Josiah Wedgwood wrote about 'Priestley's noble appointment' but expressed anxiety whether he will be able 'to go on writing and publishing with the same freedom as he now does.'[56] Indeed, Priestley thought it advisable not to write on politics and religion while in Shelburne's employ, and he confined himself to reading metaphysics and theology in Shelburne's library, as well as engaging in the chemical experimentation for which he is now famous.

It would seem that the conditions of patronage imposed upon Priestley the terms of a conservative Enlightenment, or what Gibbon was later to advise, namely, to restrict himself 'to those sciences in which real and useful improvements can be made.'[57] Gibbon seemed to predict that Priestley's invention of soda water and improvements to champagne production would add more to the world than his materialist metaphysics and radical politics. Indeed, after the French Revolution, Gibbon advocated that Priestley should be jailed for his religious and political views.[58] Priestley's radical political position derived from his dissenting faith; it was directed as much against the atheism of the *philosophes*, and the sceptical conservatism of Hume and Gibbon, as it was against religious orthodoxy.[59] Not until his exile in the United States, where many Americans were hostile to Unitarianism and the Episcopalians were the group most tolerant of his rational religion, did Priestley come to doubt his faith in the disestablishment of religion.[60]

Burke and Priestley were friends at the time of the American Revolution; they went together to hear and support Franklin's presentation of the American cause. Moreover, after Priestley had left Shelburne's employment, Burke acted as a broker to secure the patronage of the Prince of Wales for Priestley.[61] Like Tom Paine, Priestley thought Burke would be a friend of the French Revolution because he had been a friend of the American Revolution, and to his mind, the principles of the two revolutions were the same. Burke, however, saw things differently: the American Revolution conserved property and the British way of life, whereas the French was a social revolution against landed property and established religion, undermining a tradition supportive of private property, which by its very nature is unequal. Burke thought that democracy and security of private property were incompatible, whereas Shelburne, and those he patronized, saw private property and popular rule as compatible.

Bentham wrote that Shelburne was not afraid of the power of the people, and indeed he became more democratic as result of Shelburne's patronage,[62] just as Locke became more liberal as a result of the patronage of Lord Shaftesbury. Like many of the *philosophes*, Bentham admired enlightened despots; before meeting Shelburne, he was pleased that he lived and 'could write in the age of Catherine, of Joseph, of Frederic, of Gustavus, and of Leopold.' The plans of Bentham's brother Samuel for the Panoptikon had been drafted for Catherine the Great when the Benthams, like Diderot, 'went off to Russia, ardent admirers of Catherine the Great and her projected reforms-from-above.'[63] Bentham's great project for eliminating idleness, vice, and crime through architectural design, he hoped, would be realized through his relationship to Shelburne. Bentham's desire for patrons, like Voltaire's, exhited a practical bent, a scorn for mere theoreticians. Bentham thought that Plato, Descartes, Leibniz, and Kant 'were philosophers merely; he [Bentham] was a statesman.'[64]

If Bentham thought himself superior to the greatest of philosophers, Shelburne helped to confirm his high opinion of himself. Adam Smith, as noted above, wrote of the psychological benefits of patronage, namely, the concordance between the patron's estimate of his protégé's worth and the protégé's own estimate of his merits[65] – a point that Bentham underlined when he said that Shelburne had raised him from the 'bottomless pit of humiliation' and made him feel that he was 'something.'[66] The only cloud in the sunny relationship between Bentham and Shelburne appeared when, after the lord had fallen out with Barré, Bentham wished to replace him as member of parliament for Colne. Bentham wrote Shelburne a sixty-one-page letter explaining why the philosopher would be a great statesman, but Shelburne gently turned Bentham's request down. Bentham responded: 'You must allow me to snarl at you a little, now and then, while I kiss the beautiful hands you set to stroke me.'[67] Shelburne made Bentham feel the power of metamorphosis from mere philosopher to philosopher-king as messiah. In a peculiarly English version of the Enlightenment's dream of power, Bentham wrote:

> there came out to me a good man named Ld. S. and he said unto me, what shall I do to be saved? ... I said unto him to take up my book and follow me. We trudged about a long while ... till we spied a man named George who had been afflicted with an incurable blindness and deafness for many years. I said unto my apostle give him a page of my book that he may read ... then fell the scales from his eyes, and not seeing what better he could do with himself, he followed us. We had not travelled far before we saw a woman named Britannia lying by the waterside all in rags with a sleeping lion at her feet ... She started up fresher, farther and more alive than ever; the lion wagged his tail and fawned upon us like a spaniel.[68]

Bentham's dream was that utilitarianism could redeem Britannia, as soon as Shelburne persuaded King George to follow Bentham's doctrine, which Bentham humbly conceded was not his own invention: 'Priestley was the first (unless it was Beccaria) who taught my lips this sacred truth: – That the greatest happiness of the greatest number is the foundation of morals and legislation.'[69]

Burke's Doctrine of Patronage

While Bentham and Burke were jointly opposed to the natural right doctrines justifying the French Revolution, Burke thought that the ambitions of philosophers to use patrons to advance their political projects was ideological *hybris*, or even a blasphemous will to power. To him, it was vital to have a proper understanding of the relationship of patrons to clients. Patrons have rights to service and gratitude from their clients but they also have duties to the talented and needy. As Burke wrote to his patron, Earl Fitzwilliam, on 22 November 1794: 'You will certainly so use the sacred trust of Patronage, as to show it is directed, not by humour or affection, but by public principles; – that is, towards bringing the greatest possible force of weight and authority, as well as active ability and integrity, to the support of Government.'[70] Burke's doctrine followed the position adopted by an anonymous cleric, *Generosus*, who addressed the bishop of London in 1735 with the hope that the bishop would distribute his pamphlet to the nobility and gentry of Britain so that poor and meritorious clerics would get the preferments they deserve. Although the rich have a general duty to provide for the poor, one should not 'insinuate that the Revenues of the Clergy are *Charity*' but rather a reward for services rendered. *Generosus* 'would not be thought to be at all inclinable to the *levelling* scheme,' but at the same time he insisted that patrons' power of bestowing ecclesiastic preferments should not be considered an absolute property of the landowner. 'PATRONAGE is a TRUST.' Hence, 'PATRONS are obliged to dispose of their preferments with a Regard to the great *Ends* for which they were intended, and not at Liberty to serve *private* Views, to promote the Interest of a *Party*, to gratify the Inclination or Humour of the *Patron*.'[71]

The exception to Burke's rule of speaking well of patronage pertains to the East India Company, which had been a major source of patronage in Britain and was to provide the income for Macaulay and the Mills (James, John Stuart, and brothers) in the nineteenth century. Burke's efforts to impeach Warren Hastings were based on the number of Scots in the East India Company and the propensity of Scots to despotism.[72] The East India Company, under Warren Hastings, Burke declaimed, had reduced government 'to a mere Patronage,' by which he meant favouritism, nepotism, and corruption.[73] Burke supported Charles James Fox's bill to limit the power of the crown to confer many lucrative patronage posts in the Indian service, and thus curtail executive dominance in the House of Commons. Indeed, his vocal backing of this reform program marked him out, prior to the French Revolution, as one of the strongest voices against monarchical dominance of parliament. Still, Fox's bill failed because opponents thought it would simply transfer the power of conferring patronage from the crown to the governing party. Burke's prolonged campaign to convict Hastings of misgovernment and to provide the colony with good government, then, was concerned with the control over patronage in India and, indirectly, with control of the House of Commons. Speaking on Fox's bill, Burke said that he wanted a 'method of governing India well, which will not of necessity become the means of governing Great Britain ill.' Indeed, Burke claimed that 'every means, effectual to preserve India from oppression, is a guard to preserve the British constitution from its worst corruption.'[74] His fear that the balance of the British constitution could be upset by excessive royal power of patronage lasted until the French Revolution, when he ceased to be a critic of royal dominance of parliament and received a royal pension.

Burke praised Catherine, the pre-eminent patron of Enlightenment, as 'one of the greatest and wisest sovereigns Europe has ever seen,' and he tried to enlist her help in the counter-revolution to reassert the rights of monarchs in Europe.[75] However, in perhaps the most celebrated passage in the *Reflections*, Burke's championing of patronage was balanced by his fear of the will to power of Enlightenment ideologues: 'The nobility and the clergy, the one by profession, the other by patronage, kept learning in existence ... Learning paid back what it owed to nobility and to priesthood; and it paid it with usury, by enlarging their ideas and furnishing their minds. Happy if they had all continued to know their indissoluble union, and their proper place! Happy if learning, not debauched by ambition, had been satisfied to continue the instructor, and not aspired to be the master! Along with its natural protectors and guardians, learning will be cast into the mire, and trodden down under the hoofs of a swinish multitude.'[76] Shelburne's protégés did not know their proper place as ministering to the propertied; they destroyed the mutually beneficial union between opulence and genius in their desire that philosophers should be masters of the world. J.G.A. Pocock elaborates Burke's view of the natural union of opulence and genius. The Jacobins, Nazis, Red Guards, and the Khmer Rouge 'came about' from 'the decay of aristocratic patronage. When lesser men (including men of letters) followed great patrons, society was vertically divided into cliques of clientage, and the political intelligence of the follower was focused – as Burke's had once been – on the person of his leader, who was no charismatic demagogue but a natural leader in a society constructed on the model of nature.' Pocock asserts that, with the decline of aristocratic patronage, there developed 'an ideologized mass, in whom political opinions were instantaneously communicated by the electric fluid of the print medium, and the reflective caution of a managerial aristocracy could no longer delay the generation of new kinds of fanaticism.'[77] Pocock is too genteel to draw out the obvious conclusion – if contemporary aristocrats, in corporate boardrooms and governmental granting agencies, fail to patronize men of letters, then their failure will lead to an 'ideologized mass' destructive of corporate profits. However, since contemporary natural aristocrats are not as cultivated as the Marquis of Rockingham, we men of letters must spell out our mutual need to our opulent superiors.

Men of genius and learning should be grateful to be at the disposal of propertied aristocrats who, as Burke put it in *An Appeal from the New to the Old Whigs,* 'stand upon such elevated ground as to be enabled to take a large view of the widespread and infinitely diversified combinations of men and affairs in a large society; to have leisure to read, to reflect, to converse: to be enabled to draw the court and attention of the wise and learned, wherever they are to be found ...'[78] Narrow scholars and closeted philosophers can usefully serve powerful men whose practical know-how is allied to a breadth of vision. Great landed proprietors are patrons of cultural enrichment in France and in England. With respect to national churches, Burke favoured a combination of 'kingly and seignoral patronage, as now they are in England, and as they have been lately in France.' However, the French national assembly, 'without the least attention to the rights of patrons,' 'has made a degrading pensionary establishment, to which no man of liberal ideas or liberal education will destine his children.'[79] What Shelburne admired as the separation of church and state, or, in modern terms, the laicization of Catholic France, Burke saw as the construction of a church dependent upon the state, staffed by lower class servants of government – in other words, the destruction of an independent church.

Whereas Burke lamented the dissolution of the French church at the French Revolution, Shelburne regretted the effects of the revolution on the Parisian salons. Indeed, democratic revolutions had a negative effect on the patronage of the arts and sciences. Thomas Paine, whose best-selling *Common Sense* and *The Rights of Men* earned him no money because he kept the price of copies down to the costs of production, wrote successful begging letters to Washington and the Continental Congress, receiving land, money, and 'my boy Joe' [a servant] in recognition of his services to the cause of liberty.[80] In February 1784

Paine made a pitch to General Lewis Morris, a signer of the Declaration of Independence and a wealthy landed New Yorker, extolling the Old World monarchies that patronized arts, sciences, and letters.[81] When he returned to Europe, Paine sought Shelburne's patronage.[82]

While it may seem peculiar to read the militant republican praising monarchs such as Louis XIV, Catherine the Great, and George III, Paine wished republics to patronize letters as monarchies had. Indeed, President Washington's first annual message to Congress on 8 January 1790 declared: 'There is nothing which can better deserve your patronage, than the promotion of Science and Literature.'[83] Washington desired a national university for this end, while Jefferson hoped that the University of Virginia would patronize the arts in order to 'improve the taste of my countrymen, to increase their reputation, to reconcile them to the respect of the world and procure them it's [sic] praise.'[84] John Adams followed Rousseau in attributing the longevity of the Roman republic to patron-client relationships. He suggested that the United States would do well to emulate the stabilizing institution of the ancient aristocratic republic: 'The institution by which every plebeian was allowed to choose any patrician for his patron, introduced an intercourse of good offices between these orders, made the patricians emulate each other in acts of civility and humanity to their clients, and contributed to preserve the peace and harmony of Rome in so remarkable a manner, that in all contests which happened for six hundred and twenty years, they never proceeded to bloodshed.'[85] Whereas Bernard Bailyn and Gordon Wood claim the American Revolution was fought against Old World patronage, Washington, Jefferson, and Adams looked to new forms of patronage that would replace those extended by the British crown.

After the French Revolution, as Shelburne anticipated, French literature suffered from the decline in royal academies and aristocratic salons. The salons of Mme Necker and Mme de Genlis closed their doors in 1790, while the salons of Mme Condorcet, Mme de Staël, and Mme Roland continued until 1792 or 1793. During the Terror, the salons disappeared completely; however, they emerged again – chastened, to be sure – during the Directory and the Napoleonic period, with the homosocial club of the nineteenth century assuming ascendancy over the aristocratic heterosocial salon of the eighteenth century.[86] Just as Priestley was hounded from England for supporting the French Revolution, the great French chemist Antoine Laurent Lavoisier was guillotined in 1793 for being a tax-farmer in the old regime, and the Académie des Sciences was abolished. Two years later, the Institut national des Sciences and Arts was re-established to advise the Directory on works of general utility and to promote the glory of the republic, and the Académie Française was reconstituted as part of the Institut in 1803.[87] Still, while patronage was revived during the Napoleonic period, the French language lost its international standing in the republic of letters during the Revolutionary and Napoleonic eras.[88] Napoleon was a more generous patron of painters, sculptors, architects, and scientists than of intellectuals and men of letters.[89] Many of the prominent writers of the early nineteenth century, whether counterrevolutionaries, like de Bonald and de Maistre, or liberals, like Constant and Tocqueville, were aristocrats, as distinct from the *roturiers* Voltaire, Rousseau, and Diderot. The distinctive patterns of patronage of the French Enlightenment – its competing sources in the royal academies, government subventions, and aristocratic salons, and specifically the tribute bestowed on plebeian male geniuses by opulent women of taste – eroded after the French Revolution.

Émile Zola believed that the literature of the nineteenth century was emancipated from parasitism on royal and aristocratic patrons who supported authors in return for praise and obedience.[90] The French Revolution, Zola alleged, dissolved all privilege, hierarchy, respect; the book became a common commodity, and the author became an honest labourer, as in any other trade, living by his pen. Lacking great lords who accept a dedication in return for a pension, the writer now wrote for a wider reading public; indeed the decline of the salons represented the diffusion of taste to the general reading public.[91] Those who lament the decline of letters in France, he said, fail to recognize 'the justice and honesty of money.' Money has emancipated writers 'from all humiliating protection, which made the old court juggler, the old clown of the antechamber, a free citizen, a man who depends only upon himself.' The commercial marketplace of nineteenth-century France, Zola thought, would facilitate the independence of men of letters. 'We are no longer in a time when a sonnet, read in a salon, made the reputation of a writer and led him to the Academy.'[92]

Yet Zola exaggerated the break with traditional forms of patronage represented by the French Revolution. Writers continued to receive government pensions in the Napoleonic period as they did in the old regime.[93] La Société des gens de lettres was founded in 1838 and received its first government subsidy in 1846; by the end of the nineteenth century, authors were well subsidized by government in the name of public utility.[94] The salons of Mme de Staël, Mme Récamier, and Princesse Mathilde were more literary than philosophic but carried on the tradition of supporting men of letters.[95] Nevertheless, Shelburne's prognosis that the French Revolution would deprive thinkers of the patronage they needed was as acute as Burke's apprehension of impending bloodshed. The French Revolution put an end to Enlightenment. Adam Ferguson expressed the sentiments of his enlightened compatriots with anti-Enlightenment rhetoric when he referred to the French Revolution as 'Antichrist himself in the form of Democracy and Atheism.'[96]

Conclusion

The eighteenth century was a period of transition from aristocratic patronage in the republic of letters to a commercial marketplace of ideas, but the transition was more gradual than abrupt. Most of the writers of the Enlightenment received royal or aristocratic patronage at the same time as they celebrated the commercial press as the means whereby authors could secure for themselves a dignified independence. Writers thought that the expanding readership of the eighteenth century was the means to the independence of those who enlightened readers. However, a tension existed between the objectives of enlightening readers and of ensuring wide readership by appealing to their customs and current sentiments.

The growing popularity of reading altered the character of philosophy, as encyclopedias took the place of systematic philosophy. In the eighteenth century, the rationalist systems of Descartes, Hobbes, Spinoza, and Leibniz did not enjoy the favour of the empirical philosophies of Bacon, Locke, and Newton, all of whom, D'Alembert assured us in his *Preliminary Discourse* to the *Encyclopédie*, were enemies of systems. Systematic thought, for Voltaire, connoted scholasticism and sectarianism, while Enlightenment thought had an egalitarian strain. Bacon taught, in *The New Organon* (LXI), that the method of observation and experiment 'places all wits and understandings on a level.' Consider, too, Benjamin Franklin's statement that he had mastered Locke's philosophy by the age of fifteen,[1] a claim that would be even more incredible for any other philosopher. Diderot claimed that the purpose of encyclopedias was to collect the cumulative knowledge of humanity, acquired by experiment and experience but scattered around the world, and make it accessible to present generations and useful for those to come. To be sure, empirical science was more accessible to a broader reading public than systematic philosophy but it was not *universally* accessible. In his entry 'encyclopédie' in his great work, Diderot wrote that 'the general mass of men are not so made that they can understand this forward march of the human spirit.' Enlightenment was not a populist ideology. The Frankfurt School of Marxism wrongly equated Enlightenment with systematic thought and thus tended to exaggerate both its promise and its threat to humanity.[2]

Eighteenth-century philosophy tended to be more accessible to readers who were neither philosophers nor scholars than classical or seventeenth-century forms of rationalism. Systematic thought lived on in the Scottish and German universities, but the emerging feature of the British, American, and French Enlightenments was its ready accessibility to readers who were not learned, whether aristocratic patrons or common readers. When Hume and *les lumières* wrote for 'the ladies,' their gallantry was double-edged. Eighteenth-century philosophy moved closer to 'common sense' and 'public opinion' in order to lead, guide, or enlighten it. But the radical mission of enlightening public opinion had its conservative side; in combating conventional opinions, members of the Enlightenment had to appeal to widely shared views in their effort to transform the world, quite apart from their need to satisfy their royal or aristocratic patrons. Enlightenment reason was not, as Herbert Marcuse suggests, necessarily revolutionary. Admittedly, Condorcet, in a public panegyric to Benjamin Franklin on 13 November 1790, claimed that republican revolutions followed in the wake of scientific enlightenment: 'Always free in the midst of servitude, science transmits to those who cultivate it something of its noble independence, or it flees from countries subjected to arbitrary rule, or it slowly prepares the revolution which must destroy them ...'[3] But Condorcet's republican commitments caused him to lose his pensions from the Academies of Berlin and St Petersburg, and his noble independence led to his death in jail while awaiting the guillotine. Burke and Shelburne, however they differed on the desirability of the French Revolution, thought that the patronage of thought would be disrupted by the revolution. Revolutionary republicanism put an end to, rather than actualized or put into practice, the age of Enlightenment.

This study has contested Gordon Wood's and Isaac Kramnick's claim that the American Revolution was the *telos* or 'the embodiment and natural home of Enlightenment.'[4] English radicals, such as Paine, Price, and Priestley, did indeed celebrate the American Revolution as the

dawning of a new age of liberty and equality; however, if, as Bernard
Bailyn and Gordon Wood have argued, the American Revolution was
fought against Old World patronage,[5] members of the Enlightenment
were ambivalent about the results. Paine and Priestley did not find
America fertile soil for the development of thought; they had occasion
to see some truth in Kant's view: 'A high degree of civil freedom seems
advantageous to a people's *intellectual* freedom, yet it also sets up
insuperable barriers to it. Conversely, a lesser degree of civil freedom
gives intellectual freedom enough room to expand to its fullest extent.'[6] Kramnick's claim that 'Tocqueville later saw in America the
realization of the Enlightenment spirit that he traced to Descartes'[7]
does not mention Tocqueville's distinction between economic and
intellectual individualism, or the aristocrat's apprehension about
tyranny of majority opinion in the United States.

Condorcet, and many of his compatriots, supported the American
Revolution. France was an ally of America in its war with Britain, an ally
intent on avenging its loss to Britain in the Seven Years' War and
recovering its place as the dominant nation in the world. Support for
the American republic was consistent with loyalty to the French throne,
and thus should not necessarily be construed as espousal of republican
principles or rejection of aristocratic and royal patronage. Gordon
Wood's view that 'republicanism was the ideology of the Enlightenment'[8] oversimplifies the commitments of intellectuals in the eighteenth century, despite the support of French *philosophes* for the
American War of Independence. David Hume's claim that he was
American in his principles derived more from his antipathy to the
English, and his fear of the dominance of London (which he thought
would be cut down to size by the loss of American trade) in Britain,
than from support for the cause of American republicanism.[9]

What I have called the Senecan moment in eighteenth-century
thought contests Wood's and Kramnick's view that Enlightenment
thinkers tended to espouse republican ideas. Philosophers have always
been concerned with the flourishing of philosophy, as well as with
political and social justice. Blaise Pascal proclaimed the incompatibility
of justice and social order with greater clarity than any Enlightenment
thinker: 'No doubt equality of wealth is right and just; but since force
cannot be made to submit to justice, men have made it just to submit to
force; and since justice cannot be fortified, we justify force so that
justice and force go together and we have peace, which is the sovereign
good.'[10] People do not submit to blind force; they need ideas to make

that submission palatable. Philosophers' love of peace prompts an enlightened justification of the powers that be.

The French, Russian, and Chinese revolutions might be thought to have falsified Voltaire's view that all civil wars between the rich and poor ultimately end 'with the subjugation of the people, because the powerful have money, and money is master of everything in a state.'[11] These revolutions were closer to Rousseau's moral populism than to Voltaire's enlightened realism, but, with the failure of these revolutions to achieve egalitarian justice, revolutionary egalitarianism is on the wane. Henceforth, the power of money will be justified, as it has been justified throughout the ages, through the patronage of intellectuals. And, if patronage is the tribute that opulence owes to genius, 'genius' is bound to repay opulence with gratitude. Yet few intellectuals see themselves, as Voltaire and Morellet sometimes did, as hired pens or intellectual mercenaries. More often, as Pierre Bourdieu states: 'Patronage is a subtle form of domination that acts thanks to the fact that it is not perceived as such.'[12] Perhaps patronage operates most effectively in the twilight and my effort to bring it into light may be self-defeating for one who supports patronage of thought. Perhaps what I consider the Enlightenment illusion of independent thought is integral to thinking; no one considers himself or herself an intellectual mercenary or hired hand.

Although I have championed patronage of thought, and deprecated Enlightenment illusions of independent thought, attentive readers may have discerned my partiality for thinkers reluctant to bow down to the great, such as Pierre Bayle, Jean-Jacques Rousseau, and Samuel Johnson, and my respect for the ideas of Adam Smith, whose idea of a free and democratic marketplace of ideas is the central idea I contest in this book.

The eighteenth-century ideal of intellectual independence was fabricated under conditions of royal and aristocratic patronage. Thinkers depended upon patrons for political protection, for economic security, and for the recognition and dissemination of their ideas. Thought, I have argued, is a collective product, an activity carried out by individuals dependent on, and balancing expectations of, patrons, readers, publishers, and advertisers. Thought flourished where there were a multiplicity of patrons; the French Enlightenment was a product of regal patronage from Versailles, Berlin, and St Petersburg and the aristocratic patronage of Parisian *salonnières*. If Voltaire and Samuel Johnson welcomed regal patronage to avoid degrading dependence on aristocrats, Locke and Rousseau accepted aristocratic patronage to limit monarchical absolutism. The relative freedom of the English press and the absence of governmental regulation of universities could be said to constitute freedom of thought. But freedom for thought may require more than a competitive marketplace of ideas or the absence of government regulation of the press, universities, and voluntary associations. English universities lacked the patronage of an Argyll, Bute, or Dundas; they virtually closed their doors to plebeian classes and prepared the well-to-do for a clerical career. Enlightenment is the use of plebeian talent for patrician objectives. Plebeians, such as Jean-Jacques Rousseau and Samuel Johnson, who were unwilling to be so used were not parties to Enlightenment.

If Enlightenment is to be characterized, *à la* Kant, Diderot, and Bentham, by the tension of intellectual freedom and practical obedience, we can relate that tension to the patron-client relationships of the major writers of the eighteenth century. Enlightenment thinkers were unanimous in recognizing the sweetness of commerce, whether or not they supported slavery in the West Indian plantations. But commercial sugar did not supplant honeyed patronage in the eighteenth century. Nor should we to think that sweet commerce will encourage the flowering of a variety of forms of thought. Without a governmental or non-commercial sector, knowledge will come under the sway of capitalist corporations. Corporate donors will expect service and gratitude, just as eighteenth-century patrons did. If Voltaire's and Johnson's view that governmental patronage was essential to avoid degrading dependance on powerful aristocrats was a partial or one-sided truth, that partial truth must be reaffirmed in the face of the unchecked power of capitalist corporations.

William Simon's *A Time for Truth*, published in 1979, was a wholesale attack on academic independence, or what Simon took to be the monopoly of leftists in the academe and the media. Milton Friedman and Friedrich von Hayek wrote prefaces to *A Time for Truth*, claiming that successful businessmen are more open to new ideas 'than the academic intellectual who prides himself on his alleged independence of thought.'[13] Simon asserted: 'The only thing that can save the Republican party, in fact, is a counterintelligentsia.' He urged businessmen to 'rush by multimillions to the aid of liberty, in the many places where it is beleaguered.' Simon's book, Milton Friedman averred, 'will give the young intellectual whose ideas are not yet set in concrete much food for thought and strongly reinforce a change in philosophic views towards individualism ...' Foundations 'must serve as intellectual refuges for the non-egalitarian scholars and writers in our society who work largely alone in the face of overwhelming indifference and hostility. They must be given grants, grants, and more grants in exchange for books, books, and more books.'[14] Simon attenuated the loneliness of non-egalitarian scholars through his activities as president of the John N. Olin Foundation,[15] which funds the American Enterprise Institute, the Heritage Foundation, the Cato Foundation, the Manhattan Institute for Public Policy Research, and the Hoover Institute of War, Revolution and Peace. Together with other right-wing foundations, such as the Bradley Foundation, the Earhart Foundation, the Scaife Foundation, the Smith Richardson Foundation, the Liberty Foundation, and the Donner Foundation, the Olin Foundation has given weight to American and Canadian academics through 'grants, grants and more grants' and has brought together lonely individualists in right-wing institutes for public policy.[16] The Donner Foundation of Canada funds the Fraser Institute's efforts to dispense with universal health care and public broadcasting, and provides awards for those academics faithful to its mandate. Simon was clear that the cutting of funds to left-wing professors and the funding of right-wing professors does not undermine academic independence: 'This has nothing to do with trying to govern what any individual professor teaches, nor is it an attempt to "buy" docile professors who will teach what businessmen tell them to. That notion is as ridiculous as the idea that anti-capitalist professors are entitled to support from capitalism.' Although Olin scholarship students are mandated to take courses from Olin Fellows, and are required to attend visiting Olin lecturers and pose predetermined questions to the lecturers, I do not wish to suggest that these docile students are bought. Patronage is part of a gift economy. What I do question in Simon's manifesto, however, is his argument that 'business must cease the mindless subsidizing of colleges and universities whose departments of economics, government, politics and history are hostile to capitalism,'[17] if this argument is coupled to an insistence that governments reduce their support of universities and academic publications. Whether or not Simon's program has fostered a right-wing turn in American political culture, corporate support for universities is to be welcomed – but not if it simply replaces declining government funding for education and research.

A plurality of patrons is essential to impede a flattening of thought. When you have seen one corporate-sponsored individualist, you've seen 'em all. William Simon is not the 3rd Duke of Argyll, Chrétien-Guillaume de Malesherbes, or Lord Shelburne; he and his fellow corporate patrons spread more heat than light in their celebration of markets over governments. If our comparative study of eighteenth-century England, Scotland, and France has yielded a message, it is that the commercial marketplace of ideas is insufficient to generate Enlightenment. Counter-enlightenments beckon, within the United States as without.

Notes

Introduction

1 Aristotle, *Nicomachean Ethics*, 1177a–1179a; *Politics*, 1323b, 1325b.
2 Denis Diderot, *Rameau's Nephew and Other Works*, trans. Jacques Barzun and Ralph H. Bowen (Indianapolis: Hackett, 2001), 84.
3 Ibid., 36.
4 Roger Chartier, *The Order of Books*, trans. Lydia G. Cochrane (Durham, N.C.: Duke University Press, 1991), x; Chartier, *Forms and Meanings: Texts, Performances and Audiences from Codex to Computer* (Philadelphia: University of Pennsylvania Press, 1995), 1–2; Benoît Mély, *Jean-Jacques Rousseau: un intellectuel en rupture* (Paris: Minerve, 1985), 17–36; Jean Guéhenno, *Jean-Jacques Rousseau* (New York: Columbia University Press, 1967), 263; Michel Mollat, 'Les aspects économiques du mécénat en Europe (XIV–XVIII siècle),' *Revue Historique*, 273 (1985): 265–81;Vicomte Georges D'Avenel, *Les riches depuis sept cent ans: les revenus d'un intellectuel de 1200 à 1913; revenus et bénéfices, appointements et honoraires* (Paris: Colin, 1909), chapter 8. John Lough, *Writer and Public in France from the Middle Ages to the Present Day* (Oxford: Clarendon, 1978), chapter 4, asserts that writers in the eighteenth century could not make a living from their writing without patronage, while Dustin Griffin, *Literary Patronage in England, 1650–1800* (Cambridge: Cambridge University Press, 1996), 68, 282, claims that all major British writers of the eighteenth century depended upon royal or aristocratic patronage. Thomas Paine may have been an exception to this generalization; he received no money for his best-selling *Common Sense* and *Rights of Man* but successfully pressed his claim to state and federal governments in America for money, land, and a servant boy for services rendered.

5   Gordon S. Wood, *The Radicalism of the American Revolution* (New York: Alfred A. Knopf, 1992).

6   Cited in Howard D. Weinbrot, *Augustus Caesar in 'Augustan' England* (Princeton, N.J.: Princeton University Press, 1978), 124.

7   Philip Pettit, *Republicanism* (Oxford: Clarendon, 1997); Martin van Gelderen and Quentin Skinner, eds., *Republicanism: A Shared European Heritage* (Cambridge: Cambridge University Press, 2002).

8   Wood, *Radicalism of the American Revolution*, 100.

9   J.G.A. Pocock, *The Machiavellian Moment: Florentine Political Thought and the Atlantic Republican Tradition* (Princeton, N.J.: Princeton University Press, 1975).

10   Isaac Kramnick, *The Portable Enlightenment Reader* (New York: Penguin, 1995), xviii–xix.

11   Henry Steele Commanger, *The Empire of Reason: How Europe Imagined and America Realized the Enlightenment* (Garden City, N.Y.: Anchor Press, 1977), 15.

12   Benjamin Franklin, *Writings* (New York: Library of America, 1987), 787.

13   Wood, *Radicalism of the American Revolution*, 74–6; Bernard Bailyn, *The Origins of American Politics* (New York: Alfred Knopf, 1968), 109–18.

14   J.G.A. Pocock, *Barbarism and Religion: The First Decline and Fall*, vol.3 (Cambridge: Cambridge University Press, 2003), 7.

15   William Godwin, *An Enquiry concerning Political Justice*, in Mark Philp, ed., *Political and Philosophic Writings of William Godwin*, vol.3 (London: William Pickering, 1993), 475.

16   Émile Zola, 'L'argent dans la Littérature,' in *Oeuvres Complètes*, t.10 (Paris: Cercle du livres précieux, 1968), 1268–76; John Lough, *Writer and Public in France*, 199–201; René Pomeau, *On a voulu l'enterrer*, t.5, *Voltaire en Son Temps*, (Oxford: Voltaire Foundation, 1994), 366.

17   Keith Wrightson, 'Class,' in David Armitage and Michael J. Braddick, eds., *The British Atlantic World, 1500–1800* (New York: Palgrave Macmillan, 2002), 150.

18   Edmund Burke, *Letter to a Member of the Legislative Assembly*, in *Reflections on the Revolution in France*, ed. L.G. Mitchell (Oxford: Oxford University Press, 1993), 271.

19   Cited in Griffin, *Literary Patronage*, 103.

20   Cited in George Birkbeck Hill, ed., *Boswell's Life of Johnson*, vol.4 (Oxford: Clarendon, 1887), 117.

21   I can think of no English equivalent for a gender-free 'men of letters'. 'Literary people' and 'persons of letters' do not strike my ear as equivalent to *gens de lettres*.

22 'What Is Enlightenment?' in *Kant's Political Writings*, ed. Hans Reiss, trans. H.B. Nisbet (Cambridge: Cambridge University Press, 1970), 58–9.
23 Peter Mainka, *K.A. Von Zedlitz und Leipe* (Berlin: Dunker and Humbolt, 1995), 172.
24 Alexis de Tocqueville, *État social et politique de la France avant et depuis 1789*, in *Oeuvres Complètes*, ed. J.-P. Mayer (Paris: Gallimard, 1952), t.2:48–9.
25 Voltaire, *Philosophic Dictionary*, trans. Peter Gay (New York: Basic Books, 1962), 245.
26 Paul Bénichou, *The Consecration of the Writer, 1750–1830*, trans. Mark K. Jensen (Lincoln: University of Nebraska Press, 1999).
27 Roger Chartier, *Forms and Meanings*, 1–2.
28 Terry Eagleton, *Literary Theory: An Introduction* (Oxford: Basil Blackwell, 1985), 84.
29 Roger L. Emerson, 'How Not to Deal with Enlightenments,' *Historically Speaking*, 3:3 (2002): 6–7.
30 Chartier made this comment to a conference in London in 1998, shortly after seeing the movie *Shakespeare in Love*, which presents the bard's *Romeo and Juliet* as a collective project.
31 Thomas Hobbes, *Leviathan*, ed. J.C.A. Gaskin (Oxford: Oxford University Press, 1996), 229.
32 Friedrich dem Grossen, *De la Littérature Allemande* (Stuttgart: G.J. Göschen'sche Verlagshandlung, 1883), 37. Despite Frederick's view, German literature was in full bloom; Lessing, Mendelsohn, Hamann, and Kant were writing in German, while Frederick was trying to improve his French.
33 David Hume, *Essays, Moral, Political and Literary*, ed. Eugene F. Miller (Indianapolis: Liberty Classics, 1985), 113. Simone Weil also contested the purport of Frederick's claim that Augustuses make Virgils; truth and beauty are not for sale, and the patronage transaction between Augustus and Virgil kept the *Aeneid* from the standard of pure beauty of Homer's *Iliad*. 'God would be unjust if the *Aeneid*, which was composed under these conditions [receipt of patronage to enhance power and glory], were worth as much as the *Iliad*. But God is not unjust, and the *Aeneid* is very far indeed from being on an equality with the *Iliad*.' (*The Need for Roots: Prelude to a Declaration of Duties toward Mankind*, trans. Arthur Wills [Boston: Beacon Press, 1960], 233.) Weil's view that patrons cannot create what Hume called genius was, however, outside the spiritual as well as temporal horizons of the Enlightenment.
34 David Hume, *Essays, Moral, Political and Literary*, 48–49.

35 Roger Chartier, 'Student Populations in the Eighteenth Century,' trans. J. Dunkley, *British Journal for Eighteenth-Century Studies,* 2 (1979): 150.
36 John Viscount Morley, *Voltaire* (London: Macmillan, 1923), 61.
37 Jeremy Boissevain, *Friends of Friends: Networks, Manipulators and Coalitions* (Oxford: Blackwell, 1974), 19–20.
38 Michel Foucault, 'What is Enlightenment?' in Paul Rabinow, ed., *The Foucault Reader* (New York: Pantheon, 1984), 43.
39 Aristotle, *Constitution of Athens,* 43, in *The Complete Works of Aristotle,* ed. Jonathan Barnes, vol.2 (Princeton, N.J.: Princeton University Press, 1991), 2368.
40 Pierre Bourdieu and Hans Haacke, *Free Exchange* (Stanford, Calif.: Stanford University Press, 1995), 69.

1 Patronage of Philosphy

1 G. M. Ross, 'Seneca's Philosophic Influence,' in C.D.N. Costa, ed., *Seneca* (London: Routledge and Kegan Paul, 1974), 116–65.
2 Friedrich Nietzsche, *Beyond Good and Evil: Prelude to a Philosophy of the Future,* trans. W. Kaufmann (New York: Vintage, 1966), preface; 'The Problem of Socrates,' in *Twilight of the Idols,* trans. R.J. Hollingdale (Harmondsworth, U.K.: Penguin, 1968).
3 Leo Strauss, *Persecution and the Art of Writing* (Westport, Conn.: Greenwood, 1952); *What Is Political Philosophy?* (New York: Free Press, 1959).
4 Xenophon, *Memorabilia,* I.vi.13, trans. J.S. Watson, in A.D. Lindsay, ed., *Socratic Discourses* (London: J.M. Dent, 1954), 33.
5 Thomas Pangle, 'Socrates in Xenophon's Political Writings,' in Paul A. Vander Waerdt, *The Socratic Movement* (Ithaca, N.Y.: Cornell University Press, 1994), 136.
6 Denis Diderot, *Essai sur la vie de Sénèque le philosophe, sur ses écrits, et sur les règnes de Claude et de Néron,* in *Oeuvres Complètes,* ed. Roger Lewinter, t.12 (Paris: Société encyclopédique française et le Club français du livre, 1972), 692.
7 Georg Wilhelm Friedrich Hegel, *The History of Philosophy,* trans. E.S. Haldane (London: Routledge and Kegan Paul, 1955), 1:389. Hegel may have derived his view from Diogenes Laertius's *Lives,* Thomas Stanley's *The History of Philosophy* (1701), or, more likely, Johann Jakob Brucker's *Historia Critica Philosophiae* (1742–4). Stanley and Brucker develop Laertius's view that Crito was Socrates' patron. I am grateful to James Moore for this information.

8 Kenneth Dover, 'Socrates in the Clouds,' in Gregory Vlastos, ed., *The Philosophy of Socrates: A Collection of Critical Essays* (New York: Anchor Books, 1971), 73–4.

9 Paul Millett, 'Patronage and Its Avoidance in Classical Athens,' in Andrew Wallace-Hadrill, ed., *Patronage in Ancient Society* (London: Routledge, 1990), 43.

10 Cited in Francis Bacon, *The Advancement of Learning*, ed. Michael Kiernan (Oxford: Clarendon, 2000), 20. Emphasis in original.

11 Frances Bereson, 'Socrates the Man,' in K.J. Boudouris, ed., *The Philosophy of Socrates* (Athens: International Center for Greek Philosophy and Culture, 1991), 34.

12 Plato, *Euthyphro*, trans. Lane Cooper, in Edith Hamilton and Huntington Cairns, eds., *The Collected Dialogues of Plato* (New York: Pantheon–Bollinger Series LXXI, 1964), 171.

13 Plutarch, *Lives*, trans. John and William Langhorne (London: J. Mawman, 1813), 2:30.

14 Barry Strauss, 'In the Shadow of the Fortress,' in David Tabachnick, ed., *Tyranny: Ancient and Contemporary* (Lantham, Md.: Rowman and Littlefield, forthcoming).

15 Bacon, *Advancement of Learning*, 18, 20.

16 Hegel, *History of Philosophy*, 2:242, 273. Hegel's harsh verdict is that Seneca should not be discussed 'in a history of philosophy any more than of our sermons' and that 'In Seneca himself there is more folly and bombast in the way of moral reflections than genuine truth.'

17 See Brad Inwood, 'The Will in Seneca the Younger,' *Classical Philology*, 95 (2000): 44–60.

18 Hegel, *History of Philosophy*, 3:171–2.

19 Denis Diderot, *Political Writings*, ed. and trans. John Hope Mason and Robert Wokler (Cambridge: Cambridge University Press, 1992), 209.

20 Denis Diderot, *Rameau's Nephew and Other Works*, trans. Jacques Barzun and Ralph H. Bowen (Indianapolis: Hackett, 2001), 289.

21 See *Letters of Voltaire and Frederick the Great*, trans. Richard Aldington (London: Routledge, 1927), 290, 365.

22 *Voltaire's Correspondence*, ed. Theodore Besterman, letter 13221 (Genève: Institut et Musée Voltaire, 1962), 65:150.

23 René Pomeau, *On a voulu l'enterrer*, t.5, *Voltaire en son temps*, (Oxford: Voltaire Foundation, 1994), 235.

24 Ibid., 53–4; *Oeuvres Complètes de Voltaire*, t.10 (Paris: Garnier 1879), 437. "Peter was a creator; he formed man./You form heroes – such are sovereigns/Who make the character and manners of humans.

25 Alvin Kernan, *Printing Technology, Letters and Samuel Johnson* (Princeton: Princeton University Press, 1987), 105. D'Alembert's *Essai* is found in *Oeuvres Complètes de D'Alembert* (Genève: Slatkine, 1967), t.4:335–73. R.A. Leigh claims that D'Alembert's *Essai* persuaded many that Rousseau's posture of living free of patronage or pensions – D'Alembert himself had five pensions – was more than a profitable pose. See his 'Rousseau's English Pension,' in J.H. Fox, M.W. Waddicor, and D.A. Watts, eds., *Studies in Eighteenth-Century Literature* (Exeter: University of Exeter, 1975), 109–22.

26 Ernst Cassirer, *The Philosophy of the Enlightenment*, trans. Fritz Koelln and James Pettegrove (Princeton, N.J.: Princeton University Press, 1979); Isaiah Berlin, *The Age of Enlightenment: The 18th Century Philosophers* (New York: Mentor, 1963).

27 J.G.A. Pocock, 'Post-Puritan England and the Problem of the Enlightenment,' in Perez Zagorin, ed., *Culture and Politics from Puritanism to the Enlightenment* (Berkeley: University of California Press, 1980), 106; Roy Porter, 'The Enlightenment in England,' in R. Porter and M. Teich, eds., *The Enlightenment in National Context* (Cambridge: Cambridge University Press, 1981), 5.

28 J.G.A. Pocock, *Barbarism and Religion: The Enlightenments of Edward Gibbon, 1737–1764* (Cambridge: Cambridge University Press, 1999), 292–308; Roy Porter, *The Creation of the Modern Mind: The Untold Story of the British Enlightenment* (New York: W.W. Norton 2000), 9–15. We might not have to go as far as Sir James MacIntosh, who says that Gibbon 'might have been cut out of a corner of Burke's mind without his missing it,' to contest the stature of English giants.

29 John Robertson, 'The Scottish Contribution to the Enlightenment,' in Paul Wood, ed., *The Scottish Enlightenment: Essays in Reinterpretation* (Rochester, N.Y.: University of Rochester Press, 2000), 41. My emphasis.

30 Porter, *Creation of the Modern Mind*, xviii, 14–15.

31 Linda Colley, *Britons: Forging the Nation, 1707–1837* (New Haven, Conn.: Yale University Press, 1992), 123.

32 *The Letters of David Hume*, ed. J.Y.T. Greig, vol.1 (Oxford: Clarendon, 1932), 470.

33 John Spurr, *The Restoration Church, 1646–1689* (New Haven, Conn.: Yale University Press, 1991), 384; Roy Porter, *English Society in the Eighteenth Century* (Harmondsworth, U.K.: Penguin, 1982), 177–90; Lawrence Stone, *The University in Society* (Princeton, N.J.: Princeton University Press, 1974), 3–110.

34 Cassirer, *Philosophy of the Enlightenment*; Berlin, *Age of Enlightenment*;
    Peter Gay, 'Why Was the Enlightenment,' in Peter Gay, ed., *Eighteenth-Century Studies Presented to Arthur M. Wilson* (Hanover, N.H.: University
    Press of New England, 1972); Margaret C. Jacob, *The Radical
    Enlightenment: Pantheists, Freemasons and Republicans* (London: George
    Allen Unwin, 1981); Anne Goldgar, *Impolite Learning: Conduct and
    Community in the Republic of Letters, 1680–1750* (New Haven, Conn.: Yale
    University Press, 1995); Ulrich Im Hof, *The Enlightenment*, trans. William
    E. Yuill (Oxford: Blackwell, 1995); Jonathan I. Israel, *Radical
    Enlightenment: Philosophy and the Making of Modernity* (Oxford: Oxford
    University Press, 2001); T.C.W. Blanning, *The Culture of Power and the
    Power of Culture: Old Regime Europe, 1660–1789* (Oxford: Oxford
    University Press, 2002).
35 *Letters of Voltaire and Frederick the Great*, 365.
36 See, for example, Thomas O'Connor, *An Irish Theologian in Enlightenment
    France: Luke Joseph Hooke, 1714–96* (Dublin: Four Courts Press, 1995); B.W.
    Young, *Religion and Enlightenment in Eighteenth-Century England* (Oxford:
    Clarendon, 1998); Ned D. Landsman, 'Presbyterians and Provincial
    Society: The Evangelical Enlightenment in the West of Scotland, 1740–
    1775,' in John Dwyer and Richard B. Sher, eds., *Sociability and Society in
    Eighteenth-Century Scotland* (Edinburgh: Mercat Press, 1993), 194–209;
    Robert Kent Donovan, 'The Popular Party of the Church of Scotland and
    the American Revolution,' in Richard B. Sher and Jeffrey R. Smitten, eds.,
    Scotland and America in the Age of Enlightenment (Edinburgh: Edinburgh
    University Press, 1990), 81–99; Stephen Miller, *Three Deaths and
    Enlightenment Thought: Hume, Johnson, Marat* (Lewisburg, Penn.: Bucknell
    University Press, 2001).
37 Young, *Religion and Enlightenment*, 14.
38 Ibid., 20.
39 Ibid., 60.
40 Porter, *Creation of the Modern World*, 112–18; Peter Harrison, *'Religion' and
    the Religions in the Enlightenment* (Cambridge: Cambridge University Press,
    1990); J.A.I. Champion, *The Pillars of Priestcraft Shaken: The Church of
    England and Its Enemies, 1660–1730* (Cambridge: Cambridge University
    Press, 1992).
41 James O'Higgins, *Anthony Collins: The Man and His Works* (The Hague:
    Martinus Nijhoff, 1970); Robert E. Sullivan, *John Toland and the Deist
    Controversy* (Cambridge, Mass.: Harvard University Press, 1982), 230.
42 Israel, *Radical Enlightenment*, 629–30.

43 Robert Adams, 'In Search of Baron Somers,' in Perez Zagorin, ed., *Culture and Politics: From Puritanism to the Enlightenment* (Berkeley: University of California Press, 1980), 176.

44 Robert Rees Evans, *Pantheisticon: The Career of John Toland* (New York: Peter Lang, 1991), 39; also Stephen H. Daniel, *John Toland: His Methods, Manners, and Mind* (Montreal and Kingston: McGill-Queen's University Press, 1984), 11–15, 96.

45 Sullivan, *John Toland and the Deist Controversy*, 142.

46 Ibid., 94.

47 Daniel, *John Toland*, 13. Franco Venturi, *Utopia and Reform in the Enlightenment* (Cambridge: Cambridge University Press, 1971), 49–60, holds Toland to have been a major figure in the British and European Enlightenment but maintains that the Irishman appeared 'confused and contradictory' because he attempted to convey a republican message within his deist polemics.

48 Sullivan, *John Toland and the Deist Controversy*, 159–60.

49 O'Higgins, *Anthony Collins*; Sullivan, *John Toland and the Deist Controversy*, 160, 230.

50 Diderot, *Rameau's Nephew and Other Works*, 13.

51 Robert Darnton, *The Literary Underground of the Old Regime* (Cambridge, Mass.: Harvard University Press, 1982), 1–40. Also Daniel Gordon, *Citizens without Sovereignty: Equality and Sociability in French Thought, 1670–1789* (Princeton, N.J.: Princeton University Press, 1994), 4, asserts that the *lumières* were a prop, not a challenge, to absolutism. Voltaire wrote what he considered to be the most polished invasion manifesto ever written for Bonnie Prince Charlie but his Scottish admirers did not rally to Voltaire's cause.

52 *Oeuvres Complètes de Voltaire*, t.26 (Paris: Lequien, 1820), 130–1.

53 Hester Thrale Piozzi, *Dr. Johnson and Mrs. Thrale*, ed. Richard Ingrams (London: Chatto and Windus, 1984), 20–1.

54 Ann Holt, *A Life of Joseph Priestley* (London: Oxford University Press, 1931), 67.

55 Jean Le Rond d'Alembert, *Preliminary Discourse to the Encyclopedia of Diderot*, trans. Richard N. Schwab (Chicago: University of Chicago Press, 1995), 66.

56 Cited in Lord Fitzmaurice, *Life of William, Earl of Shelburne*, vol.2 (London: Macmillan, 1912), 316.

57 Julian Pitt-Rivers, *The People of the Sierra* (Chicago: University of Chicago Press, 1971), 140.

58 Cited in Karl W. Schweizer, ed., *Lord Bute: Essays in Re-Interpretation* (Leicester: Leicester University Press, 1988), 120.

59 John Trenchard and Thomas Gordon, *Cato's Letters: or Essays on Liberty, Civil and Religious, and Other Important Subjects*, no.60, 6 Jan 1721 (London: J. Walthoe *et al*, 1755), vol.2, 229.

60 Dena Goodman, *The Republic of Letters: A Cultural History of the French Enlightenment* (Ithaca, N.Y.: Cornell University Press, 1994), chapter 2.
61 Marc Bloch, *Feudal Society*, trans. L.A. Manyon (London: Routledge and Kegan Paul, 1961), 147.
62 Linda Levy Peck, *Court Patronage and Corruption in Early Stuart England* (Boston: Unwin Hyman, 1990), 3.
63 Clive T. Probyn, *The Sociable Humanist: The Life and Works of James Harris, 1709–1780* (Oxford: Clarendon, 1991), 65.
64 Ernest Gellner, 'Patrons and Clients,' in Ernest Gellner and John Waterbury, eds., *Patrons and Clients in Mediterranean Societies* (London: Duckworth, 1977), 3–4.
65 Edmund Burke, *Reflections on the Revolution in France*, ed. L.G. Mitchell (Oxford: Oxford University Press, 1993), 144.
66 Robert Kaufman, 'The Patron-Client Relationship and Macro-Politics: Problems and Prospects,' *Comparative Studies in Society and History*, 16 (1974): 285.
67 Bernard Bailyn, *The Origins of American Politics* (New York: Alfred A. Knopf, 1968), 28–31, 109–10; Gordon S. Wood, *The Radicalism of the American Revolution* (New York: Alfred A. Knopf, 1992), 57–92.
68 Edward Gibbon, *The Decline and Fall of the Roman Empire* (London: Penguin, 1936), 706.
69 Edmund Burke, *The Correspondence of Edmund Burke*, ed. R.B. McDowell (Chicago: University of Chicago Press, 1989), 8:79.
70 Peck, *Court Patronage and Corruption in Early Stuart England*, 48.
71 Marcel Mauss, *The Gift: Forms and Functions of Exchange in Archaic Societies* (London: Cohen and West, 1970), 1, 72.
72 John Waterbury, 'An Attempt to Put Patrons and Clients in Their Place,' in Gellner and Waterbury, eds., *Patrons and Clients*, 336.
73 John Brewer, *Party Ideology and Popular Politics at the Accession of George III* (Cambridge: Cambridge University Press, 1976), 5.
74 T.W. Heyck, *The Transformation of Intellectual Life in Victorian England* (London: Croom Helm, 1982), 56.
75 George Birkbeck Hill, ed., *Boswell's Life of Johnson*, vol.1 (Oxford: Clarendon, 1887), 209.
76 Cited in Jonathan Swift, *A Discourse of the Contests and Dissentions between the Nobles and Commons in Athens and Rome*, ed. Frank H. Ellis (Oxford: Clarendon, 1967), 138.
77 *Letters concerning the Present State of England. Particularly respecting the Politics, Arts, Manners and Literature of the Times* (London: J. Almon, 1772), 332–3.
78 Lawrence Stone, 'The Size and Composition of the Oxford Student Body 1580–1910,' in Stone, ed., *The University in Society*, 40.

79 Guy Fitch Lytle, 'Patronage Patterns and Oxford Colleges,' in ibid., 115, 119.
80 Lawrence Stone, 'Size and Composition,' 37; Maria Rosa di Simone,
    'Admission,' in Hilde de Ridder-Symoens, ed., *Universities in Early Modern
    Europe, 1500–1800* (Cambridge: Cambridge University Press, 1996), 310.
81 Stone, 'Size and Composition,' 11.
82 Mark H. Curtis, 'The Alienated Intellectuals of Early Stuart England,' *Past
    and Present*, 23 (1962) 25–43; John Gascoigne, *Science, Politics and
    Universities in Europe, 1600–1800* (Aldershot, U.K.: Ashgate, 1998), 393–4.
83 Trenchard and Gordon, *Cato's Letters*, vol.4, 243.
84 Olaf Pederson, 'Tradition and Innovation,' in Ridder-Symoens, ed.,
    Universities in Early Modern Europe, 1500–1800, 483.
85 Roger Hahn, *The Anatomy of a Scientific Institution: The Paris Academy of
    Scientists, 1666–1803* (Berkeley: University of California Press, 1968), 46–7.
86 Dorothy Stimson, *Scientists and Amateurs: A History of the Royal Society* (New
    York: Greenwood Press, 1968), 161–2.
87 Voltaire, *Philosophic Letters*, trans. Ernest Dilworth (Indianapolis: Bobbs-
    Merrill, 1961), 114.
88 Rousseau, *Considérations sur le Gouvernement de Pologne*, in Bernard
    Gagnebin and Marcel Raymond, ed., *Oeuvres Complètes de Jean-Jacques Rousseau*,
    t.3 (Paris: Gallimard-Pléiade, 1964), 965; also, *Du Contrat social*, IV.iv.
89 Wood, *Radicalism of the American Revolution*, 74, 76; *The Americanization of
    Benjamin Franklin* (New York: Penguin 2004), 26.
90 Adam Smith, *The Wealth of Nations*, I.x.1.
91 Jean-Jacques Rousseau, *The First and Second Discourses*, ed. Roger D.
    Masters (New York: St. Martin's Press, 1964), 212.

2 Enlightenment and Print Culture

1 Adam Smith, *An Inquiry into the Nature and Causes of the Wealth of Nations*, ed.
    R.H. Campbell and A.S. Skinner (Oxford: Clarendon, 1976), I.x.i; vol.1, 149.
2 Hume blamed his failure to secure a university position on Argyll, as we
    shall see in chapter 5. The 3rd Duke of Argyll, perhaps the central figure
    in the Scottish Enlightenment, has yet to have found a biographer. It is to
    be hoped that Roger Emerson will repair this crying need in the near
    future. See Roger L. Emerson, 'Lord Bute and the Scottish Universities
    1760–1792,' in Karl W. Schweizer, *Lord Bute: Essays in Re-interpretation*
    (Leicester: Leicester University Press, 1988), 171; and 'How Not to Deal
    with Enlightenments,' *Historically Speaking*, 3:3 (2002): 5–7. James Lees-
    Milne, in *Earls of Creation: Five Great Patrons of Eighteenth-Century Art*

(London: Hamish Hamilton, 1962), 12, writes that he might have selected Argyll in addition to Bathurst, Pembroke, Burlington, Oxford, and Leicester as one of the earls of creation: 'But one has to draw the line somewhere.'

3 *Voltaire's Correspondence*, ed. Theodore Besterman, letter 8795 (Geneva: Institut et Musée Voltaire, 1969), 45:71.

4 Ernest Campbell Mossner, *The Life of David Hume* (Austin: University of Texas Press, 1954), 4.

5 Georges, Vicomte d'Avenel, *Les riches depuis sept cent ans: Revenus et Bénéfices, Appointements et Honoraires* (Paris: Armand Colin, 1909), 301–2.

6 In *Letters concerning the Present State of England. Particularly respecting the Politics, Arts, Manners and Literature of the Times* (London: J. Almon, 1772), 321–2, George III is praised for having given 'more rewards to merit than half a score of his predecessors.' In support of this claim, the work cites 'Mr. *Hume*, the historian; who, from a very private fortune, has been thrown to affluence by several very lucrative posts.'

7 Lord Fitzmaurice, *Life of William Earl of Shelburne* (London: Macmillan, 1912), 16.

8 John Lough, *Writer and Public in France from the Middle Ages to the Present Day* (Oxford: Clarendon, 1978), 14. Also Karl Julius Holzknecht, *Literary Patronage in the Middle Ages* (New York: Octagon, 1966); and d'Avenel, *Les Riches depuis sept cent ans.*

9 Holzknecht, *Literary Patronage*, 26–31; James Carney, *The Irish Bardic Poet: A Study in the Relationship of Poet and Patron* (Dublin: Dolmen Press, 1967), 5–6.

10 Holzknecht, *Literary Patronage*, 26.

11 Ibid., 236.

12 Christine de Pisan, *Oeuvres poétiques*, t.1 (Paris: Firmin Didot, 1886), 208–33; Enid McLeod, *The Order of the Rose: The Life and Ideas of Christine de Pizan* (London: Chatto and Windus, 1976), 49–52, 96, 106; Lough, *Writer and Public in France*, 19.

13 Ann K. Warren, *Anchorites and their Patrons in Medieval England* (Berkeley: University of California Press, 1985), 127.

14 Hilary M. Carey, *Courting Disaster: Astrology at the English Court and University in the Later Middle Ages* (London: Macmillan, 1992), 154.

15 David Zaret, *Origins of Democratic Culture: Printing, Petitions and the Public Sphere in Early-Modern England* (Princeton, N.J.: Princeton University Press, 2000), 13.

16 Lucien Fevre and Henri-Jean Martin, *The Coming of the Book: The Impact of Printing, 1450–1800*, trans. David Gerard (London: New Left Books, 1976), 291–2.

17 *The Acts and Monuments of John Foxe*, cited in Eamon Duffy, *The Stripping of the Altars: Traditional Religion in England, 1400–1580* (New Haven, Conn.: Yale University Press, 1992), 77. Duffy argues that, despite Foxe, the English press largely published Catholic devotional works during the early sixteenth century.

18 Elizabeth Eisenstein, *Print Culture and Enlightenment Thought* (Chapel Hill: University of North Carolina Press, 1986), 6, 15.

19 Peter Burke, *A Social History of Knowledge from Gutenberg to Diderot* (Oxford: Polity, 2000), 22.

20 Desiderius Erasmus, *The Education of a Christian Prince*, trans. Neil M. Cheshire and Michael J. Health (Cambridge: Cambridge University Press, 1997), 3.

21 Ibid., 58, 111, 122.

22 Léon-Ernest Halkin, *Erasmus: A Critical Biography*, trans. John Tonkin (Oxford: Blackwell, 1993), 93; Cornelis Augustijn, *Erasmus: His Life, Works, and Influence*, trans. J.C. Grayson (Toronto: University of Toronto Press, 1991), 35; Lisa Jardine, *Erasmus, Man of Letters: The Construction of Charisma in Print* (Princeton, N.J.: Princeton University Press, 1993), 73.

23 John Lord Sheffield, ed., *The Miscellaneous Works of Edward Gibbon*, vol.5 (London: John Murray, 1814), 257.

24 William Robertson, *The History of the Reign of the Emperor Charles V*, in *Works*, vol.5 (London: Baldwyn, 1818), 158.

25 Francis Bacon, *The Advancement of Learning*, ed. Michael Kiernan (Oxford: Clarendon, 2000), 20.

26 Ibid., 14–15, 20–1.

27 Roger Chartier, *Forms and Meanings: Texts, Performances and Audiences from Codex to Computer* (Philadelphia: University of Pennsylvania Press, 1995), 35–6.

28 Arthur F. Marotti, 'Patronage, Poetry and Print,' in *The Yearbook of English Studies: Politics, Patronage and Literature in England*, vol.21 (Leeds: Modern Humanities Research Association, 1991), 1–3.

29 Martin Butler, "We Are One Mans All": Jonson's *The Gipsies Metamorphosed*,' in *Yearbook of English Studies*, 21:253.

30 Lough, *Writer and Public in France*, 101.

31 Sidney Lee, ed., *The Dictionary of National Biography*, vol.51 (London: Smith, Elder, 1897), 364–76.

32 Robert C. Evans, *Ben Jonson and the Poetics of Patronage* (Lewisburg, Penn.: Bucknell University Press, 1989).

33 Deborah C. Payne, 'Patronage and the Dramatic Marketplace under Charles I and II,' and Kathleen E. McLuskie, 'The Poets' Royal Exchange: Patronage and Commerce in Early Modern Drama,' in *Yearbook of English Studies*, 21:53, 138–9. See also Linda Levy Peck, *Court Patronage and Corruption in Early Stuart England* (Boston: Unwin Hyman, 1990), 3–10.

34 William Godwin, *History of the Commonwealth of England from Its Commencement to the Restoration of Charles the Second*, vol.1 (London: Henry Colburn, 1824), 78–9.

35 Roger Chartier, *The Order of Books*, trans. Lydia G. Cochrane (Cambridge: Polity Press, 1994), 43.

36 Lough, *Writer and Public in France*, 97–103; C.E.J. Caldicott, *La Carrière de Molière: entre protecteurs et éditeurs* (Amsterdam: Rodopi, 1998), 27, 41, 158–72; Chartier, *Forms and Meanings*, 37. Sharon Kettering, *Patrons, Brokers, and Clients in Seventeenth-Century France* (Oxford: Oxford University Press, 1986), does not discuss literary patronage specifically but shows how patronage was key to the centralization of France under Richelieu, Mazarin, and Colbert, as well as explaining how provincial print cultures came to be centred in Paris in the seventeenth century.

37 Roger Chartier, *Lectures et Lecteurs dans la France d'ancien régime* (Paris: Éditions du seuil, 1987), chapters 2–4; François Furèt and Jacques Ozouf: *Reading and Writing: Literacy in France from Calvin to Jules Ferry* (Cambridge: Cambridge University Press, 1982).

38 John E.N. Hersey, *Voltaire* (London: Constable, 1976), 15.

39 René Pomeau, *On a voulu l'enterrer*, t.5, *Voltaire en son temps* (Oxford: Voltaire Foundation, 1994), 366.

40 Paul Korshin, 'Types of Eighteenth-Century Literary Patronage,' *Eighteenth-Century Studies*, 7 (1974): 454–8.

41 F.J.G. Robinson and P.J. Wallis, *Book Subscription Lists: A Revised Guide* (Newcastle upon Tyne: Harold Hill, 1975), 1.

42 W.A. Speck, 'Politicians, Peers, and Publication by Subscription, 1700–1750,' in Isobel Rivers, *Books and Their Readers in Eighteenth-Century England* (Leicester: Leicester University Press, 1982), 48.

43 *Boswell's Life of Johnson*, vol.3, ed. George Birkbeck Hill (Oxford: Clarendon, 1887), 347.

44 Cited in Alvin Kernan, *Printing Technology, Letters and Samuel Johnson* (Princeton, N.J.: Princeton University Press, 1987), 10.

45 Ibid., 65-6; John Valdemir Price, 'The Reading of Philosophic Literature,' in Rivers, ed., *Books and Their Readers*, 165.

46 Robert Darnton, *The Business of Enlightenment: A Publishing History of the Encyclopédie, 1775–1800* (Cambridge, Mass.: Belknap Press, 1979), chapters 1–2.

47 Neil McKendrick, John Brewer, and J.H. Plumb, *The Birth of a Consumer Society: The Commercialization of Eighteenth-Century England* (London: Europa Publications 1982), 224–5.

48 Speck, 'Politicians, Peers, and Publication,' 66.

49 Roy M. Wiles, *Serial Publication in England before 1750* (Cambridge: Cambridge University Press, 1957), chapters 1–2.

50 Cited in Jeremy Black, *The English Press of the Eighteenth Century* (London: Croom Helm, 1987), 1.

51 James Raven, 'From Promotion to Proscription: Arrangements for Reading and Eighteenth-Century Libraries,' in James Raven, Helen Small, and Naomi Tadmor, eds., *The Practice and Representation of Reading in England before 1750* (Cambridge: Cambridge University Press, 1996), 175.

52 Lough, *Writer and Public in France*, 214.

53 Robert Darnton, *The Literary Underground of the Old Regime* (Cambridge, Mass.: Harvard University Press, 1982), 7.

54 *The Gray's-Inn Journal*, vol.2 (London: W. Faden for P. Vaillant, 1756), 56–8. The author of *Letters concerning the Present State of England*, 332–3, agreed with Murphy that the difference between the literature of the early and mid-eighteenth-centuries was attributable to superior patronage rather than superior talent.

55 Marcus Wood, '"The Abolition Blunderbuss": Free Publishing and British Abolition Propaganda,' in James Raven, ed., *Free Print and Non-Commercial Publishing since 1700* (Aldershot, U.K.: Ashgate, 2000), 67–92.

56 David Money, 'Free Flattery or Servile Tribute? Oxford and Cambridge Commemorative Poetry in the Seventeenth and Eighteenth Centuries,' in ibid., 48–66.

57 A.S. Collins, *The Profession of Letters* (London: George Routledge and Sons, 1928), 45–6.

58 Paula R. Backscheider, *Daniel Defoe: His Life* (Baltimore: Johns Hopkins University Press, 1989), 463.

59 Ibid., 58–9, 110–13, 181–2, 232, 248, 349–51, 384; Laurence Hanson, *Government and the Press, 1695–1763* (London: Humphrey Milford, 1936), 64–96, 102–3.

60 Backscheider, *Daniel Defoe*, 196.

61 Isaac D'Israeli, *Calamities of Authors; Including Some Inquiries respecting Their Moral and Literary Characters* (New York: James Eastburn, 1812), 14, 35–7.

62 *Letters concerning the Present State of England*, 321.

63 Collins, *Profession of Letters*, 11.
64 Cited in Roy Porter, *The Creation of the Modern Mind: The Untold Story of the British Enlightenment* (New York: W.W. Norton, 2000), 82.
65 Martin C. and Ruth R. Battestin, *Henry Fielding: A Life* (London: Routledge 1989), 116.
66 Frank Jenkins, *Architect and Patron: A Survey of Professional Relations and Practice from the Sixteenth Century to the Present Day* (London: Oxford University Press, 1961), xiii.
67 *Boswell's Life of Johnson*, vol.2: 313.
68 Jean-Jacques Rousseau, *The Confessions and Correspondence*, in Christopher Kelly, Roger D. Masters, and Peter G. Stillman, eds., *The Collected Writings of Rousseau*, vol.5 (Hanover, N.H.: University Press of New England, 1990), 338.
69 Raymond Birn, 'Rousseau et ses éditeurs,' *Revue d'histoire moderne et contemporaine*, 40 (1993): 120–36; *Forging Rousseau: Print, Commerce and Cultural Manipulation in the Late Enlightenment* (Oxford: Voltaire Foundation, 2001), 1–2, 9, 30–3.
70 Geoffrey Turnovsky, 'The Enlightenment Literary Market: Rousseau, Authorship, and the Book Trade,' *Eighteenth-Century Studies* 3 (2003): 391.
71 Paul Bénichou, *The Consecration of the Writer, 1750–1830*, trans. Mark K. Jensen (Lincoln: University of Nebraska Press, 1999), 14.
72 Robert Darnton, *Literary Underground of the Old Regime*, chapters 1–2, distinguishes the High Enlightenment (the denizens of aristocratic salons) from the Low Enlightenment (the hack writers, those without patronage, who inhabited Parisian cafés) and concludes that the latter, not the former, were instrumental in the French Revolution. Similarly, the Scottish Enlightenment, patronized by Whig magnates, did not support Charles Edward Stuart in 1745.
73 See dedications to Thomas Odell, *The Patron; or, the Statesman's Opera* (Dublin: S. Powell, 1729), and Samuel Foote, *The Patron: A Comedy in Three Acts* (London: P. Vaillant, 1774).
74 Robert Dodsley, *The Correspondence of Robert Dodsley 1733–64*, ed. James E. Turney (Cambridge: Cambridge University Press, 1988), 255.
75 Paul Fussell, *Samuel Johnson and the Life of Writing* (New York: Harcourt Brace Jovanovich, 1971), 174.
76 Cited in James Raven, *Judging New Wealth: Popular Publishing and Responses to Commerce in England, 1750–1800* (Oxford: Clarendon, 1992), 66.
77 Black, *English Press of the Eighteenth Century*, 246–7.
78 William B. Todd, 'Introduction,' in Paul Langford, T.O. McLoughlin, and James T. Boulton, eds., *The Writings and Speeches of Edmund Burke*, vol.1 (Oxford: Clarendon, 1997), 10.

79 Terry Belanger, 'Publishers and Writers in Eighteenth-Century England,' in Rivers, ed., *Books and Their Readers*, 17–22.

80 Chartier, *The Order of Books*, x.

81 Jean Guéhenno, *Jean-Jacques Rousseau* (New York: Columbia University Press, 1967), 263.

82 Dustin Griffin, *Literary Patronage in England, 1650–1800* (Cambridge: Cambridge University Press, 1996), 10, 68, 282.

83 Chrétien-Guillaume Lamoignon de Malesherbes, *Mémoires sur la librairie et sur la liberté de la presse (1788)* (Genève: Slatkine, 1969), 343.

84 Kernan, *Printing Technology, Letters and Samuel Johnson*, 105. D'Alembert's *Essai* is found in *Oeuvres Complètes de D'Alembert* (Genève: Slatkine, 1967), t.4:335–73.

85 Oliver Goldsmith, *Present State of Polite Learning*, cited in *Boswell's Life of Johnson*, 1:372.

86 Roger Chartier, 'The Man of Letters,' in Michel Vovelle, ed., *Enlightenment Portraits*, trans. Lydia G. Cochrane (Chicago: University of Chicago Press, 1997), 173.

87 William Shaw, *Memoirs of the Life and Writings of the Late Dr. Samuel Johnson (1785)* (New York: Garland, 1974), 74–5.

88 Henry Curwen, *A History of Booksellers: The Old and the New* (London: Chatto and Windus, 1874), 482.

89 Griffin, *Literary Patronage*, 257.

90 Voltaire, *The Age of Lewis XIV*, trans. T. Nugent (London: R. Dodsley, 1772), 172.

91 Eisenstein, *Print Culture*, 16.

92 Robert Shackleton, *Censure and Censorship: Impediments to Free Publication in the Age of Enlightenment* (Austin, Texas: Humanities Research Center, 1975), 12.

93 Lough, *Writer and Public in France*, 187.

94 J.-P. Belin, *Le Commerce des livres prohibés à Paris de 1750 à 1789* (Paris 1913; repr. New York: Burt Franklin, 1962), 109.

95 Denis Diderot, *Lettre sur le commerce de la librairie* (Paris: Grasset, 1937), 151.

96 Daniel Roche, 'Censorship and the Publishing Business,' in Robert Darnton and Daniel Roche, *The Press in France, 1775–1800* (Berkeley: University of California Press 1989), 25.

97 Shackleton, *Censure and Censorship*, 16.

98 Since most of the avenues for a life of scholarship and thought were in the hands of the Church of England, where comfortable 'livings' for gentlemen emerged in the eighteenth century, and since, from the Restoration on, plebeians ceased to go to Oxford or Cambridge, one

might say that patronage, as a hand extended to plebeians from above, was replaced by an exchange of favours among the gentry and aristocracy. Another way of putting this is that patron-client relationships became patronage as patrician cronyism.

99 Black, *English Press of the Eighteenth Century*, 246–7.

100 Voltaire, *Philosophical Letters*, trans. Ernest Dilworth (Indianapolis: Bobbs-Merrill, 1961), 58.

101 Diderot, *Lettre sur le commerce*, 156.

102 Rousseau, *Confessions*, 341.

103 Robert E. Sullivan, *John Toland and the Deist Controversy* (Cambridge, Mass.: Harvard University Press, 1982), 11.

104 Fredrick Seaton Siebert, *Freedom of the Press in England, 1476–1776: The Rise and Deline of Government Controls* (Urbana: University of Illinois Press, 1952), 267; Paul K. Monod, *Jacobitism and the English People, 1688–1788* (Cambridge: Cambridge University Press, 1989), 20, 40, 101, 121.

105 Laurence Hanson, *Government and the Press, 1695–1763* (London: Humphrey Milford, 1936), chapter 3.

106 Brewer, in McKendrick, Brewer, and Plumb, *Birth of Consumer Society*, 260; Alan Downie, 'The Growth of Government Toleration of the Press to 1790,' in Robin Myers and Michael Harris, eds., *Development of the English Book Trade, 1700–1899* (Oxford: Oxford Polytechnic Press, 1982), 37.

107 Peter Brown, *The Chathamites: A Study in the Relationship between Personalities and Ideas in the Second Half of the Eighteenth Century* (London: Macmillan, 1967), 422.

108 Battestin, *Henry Fielding*, 228.

109 Baldesar Castiglione, *The Book of the Courtier*, trans. Charles S. Singleton (New York: Anchor Books, 1959), II.46:146.

110 Hanson, *Government and the Press*, 2.

111 Battestin, *Henry Fielding*, 116.

112 Ibid., 130.

113 A parallel with Fielding's life can be found in chapter 20 of *The Parasite* (London: G. Burnet, 1765), entitled 'A Curious Dialogue That Really Occurred between a Patron and an Author,' in which the author demands pensions or else he will have to have recourse to libels.

114 Robert Darnton, *The Corpus of Clandestine Literature in France, 1769–1789* (New York: W.W. Norton, 1995).

115 Hanson, *Government and the Press*, 68.

116 John Feather, *A History of British Publishing* (London: Croom Helm, 1988), chapter 6.

117 Siebert, *Freedom of the Press*, 314.

118 Robert M. Adams, 'In Search of Baron Somers,' in Perez Zagorin, ed., *Culture and Politics from Puritanism to the Enlightenment* (Berkeley: University of California Press, 1980), 175–6, 185–7, 196–7.
119 John Toland, *The Life of John Milton, with Amytor* (London: A. Millar, 1761), 136, 138.
120 Price, 'Reading of Philosophical Literature,' in Rivers ed., *Books and Their Readers*, 165, 173.

3 Seneca in the Age of Frederick and Catherine

1 Richard Fargher, *Life and Letters in France: The Eighteenth Century* (New York: Charles Scribner's Sons, 1970), 148.
2 G.M. Ross, 'Seneca's Philosophic Influence,' in C.D.N. Costa, ed., *Seneca* (London: Routledge and Kegan Paul, 1974), 116–65. Seneca was widely admired by poets and dramatists of the seventeenth century. See John Wallace, 'John Dryden's Plays and the Conception of a Heroic Society,' in Perez Zagorin, ed., *Culture and Politics from Puritanism to the Enlightenment* (Berkeley: University of California Press, 1980), 113–34, and Linda Levy Peck, 'Benefits, Brokers and Beneficiaries: The Culture of Exchange in Seventeenth-Century England,' in B.Y. Kunze and D.D. Brautigan, eds., *Court, Country and Culture: Essays on Early Modern British History in Honor of Perez Zagorin* (Rochester: University of Rochester Press, 1992), 109–27.
3 Roger L'Estrange, *Seneca's Morals by Way of Abstract: Of Benefits* (London: Thomas Newcomb, 1678), 32.
4 John Lough, *Writer and Public in France from the Middle Ages to the Present Day* (Oxford: Clarendon, 1978), 102–7.
5 Roger Hahn, *The Anatomy of a Scientific Institution: The Paris Academy of Scientists, 1666–1803* (Berkeley: University of California Press, 1968), 9.
6 *L'Encyclopédie ou Dictionnaire Raisonné des Sciences des Arts et des Métiers*, t.7:599.
7 Voltaire, *Philosophical Letters*, trans. Ernest Dilworth (Indianapolis: Bobbs-Merrill, 1961), 36.
8 Julien Offray de la Mettrie, *Anti-Seneca or the Soveriegn Good*, in *Machine Man and Other Writings*, trans. Ann Thomson (Cambridge: Cambridge University Press, 1996), 119.
9 Ibid., 126.
10 Ibid., 123.
11 Diderot, *Oeuvres Complètes*, ed. Roger Lewinter (Paris: Société encyclopédique française et le Club français du livre, 1972), t.12:641; t.13:463.

12 La Mettrie, *Anti-Seneca or the Sovereign Good*, 135.

13 Fontenoy was hailed as a great victory for the French over the English, although French deaths were four times the British total, and Voltaire's glorification of it in a patriotic poem helped to get him into the *Académie Française*, while La Mettrie attended to the war wounded and learned how the mind is affected by shrapnel in the brain and lacerated nerves. La Mettrie's *Histoire naturelle de l'âme*, as Frederick wrote, exposed him to clerical wrath; the parlement of July 1746 ordered his work shredded and burned and forced him into permanent exile in Prussia.

14 Frederick's eulogy in Julian Offray de La Mettrie, *Man a Machine*, trans. M.W. Collins (Chicago: Open Court, 1927), xiv, xvii.

15 Voltaire, *Memoires*, in *Oeuvres Complètes de Voltaire* (Paris: Lequien, 1820), t.1:341. Voltaire's account may be exaggerated by the following facts: he liked a good story, he distrusted the overt atheism and materialism of La Mettrie – he was, as René Pomeau asserts, like Rameau's nephew to Diderot, a truth-telling scalliwag; and La Mettrie was Voltaire's rival for the love and protection of Mme Du Châtelet and the protection of Frederick. The moral of Voltaire's story is that La Mettrie practised his materialist or sensualist philosophy, and died as the result of it. La Mettrie's fellow materialist, Diderot, wanted to distance himself from the epicurean La Mettrie and so used Voltaire's account to support his assessment of La Mettrie's *Anti-Sénèque*.

16 *Letters of Voltaire and Frederick the Great*, trans. Richard Aldington (London: Routledge, 1927), 72.

17 Denis Diderot's *Essai sur la vie de Sénèque le philosophe, sur ses écrits, et sur les règnes de Claude et de Néron* is found in *Oeuvres Complètes*, t.12:509–744; and his *Essai sur les règnes de Claude et de Néron, et sur les moeurs et les écrits de Sénèque, pour servir d'introduction à la lecture de ce philosophe* is in *Oeuvres Complètes*, t.13:279–626.

18 Lucius Annaeus Seneca, *De Beneficiis, On Benefits*, III.xviii.1, trans. John W. Bashore, in *Moral Essays*, vol.3 (Cambridge: Harvard University Press, 1935), 159.

19 Marcus Tullius Cicero, *The Offices*, trans. Thomas Lockman (London: J.M. Dent, 1960), I.iii–I.vii.

20 G.E.M. de Ste. Croix, 'Suffragium: From Vote to Patronage,' *British Journal of Sociology*, 5 (1974): 40.

21 Edmund Burke, *Reflections on the Revolution in France*, ed. L.G. Mitchell (Oxford: Oxford University Press, 1993), 144.

22 Richard P. Saller, *Personal Patronage under the Early Empire* (Cambridge: Cambridge University Press, 1982), 4.

23 Ronald Weissman, 'Taking Patronage Seriously: Mediterranean Values and Renaissance Society,' in F.W. Kent, Patricia Simon, and J.C. Eade, eds., *Patronage, Art, and Society in Renaissance Italy* (Oxford: Clarendon, 1987), 35.

24 Miriam T. Griffin, *Seneca: A Philosopher in Politics* (Oxford: Clarendon, 1976), 237. The role of patronage in fostering the illusion of class collaborationism is discussed in Sydel Silverman, 'Patronage as Myth,' and James Scott, 'Patronage as Exploitation,' in Ernest Gellner and John Waterbury, eds., *Patrons and Clients in Mediterranean Societies* (London: Duckworth, 1977), 7–39.

25 Charles Louis de Secondat, Baron de Montesquieu, *Lettres Persanes*, ed. Paul Vernière (Paris: Garnier, 1960), 215.

26 By 'moment,' I mean the Hegelian sense of a dynamic moment within an intellectual system, and not the momentous moment of Machiavellian founding – hence, the antithesis with Pocock's Machiavellian moment should not be interpreted as denoting an acceptance of Pocock's connotations of time and history making.

27 Peter France, *Politeness and Its Discontents: Problems in French Classical Culture* (Cambridge: Cambridge University Press, 1992), 128.

28 J.G.A. Pocock equates 'the age of Enlightenment' with that of 'the standing army' in *Barbarism and Religion: The First Decline and Fall*, vol.3 (Cambridge: Cambridge University Press, 2003), 310–11.

29 *The Works of William Robertson*, vol.4 (London: Baldwyn, 1818), 230.

30 Voltaire, 'Equality' in *Philosophical Dictionary*, trans. Peter Gay (New York: Basic Books, 1962), 246.

31 Ibid., 418.

32 *The Complete Works of Voltaire*, ed. Theodore Besterman (Oxford: Voltaire Foundation, 1975), 124:160. Voltaire also wrote to Frederick on 9 December 1774: 'Your Majesty consoles with a stroke of the pen for the outcries of the superstitious and implacable rabble.'

33 *Voltaire and Catherine the Great: Selected Correspondence*, trans. A. Lentin (Cambridge, U.K.: Oriental Research Partners, 1974), 14.

34 Ibid., 14; Robert E. McGrew, *Paul 1 of Russia, 1754–1801* (Oxford: Clarendon, 1992), 41.

35 Diderot, *Essai sur les règnes de Claude et de Néron*, in *Oeuvres Complètes*, t.13:324.

36 Robert Niklaus, *A Literary History of France: The Eighteenth Century, 1715–1789* (London: Ernest Benn, 1970), 162; David P. Bien, *The Calas Affair: Persecution, Toleration, and Heresy in Eighteenth-Century Toulouse* (Princeton, N.J.: Princeton University Press, 1960).

37 Bien, *The Calas Affair*, 82.
38 Fargher, *Life and Letters in France*, 85.
39 *Letters of Voltaire and Frederick the Great*, 29, 75, 131.
40 Cited in Peter Gay, *Voltaire's Politics: The Poet as Realist* (Princeton, N.J.: Princeton University Press, 1959), 147.
41 Nancy Mitford, *Madame de Pompadour* (London: Hamish Hamilton, 1968), 260.
42 René Pomeau et Christiane Mervaud, *De la Cour au jardin* (Oxford: Voltaire Foundation, 1991), 346.
43 *Letters of Voltaire and Frederick the Great*, 31.
44 Joseph de Maistre, *Against Rousseau*, trans. Richard A. Lebrun (Montreal: McGill-Queen's University Press, 1996), 100, 149.
45 Saller, *Personal Patronage*, 23, 207.
46 Voltaire, *Essai sur les moeurs et l'esprit des nations et sur les principaux faits de histoire depuis Charlemagne jusqu' à Louis XIII* (Paris: Garnier, 1963), t.1:68–70, 217–20; t.2:286.
47 D. McAlendon, 'Senatorial Opposition to Claudius and Nero,' *American Journal of Philology*, 77 (1956): 131.
48 Miriam T. Griffin, *Seneca: A Philosopher in Politics* (Oxford: Clarendon, 1976), 286.
49 J.P. Sullivan, *Literature and Politics in the Age of Nero* (Ithaca, N.Y.: Cornell University Press, 1985), 19.
50 Jocelyn M.C. Toynbee, 'Dictators and Philosophers in the First Century A.D.,' *Greece and Rome*, 13 (1944): 46–9. Musonius Rufus was banished by Nero, Thraesea Paetus was killed by Nero for his abstention from public life, and Seneca was ordered to kill himself for his association with Pisonian conspirators against Nero.
51 Ronald Syme, 'Some Friends of the Caesars,' *American Journal of Philology*, 77 (1956): 264.
52 Miriam T. Griffin, *Nero: The End of a Dynasty* (New Haven, Conn.: Yale University Press, 1984), 95.
53 Saller, *Personal Patronage*, 119.
54 Brad Inwood, 'Politics and Paradox in Seneca's *De beneficiis*,' in André Laks and Malcolm Schofield eds., *Justice and Generosity: Studies in Hellenistic Social and Political Philosophy* (Cambridge: Cambridge University Press, 1995), 252–4.
55 Ibid., 19.
56 Joseph Antony Amato, *Guilt and Gratitude: A Study of the Origins of Contemporary Conscience* (Westport, Conn.: Greenwood Press, 1982), xviii–xix.

57 Bernard W. Henderson, in *The Life and Principate of the Emperor Nero* (Philadelphia: J.B. Lippincott, 1903), 279–81, accuses Seneca of ingratitude for participating in the Pisonian conspiracy; Gerard Walter, in *Nero*, trans. Emma Craufurd (London: Allen and Unwin, 1957), chapter 10, claims that Seneca knew that his brother, Mela, and Mela's son, Lucan, wanted to place Seneca on the throne; Vasily Rudich, in *Dissidence and Literature under Nero: The Price of Rhetoricization* (London: Routledge, 1997), 104–5, writes that Seneca was not actively involved in the conspiracy but knew of it.

58 Edward Hyde, Earl of Clarendon, *A Brief View and Survey of the Dangerous and Pernicious Errors to Church and State, in Mr. Hobbes's Book, Entitled Leviathan* (Oxford: Printed at the Theater, 1676), 181–2.

59 *The Correspondence of John Locke*, ed. E.S. De Beer (Oxford: Clarendon, 1976), 2:662.

60 Jean S. Yolton, ed., *A Locke Miscellany: Locke Biography and Criticism for All* (Bristol: Thoemmes, 1990), 255.

61 Christopher Kelly, Roger D. Masters, and Peter G. Stillman, eds. *The Collected Writings of Rousseau*, vol.5, trans. Christopher Kelly (Hanover, N.H.: University Press of New England, 1995), 573, 582.

62 Cited in Amato, *Guilt and Gratitude*, 27. Ralph W. Emerson's essay 'Gifts' echoed this sentiment: 'It is not the office of a man to receive gifts ... We wish to be self-sustained. We do not forgive a giver. The hand that feeds us is in some danger of being bitten.'

63 Edmund Burke, *Letter to a Noble Lord*, in *The Works*, vol.8 (London: Rivington, 1826), 51.

64 'What Is Enlightenment?' in *Kant's Political Writings*, ed. Hans Reiss, trans. H.B. Nisbet (Cambridge: Cambridge University Press, 1970), 58–9.

65 Diderot, *Regrets at Parting with my Old Dressing Gown*, in *Rameau's Nephew and Other Works*, trans. Jacques Barzun and Ralph H. Bowen (Indianapolis: Hackett, 2001), 309–17.

66 Ibid., 251; Toynbee, 'Dictators and Philosophers,' 46; Sullivan, *Literature and Politics*, 120; Rudich, *Dissidence and Literature*, 46, 57–66; Manfred Fuhrmann, *Seneca und Kaiser Nero: Eine Biographie* (Berlin: Alexander Fest, 1997), 175–96.

67 Lucius Annaeus Seneca, *Ad Lucilium: Epistulae Morales*, trans. Richard M. Gummere (London: William Heinemann, 1920), 2:105, 109–11.

68 John Lough, *The Philosophes and Post-Revolutionary France* (Oxford: Clarendon, 1982), 11.

69 Robert Darnton, *The Business of Enlightenment: A Publishing History of the Encylopédie, 1775–1800* (Cambridge, Mass.: Belnap Press, 1979), 8.

70 Kant, 'What Is Enlightenment?', 59.
71 Cited in G.P. Gooch, *Frederick the Great: The Ruler, The Writer, The Man* (Hamden, Conn.: Archon Books, 1962), 144; T.C.W. Blanning, 'Frederick the Great and Enlightened Absolutism,' in H.M. Scott ed., *Enlightened Absolutism* (Ann Arbor: University of Michigan Press, 1990), 282.
72 David Fraser, *Frederick the Great: King of Prussia* (London: Allen Lane, 2000), 488. Rousseau later regretted his rustic arrogance and considered Frederick to be enlightened and worthy of being his patron.
73 Seneca, *Ad Lucilium*, 1:89.
74 Pierre C. Oustinoff, 'Notes on Diderot's Fortunes in Russia,' *Diderot Studies*, 1 (1949): 122.
75 Jeremy Bentham, *A Fragment on Government*, ed. J.H. Burns and H.L.A. Hart (Cambridge: Cambridge University Press, 1988), 10.
76 Diderot, *Oeuvres Complètes*, t.10:249.
77 Amato, *Guilt and Gratitude*, 63.
78 Edward Andrew, *Protestant Conscience, Enlightenment Reason and Modern Subjectivity* (Toronto: University of Toronto Press, 2001), chapters 6–7.
79 John Millar, *An Historical View of the English Government* (Dublin: Zachariah Jackson, 1789), 8.
80 René Pomeau, *On a voulu l'enterrer*, t.5 *Voltaire en Son Temps* (Oxford: Voltaire Foundation, 1994), 55–6, 206.
81 Daniel Brewer, *The Discourse of Enlightenment in Eighteenth-Century France: Diderot and the Art of Philosophizing* (Cambridge: Cambridge University Press, 1990), 15.
82 Jean Starobinski, *Blessings in Disguise; Or, the Morality of Evil* (Cambridge, Mass.: Harvard University Press, 1995), 45.
83 *The Complete Writings of Thomas Paine*, ed. Philip Foner (New York: Citadel Press, 1945), 1246.
84 Edward Gibbon, *Memoirs*, vol.1 (London: Hunt and Clarke, 1817), 256.
85 Ibid., 255; also 2:243–4. Interestingly, one page after asserting that Gibbon lived independent of patrons, J.G.A. Pocock, in *Barbarism and Religion*, 3:7–8, refers to Lord North as Gibbon's patron.

4 Patronage and the Modes of Liberal Tolerance: Bayle, Care, and Locke

1 Voltaire, *Philosophical Dictionary*, trans. Peter Gay (New York: Basic Books, 1962), 2:421.
2 *The Miscellaneous Works of Edward Gibbon, Esq. In 5 Volumes*, ed. John Lord Sheffield (London: John Murray, 1814), 1:69.

3 Léo Pierre Courtines, *Bayle's Relations with England and the English* (New York: Columbia University Press, 1938), 118.

4 H.C. Hazewinkel, 'Pierre Bayle à Rotterdam,' in Paul Dibon ed., *Pierre Bayle: Le Philosophe de Rotterdam* (Paris: Vrin, 1959), 21–4.

5 Howard Robinson, in *Bayle the Sceptic* (New York: Columbia University Press, 1931), H.T. Mason, in *Pierre Bayle and Voltaire* (Oxford: Oxford University Press, 1963), and Craig B. Brush, in *Montaigne and Bayle: Variations on the Theme of Scepticism* (The Hague: Martinus Nijhoff, 1966), present the case for placing Bayle in the sceptical tradition from Montaigne to Voltaire; however, following Elisabeth Labrouse's *Pierre Bayle* (La Haye: Martinus Nijhoff, 1963), John Kilcullen, in *Sincerity and Truth: Essays on Arnauld, Bayle and Toleration* (Oxford: Clarendon, 1988), and Thomas M. Lennon, in *Reading Bayle* (Toronto: University of Toronto Press, 1999), have placed greater emphasis on Bayle's inner certainty. Bayle was sceptical in that he thought conscience or the inner light could err but was Protestant in that he was certain that individuals should rely on their own judgment, however fallible, rather than any external authority and that no better guide than conscience is available to human beings. That is, Bayle's position combined a belief in the sanctity of one's own judgment with scepticism about the correctness of moral judgment, one's own or that of the church, canon lawyers, and philosophers.

6 *Miscellaneous Works of Edward Gibbon*, 1:69–70.

7 Robinson, *Bayle the Sceptic*, 43, 56.

8 Pierre Bayle, *Critique générale de l'Histoire du Calvinisme de Mr. Maimbourg* (Ville-Franche: Pierre le Blanc, 1683), 1, 3, 84.

9 Pierre Bayle, *An Historical and Critical Dictionary*, trans. P. DesMaiseaux et al. (London: C. Harper et al., 1710), 4:2785–8.

10 Pierre Bayle, *A General Dictionary*, trans. P. DesMaiseaux *et al.* (London: James Bettenham, 1734–41), 6:555.

11 Bayle, *Historical and Critical Dictionary*, 2797. Bayle wrote that Mersenne attempted to convert Hobbes on his deathbed and Hobbes responded that Mersenne 'can entertain me in a more agreeable manner. When did you see Mr. Gassendi?' (3:1679). Distinguishing himself from Averroes, who died 'as a philosopher' – not a believer – Bayle wrote to Jean Terson: 'Je meurs en Philosophe Chrétien, persuadé et pénétré des bontés et de la miséricorde de Dieu .' See Labrousse, *Pierre Bayle*, 1:267–9.

12 Pierre Bayle, *Philosophical Commentary*, trans. Amie Godman Tannenbaum (New York: Peter Lang, 1987), 18.

13 Elisabeth Labrousse, *Bayle*, trans. Denys Potts (Oxford: Oxford University Press, 1983), 78; Labrousse, *Pierre Bayle*, 517.

14 Bayle, *General Dictionary*, vol.2:657.

15 Pierre Jurieu, *Des Droits des deux Souverains en matière de Religion, La Conscience et le Prince* (Rotterdam: Henri de Graff, 1687), 13–14, 70–1, 257, 284–97; Guy Howard Dodge, *The Political Theory of the Huguenots of the Dispersion: With Special Reference to the Thought and Influence of Pierre Jurieu* (New York: Columbia University Press, 1947), 205; R.J. Howells, *Pierre Jurieu: Antinomian Radical* (Durham, U.K.: University of Durham, 1983), 54.

16 Robert M. Adams, 'In Search of Baron Somers,' in Perez Zagorin, ed., *Culture and Politics from Puritanism to the Enlightenment* (Berkeley: University of California Press, 1980), 176.

17 Ben Rogers, 'In Praise of Vanity: The Augustinian Analysis of the Benefits of Vice from Port-Royal to Mandeville,' PhD thesis, University of Oxford, 1994, chapter 7. Bayle used '*Timeo Danaos*' in *Critique générale*, 58–9, with respect to the corrupting effect of patronage.

18 Courtines, *Bayle's Relations with England and the English*, 56; Labrousse, *Bayle*, 46.

19 Courtines, *Bayle's Relations with England*, 137–8; Labrousse, *Bayle*, 45; Charles Lenient, *Étude sur Bayle* (Paris: Giraudet et Jouaust, 1855), 224. Lenient and Courtines also asserted that Bayle turned down patronage from the Earl of Hermington but I have been unable to identify this individual.

20 Ruth Whelan, *The Anatomy of Superstition: A Study of the Historical Theory and Practice of Pierre Bayle* (Oxford: Voltaire Foundation, 1989), 105, 185; Courtines, *Bayle's Relations with England*, 57.

21 Bayle, *Philosophic Commentary*, 146.

22 Labrousse, *Pierre Bayle*, 2:517.

23 Robinson, *Bayle the Sceptic*, 82.

24 John Locke, *Letters concerning Toleration* (London: A. Millar, 1765), 36.

25 Ibid.

26 Robinson, *Bayle the Sceptic*, 81.

27 Bayle, *Philosophic Commentary*, 115.

28 Courtines, *Bayle's Relations with England*, 51.

29 Bayle, *Historical and Critical Dictionary*, 629–30.

30 Anthony À Wood, *Athenae Oxonsienses* (London: T. Bennett, 1692), 1:471, 599; 2:460.

31 George Hilton Jones, *Convergent Forces: Immediate Causes of the Revolution of 1688 in England* (Ames: Iowa State University Press, 1990), 80.

32 Lois G. Schwoerer, *The Ingenious Mr. Henry Care: Restoration Publicist* (Baltimore: Johns Hopkins University Press, 2001), xix–xx.

33   Ibid., xvi.
34   Blair Worden, 'Marchamont Nedham and the Beginnings of English Republicanism, 1649–1656,' in David Wootton, ed., *Republicanism, Liberty and Commercial Society, 1649–1776* (Stanford, Calif.: Stanford University Press, 1994), 60.
35   Schwoerer, *Ingenious Mr. Henry Care*, 24–7.
36   Ibid., 32, 37, 81.
37   Ibid., 189.
38   Ibid., 204.
39   J.R. Jones, *The Revolution of 1688 in England* (London: Weidenfeld and Nicolson, 1972), 112.
40   Ibid., 105, 113.
41   Schwoerer, *Ingenious Mr. Henry Care*, 196.
42   Richard Vernon, *The Career of Toleration: John Locke, Jonas Proast and After* (Montreal and Kingston: McGill-Queen's University Press, 1997), 3.
43   Maurice Cranston, 'John Locke and the Case for Toleration,' in Susan Mendus and David Edwards, eds., *On Toleration* (Oxford: Clarendon, 1987), 102.
44   John Locke, *Two Tracts of Government*, ed. Philip Abrams (Cambridge: Cambridge University Press, 1967), 175; Peter Laslett attributes the transformation of Locke's 'traditionalist and authoritarian views' on religious toleration to Shaftesbury. See John Locke, *Two Treatises of Government*, ed. Peter Laslett (Cambridge: Cambridge University Press, 1960), 29. A similar view is expressed by G.A.J. Rogers, *Locke's Enlightenment: Aspects of the Origin, Nature and Impact of his Philosophy* (Hildesheim, Germany: Georg Olms Verlag, 1998), 8.
45   W.M. Spellman, *John Locke* (New York: St Martin's Press, 1997), 15. Perhaps the grammatical structure of these sentences indicates the difficulty Spellman encountered in negotiating the fact of Shaftesbury's liberalization of Locke with his claim that Locke was an independent thinker and an adviser to Shaftesbury.
46   Maurice Cranston, *John Locke: A Biography* (London: Longmans Green, 1957), 107.
47   K.H.D. Haley, *The First Earl of Shaftesbury* (Oxford: Clarendon, 1968), 226.
48   John Locke, *The Works in Ten Volumes*, vol.10 (London: W. Otridge, 1812), 205–7.
49   Locke, *Letters concerning Toleration*, 63, 70.
50   John Locke, *Two Treatises of Government*, II. 40, 42. David Armitage, 'Locke's Carolina Re-visited,' paper presented to North American Conference on British Studies, Toronto, 2 November 2001.

51 Jeremy Waldron, *God, Locke and Equality: Christian Foundations of John Locke's Political Thought* (Cambridge: Cambridge University Press, 2002), 203–5.

52 Ibid., 191, 205.

53 Haley, *First Earl*, 205–6, 215.

54 Ibid., 215.

55 Cranston, *John Locke*, 246.

56 Pierre Coste, 'The Character of Mr. Locke,' in Jean S. Yolton, ed., *A Locke Miscellancy: Locke Biography and Criticism for All* (Bristol: Thoemmes, 1990), 339.

57 Cranston, *John Locke*, 290.

58 Rogers, *Locke's Enlightenment*, 21.

59 *Oeuvres Complètes de Voltaire*, t.20 (Paris: Garnier, 1879), 518.

60 Locke, *Letters concerning Toleration*, 58.

61 Mark Goldie, 'John Locke's Circle and James II,' *Historical Journal*, 35 (1992): 557–86.

62 J.R. Jones writes, in *The Revolution of 1688 in England* (London: Weidenfeld and Nicolson, 1972), 113: 'Protestant landowners began to fear a reversal of the Restoration land settlement.' Maurice Ashley thinks that James was extremely anxious to reassure Protestant landowners that the distribution of lands in Ireland would not be undermined. See *James II* (London: J.M. Dent, 1977), 188.

63 Lawrence Stone, 'The Results of the English Revolutions of the Seventeenth Century,' in J.G.A. Pocock, ed., *Three British Revolutions: 1641, 1688, 1776* (Princeton, N.J.: Princeton University Press, 1980), 63.

64 James II, *Declaration of Indulgence*, cited in Maurice Ashley, *The Glorious Revolution of 1688* (London: Hodder and Stoughton, 1966), 199.

65 Cited in Cranston, *John Locke*, 284.

66 John Locke, 'On Allegiance and the Revolution,' in Mark Goldie, ed., *Political Essays* (Cambridge: Cambridge University Press, 1997), 308.

67 Ibid., 307–8, 312–13.

68 Voltaire, *Philosophical Letters*, trans. Ernest Dilworth (Indianapolis: Bobbs-Merrill, 1961), 19.

69 Cited in Ulrich Im Hof, *The Enlightenment*, trans. William E. Yuill (Oxford: Blackwell, 1995), 98.

70 My sole point of agreement with Jeremy Waldron's *God, Locke and Equality*, is his claim, against John Dunn, that Locke's ideas are not exclusively of interest to historians of ideas.

5   Voltaire and His Female Protectors

1 Ira O. Wade, *Studies on Voltaire with Some Unpublished Papers of Mme Du Châtelet* (New York: Russell and Russell, 1967), 135–6.
2 Introduction, n.3.
3 Jean Orieux, *Voltaire*, trans. Barbara Bray and Helen R. Lane (New York: Doubleday, 1979), 384–5; John E.N. Hersey, *Voltaire* (London: Constable, 1976), 326.
4 Mary Trouille, 'Eighteenth-Century Amazons of the Pen: Stéphanie de Genlis and Olympe de Gouges,' in Roland Bonnel and Catherine Rubinger, eds., *Femmes Savantes et Femmes d'Esprit: Women Intellectuals of the Eighteenth Century*, eds. (New York: Peter Lang, 1994), 341–70; Dominique Godineau, 'The Woman,' in Michel Vovelle, ed., *Enlightenment Portraits*, trans. Lydia G. Cochrane (Chicago: University of Chicago Press, 1997), 416–23; Claire Tomalin, *The Life and Death of Mary Wollstonecraft* (Harmondsworth, U.K.: Penguin, 1985), 195–202; Olympe de Gouges, *The Rights of Women*, trans. Val Stevenson (London: Pythia Press, 1989).
5 Alberto Elena, 'An Introduction to Laura Bassi,' *Isis*, 82 (1991): 510–18; Judith P. Zinsser, 'Émilie du Châtelet: Genius, Gender and Political Authority,' in Hilda L. Smith, ed., *Women Writers and the Early Modern British Political Tradition* (Cambridge: Cambridge University Press, 1998), 176; on the homosexuality of Lambertini – later to be Pope Benedict XIV – see Roger Peyrefitte, *Voltaire et Frédéric II*, t.1 (Paris: Albin Michel, 1992), 151.
6 Tomalin, *Life and Death of Mary Wollstonecraft*, 94.
7 Jean Le Rond d'Alembert, *Preliminary Discourse to the Encyclopedia of Diderot*, trans. Richard N. Schwab (Chicago: University of Chicago Press, l995), 66.
8 D'Alembert's hypothesis that aristocrats patronized men of letters to get a cheap education would seem to apply to Lord Shelburne, who invited Price, Priestley, Hume, Smith, Franklin, and Bentham to Bowood to broaden his education, but not to Baron Somers, who patronized Locke, Toland, Tindal, and Addison but was their intellectual equal. See Robert M. Adams, 'In Search of Baron Somers,' in Perez Zagorin, *Culture and Politics from Puritanism to the Enlightenment* (Berkeley: University of California Press, 1980). Although Somers and Shelburne had political reasons for patronizing thinkers, they might be compared to more typically English aristocrats who employed as gardeners expert cricketers, such as 'Lumpy' Stevens, the most feared bowler of the eighteenth century, or John Minshull, the first batsman to score a century. Aristocrats liked to play with the best, as long as the players knew their station (see

David Underdown, *The Start of Play: Cricket and Culture in Eighteenth-Century England* [Harmondsworth: Penguin, 2000], 144–9). But the English rarely played with the mind. Somers and Shelburne were distrusted by their contemporaries as too clever by half.

9 Daniel Gordon, 'Beyond the Social History of Ideas: Morellet and the Enlightenment,' in Jeffrey Merrick and Dorothy Medlin, eds., *André Morellet (1727–1819) in the Republic of Letters and the French Revolution* (New York: Peter Lang, 1995), 51. Also Dena Goodman, *The Republic of Letters: A Cultural History of the French Enlightenment* (Ithaca, N.Y.: Cornell University Press, 1994), chapter 2.

10 Madame du Châtelet, *Discours sur le bonheur* (Paris: Payot and Rivages, 1995), 53.

11 Elisabeth Badinter and Robert Badinter, *Condorcet: Un intellectuel en politique* (Paris: Fayard, 1988), 33–4; Marisa Linton, *The Politics of Virtue in Enlightenment France* (Basingstoke: Palgrave, 2001), 68.

12 Émilie du Châtelet, *Institutions de physique* (Paris: Prault, 1740), 2.

13 Du Châtelet; *Discours sur le bonheur*, 66; René Vaillot, *Avec Madame du Châtelet* (Oxford: Voltaire Foundation, 1988), 245, 387.

14 Zinsser, 'Émilie du Châtelet', 176.

15 Julien Offray de la Mettrie, *Oeuvres Philosophiques*, t.2 (Paris: Fayard, 1984), 108. I am grateful to Ian Hacking for drawing my attention to La Mettrie's love letter to du Châtelet.

16 Immanuel Kant, *Observations on the Feeling of the Beautiful and Sublime*, trans. John T. Goldthwait (Berkeley: University of California Press, 1960), 78.

17 Julien Offray de la Mettrie, *Histoire naturelle de l'âme* (Oxford [Paris], 1747), 1–12.

18 Peter Gay, *Voltaire's Politics: The Poet as Realist* (Princeton, N.J.: Princeton University Press, 1959), 78.

19 Voltaire, *Mémoires*, in *Oeuvres Complètes de Voltaire*, t.1 (Paris: Lequien, 1820), 295.

20 André Maurois, *Voltaire*, trans. Hamish Miles (Edinburgh: Peter Davies, 1932), 117.

21 *Oeuvres Complètes de Voltaire*, t.1:343, 350.

22 Hersey, *Voltaire*, 46, 86, 88.

23 René Vaillot, *Madame du Châtelet* (Paris: Albin Michel, 1978), 194–5; Zinsser, 'Émilie du Châtelet,' 175.

24 Vaillot, *Madame du Châtelet*, 274–5; Vaillot, *Avec Madame du Châtelet*, 297, 304–5; Gilbert Mercier, *Madame Voltaire* (Paris: Éditions de Fallois, 2001), 224.

25 Pomeau's introduction to Vaillot, *Avec Madame du Châtelet*, 2.

26 Orieux, *Voltaire*, 39.

27 Vaillot, *Madame du Châtelet*, 94, 99; Vaillot, *Avec Madame du Châtelet*, 15.

28 Vaillot, *Madame du Châtelet*, 202–3, 212–13, 218.

29 Peyrefitte, *Voltaire et Frédéric II*, 61–74. Voltaire referred to Frederick as 'Moderne Alcibiade ... Protecteur de Socrate,' with other references to Ephestion and Alexander, and Caesar and Nicomedes.

30 *Oeuvres Complètes de Voltaire*, t.1:305.

31 Ibid., 310.

32 Letter D1331, in *The Complete Works of Voltaire*, ed. Theodore Besterman (Genève: Institut et Musée Voltaire, 1968–2001), t.88:312.

33 Vaillot, *Avec Madame du Châtelet*, 198–9.

34 Letter D9530, in *Complete Works of Voltaire*, t.48, 93.

35 Jean-Jacques Rousseau, *The Confessions and Correspondence*, in Christopher Kelly, Roger D. Masters, and Peter G. Stillman, eds., *The Collected Writings of Rousseau*, vol.5, trans. Cristopher Kelly. (Hanover, N.H.: University Press of New England, 1990), 243.

36 Ibid., 505.

37 Voltaire, *Dictionnaire philosophique*, cited in Robert Darnton, *The Literary Underground of the Old Regime* (Cambridge, Mass: Harvard University Press, 1982), 13.

38 John Lough, *The Philosophes and Post-Revolutionary France* (Oxford: Clarendon, 1980), 57.

39 For a fine account of the remarkable women in female salons in eighteenth-century Britain, see Sylvia Harcstock Myers, *The Bluestocking Circle: Women, Friendship and the Life of the Mind in Eighteenth-Century England* (Oxford: Clarendon, 1990).

40 Guy Chaussinand-Nogaret, *Histoire des élites en France du XVIè au XXè siècle: l'honneur, le mérite, l'argent* (Paris: Tallandier, 1991), 303, 312. The masculinized sociability of the nineteenth-century *cercles* and cabarets is emphasized in the articles comprising *Femmes dans la cité, 1815–1871* (Paris: Créaphis, 2000).

41 Goodman, *The Republic of Letters*, 130.

42 Roger Chartier, 'The Man of Letters,' in Vovelle, ed., *Enlightenment Portraits*, 154; Francis Steegmuller, *A Woman, a Man, and Two Kingdoms: The Story of Madame d'Épinay and the Abbé Galiani* (New York: Alfred Knopf, 1991), 111.

43 Chartier, 'The Man of Letters,' 154; Robert Darnton, *The Great Cat Massacre and Other Episodes in French Cultural History* (London: Allen Lane,

1984), 154; Carla Hesse, *The Other Enlightenment: How French Women Became Modern* (Princeton, N.J.: Princeton University Press, 2001), 38, estimates that only 2 per cent of writers in the *ancien régime* were female but that the percentage had doubled to 4 per cent by 1820.

44 Darnton, *Great Cat Massacre*, 154; Bonnel and Rubinger, ed., *Femmes Savantes et Femmes d'Esprit*, 5.

45 The leading *salonnières* of the nineteenth century, Mme de Staël, Mme Récamier, and Princesse Mathilde, lived apart from their husbands. See Jean-Denis Bredin, *Une singulière famille: Jacques Necker, Suzanne Necker et Germaine de Staël* (Paris: Fayard, 1999); Françoise Wagener, *Madame Récamier: 1777–1849* (Paris: Flammarion, 2000); Laura Rièse, *Les salons littéraires parisiens du second empire à nos jours* (Toulouse: Privat, 1962). For the grand *salonnières* of the eighteenth century, see Roger Marchal, *Madame de Lambert et son milieu* (Oxford: Voltaire Foundation, 1991); Jean Sareil, *Les Tencin* (Genève: Librairie Droz, 1969); Pierre, Comte de Ségur, *Le Royaume de la rue Saint-Honoré: Mme Geoffrin et sa fille* (Paris: Calmann-Lévy, 1897); Benedetta Craveri, *Madame du Deffand and Her World*, trans. Teresa Waugh (London: Peter Holban, 1994); Jacqueline Hellegouarc'h, *L'esprit de société: cercles et 'salons' parisiens au XVIIIè siècle* (Paris: Garnier, 2000).

46 Vaillot, *Madame du Châtelet*, 38; Zinsser, 'Émilie du Châtelet,' 175.

47 De Ségur, *Le Royaume de la rue Saint-Honore*, 27–9.

48 The centrality of the salons to the French Enlightenment has been ably described by Goodman, *The Republic of Letters*, chapter 2; Daniel Roche, *La France des Lumières* (Paris: Fayard, 1993), 398–402; Chartier, 'The Man of Letters', 154–61.

49 Robert Darnton, 'An Exemplary Literary Career,' in Merrick and Medlin, eds., *André Morellet*, 12.

50 Sareil, *Les Tencin*, 218, 397.

51 Roche, *La France des Lumières*, 398–9.

52 Darnton, 'An Exemplary Literary Career,' 12.

53 Frank Hamel, *An Eighteenth-Century Marquise: A Study of Émilie Du Châtelet and her Times* (New York: James Pott, 1911), 118–19; Mercier, *Madame Voltaire*, 221; Vaillot, *Avec Madame Du Châtelet*, 204.

54 Cited in Goodman, *Republic of Letters*, 41.

55 Roche, *La France des Lumières*, 461.

56 Rousseau, *The Confessions and Correspondence*, in *The Collected Writings of Rousseau*, 5:243.

57 Robert W. Gutman, *Mozart: A Cultural Biography* (New York: Harcourt Brace, 1999), xxi.

58 Edmond and Jules de Goncourt, *The Woman of the Eighteenth Century*, trans. Jacques le Clercq and Ralph Roeder (London: George Allen and Unwin, 1928), 243, 262–5.

59 David Hume, 'Of Essay Writing,' in Eugene F. Miller, ed., *Essays, Moral, Political and Literary* (Indianapolis: Liberty Classics, 1985), 535–6.

60 Dena Goodman, 'Enlightenment Salons: The Convergence of Female and Philosophic Ambitions,' *Eighteenth-Century Studies*, 22 (1989): 329–50; Goodman, *The Republic of Letters*, chapters 2, 6.

61 Cited in Roy Porter, *English Society in the Eighteenth Century* (Harmondsworth: Penguin, 1982), 36.

62 Lord Fitzmaurice, *Life of William Earl of Shelburne* (London: Macmillan, 1912), 425–26.

63 Mary Wollstonecraft, *A Vindication of the Rights of Men with a Vindication of the Rights of Woman and Hints*, ed. Sylvana Tomaselli (Cambridge: Cambridge University Press, 1995), 67.

64 *Oeuvres Complètes de Voltaire*, t.33 (Paris: Garnier, 1877–83), 294.

65 Vaillot, *Madame du Châtelet*, 193; Vaillot, *Avec Madame du Châtelet*, 121, 163.

66 Thomas L. Hankins, *Jean D'Alembert: Science and the Enlightenment* (Oxford: Clarendon, 1976), 15.

67 Roger Chartier, *The Cultural Origins of the French Revolution*, trans. Lydia G. Cochrane (Durham, N.C.: Duke University Press, 1991), 157; Roche, *France des Lumières*, 399.

68 Cited in Ulrich Im Hof, *The Enlightenment*, trans. William E. Yuill (Oxford: Blackwell, 1995), 115.

69 Robert Shackleton, *Montesquieu: A Critical Biography* (London: Oxford University Press, 1961), 55.

70 Charles Duclos, *Considérations sur les Moeurs de se siècle (1750)*, ed. F.C. Green (Cambridge: Cambridge University Press, 1939), 135.

71 Richard Fargher, *Life and Letters in France: The Eighteenth Century* (New York: Charles Scribner's Sons, 1970), 63; Anne Goldgar, *Impolite Learning: Conduct and Community in the Republic of Letters, 1680–1750* (New Haven, Conn.: Yale University Press, 1995), 231.

72 Cited in Roche, *La France des Lumières*, 401. Robert Sparling would have me note that such superficiality is not unknown in academic conferences and that complex philosophic arguments are not common at meetings of the Canadian Political Science Association.

73 J.-P. Belin, *Le Commerce des livres prohibés à Paris de 1750 à 1789* (New York: Burt Franklin, 1962), 107–08; Sareil, *Les Tencin*, 387.

74 Shackleton, *Montesquieu*, 85–6; Sareil, *Les Tencin*, 387, 395.

75 Shackleton, *Montesquieu*, 189; Sareil, *Les Tencin*, 395–6.

76 Vaillot, *Avec Madame du Châtelet*, 234–5.

77 *Oeuvres Complètes de Voltaire* (1820), t.1: 334.

78 Alden R. Gordon, 'Searching for the Elusive Madame de Pompadour,' *Eighteenth-Century Studies*, 37:1 (fall 2003): 109.

79 Chartier, 'Man of Letters,' 166; Nancy Mitford, *Madame de Pompadour* (London: Hamish Hamilton, 1968), 151–3.

80 Robert Niklaus, *A Literary History of France: The Eighteenth Century* (London: Ernest Benn, 1970), 158.

81 Shackleton, *Montesquieu*, 359; Mitford, *Madame de Pompadour*, 157; Norman Torrey, *The Spirit of Voltaire* (New York: Columbia University Press, 1938), 133–9; Orieux, *Voltaire*, 201.

82 Charles Louis de Secondat, Baron de Montesquieu, *Lettres Persanes*, ed. Paul Vernière (Paris: Garnier, 1960), 7.

83 Torrey, *Spirit of Voltaire*, 133.

84 Ibid., 119–20; René Pomeau, *Ecraser l'Infâme: Voltaire en son temps*, t.4 (Oxford: Voltaire Foundation, 1994), 176.

85 Darnton, *Great Cat Massacre*, 155.

86 Vaillot, *Avec Madame du Châtelet*, 215–16; Mitford, *Madame de Pompadour*, 43.

87 Craveri, *Madame du Deffand*, 7, 12, 103, 337.

88 Sareil, *Les Tencin*, 154.

89 Gutman, *Mozart*, 38.

90 *Voltaire and Catherine the Great: Selected Correspondence*, trans. A. Lentin (Cambridge: Oriental Research Partners, 1974), 14.

91 John T. Alexander, *Catherine the Great: Life and Legend* (Oxford: Oxford University Press, 1989), 93.

92 *Letters concerning the Present State of England. Particularly respecting the Politics, Arts, Manners and Literature of the Times* (London: J. Almon, 1772), 319.

93 Steegmuller, *A Woman, a Man and Two Kingdoms*, 217.

94 Horace Walpole, *Memoirs of the Reign of King George the Third*, vol.2 (London: Lawrence and Bullen, 1894), 25.

95 Letter D18438, in *Voltaire's Correspondence*, 85:143.

96 Cited in Fargher, *Life and Letters in France*, 161.

97 John Bowring, ed., *The Works of Jeremy Bentham*, vol.10 (New York: Russell and Russell, 1962), 162.

98 Jean Sareil, *Voltaire et les grands* (Genève: Droz, 1978), 135–45.

99 J.H. Brumfitt, 'Voltaire Historian and the Royal Mistresses,' in Maxine G. Cutler, ed., *Voltaire, the Enlightenment and the Comic Mode: Essays in Honor of Jean Sareil* (New York: Peter Lang, 1990), 11–26.

100 Cited in Isaac Kramnick, ed., *The Portable Enlightenment Reader* (New York: Penguin, 1995), 131.
101 Robert S. Tate, 'Voltaire and the Question of Law and Order,' in J.H. Fox, M.H. Waddicor, and D.A. Watts, eds., *Studies in Eighteenth-Century Literature Presented to Robert Niklaus* (Exeter: University of Exeter Press, 1975), 279.
102 Stuart Andrews, ed., *Enlightened Despotism* (London: Longmans, 1967), 141.
103 Jean Starobinski, *Blessings in Disguise; or, The Morality of Evil* (Cambridge, Mass.: Harvard University Press, 1995), 45.
104 Bonnie Anderson and Judith P. Zinsser, *A History of Their Own: Women in Europe from Prehistory to the Present*, vol.2 (New York: Harper and Row, 1988), 115.
105 Gay, *Voltaire*, 136.
106 John Gray, *Voltaire and Enlightenment* (London: Phoenix, 1998), 9.
107 René Pomeau et Christiane Mervaud, *De la Cour au jardin*, t.3, *Voltaire en son temps*, (Oxford: Voltaire Foundation, 1991), 72.
108 *Letters of Voltaire and Frederick the Great*, trans. by Richard Aldington (London: Routledge, 1927), 301.
109 *Voltaire and Catherine*, 52.
110 Ibid., 68.
111 René Pomeau, '*Ecraser l'Infâme*,' t.4, *Voltaire en son temps*, 373; *On a voulu l'enterrer*, t.5, *Voltaire en son temps* (Oxford: Voltaire Foundation, 1994), 61.
112 *Voltaire and Catherine*, 68, 80.
113 Cited in Kramnick ed., *The Portable Enlightenment Reader*, 533–4.
114 Alexander, *Catherine the Great*, 173. Diderot's *Observations sur le Nakaz*, sent to Catherine only after his death, so angered her that she ordered it destroyed. See Denis Diderot, *Political Writings*, trans. John Hope Mason and Robert Wokler (Cambridge: Cambridge University Press, 1992), 83–169.
115 Pomeau, *On a voulu l'enterrer*, 98–9.
116 *Voltaire and Catherine*, 152.
117 Ibid., 143.
118 Ibid., 147–9.
119 *Voltaire and Catherine*, 15.
120 Pomeau et Mervaud, *De la Cour au jardin*, 325.
121 Brunfitt, 'Voltaire Historian and the Royal Mistresses,' 12.
122 Orieux, *Voltaire*, 384–5.

6 Scottish Universities and Their Patrons: Argyll, Bute, and Dundas

1 Adam Smith, *An Inquiry into the Nature and Causes of the Wealth of Nations*, ed. R.H. Campbell and A.S. Skinner (Oxford: Clarendon, 1976), V.i.9.37–9: 809–11.

2 John Gascoigne, *Science, Politics and Universities in Europe, 1600–1800* (Aldershot, U.K.: Ashgate, 1998), chapter 9, 2; Walter Rüegg, 'Themes,' in Rüegg ed., *A History of the University in Europe*, vol.2 (Cambridge: Cambridge University Press, 1996), 13.

3 Roy Porter, 'The Scientific Revolution and Universities,' and Notker Hammerstein, 'The Enlightenment,' in Rüegg ed., *A History of the University in Europe*, 2: 532–3, 542, 631. Roger Chartier, Marie-Madeleine Compère, and Dominique Julia, *L'Education en France du XVIe au XVIIIe siècle* (Paris: Société d'édition, 1976), 207.

4 R.S. Westfall, *Never at Rest: A Biography of Isaac Newton* (Cambridge: Cambridge University Press, 1980), 190.

5 Gascoigne, *Science, Politics and Universities*, chapter 1.

6 R.A. Houston, 'Scottish Education and Literacy, 1600–1800: An International Perspective,' in T.M. Devine, *Improvement and Enlightenment: Proceedings of the Scottish Studies Seminar, University of Strathclyde, 1987–88* (Edinburgh: John Donald, 1989), 50.

7 Ronald Sunter, *Patronage and Politics in Scotland, 1707–1832* (Edinburgh: John Donald, 1986), 22, 42.

8 Charles Camic, *Experience and Enlightenment: Socialization for Cultural Change in Eighteenth-Century Scotland* (Edinburgh: Edinburgh University Press, 1983), Andrew Hook and Richard B. Sher, eds., 204, 208.

9 Roger L. Emerson, 'Politics and the Glasgow Professors, 1690–1800,' in Andrew Hook and Richard B. Sher, eds., *The Glasgow Enlightenment* (East Lothian: Tuckwell Press, 1995), 30; Roger L. Emerson, 'How Not to Deal with Enlightenments,' *Historically Speaking* 3:3 (2002): 7; 'Lord Bute and the Scottish Universities, 1760–1792,' in Karl W. Schweitzer, ed., *Lord Bute: Essays in Re-interpretation* (Leicester: Leicester University Press, 1988), 171.

10 T.C. Smout, 'Problems of Nationalism, Identity and Improvement in Later Eighteenth-Century Scotland,' in Devine, *Improvement and Enlightenment*, 13.

11 Richard B. Sher, *Church and University in the Scottish Enlightenment: The Moderate Literati of Edinburgh* (Princeton, N.J.: Princeton University Press, 1985), 151.

12 Ibid., 36, 262.

13 Stephen Shapin, 'Property, Patronage and the Politics of Science: The Founding of the Royal Society of Edinburgh,' *British Journal for the History of Science*, 7 (1974): 7.

14 Roger L. Emerson, *Patronage and Politics: The Aberdeen Universities in the Eighteenth Century* (Aberdeen: Aberdeen University Press, 1992), 7–8; Jane Rendell, *The Origins of the Scottish Enlightenment* (London: Macmillan, 1978), 47–8.

15 Rendell, *Origins*, 19–21, 70–3; Philip Flynn, *Enlightenment Scotland: A Study and Selection of Scottish Philosophical Prose from the Eighteenth and Early Nineteenth Centuries* (Edinburgh: Scottish Academic Press, 1992), xi; George Grinell, 'Newton's *Principia* as Whig Propaganda,' in Paul Fritz and David Williams, eds., *City and Society in the Eighteenth Century* (Toronto: Hakkert, 1973), 181–92.

16 Nicholas Phillipson, 'Culture and Society in the 18th Century Province: The Case of Edinburgh and the Scottish Enlightenment,' in Lawrence Stone, ed., *The University in Society* (Princeton, N.J.: Princeton University Press, 1974), 421–31.

17 Michael Fry, *Patronage and Principle: A Political History of Modern Scotland* (Aberdeen: Aberdeen University Press, 1987), 7, 256, and *The Dundas Despotism* (Edinburgh: Edinburgh University Press, 1992), 14, 55.

18 David Allan, *Virtue, Learning and the Scottish Enlightenment: Ideas of Scholarship in Early Modern History* (Edinburgh: Edinburgh University Press, 1993), 86.

19 *The Letters of David Hume*, ed. J.Y.T. Greig, vol.1 (Oxford: Clarendon, 1932), 255.

20 Ernest Campbell Mossner, *The Life of David Hume* (Austen: University of Texas Press, 1954), 606; see also James G. Basker, 'Scotticisms and the Problem of Cultural Identity,' in John Dwyer and Richard B. Sher, eds., *Sociability and Society in Eighteenth-Century Scotland* (Edinburgh: Mercat Press, 1993), 80–95.

21 Christopher Berry, *Social Theory of the Scottish Enlightenment* (Edinburgh: Edinburgh University Press, 1997), 13–14.

22 Archibald Bruce, *The Patron's A, B, C: or, the Shorter Catechism Attempted after a New Plan* (Glasgow: J. Duncan, 1771), 5–6.

23 Cited in Camic, *Experience and Enlightenment*, 208.

24 John Trenchard and Thomas Gordon, *Cato's Letters: Or Essays on Liberty, Civil and Religious, and Other Important Subjects* (London: J. Walthoe et al., 1755), liv.

25 Sher, *Church and University*, 33, 40. Ferguson, unlike Robertson, Smith, and Hume, favoured a citizen's militia over a professional standing army but saw the Scots militia as a conservative institution, with the ranks in the

army corresponding to the established order of subordination. The Senecan moment predominated over the Machiavellian moment in eighteenth-century Scotland.

26 Mossner, *The Life of David Hume*, 539–40.

27 Ibid., 5.

28 David Hume, 'Rise of the Arts and Sciences,' in *Essays Moral, Political and Literary*, ed. Eugene F. Miller (Indianapolis: Liberty Classics, 1985), 113.

29 *Letters of David Hume*, ed. J.Y.T. Greig, 2:309–12.

30 T.W. Heyck, *The Transformation of Intellectual Life in Victorian England* (London: Croom Helm, 1982), 56.

31 *Letters of David Hume*, 1:25, 27, 28.

32 Ibid., 249–50.

33 Ibid., 113.

34 David Hume, *The History of England from the Invasion of Julius Caesar to the Abdication of James the Second*, vol.6 (Boston: Phillips, Samson, 1856), 250–1, 301–2. Also David Wootton, 'David Hume, "the Historian,"' in David F. Norton., *The Cambridge Companion to Hume* (Cambridge: Cambridge University Press, 1993), 303.

35 *Letters of David Hume*, 1:214.

36 Mark Salber Phillips, *Society and Sentiment: Genres of Historical Writing in Britain, 1740–1820* (Princeton, N.J.: Princeton University Press, 2000), 60.

37 A whig, as Boswell knew, meant a Scottish drover of cattle (as distinct from a tory, or Irish thief). The 3rd Duke of Argyll was the Whig of Whigs.

38 In giving Boswell credit for creating Johnson as the greatest of eighteenth-century Englishmen, I have perhaps overstated the case, but D'Alembert no longer enjoys the reputation he had as the wittiest of *les lumières*. As Thomas Hankins (*Jean D'Alembert: Science and Enlightenment* [Oxford: Clarendon, 1970], 16) writes: 'D'Alembert had no Boswell to record his conversations.'

39 *Letters of David Hume*, 1:164–5.

40 Ibid., 280.

41 *The Correspondence of Adam Smith*, ed. Ernest Campbell Mossner and Ian Simpson Ross (Oxford: Clarendon, 1987), 6, 13.

42 Ibid., 33, 35.

43 Sher, *Church and University*, 95; Roger L. Emerson, 'Archibald Campbell, 3rd Duke of Argyll (1682–1761): Patronage and the Creation of the Scottish Enlightenment,' unpublished paper, 17.

44 Emerson, 'How Not to Deal with Enlightenments,' 7, and 'Politics and the Glasgow Professors', 31.

45 *Letters of David Hume*, 1:2–4.

46 Ibid., 2:209.

47 Ibid., 1:244.
48 Ibid., 4.
49 Mossner, *Life of David Hume*, 308.
50 Hume, *Essays Moral, Political and Literary*, 533–6.
51 Ibid., 563. Hume's female readership is emphasized by Wootton, 'David Hume, "the Historian,"' 282, and by Jerome Christensen, *Practicing Enlightenment: Hume and the Formation of a Literary Career* (Madison: University of Wisconsin Press, 1987), 18, 95–8.
52 Mark A. Thompson, *The Secretaries of State, 1681–1782* (Oxford: Clarendon, 1932), 134.
53 *Correspondence of Adam Smith*, 91, 93.
54 Mossner, *Life of David Hume*, 493.
55 *Letters of David Hume*, 1:428.
56 Mossner, *Life of David Hume*, 539–49.
57 Ibid., 504.
58 *Letters of David Hume*, 1:207.
59 Ibid., 364–5.
60 *Correspondence of Adam Smith*, 112–13.
61 Fry, *The Dundas Despotism*, 184.
62 Cited in Phillips, *Society and Sentiment*, 318.
63 Shapin, 'Property, Patronage and the Politics of Science', 12–13.
64 *Correspondence of Adam Smith*, 323–4.
65 Barbara M. Benedict, '"Service to the Public": William Creech and Sentiment for Sale,' in Dwyer and Sher ed., *Sociability and Society in Eighteenth-Century Scotland*, 119–46.
66 Adam Smith, *The Theory of Moral Sentiments*, ed. D.D. Raphael and A.L. Macfie (Indianapolis: Liberty Fund, 1982), 68, 95.
67 Ibid., 162.
68 Ibid., 95.
69 *Letters of David Hume*, 305.
70 Ian Simpson Ross, 'Adam Smith's "Happiest" Years as a Glasgow Professor,' in Hook and Sher, eds., *Glasgow Enlightenment*, 80.
71 Ibid., 81.
72 *Correspondence of Adam Smith*, 37.
73 Sher, *Church and University*, 120.
74 Ibid., 252–3.
75 Emerson, 'Politics and the Glasgow Professors,' 26.
76 Camic, *Experience and Enlightenment*, 213.
77 Peter Brown, *The Chathamites: A Study in the Relationship between Personalities and Ideas in the Second Half of the Eighteenth Century* (London: Macmillan, 1967), 152.

78 Berry, *Social Theory*, 14–15; George Pottinger, *Heirs of the Enlightenment: Edinburgh Reviewers and Writers, 1800–1830* (Edinburgh: Scottish Academic Press, 1992), 33; Fry, *Dundas Despotism*, 69; Sher, *Church and University*, 114, 127–9.

79 Sher, *Church and University*, 299. It is with malicious pleasure that I report that librarians of Cambridge University Library had to slit open the pages of the 1818 edition of Robertson's *History of Charles V*, the book that had the largest advance from publishers until that time.

7 Independence in Theory and Practice: D'Alembert and Rousseau

1 Sharon Kettering, *Patrons, Brokers, and Clients in Seventeenth-Century France* (Oxford: Oxford University Press, 1986), 30.

2 Jean Guéhenno, *Jean-Jacques Rousseau*, vol.1 (New York: Columbia University Press, 1967), 361.

3 Jean-Jacques Rousseau, *The Confessions and Correspondence*, in Christopher Kelly, Roger D. Masters, and Peter G. Stillman, eds., *The Collected Writings of Rousseau*, vol.5, trans. Christopher Kelly (Hanover, N.H.: University Press of New England, 1990), 243.

4 Ibid., 280.

5 Ibid.

6 Maurice Cranston, *Jean-Jacques: The Early Life and Work of Jean-Jacques Rousseau 1712–1754* (London: Allen Lane, 1983), 214.

7 Rousseau, *Confessions*, in *The Collected Writings*, 5:640.

8 Arthur M. Wilson, *Diderot: The Testing Years, 1713–59* (New York: Oxford University Press, 1957), 97.

9 Rousseau, *Confessions*, in *The Collected Writings* 5:323–4.

10 Ibid., 324.

11 Geoffrey Turnovsky, 'The Enlightenment Literary Market: Rousseau, Authorship, and the Book Trade,' *Eighteenth-Century Studies*, 3 (2003): 388–410.

12 Guéhenno, *Jean-Jacques Rousseau*, 1:282.

13 *Oeuvres Complètes de D'Alembert*, t.4 (Genève: Slatkine, 1967), 335–73; praise of the Marquis d'Argenson is on 358–9. Thomas L. Hankins, *Jean D'Alembert: Science and Enlightenment* (Oxford: Clarendon, 1976), 73, indicates that D'Alembert dedicated four works to the Comte d'Argenson and described him as 'the only man of position to whom he owed any obligation.'

14 Rousseau, *Confessions*, in *The Collected Writings*, 5:429.

15 Jean-Jacques Rousseau, *The First and Second Discourses*, ed. Roger D. Masters (New York: St. Martin's Press, 1964), 63–4.

16 R.A. Leigh, 'Rousseau's English Pension,' in J.H. Fox, M.H. Waddicor, and D.A. Watts, eds., *Studies in Eighteenth-Century Literature Presented to Robert Niklaus* (Exeter: University of Exeter Press, 1975), 110; George R. Havens, 'Diderot, Rousseau, and the Discours sur l'Inégalité,' *Diderot Studies* 3 (1961):227–8.

17 Rousseau, *Confessions*, in *The Collected Writings*, 5:319.

18 Bernard Williams, *Truth and Truthfulness: An Essay in Genealogy* (Princeton, N.J.: Princeton University Press, 2002), 123, 199.

19 Edmund Burke, *Letter to a Member of the National Assembly*, in Edmund Burke, *Reflections on the Revolution in France*, ed. L.G. Mitchell (New York: Penguin, 1993), 271.

20 Benoît Mély, *Jean-Jacques Rousseau: un intellectuel en rupture* (Paris: Minerve, 1985), 24.

21 Guéhenno, *Jean-Jacques Rousseau*, 1:287.

22 Ibid., 289.

23 Peter France, *Politeness and Its Discontents: Problems in French Classical Culture* (Cambridge: Cambridge University Press, 1992), 107.

24 Leigh, 'Rousseau's English Pension,' 110.

25 Benedetta Craveri, *Madame du Deffand and Her World*, trans. Teresa Waugh (London: Peter Halban, 1994), 98; Dena Goodman, *The Republic of Letters: A Cultural History of the French Enlightenment* (Ithaca, N.Y.: Cornell University Press, 1994), 36–7.

26 *Oeuvres Complètes de D'Alembert*, t.4: 367.

27 Mély, *Jean-Jacques Rousseau*, 51.

28 Daniel Roche, *La France des Lumières* (Paris: Fayard, 1993), 489.

29 T.W. Heyck, *The Transformation of Intellectual Life in Victorian England* (London: Croom Helm, 1982), 32. Mill's cosy billet with the East India Company enabled him to write on company time while maintaining his independence; Rousseau's music copying provided less income and leisure.

30 *Rousseau: Judge of Jean-Jacques: Dialogues*, in *The Collected Writings*, 1:139, 142.

31 Mély, *Jean-Jacques Rousseau*, 56.

32 Guéhenno, *Jean-Jacques Rousseau*, 259.

33 Rousseau, *Confessions*, in *The Collected Writings*, 5:299.

34 Ibid., 551–2.

35 Ibid., 338.

36 Raymond Birn, 'Rousseau et ses éditeurs,' *Revue d'histoire moderne et contemporaine*, 40 (1993):120–36, and *Forging Rousseau: Print, Commerce and Cultural Manipulation in the Late Enlightenment* (Oxford: Voltaire Foundation, 2001), 1–2, 9, 30–3.

37 Georges, Vicomte d'Avenel, *Les riches depuis sept cent ans: Revenus et Bénéfices, Appointements et Honoraires* (Paris: Armand Colin, 1909), 306.

38 Birn, 'Rousseau et ses éditeurs', 121.

39 *Rousseau: Judge of Jean-Jacques*, in *The Collected Writings*, 1:133. This number seems improbably high.

40 Mély, *Jean-Jacques Rousseau*, 220.

41 *Rousseau Judge of Jean-Jacques*, in *The Collected Writings*, 1:139–40.

42 Cited in Mély, *Jean-Jacques Rousseau*, 10.

43 *Oeuvres Complètes de D'Alembert*, t.4: 340.

44 Ibid., 341–2.

45 Ibid., 344–6.

46 Ibid., 348, 353.

47 Ibid., 357.

48 Ibid., 358–9, 371.

49 Ibid., 367, 369.

50 Rousseau, *The First and Second Discourses*, 370–2.

51 Ibid., 212.

52 Martin Thom, *Republics, Nations and Tribes* (London: Verso, 1995), 74.

53 Bernard Gagnebin and Marcel Raymond, eds., *Oeuvres Complètes de Jean-Jacques Rousseau*, t.3, (Paris: Gallimard-Pléiade, 1964), 965.

54 Rousseau, *Reveries of a Solitary Walker*, in *The Collected Writings*, 8:52.

55 Rousseau, *Emile*, trans. Barbara Foxley (London: Everyman, 2001), 234.

56 Ibid., 375–6.

57 David Fraser, *Frederick the Great: King of Prussia* (London: Allen Lane, 2000), 488.

58 Guéhenno, *Jean-Jacques Rousseau*, 2:98.

59 T.W.C. Blanning, 'Frederick the Great and Enlightened Absolutism,' in H.M. Scott, ed., *Enlightened Absolutism* (Ann Arbor: University of Michigan Press, 1990), 281–2. Blanning may have overemphasized the pacific strain in Frederick's foreign policy, since Prussia did not have overseas colonies and hence did not fight wars there as other European powers did.

60 Rousseau, *Confessions*, in *The Collected Writings*, 5:502.

61 Guéhenno, *Jean-Jacques Rousseau*, 2:174.

62 Hume, *The Letters of David Hume*, ed. J.Y.T. Greig (Oxford: Clarendon, 1932), 1:527.

63 Cited in Mark J. Temmer, *Samuel Johnson and Three Infidels* (Athens: University of Georgia Press, 1988), 41.

64 Rousseau's letter to Beaumont, cited in Mély, *Jean-Jacques Rousseau*, 10.

65 Vittorio Alfieri, *The Prince and Letters*, trans. Beatrice Corrigan and Julius A. Molinaro (Toronto: University of Toronto Press, 1972), 30–1.

66 Voltaire defended his participation in the slave trade in *Essai sur les moeurs et l'esprit des nations et sur les principaux faits de l'histoire depuis Charlesmagne jusqu'à Louis XIII* (Paris: Garnier, 1963), 805. His currency speculation in Prussia and the Netherlands was probably illegal, despite Voltaire's acquittal in court, and certainly morally questionable, and the profits he made supplying armies seem inconsistent with the pacifism he preached.

67 Robert Shackleton, *Montesquieu: A Critical Biography* (London: Oxford Univeristy Press, 1961), 14–15, 81–4, 207.

68 Mély, *Jean-Jacques Rousseau*, 59-60.

69 Rousseau, *Confessions and Correspondence*, in *The Collected Writings of Rousseau*, 5:441, 573, 582.

70 Mély, *Jean-Jacques Rousseau*, 62, 282.

71 Ibid., 311; Guéhenno, *Jean-Jacques Rousseau*, 1:402, 424.

72 Cited in Jean Fabien Spitz, 'From Civism to Civility: D'Holbach's Critique of Republican Virtue,' trans. John Fletcher, in Martin van Gelderen and Quentin Skinner, eds., *Republicanism: A Shared European Heritage*, vol.2 (Cambridge: Cambridge University Press, 2002), 113.

73 Ibid., 332; Guéhenno, *Jean-Jacques Rousseau*, 1:335.

74 I have read no one so unromantic as to suggest that the source of the great love of Rousseau's life, which he fictionalized as Julie and St Preux, was based on his rivalry with Voltaire. But just how great it would have been to have cuckolded the cuckold of the leading man of letters in France!

75 Mély, *Jean-Jacques Rousseau*, 86. Rousseau's account of his refusal to go to Geneva, and his break with Grimm, Diderot, and D'Épinay, can be found in *Confessions*, in *The Collected Writings*, 5:345–423.

76 Birn, 'Rousseau et ses éditeurs,' 124–7; Birn, *Forging Rousseau*, 1–2; Guéhenno, *Jean-Jacques Rousseau*, 2:48; Mély, *Jean-Jacques Rousseau*, 112.

77 Christopher Kelly, *Rousseau as Author: Consecrating One's Life to the Truth* (Chicago: University of Chicago Press, 2003), 22.

78 Rousseau, *Confessions*, in *The Collected Writings*, 5:340–1.

79 Guy Chaussinaand-Nogaret, *Choiseul:Naissance de la gauche* (Paris: Perrin, 1995), 126, 149–52.

80 Guéhenno, *Jean-Jacques Rousseau*, 2:196.

81 Rousseau, *Confessions*, in *The Collected Writings*, 5:547; *Rousseau: Judge of Jean-Jacques*, ibid., 1:237; *Reveries*, ibid., 52.

82 Rousseau, *Confessions*, in *The Collected Writings*, 5:504–5.

83 Turnovsky, 'The Enlightenment Literary Market,' 392.

84 *Rousseau: Judge of Jean-Jacques*, in *The Collected Writings*, 1:207.

85 Rousseau, *Confessions*, 5:437.

86 *Letters of David Hume*, 1:374.
87 *Rousseau: Judge of Jean-Jacques*, in *The Collected Writings*, 1:91.
88 Mély, *Jean-Jacques Rousseau*, 220.
89 Robert Wokler, *Rousseau* (Oxford: Oxford University Press, 1995), 110.
90 Birn, *Forging Rousseau*, 232.
91 Voltaire, *Philosophical Dictionary*, trans. Peter Gay (New York: Basic Books, 1962), 245.

8 Samuel Johnson and the Question of Englightenment in England

1 Roy Porter, *The Creation of the Modern Mind: The Untold Story of the British Enlightenment* (New York: W.W. Norton, 2000).
2 Franco Venturi, *Utopia and Reform in the Enlightenment* (Cambridge: Cambridge University Press, 1971), 132–3; Lester Crocker, 'The Enlightenment: Problems of Interpretation,' in R. Ajello, M. Firpo, L. Guerci, and G. Ricuperati, eds., *L'Età Dei Lumi: Studi Storici sul settecento Europeo in Onore di Franco Venturi*, vol.1 (Napoli: Jovene, 1985), 28.
3 This generalization might be qualified insofar, at the Eleventh International Conference on the Enlightenment in Los Angeles on 3–10 August 2003, panels on Johnson and the 'Globalization of Literature' were held and the papers presented included such topics as Johnson's contributions to Catalan culture and to Japanese culture.
4 J.G.A. Pocock, 'Clergy and Commerce: The Conservative Enlightenment in England,' in Ajello et al., eds., *L'Età Dei Lumi*, vol.2:526.
5 B.W.Young, *Religion and Enlightenment in Eighteenth-Century England* (Oxford: Clarendon, 1998), 71.
6 Pocock, 'Clergy and Commerce,' 529.
7 Stephen Miller, *Three Deaths and Enlightenment Thought: Hume, Johnson, Marat* (Lewisburg, Penn.: Bucknell University Press, 2001), 100.
8 Ned D. Landsman, 'Presbyterians and Provincial Society: The Evangelical Enlightenment in the West of Scotland, 1740–1775,' in John Dwyer and Richard B. Sher eds., *Sociability and Society in Eighteenth-Century Scotland* (Edinburgh: Mercat Press, 1993), 194–209; Robert Kent Donovan, 'The Popular Party of the Church of Scotland and the American Revolution,' in Richard B. Sher and Jeffrey R. Smitten eds., *Scotland and America in the Age of Enlightenment* (Edinburgh: Edinburgh University Press, 1990), 81–99.
9 Miller, *Three Deaths*, 100.
10 Daniel Roche, *La France des Lumières* (Paris: Fayard, 1993), 388–9; Daniel Mornet, *French Thought in the Eighteenth Century*, trans. Lawrence M. Levin (New York: Archon Books, 1969), 181; R.R. Palmer, *The Improvement of*

Mankind: Education and the French Revolution (Princeton, N.J.: Princeton University Press, 1985), 20–2, 128–9.

11 Cited in Peter Gay, *Voltaire's Politics: The Poet as Realist* (Princeton, N.J.: Princeton University Press, 1959), 222.

12 Kaya Tianen-Antilla, *The Problem of Humanity: The Blacks in the European Enlightenment* (Helsinki: Finnish Historical Society, 1994). Tianen-Antilla concludes (346): 'It would be rather daring to regard Enlightenment thinkers as racist, in spite of the fact that they presented arguments about the Africans which would these days be considered as discriminatory.'

13 Harvey Chisick, 'David Hume and the Common People,' in Peter Jones, ed., *The 'Science of Man' in the Scottish Enlightenment: Hume, Reid and Their Contemporaries* (Edinburgh: Edinburgh University Press, 1989), 21.

14 Alvin Kernan, *Printing Technology, Letters and Samuel Johnson* (Princeton, N.J.: Princeton University Press, 1987), 4, 20, 93, 105.

15 Cited in Dustin Griffin, *Literary Patronage in England, 1650–1800* (Cambridge: Cambridge University Press, 1996), 246.

16 Edward Gibbon, *Memoirs* (London: Hunt and Clarke, 1827), 256.

17 *The Political Writings of Dr. Johnson: A Selection*, ed. J. P. Hardy (London: Routledge and Kegan Paul, 1968), 39.

18 Thrale, Hester Lynch, *Thraliana: The Diary of Mrs. Hester Lynch Thrale*, vol.1, ed. Katherine C. Balderson (Oxford: Clarendon, 1951), 183.

19 Jeremy Black, *The English Press in the Eighteenth Century* (London: Croom Helm, 1987), 246–7.

20 Samuel Johnson, *The Idler and The Adventurer*, in *Works of Samuel Johnson*, ed. W.J. Bate, John M. Bullitt, and L. F. Powell (New Haven, Conn.: Yale University Press, 1963), 2:457.

21 *Boswell's Life of Johnson*, ed. George Birkbeck Hill (Oxford: Clarendon, 1887), 2:66.

22 Sir John Hawkins, *The Life of Samuel Johnson, LL.D*, ed. Bertram H. Davis (New York: Macmillan, 1961), 194–5.

23 Paul Fussell, *Samuel Johnson and the Life of Writing* (New York: Harcourt Brace Jovanovich, 1971), 3.

24 *Boswell's Life of Johnson*, 1:71.

25 Lawrence Stone, 'The Size and Composition of the Oxford Student Body, 1580–1910,' in Lawrence Stone, ed., *The University in Society* (Princeton, N.J.: Princeton University Press, 1974), 19–23, 37–40; Marie Rosa di Simone, 'Admission,' in Walter Rüegg, ed., *A History of the University in Europe*, vol.2 (Cambridge: Cambridge University Press, 1996), 316. See also John Spurr, *The Restoration Church, 1646–1689* (New Haven, Conn.: Yale University Press, 1991), 384.

26 *Boswell's Life of Johnson*, 5:35.

27 Ibid., 1:74.

28 Ibid., 80.

29 Fussell, *Samuel Johnson*, 11.

30 *Boswell's Life of Johnson*, 1:133.

31 Jacob Leed, 'Johnson, Chesterfield and Patronage: A Response to Paul Korshin,' *Studies in Burke and His Time*, 13 (1971): 2012.

32 Paul J. Korshin, 'Types of Eighteenth-Century Literary Patronage,' *Eighteenth-Century Studies*, 7 (1974), 470–1.

33 *Boswell's Life of Johnson*, 4:338.

34 Bate, Bullit, and Powell, ed., *Works of Samuel Johnson*, vol.5:105.

35 Ibid., vol.1: 262–3.

36 Ibid., vol.2: 10.

37 Jacob Leed, 'Patronage in the *Rambler*,' *Studies in Burke and His Time*, 14 (1972): 5.

38 *The Rambler*, in *Works of Samuel Johnson*, 4:120.

39 *Boswell's Life of Johnson*, 5:59.

40 *The Letters of David Hume*, ed. J.Y.T. Greig (Oxford: Clarendon, 1932), 1:262.

41 Cited in Fussell, *Samuel Johnson*, 174.

42 John Courtney, *A Poetical Review of the Literary & Moral Characters of the Late Samuel Johnson* (London: 1786), 10–11, 25.

43 Fussell, *Samuel Johnson*, 82; *Boswell's Life of Johnson*, 2:1.

44 Griffin, *Literary Patronage in England*, 206.

45 Ernest Campbell Mossner, *The Life of David Hume* (Austin: University of Texas Press, 1954), 361.

46 Kernan, *Printing Technology, Letters and Samuel Johnson*, 32.

47 *Boswell's Life of Johnson*, 1:373.

48 Ibid., 372.

49 Joel J. Gould, 'John Wilkes and the Writings of "Pensioner Johnson,"' *Studies in Burke and His Time*, 18 (1977): 85–98.

50 *Boswell's Life of Johnson*, 1:429.

51 Ibid., 2:313. *Taxation No Tyranny* is contained in Hardy, *The Political Writings of Dr. Johnson*, 100–32. Johnson opposed American independence because he favoured rights for French Catholics in the Quebec Act of 1774 and because he supported Amerindian land claims and opposed black slavery. Johnson wrote: 'Let us restore to the French what we have taken from them. We shall see our Colonists at our feet, when they have an enemy so near them. Let us give the Indians arms, and teach them discipline, and encourage them now and then to plunder a Plantation.

Security and leisure are the parents of sedition.' Johnson found it distasteful that 'we hear the loudest yelps for liberty among the drivers of negroes' and recommended that the slaves be freed. 'If they are furnished with fire-arms for defence, and utensils for husbandry, and settled in some simple form of government within the country, they may be more grateful and honest than their masters.' Boswell, who supported American independence, black slavery, and opposed Catholic and Indian rights, might be said to be more typical of Enlightenment views, but doubtless national, as well as individual, differences among French, English, Scots, and Americans have to be taken into account. Benjamin Franklin dismissed Johnson's argument as that of 'a court pensioner' and responded to it by forging a document, allegedly written by a Senecan chief to the governor of Canada, listing the scalps of the men, women and children his tribesmen had taken for the English. See Gordon Wood, *The Americanization of Benjamin Franklin* (New York: Penguin, 2004), 160. It appears folly to commend Johnson's arguments against American independence when the Americans won on the battlefield, but, just as Johnson loved the University of Salamanca for declaring unlawful Spanish conquest of the Incas and Aztecs, I see merits in Johnson's taking the losing side on America. My point is that the arguments of Henry Care and Johnson cannot be dismissed because they were pensioners of government, and, while Locke, Franklin, and Paine were on the winning side, their arguments are not more interesting than Care's or Johnson's.

52 *Boswell's Life of Johnson*, 1:442–3.
53 Ibid., 2:153, 355; 4:118.
54 Ibid., 4:118; 2:153.
55 Cited in Donald J. Greene, *The Politics of Samuel Johnson* (New Haven, Conn.: Yale University Press, 1960), 3.
56 *Boswell's Life of Johnson*, 2:355.
57 Ibid., 2:457; Thrale, *Thraliana*, 1:46–7.
58 *Boswell's Life of Johnson*, 1:454.
59 Johnson, *Political Writings of Dr. Johnson*, 47.
60 *Boswell's Life of Johnson*, 2:157–8.
61 William Shaw, *Memoirs of the Life and Writings of the Late Dr. Samuel Johnson (1785)* (New York: Garland, 1974), 178–9.
62 Thrale, *Thraliana*, 1:329.
63 Ibid., 16.
64 Hawkins, *Life of Samuel Johnson*, 203–4.
65 Hester Thrale frequently compared Johnson and Rousseau with respect to Christian penance administered at the hands of women (via flogging).

See Richard Ingram, ed., *Dr. Johnson by Mrs. Thrale* (London: Chatto and
Windus, 1984) 22, 67, 111–12; Thrale, *Thraliana*, 1:203, 384–6; 2:765–6.
66 Hawkins, *Life of Samuel Johnson*, 176.

9 Irish Antagonists: Burke and Shelburne

1 Lord Fitzmaurice, *Life of William Earl of Shelburne*, vol.1 (London:
   Macmillan, 1912), 427.
2 David O. Thomas, *The Honest Mind: The Thought and Work of Richard Price*
   (Oxford: Clarendon, 1977), 145.
3 Fitzmaurice, *Life of William Earl of Shelburne*, 2:337–8.
4 Peter Brown, *The Chathamites: A Study in the Relationship between Personalities
   and Ideas in the Second Half of the Eighteenth Century* (London: Macmillan,
   1967), 104.
5 Mary P. Mack, *Jeremy Bentham: An Odyssey of Ideas, 1748–1792* (London:
   Heinemann, 1962), 370; Bentham, *The Works of Jeremy Bentham*, vol.10, ed.
   John Bowring (New York: Russell and Russell, 1962), 186.
6 *Boswell's Life of Johnson*, ed. George Birkbeck Hill (Oxford: Clarendon,
   1887), 3:35–6.
7 Hester Thrale, *Thraliana: The Diary of Mrs. Hester Lynch Thrale*, ed.
   Katherine C. Balderston (Oxford: Clarendon, 1951), 1:81.
8 John Norris, *Shelburne and Reform* (London: Macmillan, 1963), 5–6.
9 *The Correspondence of Adam Smith*, ed. Ernest Campbell Mossner and Ian
   Simpson Ross (Oxford: Clarendon, 1987), 258.
10 Conor Cruise O'Brien, *The Great Melody: A Thematic Biography and
   Commentated Anthology of Edmund Burke* (London: Sinclair-Stevenson,
   1992), 235–43.
11 Ibid., 50, 235.
12 Brown, *The Chathamites*, 90.
13 Edmund Burke, *Letter to a Noble Lord*, in Paul Langford, L.G. Mitchell, and
   William B. Todd, eds., *The Writings and Speeches of Edmund Burke*, vol.9
   (Oxford: Clarendon, 1989), 177.
14 Norris, *Shelburne and Reform*, 132–4.
15 Fitzmaurice, *Life of William, Earl of Shelburne*, 2:420–1.
16 Jenny Uglow, *The Lunar Men: Five Friends Whose Curiosity Changed the World*
   (New York: Farrar, Straus and Giroux, 2002), 446.
17 Edmund Burke, *Reflections on the Revolution in France*, ed. L.G. Mitchell
   (Oxford: Oxford University Press, 1993), 11; Mitchell writes (xiii) that 'no
   passage in the *Reflections* is more bitter than that which discusses these
   men' [Shelburne's circle at Bowood].

18 Burke, *Reflections*, 8.
19 Thomas, *The Honest Mind*, 314.
20 Burke, *Letter to a Noble Lord*, 162. See Isaac Kramnick, *The Rage of Edmund Burke: Portrait of an Ambivalent Conservative* (New York: Basic Books, 1977), for a fine account of the connection between Burke's rage and the ambiguity of his class identification.
21 Thomas, *The Honest Mind*, 313.
22 *Boswell's Life of Johnson*, 4:174.
23 Cited in Jennifer M. Walsh, *Edmund Burke and International Relations: The Commonwealth of Europe and the Crusade against the French Revolution* (New York: St Martin's Press, 1995), 10.
24 Thomas Love Peacock, *Nightmare Abbey* (1818), in *Nightmare Abbey and Crotchet Castle* (London: Hamish Hamilton, 1947), 58.
25 Karl Marx, *Capital: A Critical Analysis of Capitalist Production*, trans. Samuel Moore and Edward Aveling (Moscow: Foreign Languages Publishing House, 1959), 1:760.
26 Burke, *Letter to a Noble Lord*, 160.
27 O'Brien, *The Great Melody*, 135.
28 Ibid., 162.
29 Frederick G. Whelan, *Edmund Burke and India: Political Morality and Empire* (Pittsburgh: University of Pittsburgh Press, 1996), 118.
30 Ian Crowe, 'Introduction: Principles and Circumstances,' in Ian Crowe, ed., *Edmund Burke: His Life and Legacy* (Dublin: Four Courts Press, 1997), 15.
31 Ibid., 413.
32 Cited in Walsh, *Edmund Burke and International Relations*, 90.
33 Crowe, *Edmund Burke*, 15.
34 O'Brien, *The Great Melody*, 463, 502.
35 Burke, 'Speech on Economical Reform,' in *The Writings and Speeches of Edmund Burke*, ed. Langford, Mitchell, and Todd, 3:528.
36 Sir Lewis Namier, *England in the Age of the American Revolution* (London: Macmillan, 1966), 179.
37 Lewis Namier, *The Structure of Politics at the Accession of George III* (London: Macmillan, 1957), 10.
38 Burke's speech in the House of Commons in February 1769, cited in John Brewer, *Party Ideology and Popular Politics at the Accession of George III* (Cambridge: Cambridge University Press, 1976), 71.
39 Christopher Reid, *Edmund Burke and the Practice of Political Writing* (Dublin: Gill and Macmillan, 1985), 76.
40 Brown, *The Chathamites*, 56.

41 Neither J.G.A. Pocock nor Conor Cruise O'Brien, who assess Namier's view of Burke, mention Burke's use of Jews as symbols of the rootless ideology and anti-clericalism of the French Revolution. Since Namier's admiration for aristocratic eighteenth-century British politics may have been a reaction to the racist populism he fled in his lifetime, I think it unlikely that he would have ignored Burke's anti-Semitism, as Pocock and O'Brien have.

42 Hill, ed., *Boswell's Life of Johnson*, 5:358.

43 Bowring, ed., *Works of Jeremy Bentham*, 1:249; 10:116–17.

44 O'Brien, *The Great Melody*, 93–4, 462–3.

45 Ibid., 231.

46 Ibid., 452.

47 Reid, *Edmund Burke*, 79–81.

48 Brown, *The Chathamites*, 196, 225–6.

49 Hill, ed., *Boswell's Life of Johnson*, 4:338.

50 Thomas, *The Honest Mind*, 147; also, 316.

51 Uglow, *The Lunar Men*, xiii.

52 Ibid., 195–8, 218–19.

53 Brown, *The Chathamites*, 123.

54 Joseph Priestley, *The History and Present State of Electricity with Original Experiments* (London: C. Bathurst et al. 1775), xv–xvi. This work was first published in 1767, before Price introduced Priestley to Shelburne in 1772, the year before Shelburne employed Priestley.

55 Robert E. Schofield, *The Enlightenment of Joseph Priestley: A Study of His Life and Work from 1733 to 1773* (University Park: Pennsylvania State University Press, 1997), 271.

56 Ibid.

57 Cited in Stewart Crehan, *Blake in Context* (Dublin: Gill and Macmillan, 1984), 290.

58 I am grateful to J.G.A. Pocock for this information.

59 Ann Holt, *A Life of Joseph Priestley* (London: Oxford University Press, 1931), 93, 139.

60 Ibid., 211–12; Schofield, *Enlightenment*, 275.

61 Thomas, *The Honest Mind*, 312; Carl B. Cone, *Burke and the Nature of Politics: The Age of the French Revolution*, vol.2 (Lexington: University of Kentucky Press, 1964), 291.

62 Mack, *Jeremy Bentham*, 380.

63 Ibid., 112, 362.

64 Ibid., 130.
65 Adam Smith, *The Theory of Moral Sentiments*, ed. D.D. Raphael and A.L. Macfie (Indianapolis: Liberty Fund, 1982), 95.
66 Bentham, *Works of Jeremy Bentham,*, 10:115.
67 Ibid., 245.
68 Bentham papers, cited in Norris, *Shelburne and Reform*, 142.
69 Bentham, *Works of Jeremy Bentham*, 10:142.
70 Burke, *The Correspondence of Edmund Burke*, ed. R.B. McDowell, vol.8 (Chicago: University of Chicago Press, 1989), 79. As a morally justifiable practice, patronage is distinct from all-too-human nepotism, as was the case when Burke, as postmaster general in 1782, got a Treasury position for his son Richard, or when Benjamin Franklin, as postmaster general for North America in 1753, appointed all his friends and relatives to positions under his control.
71 Generosus, *The Nature of Patronage and the Duty of Patrons* (Edinburgh: John Traill, 1735), 6, 12–13. Generosus's opposition to partisanship may appear to conflict with Burke's commitments to political parties, but Generosus's conception of merit included a firm commitment to High Anglicanism.
72 Linda Colley, *Britons: Forging the Nation, 1707–1837* (New Haven, Conn.: Yale University Press, 1992), 130.
73 Whelan, *Edmund Burke and India*, 84.
74 Ibid., 49, 116.
75 Cited in Stuart Andrews ed., *Enlightened Despotism* (London: Longmans, 1967),159–62.
76 Burke, *Reflections*, 79.
77 J.G.A. Pocock, introduction to Edmund Burke, *Reflections on the Revolution in France*, (Indianapolis, Ind.: Hackett, 1987), xxxvii–xxxviii.
78 Burke, *The Writings and Speeches of the Right Honourable Edmund Burke in Twelve Volumes* (Toronto: G.N. Morang, 1901), 175.
79 Burke, *Reflections*, 148–9.
80 John Keane, in *Tom Paine: A Political Life* (Boston: Little Brown, 1995), 269, writes that little is known of Joe's age and skin colour; see also W.E. Woodward, *Tom Paine: America's Grandfather, 1737–1809* (New York: E.P. Dutton, 1945), 153–4. David Freeman Hawke, *Paine* (New York: Harper and Row, 1974), 167, 376, asserts that the servant was black.
81 *The Complete Writings of Thomas Paine*, ed. Philip F. Foner (New York: Citadel Press, 1945), 1246.
82 Ibid., 1265–6.

83 Thomas and Lorraine Pangle, *The Learning of Liberty* (Lawrence: University Press of Kansas, 1993), 113.

84 Ibid., 149–62.

85 John Adams, *A Defence of the Constitution of Government of the United States of America*, vol.1 (London: John Stockdale, 1794), 217.

86 Guy Chaussinand-Nogaret, *Histoire des élites en France du XVIè au XXè siècle: l'honneur, le mérite, l'argent* (Paris: Tallandier, 1991), 303–12.

87 Roger Hahn, *The Anatomy of a Scientific Institution: The Paris Academy of the Sciences, 1666–1803* (Berkeley: University of California Press, 1972); Martin S. Staum, *Minerva's Message: Stabilizing the French Revolution* (Montreal and Kingston: McGill-Queen's University Press, 1996).

88 John Lough, *Writer and Public in France* (Oxford: Clarendon, 1978), 275.

89 Annie Jourdan, *Napoléon, héros, imperator, mécène* (Paris: Aubier, 1998).

90 Émile Zola, 'L'argent dans la Littérature,' in *Oeuvres Complètes*, t.10 (Paris: Cercle du livres précieux, 1968), 1268.

91 Ibid., 1269, 1270, 1276.

92 Ibid., 1277, 1279.

93 G. Vauthier, 'Les pensions aux écrivains, 1806–1810,' *Revue des études napoléoniennes*, 2 (1914):297–303.

94 Lough, *Writer and Public in France*, 314–15.

95 Roxana M. Verona, *Les 'Salons de Sainte-Beuve': le critique et ses muses* (Paris: Honoré Champion, 1999).

96 Richard B. Sher, *Church and University in the Scottish Enlightenment: The Moderate Literati of Edinburgh* (Princeton, N.J.: Princeton University Press, 1985), 305.

Conclusion

1 Benjamin Franklin, *The Writings*, ed. Albert Henry Smyth (New York: Macmillan, 1907), 10:148.

2 Theodor Adorno and Max Horkheimer, *Dialectic of Enlightenment*, trans. John Cumming (New York: Herder and Herder, 1972); Herbert Marcuse, *Reason and Revolution: Hegel and the Rise of Social Theory* (Boston: Beacon Press, 1968).

3 Cited in Roger Hahn, *The Anatomy of a Scientific Institution: The Paris Academy of the Sciences, 1666–1803* (Berkeley: University of California Press, 1971), 165.

4 Isaac Kramnick, *The Portable Enlightenment Reader* (New York: Penguin, 1995), xviii-xix; Gordon S. Wood, *The Radicalism of the American Revolution* (New York: Alfred A. Knopf, 1992), 100.

5   Bernard Bailyn, *The Origins of American Politics* (New York: Alfred A. Knopf, 1968), 28–31, 109–10; Wood, *Radicalism of the American Revolution*, 57–92.

6   Kant, 'What Is Enlightenment?' in *Kant's Political Writings*, ed. Hans Reiss, trans. H.B. Nisbet (Cambridge: Cambridge University Press, 1970), 59.

7   Kramnick, *Portable Enlightenment Reader*, xix.

8   Wood, *The Radicalism of the American Revolution*, 100.

9   Donald W. Livingstone, 'Hume, English Barbarism and American Independence,' in Richard B. Sher and Jeffrey R. Smitten, eds., *Scotland and America in the Age of Enlightenment* (Edinburgh: Edinburgh University Press, 1990), 133–47.

10   Blaise Pascal, *Pensées*, trans. M. Turnell (New York: Harper and Brothers, 1962), 151.

11   Voltaire, 'Equality,' in *Philosophical Dictionary*, trans. Peter Gay (New York: Basic Books, 1962), 246.

12   Pierre Bourdieu and Hans Haacke, *Free Exchange* (Stanford, Calif.: Stanford University Press, 1995), 54.

13   William Simon, *A Time for Truth* (New York: McGraw-Hill, 1979), xi.

14   Ibid., xiv, 238, 230, 231.

15   One might compare John Olin to Alfred Nobel, since their foundations were based on armaments and petrochemicals, but the Olin Foundation does not reward peacemakers and its standards of excellence are more uniform ideologically than those of the Nobel Foundation. Though Catherine the Great's patronage of philosophers served to cover her murderous past, Nobel still seems closer to the great patron of the Enlightenment than Olin.

16   See Derk Arend Wilcox, Joshua Sheckman, and Penelope Naas, eds., *The Right Guide: A Guide to Conservative and Right of Centre Organizations* (Ann Arbor, Mich: Economics America, 1993). Anne Norton, *Leo Strauss and the Politics of the American Empire*, (New Haven, Conn.: Yale University Press, 2004), 11–12, points out the role of the Olin, Bradley, Scaife, and Earheart foundations in patronizing Straussian thinkers and promoting the rise of right-wing thought in the United States.

17   Simon, *Time for Truth*, 231–2.

Bibliography

Adams, Robert. 'In Search of Baron Somers.' In Perez Zagorin, ed., *Culture and Politics from Puritanism to the Enlightenment*. Berkeley: University of California Press, 1980.

Adorno, Theodor, and Max Horkheimer. *Dialectic of Enlightenment*. Trans. John Cumming. New York: Herder and Herder, 1972.

Alembert, Jean Le Rond d'. *Preliminary Discourse to the Encyclopedia of Diderot*. Trans. Richard N. Schwab. Chicago: University of Chicago Press, l995.

– *Oeuvres complètes de D'Alembert*. Geneva: Slatkine, 1967.

Alexander, John T. *Catherine the Great: Life and Legend*. Oxford: Oxford University Press, 1989.

Alfieri, Vittorio. *The Prince and Letters*. Trans. Beatrice Corrigan and Julius A. Molinaro. Toronto: University of Toronto Press, 1972.

Allan, David. *Virtue, Learning and the Scottish Enlightenment: Ideas of Scholarship in Early Modern History*. Edinburgh: Edinburgh University Press, 1993.

Amato, Joseph Antony. *Guilt and Gratitude: A Study of the Origins of Contemporary Conscience*. Westport, Conn.: Greenwood Press, 1982.

Anderson, Bonnie, and Judith P. Zinsser. *A History of Their Own: Women in Europe from Prehistory to the Present*. New York: Harper and Row, 1988.

Andrew, Edward. *Protestant Conscience, Enlightenment Reason and Modern Subjectivity*. Toronto: University of Toronto Press, 2001.

Andrews, Stuart, ed. *Enlightened Despotism*. London: Longmans, 1967.

Aristotle. *The Complete Works of Aristotle*. Ed. Jonathan Barnes. Princeton, N.J.: Princeton University Press, 1991.

Armitage, David. 'Locke's Carolina Re-visited.' Paper presented to North American Conference on British Studies, Toronto, 2 November 2001.

Ashley, Maurice. *The Glorious Revolution of 1688*. London: Hodder and Stoughton, 1966.

– *James II*. London: J.M. Dent, 1977.

Augustijn, Cornelis. *Erasmus: His Life, Works and Influence*. Trans. J.C. Grayson. Toronto: University of Toronto Press, 1991.

Avenel, Georges d', Vicomte. *Les riches depuis sept cent ans: les revenus d'un intellectuel de 1200 à 1913; revenus et bénéfices, appointements et honoraires*. Paris: Colin, 1909.

Backscheider, Paula R. *Daniel Defoe: His Life*. Baltimore: Johns Hopkins University Press, 1989.

Bacon, Francis. *The Advancement of Learning*. Ed. Michael Kiernan. Oxford: Clarendon, 2000.

Badinter, Elisabeth, and Robert Badinter. *Condorcet: Un intellectuel en politique*. Paris: Fayard, 1988.

Bailyn, Bernard. *The Origins of American Politics*. New York: Alfred Knopf, 1968.

Basker, James G. 'Scotticisms and the Problem of Cultural Identity.' In John Dwyer and Richard B. Sher, eds. *Sociability and Society in Eighteenth-Century Scotland*. Edinburgh: Mercat Press, 1993.

Battestin, Martin C., and Ruth R. *Henry Fielding: A Life*. London: Routledge, 1989.

Bayle, Pierre. *Critique générale de l'Histoire du Calvinisme de Mr. Maimbourg*. Ville-Franche: Pierre le Blanc, 1683.

– *A General Dictionary*. Trans. P. DesMaiseaux et al. London: James Bettenham, 1734–41.

– *An Historical and Critical Dictionary*. Trans. P. DesMaiseaux et al. London: C. Harper et al., 1710.

– *Philosophical Commentary*. Trans. Amie Godman Tannenbaum. New York: Peter Lang, 1987.

Belanger, Terry. 'Publishers and Writers in Eighteenth-Century England.' In Isabel Rivers, ed., *Books and Their Readers in Eighteenth-Century England*. Leicester: Leicester University Press, 1982.

Belin, J.-P. *Le Commerce des livres prohibés à Paris de 1750 à 1789*. Paris, 1913; rep. New York: Burt Franklin, 1962.

Benedict, Barbara M. 'Service to the Public': William Creech and Sentiment for Sale.' In John Dwyer and Richard B. Sher, eds., *Sociability and Society in Eighteenth-Century Scotland*. Edinburgh: Mercat Press, 1993.

Bénichou, Paul. *The Consecration of the Writer, 1750–1830*. Trans. Mark K. Jensen. Lincoln: University of Nebraska Press, 1999.

Bentham, Jeremy. *A Fragment on Government*. Eds. J.H. Burns and H.L.A. Hart. Cambridge: Cambridge University Press, 1988.

– *The Works of Jeremy Bentham*. Ed. John Bowring. New York: Russell and Russell, 1962.

Berenson, Frances. 'Socrates the Man.' In K. J. Boudouris, ed., *The Philosophy of Socrates*. Athens: International Center for Greek Philosophy and Culture, 1991·

Berlin, Isaiah. *The Age of Enlightenment: The 18th Century Philosophers*. New York: Mentor, 1963.

Berry, Christopher. *Social Theory of the Scottish Enlightenment*. Edinburgh: Edinburgh University Press, 1997.

Bien, David P. *The Calas Affair: Persecution, Toleration, and Heresy in Eighteenth-Century Toulouse*. Princeton: Princeton University Press, 1960.

Birn, Raymond. *Forging Rousseau: Print, Commerce and Cultural Manipulation in the Late Enlightenment*. Oxford: Voltaire Foundation, 2001.

– 'Rousseau et ses éditeurs.' *Revue d'histoire moderne et contemporaine*, 40 (1993).

Black, Jeremy. *The English Press of the Eighteenth Century*. London: Croom Helm, 1987.

Blanning, T.C.W. *The Culture of Power and the Power of Culture: Old Regime Europe 1660–1789*. Oxford: Oxford University Press, 2002.

– 'Frederick the Great and Enlightened Absolutism.' In H.M. Scott, ed., *Enlightened Absolutism*. Ann Arbor: University of Michigan Press, 1990.

Bloch, Marc. *Feudal Society*. Trans. L.A. Manyon. London: Routledge and Kegan Paul, 1961.

Boissevain, Jeremy. *Friends of Friends: Networks, Manipulators and Coalitions*. Oxford: Blackwell, 1974.

Boswell, James. *Boswell's Life of Johnson*. Ed. George Birkbeck Hill. Oxford: Clarendon, 1887.

Bourdieu, Pierre, and Hans Haacke. *Free Exchange*. Stanford, Calif.: Stanford University Press, 1995.

Bredin, Jean-Denis. *Une singulière famille: Jacques Necker, Suzanne Necker et Germaine de Staël*. Paris: Fayard, 1999.

Brewer, Daniel. *The Discourse of Enlightenment in Eighteenth-Century France: Diderot and the Art of Philosophizing*. Cambridge: Cambridge University Press, 1990.

Brewer, John. *Party Ideology and Popular Politics at the Accession of George III*. Cambridge: Cambridge University Press, 1976.

Brown, Peter. *The Chathamites: A Study in the Relationship between Personalities and Ideas in the Second Half of the Eighteenth Century*. London: Macmillan, 1967.

Bruce, Archibald. *The Patron's A, B, C: or, the Shorter Catechism Attempted after a New Plan*. Glasgow: J. Duncan, 1771.

Brumfitt, J.H. 'Voltaire Historian and the Royal Mistresses.' In Maxine G. Cutler, ed., *Voltaire, the Enlightenment and the Comic Mode: Essays in Honor of Jean Sareil*. New York: Peter Lang, 1990.

Brush, Craig B. *Montaigne and Bayle: Variations on the Theme of Scepticism*. The Hague: Martinus Nijhoff, 1966.

Burke, Edmund. *The Correspondence of Edmund Burke*. Ed. R.B. McDowell. Chicago: University of Chicago Press, 1989.
– *Reflections on the Revolution in France*. Ed. L.G. Mitchell. Oxford: Oxford University Press, 1993.
– *Reflections on the Revolution in France*. Ed. J.G.A. Pocock. Indianapolis: Hackett, 1987.
– *The Works*. London: Rivington, 1826.
– *The Writings and Speeches of Edmund Burke*. Ed. Paul Langford, L.G. Mitchell, and William B. Todd. Oxford: Clarendon, 1989.
– The Writings and Speeches of the Right Honourable Edmund Burke in Twelve Volumes. Toronto: G.N. Morang, 1901.
Burke, Peter. *A Social History of Knowledge from Gutenberg to Diderot*. Oxford: Polity, 2000.
Butler, Martin. '"We Are One Mans All": Jonson's *The Gipsies* Metamorphosed.' In *The Yearbook of English Studies: Politics, Patronage and Literature in England*, vol. 21. Leeds: Modern Humanities Research Association, 1991.
Caldicott, C.E.J. *La Carrière de Molière: entre protecteurs et éditeurs*. Amsterdam: Rodopi, 1998.
Camic, Charles. *Experience and Enlightenment: Socialization for Cultural Change in Eighteenth-Century Scotland*. Edinburgh: Edinburgh University Press, 1983.
Carey, Hilary M. *Courting Disaster: Astrology at the English Court and University in the Later Middle Ages*. London: Macmillan, 1992.
Carney, James. *The Irish Bardic Poet: A Study in the Relationship of Poet and Patron*. Dublin: Dolmen Press, 1967.
Cassirer, Ernst. *The Philosophy of the Enlightenment*. Trans. Fritz Koelln and James Pettegrove. Princeton, N.J.: Princeton University Press, 1979.
Castiglione, Baldesar. *The Book of the Courtier*. Trans. Charles S. Singleton. New York: Anchor Books, 1959.
Champion, J.A.I. *The Pillars of Priestcraft Shaken: The Church of England and Its Enemies, 1660–1730*. Cambridge: Cambridge University Press, 1992.
Chartier, Roger. *The Cultural Origins of the French Revolution*. Trans. Lydia G. Cochrane Durham, N.C.: Duke University Press, 1991.
– *Forms and Meanings: Texts, Performances and Audiences from Codex to Computer*. Philadelphia: University of Pennsylvania Press, 1995.
– *Lectures et Lecteurs dans la France d'ancien régime*. Paris: Éditions du seuil, 1987.
– 'The Man of Letters.' In Michel Vovelle, ed., and Lydia G. Cochrane, trans, *Enlightenment Portraits*. Chicago: University of Chicago Press, 1997.
– *The Order of Books*. Trans. Lydia G. Cochrane. Durham, N.C.: Duke University Press, 1991.

– 'Student Populations in the Eighteenth Century.' Trans. J. Dunkley. *British Journal for Eighteenth-Century Studies*, 2 (1979).

Chartier, Roger, Marie-Madeleine Compère, and Dominique Julia. *L'Education en France du XVIe au XVIIIe siècle*. Paris: Société d'édition, 1976.

Châtelet, Madame du. *Discours sur le bonheur*. Paris: Payot and Rivages, 1995.

– *Institutions de physique*. Paris: Prault, 1740.

Chaussinand-Nogaret, Guy. *Choiseul: Naissance de la gauche*. Paris: Perrin, 1995.

– *Histoire des élites en France du XVIè au XXè siècle: l'honneur, le mérite, l'argent*. Paris: Tallandier, 1991.

Chisick, Harvey. 'David Hume and the Common People.' In Peter Jones, ed., *The 'Science of Man' in the Scottish Enlightenment: Hume, Reid and Their Contemporaries*. Edinburgh: Edinburgh University Press, 1989.

Christensen, Jerome. *Practicing Enlightenment: Hume and the Formation of a Literary Career*. Madison: University of Wisconsin Press, 1987.

Cicero, Marcus Tullius. *The Offices*. Trans. Thomas Lockman. London: J.M. Dent, 1960.

Colley, Linda. *Britons: Forging the Nation, 1707–1837*. New Haven, Conn.: Yale University Press, 1992.

Collins, A.S. *The Profession of Letters*. London: George Routledge and Sons, 1928.

Commanger, Henry Steele. *The Empire of Reason: How Europe Imagined and America Realized the Enlightenment*. Garden City, N.Y.: Anchor Press, 1977.

Cone, Carl B. *Burke and the Nature of Politics: The Age of the French Revolution*. Lexington: University of Kentucky Press, 1964.

Corbin, Alain, Jacqueline Lalouette, and Michèle Riot-Sarcey, eds. *Femmes dans la cité, 1815–1871*. Paris: Créaphis, 1997.

Coste, Pierre. 'The Character of Mr. Locke.' In Jean S. Yolton, ed., *A Locke Miscellany: Locke Biography and Criticism for All*. Bristol: Thoemmes, 1990.

Courtines, Léo Pierre. *Bayle's Relations with England and the English*. New York: Columbia University Press, 1938.

Courtney, John. *A Poetical Review of the Literary & Moral Characters of the Late Samuel Johnson*. London: 1786.

Cranston, Maurice. *Jean-Jacques: The Early Life and Work of Jean-Jacques Rousseau, 1712–1754*. London: Allen Lane, 1983.

– *John Locke: A Biography*. London: Longmans Green, 1957.

– 'John Locke and the Case for Toleration.' In Susan Mendus and David Edwards, eds., *On Toleration*. Oxford: Clarendon, 1987.

Craveri, Benedetta. *Madame du Deffand and Her World*. Trans. Teresa Waugh. London: Peter Holban, 1994.

Crehan, Stewart. *Blake in Context*. Dublin: Gill and Macmillan, 1984.

Crocker, Lester. 'The Enlightenment: Problems of Interpretation.' In R. Ajello, M. Firpo, L. Guerci, and G. Ricuperati, eds., *L'Età Dei Lumi: Studi Storici sul settecento Europeo in Onore di Franco Venturi*. Napoli: Jovene, 1985.

Crowe, Ian, ed. *Edmund Burke: His Life and Legacy*. Dublin: Four Courts Press, 1997.

Curtis, Mark H. 'The Alienated Intellectuals of Early Stuart England,' *Past and Present*, 23 (1962).

Curwen, Henry. *A History of Booksellers: The Old and the New*. London: Chatto and Windus, 1874.

Daniel, Stephen H. *John Toland: His Methods, Manners, and Mind*. Montreal and Kington: McGill-Queen's University Press, 1984.

Darnton, Robert. *The Business of Enlightenment: A Publishing History of the Encyclopédie, 1775–1800*. Cambridge, Mass.: Belknap Press, 1979.

– *The Corpus of Clandestine Literature in France 1769–1789*. New York: W.W. Norton, 1995.

– 'An Exemplary Literary Career.' In Jeffrey Merrick and Dorothy Medlin, eds., *André Morellet (1727–1819) in the Republic of Letters and the French Revolution*. New York: Peter Lang, 1995.

– *The Great Cat Massacre and Other Episodes in French Cultural History*. London: Allen Lane, 1984.

– *The Literary Underground of the Old Regime*. Cambridge, Mass.: Harvard University Press, 1982

Diderot, Denis. *Rameau's Nephew and Other Works*. Trans. Jacques Barzun and Ralph H. Bowen. Indianapolis: Hackett, 2001.

– *Lettre sur le commerce de la librarie*. Paris: Grasset, 1937.

– *Oeuvres Complètes*. Ed. Roger Lewinter. Paris: Société encyclopédique française et le Club français du livre, 1972.

– *Political Writings*. Ed. and trans. John Hope Mason and Robert Wokler. Cambridge: Cambridge University Press, 1992.

D'Israeli, Isaac. *Calamities of Authors; including Some Inquiries respecting Their Moral and Literary Characters*. New York: James Eastburn, 1812.

Dodge, Guy Howard. *The Political Theory of the Huguenots of the Dispersion: With Special Reference to the Thought and Influence of Pierre Jurieu*. New York: Columbia University Press, 1947.

Dodsley, Robert. *The Correspondence of Robert Dodsley, 1733–64*. Ed. James E. Turney. Cambridge: Cambridge University Press, 1988.

Donovan, Robert Kent. 'The Popular Party of the Church of Scotland and the American Revolution.' In Richard B. Sher and Jeffrey R. Smitten, eds.,

Scotland and America in the Age of Enlightenment. Edinburgh: Edinburgh
University Press, 1990·

Dover, Kenneth. 'Socrates in the Clouds.' In Gregory Vlastos, ed., *The
Philosophy of Socrates: A Collection of Critical Essays.* New York: Anchor Books,
1971.

Downie, Alan. 'The Growth of Government Toleration of the Press to 1790.' In
Robin Myers and Michael Harris, eds., *Development of the English Book Trade,
1700–1899.* Oxford: Oxford Polytechnic Press, 1982.

Duclos, Charles. *Considérations sur les Moeurs de ce siècle (1750).* Ed. F.C. Green.
Cambridge: Cambridge University Press, 1939.

Duffy, Eamon. *The Stripping of the Altars: Traditional Religion in England, 1400–
1580.* New Haven, Conn.: Yale University Press, 1992.

Eagleton, Terry. *Literary Theory: An Introduction.* Oxford: Basil Blackwell, 1985.

Eisenstein, Elizabeth. *Print Culture and Enlightenment Thought.* Chapel Hill:
University of North Carolina Press, 1986.

Elena, Alberto. 'An Introduction to Laura Bassi.' *Isis,* 82 (1991): 510–18.

Emerson, Ralph Waldo. *The Essential Writings of Ralph Waldo Emerson.* New York:
Modern Library, 2000.

Emerson, Roger L. 'Archibald Campbell, 3rd Duke of Argyll (1682–1761):
Patronage and the Creation of the Scottish Enlightenment.' Unpublished
paper.

– 'How Not to Deal with Enlightenments.' *Historically Speaking* 3:3 (2002).

– 'Lord Bute and the Scottish Universities 1760–1792.' In Karl W. Schweizer,
ed., *Lord Bute: Essays in Re-interpretation.* Leicester: Leicester University Press,
1988.

– *Patronage and Politics: The Aberdeen Universities in the Eighteenth Century.*
Aberdeen: Aberdeen University Press, 1992.

– 'Politics and the Glasgow Professors, 1690–1800.' In Andrew Hook and Richard
B. Sher, eds. *The Glasgow Enlightenment.* East Lothian: Tuckwell Press, 1995.

L'Encyclopédie ou Dictionnaire Raisonné des Sciences des Arts et des Métiers. Nouvelle
impression en facsimile de la première edition de 1751–1780. Stuttgart-Bad
Cannstatt: Friedrich Fromman Verlag, 1966.

Erasmus, Desiderius. *The Education of a Christian Prince.* Trans. Neil M. Cheshire
and Michael J Health. Cambridge: Cambridge University Press, 1997.

Evans, Robert C. *Ben Jonson and the Poetics of Patronage.* Lewisburg, Penn.:
Bucknell University Press, 1989.

Evans, Robert Rees. *Pantheisticon: The Career of John Toland.* New York: Peter
Lang, 1991.

Fargher, Richard. *Life and Letters in France: The Eighteenth Century.* New York:
Charles Scribner's Sons, 1970.

Feather, John. *A History of British Publishing*. London: Croom Helm, 1988.

Fevre, Lucien, and Henri-Jean Martin. *The Coming of the Book: The Impact of Printing 1450–1800*. Trans. David Gerard. London: New Left Books, 1976.

Fitzmaurice, Lord. *Life of William, Earl of Shelburne*. London: Macmillan, 1912.

Flynn, Philip. *Enlightenment Scotland: A Study and Selection of Scottish Philosophical Prose from the Eighteenth and Early Nineteenth Centuries*. Edinburgh: Scottish Academic Press, 1992.

Foote, Samuel. *The Patron: A Comedy in Three Acts*. London: P. Vaillant, 1774.

Foucault, Michel. 'What Is Enlightenment?' In Paul Rabinow, ed., *The Foucault Reader*. New York: Pantheon, 1984.

France, Peter. *Politeness and Its Discontents: Problems in French Classical Culture*. Cambridge: Cambridge University Press, 1992.

Franklin, Benjamin. *The Writings*, ed. Albert Henry Smyth. New York: Macmillan, 1907.

–*Writings*. New York: Library of America, 1987.

Fraser, David. *Frederick the Great: King of Prussia*. London: Allen Lane, 2000.

Friedrich der Grosse. *De la Littérature Allemande*. Stuttgart: G.J. Göschen'sche Verlagshandlung, 1883.

Fry, Michael. *Patronage and Principle: A Political History of Modern Scotland*. Aberdeen: Aberdeen University Press, 1987.

– *The Dundas Despotism*. Edinburgh: Edinburgh University Press, 1992.

Fuhrmann, Manfred. *Seneca und Kaiser Nero: Eine Biographie*. Berlin: Alexander Fest, 1997.

Furet, François, and Jacques Ozouf. *Reading and Writing: Literacy in France from Calvin to Jules Ferry*. Cambridge: Cambridge University Press, 1982.

Fussell, Paul. *Samuel Johnson and the Life of Writing*. New York: Harcourt Brace Jovanovich, 1971.

Gascoigne, John. *Science, Politics and Universities in Europe, 1600–1800*. Aldershot, U.K.: Ashgate, 1998.

Gay, Peter. 'Why Was the Enlightenment.' In Peter Gay, ed., *Eighteenth-Century Studies Presented to Arthur M. Wilson*. Hanover, N.H.: University Press of New England, 1972.

– *Voltaire's Politics: The Poet as Realist*. Princeton, N.J.: Princeton University Press, 1959.

Gellner, Ernest. 'Patrons and Clients.' In Ernest Gellner and John Waterbury, eds., *Patrons and Clients in Mediterranean Societies*. London: Duckworth, 1977.

Generosus. *The Nature of Patronage and the Duty of Patrons*. Edinburgh: John Traill, 1735.

Gibbon, Edward. *The Decline and Fall of the Roman Empire*. London: Penguin, 1936.

– *Memoirs*. London: Hunt and Clarke, 1817.

– *The Miscellaneous Works of Edward Gibbon, Esq. In 5 Volumes.* Ed. John Lord Sheffield. London: John Murray, 1814.

Godineau, Dominique. 'The Woman.' In Michel Vovelle, ed. and Lydia G. Cochrane, trans. *Enlightenment Portraits.* Chicago: University of Chicago Press, 1997.

Godwin, William. *An Enquiry concerning Political Justice.* In Mark Philp, ed., *Political and Philosophic Writings of William Godwin.* London: William Pickering, 1993.

– *History of the Commonwealth of England from Its Commencement to the Restoration of Charles the Second.* London: Henry Colburn, 1824.

Goldgar, Anne. *Impolite Learning: Conduct and Community in the Republic of Letters, 1680–1750.* New Haven, Conn.: Yale University Press, 1995.

Goldie, Mark. 'John Locke's Circle and James II.' *Historical Journal* 35 (1992).

Goncourt, Edmond, and Jules de Goncourt. *The Woman of the Eighteenth Century.* Trans. Jacques le Clercq and Ralph Roeder. London: George Allen and Unwin 1928.

Gooch, G.P. *Frederick the Great: The Ruler, The Writer, The Man.* Hamden, Conn.: Archon Books, 1962.

Goodman, Dena. 'Enlightenment Salons: The Convergence of Female and Philosophic Ambitions.' *Eighteenth-Century Studies* 22 (1989).

– *The Republic of Letters: A Cultural History of the French Enlightenment.* Ithaca, N.Y.: Cornell University Press, 1994.

Gordon, Alden R. 'Searching for the Elusive Madame de Pompadour.' *Eighteenth-Century Studies,* 37:1 (fall 2003).

Gordon, Daniel. 'Beyond the Social History of Ideas: Morellet and the Enlightenment.' In Jeffrey Merrick and Dorothy Medlin, eds., *André Morellet (1727–1819) in the Republic of Letters and the French Revolution.* New York: Peter Lang, 1995.

– *Citizens without Sovereignty: Equality and Sociability in French Thought, 1670–1789.* Princeton, N.J.: Princeton University Press, 1994.

Gouges, Olympe de. *The Rights of Women.* Trans. Val Stevenson. London: Pythia Press, 1989.

Gould, Joel J. 'John Wilkes and the Writings of "Pensioner Johnson."' *Studies in Burke and His Time,* 18 (1977).

Gray, John. *Voltaire and Enlightenment.* London: Phoenix, 1998.

The Gray's-Inn Journal. London: W. Faden for P. Vaillant, 1756.

Greene, Donald J. *The Politics of Samuel Johnson.* New Haven, Conn.: Yale University Press, 1960.

Griffin, Dustin. *Literary Patronage in England, 1650–1800.* Cambridge: Cambridge University Press, 1996.

Griffin, Miriam T. *Nero: The End of a Dynasty*. New Haven, Conn.: Yale University Press, 1984.

– *Seneca: A Philosopher in Politics*. Oxford: Clarendon, 1976.

Grinell, George. 'Newton's *Principia* as Whig Propaganda.' In Paul Fritz and David Williams, eds., *City and Society in the Eighteenth Century*. Toronto: Hakkert, 1973.

Guéhenno, Jean. *Jean-Jacques Rousseau*. Trans. John and Doreen Weightman. 2 vols. New York: Columbia University Press, 1967.

Gutman, Robert W. *Mozart: A Cultural Biography*. New York: Harcourt Brace, 1999.

Hahn, Roger. *The Anatomy of a Scientific Institution: The Paris Academy of Scientists, 1666–1803*. Berkeley: University of California Press, 1968.

Haley, K.H.D. *The First Earl of Shaftesbury*. Oxford: Clarendon, 1968.

Halkin, Léon-Ernest. *Erasmus: A Critical Biography*. Trans. John Tonkin. Oxford: Blackwell, 1993.

Hamel, Frank. *An Eighteenth-Century Marquise: A Study of Émilie Du Châtelet and Her Times*. New York: James Pott, 1911.

Hammerstein, Notker. 'The Enlightenment.' In Walter Rüegg, ed., *A History of the University in Europe*. Cambridge: Cambridge University Press, 1996.

Hankins, Thomas L. *Jean D'Alembert: Science and the Enlightenment*. Oxford: Clarendon, 1976.

Hanson, Laurence. *Government and the Press, 1695–1763*. London: Humphrey Milford, 1936.

Harrison, Peter. *'Religion' and the Religions in the Enlightenment*. Cambridge: Cambridge University Press, 1990.

Havens, George R. 'Diderot, Rousseau, and the Discours sur l'Inégalité.' *Diderot Studies*, 3 (1961).

Hawke, David Freeman. *Paine*. New York: Harper and Row, 1974.

Hawkins, Sir John. *The Life of Samuel Johnson, LL.D.* Ed. Bertram H. Davis. New York: Macmillan, 1961.

Hayes, Julia C. *Reading the French Enlightenment*. Cambridge: Cambridge University Press, 1999.

Hazewinkel, H.C. 'Pierre Bayle à Rotterdam.' In Paul Dibon, ed., *Pierre Bayle: Le Philosophe de Rotterdam*. Paris: Vrin, 1959

Hegel, Georg Wilhelm Friedrich. *The History of Philosophy*. Trans. E.S. Haldane. London: Routledge and Kegan Paul, 1955.

Hellegouarc'h, Jacqueline. *L'esprit de société: cercles et 'salons' parisiens au XVIIIè siècle*, Paris: Garnier, 2000.

Henderson, Bernard W. *The Life and Principate of the Emperor Nero*. Philadelphia: J.B. Lippincott, 1903.

Hersey, John E.N. *Voltaire.* London: Constable, 1976.

Hesse, Carla. *The Other Enlightenment: How French Women Became Modern.* Princeton: Princeton University Press, 2001.

Heyck, T.W. *The Transformation of Intellectual Life in Victorian England.* London: Croom Helm, 1982.

Hobbes, Thomas. *Leviathan.* Ed. J.C.A. Gaskin. Oxford: Oxford University Press, 1996.

Holt, Ann. *A Life of Joseph Priestley.* London: Oxford University Press, 1931.

Holzknecht, Karl Julius. *Literary Patronage in the Middle Ages.* New York: Octagon, 1966.

Houston, R.A. 'Scottish Education and Literacy, 1600–1800: An International Perspective.' In T.M. Devine, ed., *Improvement and Enlightenment: Proceedings of the Scottish Studies Seminar, University of Strathclyde 1987–88.* Edinburgh: John Donald, 1989.

Howells, R.J. *Pierre Jurieu: Antinomian Radical.* Durham, U.K.: University of Durham, 1983.

Hume, David. *Essays, Moral, Political and Literary.* Ed. Eugene F. Miller. Indianapolis: Liberty Classics, 1985.

– *The History of England from the Invasion of Julius Caesar to the Abdication of James the Second.* Boston: Phillips, Samson, 1856.

– *The Letters of David Hume.* Ed. J.Y.T. Greig. Oxford: Clarendon, 1932.

Hyde, Edward, Earl of Clarendon. *A Brief View and Survey of the Dangerous and Pernicious Errors to Church and State, in Mr. Hobbes's Book, Entitled Leviathan.* Oxford: Printed at the Theater, 1676.

Im Hof, Ulrich. *The Enlightenment.* Trans. William E. Yuill. Oxford: Blackwell, 1995.

Ingrams, Richard, ed. *Dr. Johnson by Mrs. Thrale* London: Chatto and Windus, 1984.

Inwood, Brad. 'Politics and Paradox in Seneca's *De beneficiis.*' In André Laks and Malcolm Schofield, eds., *Justice and Generosity: Studies in Hellenistic Social and Political Philosophy.* Cambridge: Cambridge University Press, 1995.

– 'The Will in Seneca the Younger.' *Classical Philology,* 95 (2000).

Israel, Jonathan I. *Radical Enlightenment: Philosophy and the Making of Modernity.* Oxford: Oxford University Press, 2001.

Jacob, Margaret C. *The Radical Enlightenment: Pantheists, Freemasons and Republicans.* London: George Allen and Unwin, 1981.

Jardine, Lisa. *Erasmus, Man of Letters: The Construction of Charisma in Print.* Princeton: Princeton University Press, 1993.

Jenkins, Frank. *Architect and Patron: A Survey of Professional Relations and Practice from the Sixteenth Century to the Present Day.* London: Oxford University Press, 1961.

Johnson, Samuel. *The Political Writings of Dr. Johnson: A Selection.* Ed. J.P. Hardy. London: Routledge and Kegan Paul, 1968.

– *Works.* Eds. W.J. Bate, John M. Bullitt, and L.F. Powell. New Haven: Yale University Press, 1963.

Jones, George Hilton. *Convergent Forces: Immediate Causes of the Revolution of 1688 in England.* Ames: Iowa State University Press, 1990.

Jones, J.R. *The Revolution of 1688 in England.* London: Weidenfeld and Nicolson, 1972.

Jourdan, Annie. *Napoléon, héros, imperator, mécène.* Paris: Aubier, 1998.

Jurieu, Pierre. *Des droits des deux souverains en matière de religion, la conscience et le prince.* Rotterdam: Henri de Graff, 1687.

Kant, Immanuel. *Kant's Political Writings.* Ed. Hans Reiss, trans. H.B. Nisbet. Cambridge: Cambridge University Press, 1970.

– *Observations on the Feeling of the Beautiful and Sublime.* Trans. John T. Goldthwait. Berkeley: University of California Press, 1960.

Kaufman, Robert, 'The Patron-Client Relationship and Macro-Politics: Problems and Prospects.' *Comparative Studies in Society and History,* 16 (1974).

Keane, John. *Tom Paine: A Political Life.* Boston: Little Brown, 1995.

Kelly, Christopher. *Rousseau as Author: Consecrating One's Life to the Truth.* Chicago: University of Chicago Press, 2003.

Kernan, Alvin. *Printing Technology, Letters and Samuel Johnson.* Princeton: Princeton University Press, 1987.

Kettering, Sharon. *Patrons, Brokers, and Clients in Seventeenth-Century France.* Oxford: Oxford University Press, 1986.

Kilcullen, John. *Sincerity and Truth: Essays on Arnauld, Bayle and Toleration.* Oxford: Clarendon, 1988.

Korshin, Paul. 'Types of Eighteenth-Century Literary Patronage.' *Eighteenth-Century Studies,* 7 (1974).

Kramnick, Isaac, ed. *The Portable Enlightenment Reader.* New York: Penguin, 1995.

– *The Rage of Edmund Burke: Portrait of an Ambivalent Conservative.* New York: Basic Books, 1977.

Labrouse, Elisabeth. *Bayle.* Trans. Denys Potts. Oxford: Oxford University Press, 1983.

– *Pierre Bayle.* La Haye: Martinus Nijhoff, 1963.

Landsman, Ned D. 'Presbyterians and Provincial Society: The Evangelical Enlightenment in the West of Scotland, 1740–1775.' In John Dwyer and Richard B. Sher, eds., *Sociability and Society in Eighteenth-Century Scotland.* Edinburgh: Mercat Press, 1993.

Lee, Sidney, ed. *The Dictionary of National Biography.* London: Smith, Elder, 1897.

Leed, Jacob. 'Johnson, Chesterfield and Patronage: A Response to Paul Korshin.' *Studies in Burke and His Time*, 13 (1971).

– 'Patronage in the *Rambler.*' *Studies in Burke and His Time* 14 (1972).

Lees-Milne, James. *Earls of Creation: Five Great Patrons of Eighteenth-Century Art.* London: Hamish Hamilton, 1962.

Leigh, R.A. 'Rousseau's English Pension.' In J.H. Fox, M.W. Waddicor, and D.A. Watts, eds., *Studies in Eighteenth-Century Literature.* Exeter: University of Exeter, 1975.

Lenient, Charles. *Étude sur Bayle.* Paris: Giraudet et Jouaust, 1855.

Lennon, Thomas M. *Reading Bayle.* Toronto: University of Toronto Press, 1999.

L'Estrange, Roger. *Seneca's Morals by Way of Abstract: Of Benefits.* London: Thomas Newcomb, 1678.

Letters concerning the Present State of England. Particularly respecting the Politics, Arts, Manners and Literature of the Times. London: J. Almon, 1772.

Linton, Marisa. *The Politics of Virtue in Enlightenment France.* Basingstoke, U.K.: Palgrave, 2001.

Livingstone, Donald W. 'Hume, English Barbarism and American Independence.' In Richard B. Sher and Jeffrey R. Smitten, eds., *Scotland and America in the Age of Enlightenment.* Edinburgh: Edinburgh University Press, 1990.

Locke, John. *The Correspondence of John Locke.* Ed. E.S. De Beer. Oxford: Clarendon, 1976.

– *Letters concerning Toleration.* London: A. Millar, 1765.

– *Political Essays.* Ed. Mark Goldie. Cambridge: Cambridge University Press, 1997.

– *Two Tracts of Government.* Ed. Philip Abrams. Cambridge: Cambridge University Press, 1967.

– *Two Treatises of Government.* Ed. Peter Laslett. Cambridge: Cambridge University Press, 1960.

– *The Works in Ten Volumes.* London: W. Otridge, 1812.

Lough, John. *The Philosophes and Post-Revolutionary France.* Oxford: Clarendon, 1982.

– *Writer and Public in France from the Middle Ages to the Present Day.* Oxford: Clarendon, 1978.

Mack, Mary P. *Jeremy Bentham: An Odyssey of Ideas, 1748–1792.* London: Heinemann, 1962.

Mainka, Peter. *K.A. Von Zedlitz und Leipe.* Berlin: Dunker and Humbolt, 1995.

Maistre, Joseph de. *Against Rousseau.* Trans. Richard A. Lebrun. Montreal and Kingston: McGill-Queens University Press, 1996.

Malesherbes, Chrétien-Guillaume Lamoignon de. *Mémoires sur la librairie et sur la liberté de la presse (1788).* Genève: Slatkine, 1969.

Marchal, Roger. *Madame de Lambert et son milieu*. Oxford: Voltaire Foundation, 1991.

Marcuse, Herbert. *Reason and Revolution: Hegel and the Rise of Social Theory*. Boston: Beacon Press, 1968.

Marotti, Arthur F. 'Patronage, Poetry and Print.' In *The Yearbook of English Studies: Politics, Patronage and Literature in England*, vol. 21. Leeds: Modern Humanities Research Association, 1991.

Marx, Karl. *Capital: A Critical Analysis of Capitalist Production*. Trans. Samuel Moore and Edward Aveling. Moscow: Foreign Languages Publishing House, 1959.

Mason, H.T. *Pierre Bayle and Voltaire*. Oxford: Oxford University Press, 1963.

Maurois, André. *Voltaire*, trans. Hamish Miles. Edinburgh: Peter Davies, 1932.

Mauss, Marcel. *The Gift: Forms and Functions of Exchange in Archaic Societies*. London: Cohen and West, 1970.

McAlendon, D. 'Senatorial Opposition to Claudius and Nero.' *American Journal of Philology*, 77 (1956).

McGrew, Robert E. *Paul 1 of Russia, 1754–1801*. Oxford: Clarendon, 1992.

McKendrick, Neil, John Brewer, and J.H. Plumb. *The Birth of a Consumer Society: The Commercialization of Eighteenth-Century England*. London: Europa Publications, 1982.

McLeod, Enid. *The Order of the Rose: The Life and Ideas of Christine de Pizan*. London: Chatto and Windus, 1976.

McLuskie, Kathleen E. 'The Poets' Royal Exchange: Patronage and Commerce in Early Modern Drama.' *The Yearbook of English Studies: Politics, Patronage and Literature in England*, vol.21. Leeds: Modern Humanities Research Association, 1991.

Mély, Benoît. *Jean-Jacques Rousseau: un intellectuel en rupture*. Paris: Minerve, 1985.

Mercier, Gilbert. *Madame Voltaire*. Paris: Éditions de Fallois, 2001.

Mettrie, Julien Offray de la. *Anti-Seneca or the Soveriegn Good*. In *Machine Man and Other Writings*. Trans. Ann Thomson. Cambridge: Cambridge University Press, 1996.

– *Histoire naturelle de l'âme*. Oxford [Paris], 1747.

– *Man a Machine*. Trans. M.W. Collins. Chicago: Open Court, 1927.

– *Oeuvres Philosophiques*. Paris: Fayard, 1984.

Millar, John. *An Historical View of the English Government*. Dublin: Zachariah Jackson, 1789.

Miller, Stephen. *Three Deaths and Enlightenment Thought: Hume, Johnson, Marat*. Lewisburg, Penn.: Bucknell University Press, 2001.

Millett, Paul. 'Patronage and Its Avoidance in Classical Athens.' In Andrew Wallace-Hadrill, ed., *Patronage in Ancient Society*. London: Routledge, 1990.

Mitford, Nancy. *Madame de Pompadour*. London: Hamish Hamilton, 1968.

Mollat, Michel. 'Les aspects économiques du mécénat en Europe (XIV–XVIII siècle).' *Revue Historique*, 273 (1985).

Money, David. 'Free Flattery or Servile Tribute? Oxford and Cambridge Commemorative Poetry in the Seventeenth and Eighteenth Centuries.' In James Raven, ed., *Free Print and Non-Commercial Publishing since 1700*. Aldershot, U.K.: Ashgate, 2000.

Monod, Paul K. *Jacobitism and the English People, 1688–1788*. Cambridge: Cambridge University Press, 1989.

Montesquieu, Charles Louis de Secondat, Baron de. *Lettres Persanes*. Ed. Paul Vernière. Paris: Garnier, 1960.

Morley, John Viscount. *Voltaire*. London: Macmillan, 1923.

Mornet, Daniel. *French Thought in the Eighteenth Century*. Trans. Lawrence M. Levin. New York: Archon Books, 1969.

Mossner, Ernest Campbell. *The Life of David Hume*. Austin: University of Texas Press, 1954.

Myers, Sylvia Harcstock. *The Bluestocking Circle: Women, Friendship and the Life of the Mind in Eighteenth-Century England*. Oxford: Clarendon, 1990.

Namier, Sir Lewis. *England in the Age of the American Revolution*. London: Macmillan, 1966.

– *The Structure of Politics at the Accession of George III*. London: Macmillan, 1957.

Nietzsche, Friedrich. *Beyond Good and Evil: Prelude to a Philosophy of the Future*. Trans. W. Kaufmann. New York: Vintage, 1966.

– *Twilight of the Idols*. Trans. R.J. Hollingdale. Harmondsworth: Penguin, 1968.

Niklaus, Robert. *A Literary History of France: The Eighteenth Century, 1715–1789*. London: Ernest Benn, 1970.

Norris, John. *Shelburne and Reform*. London: MacMillan, 1963.

Norton, Anne. *Leo Strauss and the Politics of the American Empire*. New Haven, Conn.: Yale University Press, 2004.

O'Brien, Conor Cruise. *The Great Melody: A Thematic Biography and Commentated Anthology of Edmund Burke*. London: Sinclair-Stevenson, 1992.

O'Connor, Thomas. *An Irish Theologian in Enlightenment France: Luke Joseph Hooke, 1714–96*. Dublin: Four Courts Press, 1995.

Odell, Thomas. *The Patron; or, the Statesman's Opera*. Dublin: S. Powell, 1729.

O'Higgins, James, *Anthony Collins: The Man and His Work*. The Hague: Martinus Nijhoff, 1970.

Orieux, Jean. *Voltaire*. Trans. Barbara Bray and Helen R. Lane. New York: Doubleday, 1979.

Oustinoff, Pierre C. 'Notes on Diderot's Fortunes in Russia.' *Diderot Studies*, 1 (1949).

Paine, Thomas. *The Complete Writings of Thomas Paine*. Ed Philip Foner. New York: Citadel Press, 1945.

Palmer, R.R. *The Improvement of Mankind: Education and the French Revolution*. Princeton: Princeton University Press, 1985.

Pangle, Thomas. 'Socrates in Xenophon's Political Writings.' In Paul A. Vander Waerdt, ed., *The Socratic Movement*. Ithaca: Cornell University Press, 1994.

Pangle, Lorraine and Thomas. *The Learning of Liberty*. Lawrence: University Press of Kansas, 1993.

The Parasite. London: G. Burnet, 1765.

Pascal, Blaise. *Pensées*. Trans. M. Turnell. New York: Harper and Brothers, 1962.

Payne, Deborah C. 'Patronage and the Dramatic Marketplace under Charles I and II.' *Yearbook of English Studies: Politics, Patronage and Literature in England*, vol.21. Leeds: The Modern Humanities Research Association, 1991.

Peacock, Thomas Love. *Nightmare Abbey and Crotchet Castle*. London: Hamish Hamilton, 1947.

Peck, Linda Levy. 'Benefits, Brokers and Beneficiaries: The Culture of Exchange in Seventeenth-Century England.' In B.Y. Kunze and D.D. Brautigan, eds., *Court, Country and Culture: Essays on Early Modern British History in Honor of Perez Zagorin*. Rochester: University of Rochester Press, 1992.

– *Court Patronage and Corruption in Early Stuart England*. Boston: Unwin Hyman, 1990.

Pederson, Olaf. 'Tradition and Innovation.' In Hilde de Ridder-Symoens, ed., *Universities in Early Modern Europe, 1500–1800*. Cambridge: Cambridge University Press, 1996.

Pettit, Philip. *Republicanism*. Oxford: Clarendon, 1997.

Peyrefitte, Roger. *Voltaire et Frédéric II*. Paris: Albin Michel, 1992.

Phillips, Mark Salber. *Society and Sentiment: Genres of Historical Writing in Britain, 1740–1820*. Princeton: Princeton University Press, 2000.

Phillipson, Nicholas. 'Culture and Society in the 18th Century Province: The Case of Edinburgh and the Scottish Enlightenment.' In Lawrence Stone, ed., *The University in Society*. Princeton: Princeton University Press, 1974.

Piozzi, Hester Thrale. *Dr. Johnson and Mrs. Thrale*. Ed. Richard Ingrams. London: Chatto and Windus, 1984.

Pisan, Christine de. *Oeuvres poétiques*. Paris: Firmin Didot, 1886.

Pitt-Rivers, Julian. *The People of the Sierra*. Chicago: University of Chicago Press, 1971.

Plato. *Euthyphro*. Trans. Lane Cooper. In Edith Hamilton and Huntington Cairns, ed., *The Collected Dialogues of Plato*. New York: Pantheon–Bollinger Series LXXI, 1964.

Plutarch. *Lives*. Trans. John and William Langhorne. London: J. Mawman, 1813.

Pocock, J.G.A. *Barbarism and Religion: The Enlightenments of Edward Gibbon, 1737–1764*. Cambridge: Cambridge University Press, 1999.

– *Barbarism and Religion: The First Decline and Fall*. Cambridge: Cambridge University Press, 2003.

– 'Clergy and Commerce: The Conservative Enlightenment in England.' In R. Ajello, M. Firpo, L. Guerci, and G. Ricuperati, eds., *L'Età Dei Lumi: Studi Storici sul settecento Europeo in Onore di Franco Venturi*. Naples: Jovene, 1985.

– *The Machiavellian Moment: Florentine Political Thought and the Atlantic Republican Tradition*. Princeton: Princeton University Press, 1975.

– 'Post-Puritan England and the Problem of the Enlightenment.' In Perez Zagorin, ed., *Culture and Politics from Puritanism to the Enlightenment*. Berkeley: University of California Press, 1980.

Pomeau, René. *Voltaire en son temps*. 5 vols. Oxford: Voltaire Foundation, 1985–94.

Porter, Roy. *The Creation of the Modern Mind: The Untold Story of the British Enlightenment*. New York: W.W. Norton, 2000.

– 'The Enlightenment in England.' In R. Porter and M. Teich, eds., *The Enlightenment in National Context*. Cambridge: Cambridge University Press, 1981.

– *English Society in the Eighteenth Century*. Harmondsworth, U.K.: Penguin, 1982.

– 'The Scientific Revolution and Universities.' In Walter Rüegg, ed., *A History of the University in Europe*. Cambridge: Cambridge University Press, 1996.

Price, John Valdemir. 'The Reading of Philosophic Literature.' In Isobel Rivers, ed., *Books and Their Readers in Eighteenth-Century England*. Leicester: Leicester University Press, 1982.

Priestley, Joseph. *The History and Present State of Electricity with Original Experiments*. London: C. Bathurst et al., 1775.

Probyn, Clive T. *The Sociable Humanist: The Life and Works of James Harris, 1709–1780*. Oxford: Clarendon, 1991.

Raven, James. *Judging New Wealth: Popular Publishing and Responses to Commerce in England, 1750–1800*. Oxford: Clarendon, 1992.

– 'From Promotion to Proscription: Arrangements for Reading and Eighteenth-Century Libraries.' In James Raven, Helen Small, and Naomi Tadmor, eds., *The Practice and Representation of Reading in England before 1750*. Cambridge: Cambridge University Press, 1996.

Reid, Christopher. *Edmund Burke and the Practice of Political Writing*. Dublin: Gill and Macmillan, 1985.

Rendell, Jane. *The Origins of the Scottish Enlightenment*. London: Macmillan, 1978.

Rièse, Laura. *Les salons littéraires parisiens du second empire à nos jours.* Toulouse: Privat, 1962.

Robertson, John. 'The Scottish Contribution to the Enlightenment.' In Paul Wood, ed., *The Scottish Enlightenment: Essays in Reinterpretation.* Rochester: University of Rochester Press, 2000.

Robertson, William. *The Works of William Robertson.* London: Baldwyn, 1818.

Robinson, F.J.G., and P.J. Wallis. *Book Subscription Lists: A Revised Guide.* Newcastle upon Tyne: Harold Hill, 1975.

Robinson, Howard. *Bayle the Sceptic.* New York: Columbia University Press, 1931.

Roche, Daniel. 'Censorship and the Publishing Business.' In Robert Darnton and Daniel Roche, ed., *The Press in France 1775–1800.* Berkeley: University of California Press, 1989.

– *La France des Lumières.* Paris: Fayard, 1993.

Rogers, Ben. 'In Praise of Vanity: The Augustinian Analysis of the Benefits of Vice from Port-Royal to Mandeville.' PhD thesis, University of Oxford, 1994.

Rogers, G.A.J. *Locke's Enlightenment: Aspects of the Origin, Nature and Impact of His Philosophy.* Hildesheim, Germany: Georg Olms Verlag, 1998.

Ross, G.M. 'Seneca's Philosophic Influence.' In C.D.N. Costa, ed., *Seneca.* London: Routledge and Kegan Paul, 1974.

Ross, Ian Simpson. 'Adam Smith's "Happiest" Years as a Glasgow Professor.' In Andrew Hook and Richard B. Sher, eds., *Glasgow Enlightenment.* East Lothian, U.K.: Tuckwell Press, 1995.

Rousseau, Jean-Jacques. *The Collected Writings of Rousseau.* Eds. Christopher Kelly, Roger D. Masters, and Peter G. Stillman. 10 vols. Hanover, N.H.: University Press of New England, c.1990–.

– *Emile.* Trans. Barbara Foxley. London: Everyman, 2001.

– *The First and Second Discourses.* Ed. Roger D. Masters. New York: St Martin's Press, 1964.

– *Oeuvres Complètes de Jean-Jacques Rousseau.* Ed. Bernard Gagnebin and Marcel Raymond. Paris: Gallimard-Pléiade, 1964.

Rudich, Vasily. *Dissidence and Literature under Nero: The Price of Rhetoricization.* London: Routledge, 1997.

Rüegg, Walter. 'Themes.' In Walter Rüegg, ed., *A History of the University in Europe.* Cambridge: Cambridge University Press, 1996.

Ste Croix, G.E.M. de. 'Suffragium: From Vote to Patronage.' *British Journal of Sociology,* 5 (1974).

Saller, Richard P. *Personal Patronage under the Early Empire.* Cambridge: Cambridge University Press, 1982.

Sareil, Jean. *Les Tencin.* Geneva: Librairie Droz, 1969.

– *Voltaire et les grands.* Geneva: Librairie Droz, 1978.

Schofield, Robert E. *The Enlightenment of Joseph Priestley: A Study of His Life and Work from 1733 to 1773.* University Park: Pennsylvania State University Press, 1997.

Schweizer, Karl W., ed. *Lord Bute: Essays in Re-Interpretation.* Leicester: Leicester University Press, 1988.

Schwoerer, Lois G. *The Ingenious Mr. Henry Care: Restoration Publicist.* Baltimore: Johns Hopkins University Press, 2001.

Scott, James. 'Patronage as Exploitation.' In Ernest Gellner and John Waterbury, eds., *Patrons and Clients in Mediterranean Societies.* London: Duckworth, 1977.

Ségur, Pierre, Comte de. *Le Royaume de la rue Saint-Honoré: Mme Geoffrin et sa fille.* Paris: Calmann-Lévy, 1897.

Seneca, Lucius Annaeus. *Ad Lucilium: Epistulae Morales.* Trans. Richard M. Gummere. London: William Heinemann, 1920.

– *De Beneficiis, On Benefits.* Trans. John W. Bashore. In *Moral Essays.* Cambridge, Mass.: Harvard University Press, 1935.

Shackleton, Robert. *Censure and Censorship: Impediments to Free Publication in the Age of Enlightenment.* Austin, Texas: Humanities Research Center, 1975.

– *Montesquieu: A Critical Biography.* London: Oxford University Press, 1961.

Shapin, Stephen. 'Property, Patronage and the Politics of Science: The Founding of the Royal Society of Edinburgh.' *British Journal for the History of Science,* 7 (1974).

Shaw, William. *Memoirs of the Life and Writings of the Late Dr. Samuel Johnson (1785).* New York: Garland, 1974.

Sher, Richard B. *Church and University in the Scottish Enlightenment: The Moderate Literati of Edinburgh.* Princeton: Princeton University Press, 1985.

Siebert, Fredrick Seaton. *Freedom of the Press in England, 1476–1776: The Rise and Decline of Government Controls.* Urbana: University of Illinois Press, 1952.

Silverman, Sydel. 'Patronage as Myth.' In Ernest Gellner and John Waterbury, eds., *Patrons and Clients in Mediterranean Societies.* London: Duckworth, 1977.

Simon, William. *A Time for Truth.* New York: McGraw-Hill, 1979.

Simone, Maria Rosa di. 'Admission.' In Hilde de Ridder-Symoens, ed., *Universities in Early Modern Europe 1500–1800.* Cambridge: Cambridge University Press, 1996.

Skinner, Quentin and Martin van Gelderen, eds. *Republicanism: A Shared European Heritage.* Cambridge: Cambridge University Press, 2002.

Smith, Adam. *The Correspondence of Adam Smith.* Ed. Ernest Campbell Mossner and Ian Simpson Ross. Oxford: Clarendon, 1987.

– *An Inquiry into the Nature and Causes of the Wealth of Nations.* Ed. R.H. Campbell and A.S. Skinner. Oxford: Clarendon, 1976.

– *The Theory of Moral Sentiments.* Ed. D.D. Raphael and A.L. Macfie. Indianapolis: Liberty Fund, 1982.

Smout, T.C. 'Problems of Nationalism, Identity and Improvement in later Eighteenth-Century Scotland.' In T.M. Devine, ed., *Improvement and Enlightenment: Proceedings of the Scottish Studies Seminar, University of Strathclyde, 1987–88.* Edinburgh: John Donald, 1989.

Speck, W.A. 'Politicians, Peers, and Publication by Subscription, 1700–1750.' In Isobel Rivers, ed., *Books and Their Readers in Eighteenth-Century England.* Leicester: Leicester University Press, 1982.

Spellman, W.M. *John Locke.* New York: St Martin's Press, 1997.

Spitz, Jean Fabien. 'From Civism to Civility: D'Holbach's Critique of Republican Virtue.' Trans. John Fletcher. In Martin van Gelderen and Quentin Skinner eds., *Republicanism: A Shared European Heritage.* Cambridge: Cambridge University Press, 2002.

Spurr, John. *The Restoration Church, 1646–1689.* New Haven, Comm.: Yale University Press, 1991.

Starobinski, Jean. *Blessings in Disguise; or, the Morality of Evil.* Cambridge, Mass.: Harvard University Press, 1995.

Staum, Martin S. *Minerva's Message: Stabilizing the French Revolution.* Montreal and Kingston: McGill-Queen's University Press, 1996.

Steegmuller, Francis. *A Woman, a Man, and Two Kingdoms: The Story of Madame d'Épinay and the Abbé Galiani.* New York: Alfred Knopf, 1991.

Stimson, Dorothy. *Scientists and Amateurs: A History of the Royal Society.* New York: Greenwood Press, 1968.

Stone, Lawrence. 'The Results of the English Revolutions of the Seventeenth Century.' In J.G.A. Pocock, ed., *Three British Revolutions: 1641, 1688, 1776.* Princeton: Princeton University Press, 1980.

– *The University in Society.* Princeton: Princeton University Press, 1974.

Strauss, Barry. 'In the Shadow of the Fortress.' In David Tabachnick, ed., *Tyranny: Ancient and Modern.* Lantham, Md.: Rowman and Littlefield, forthcoming.

Strauss, Leo. *Persecution and the Art of Writing.* Westport, Conn.: Greenwood, 1952.

– *What Is Political Philosophy?* New York: Free Press, 1959.

Sullivan, J.P. *Literature and Politics in the Age of Nero.* Ithaca: Cornell University Press, 1985.

Sullivan, Robert E. *John Toland and the Deist Controversy.* Cambridge: Harvard University Press, 1982.

Sunter, Ronald. *Patronage and Politics in Scotland, 1707–1832.* Edinburgh: John Donald, 1986.

Swift, Jonathan. *A Discourse of the Contests and Dissentions between the Nobles and Commons in Athens and Rome.* Ed. Frank H. Ellis. Oxford: Clarendon, 1967.

Syme, Ronald. 'Some Friends of the Caesars.' *American Journal of Philology,* 77 (1956).

Tate, Robert S. 'Voltaire and the Question of Law and Order.' In J.H. Fox, M.H. Waddicor, and D.A. Watts, eds., *Studies in Eighteenth-Century Literature Presented to Robert Niklaus.* Exeter: University of Exeter Press, 1975.

Temmer, Mark J. *Samuel Johnson and Three Infidels.* Athens: University of Georgia Press, 1988.

Thom, Martin. *Republics, Nations and Tribes.* London: Verso, 1995.

Thomas, David O. *The Honest Mind: The Thought and Work of Richard Price.* Oxford: Clarendon, 1977.

Thompson, Mark A. *The Secretaries of State, 1681–1782.* Oxford: Clarendon, 1932.

Thrale, Hester Lynch. *Thraliana: The Diary of Mrs. Hester Lynch Thrale.* Ed. Katherine C. Balderson. Oxford: Clarendon, 1951.

Tianen-Antilla, Kaya. *The Problem of Humanity: The Blacks in the European Enlightenment.* Helsinki: Finnish Historical Society, 1994.

Tocqueville, Alexis de. *État social et politique de la France avant et depuis 1789.* In J.-P. Mayer, ed., *Oeuvres Complètes.* Paris: Gallimard, 1952.

Todd, William B. 'Introduction.' In Paul Langford, T.O. McLoughlin, and James T. Boulton, eds., *The Writings and Speeches of Edmund Burke.* Oxford: Clarendon, 1997.

Toland, John. *The Life of John Milton, with Amytor.* London: A. Millar, 1761.

Tomalin, Claire. *The Life and Death of Mary Wollstonecraft.* Harmondsworth: Penguin, 1985.

Toynbee, Jocelyn M.C. 'Dictators and Philosophers in the First Century A.D.' *Greece and Rome* 13 (1944).

Trenchard, John, and Thomas Gordon. *Cato's Letters: or Essays on Liberty, Civil and Religious, and Other Important Subjects.* London: J. Walthoe et al., 1755.

Trouille, Mary. 'Eighteenth-Century Amazons of the Pen: Stéphanie de Genlis & Olympe de Gouges.' In Roland Bonnel and Catherine Rubinger, eds., *Femmes Savantes et Femmes d'Esprit: Women Intellectuals of the Eighteenth Century.* New York: Peter Lang, 1994.

Turnovsky, Geoffrey. 'The Enlightenment Literary Market: Rousseau, Authorship, and the Book Trade.' *Eighteenth-Century Studies,* 3 (2003).

Uglow, Jenny. *The Lunar Men: Five Friends Whose Curiosity Changed the World.* New York: Farrar, Straus and Giroux, 2002.

Underdown, David. *The Start of Play: Cricket and Culture in Eighteenth-Century England.* Harmondsworth: Penguin, 2000.

Vaillot, René. *Avec Madame du Châtelet.* Oxford: Voltaire Foundation, 1988.

Vauthier, G. 'Les pensions aux écrivains, 1806–1810.' *Revue des études napoléoniennes* 2 (1914).

Venturi, Franco. *Utopia and Reform in the Enlightenment.* Cambridge: Cambridge University Press, 1971.

Vernon, Richard. *The Career of Toleration: John Locke, Jonas Proast and After.* Montreal and Kingston: McGill-Queen's University Press, 1997.

Verona, Roxana M. *Les 'Salons de Sainte-Beuve': le critique et ses muses.* Paris: Honoré Champion, 1999.

Voltaire, François-Marie Arouet de. *The Age of Lewis XIV.* Trans. T. Nugent. London: R. Dodsley, 1772.

– *The Complete Works of Voltaire.* Ed. Theodore Besterman. Genève: Institut et Musée Voltaire, 1968–2001.

– *Essai sur les moeurs et l'esprit des nations et sur les principaux faits de l' histoire depuis Charlemagne jusqu' à Louis XIII.* Paris: Garnier, 1963.

– *Letters of Voltaire and Frederick the Great.* Trans. Richard Aldington. London: Routledge, 1927.

– *Oeuvres Complètes de Voltaire.* Paris: Lequien, 1820.

– *Oeuvres Complètes de Voltaire.* Paris: Garnier, 1879.

– *Philosophical Dictionary.* Trans. Peter Gay. New York: Basic Books, 1962.

– *Philosophic Letters.* Trans. Ernest Dilworth. Indianapolis: Bobbs-Merrill, 1961.

– *Voltaire and Catherine the Great: Selected Correspondence.* Trans. A. Lentin. Cambridge, U.K.: Oriental Research Partners, 1974.

– *Voltaire's Correspondence.* Ed. Theodore Besterman. Geneva: Institut et Musée Voltaire, 1962.

Wade, Ira O. *Studies on Voltaire with Some Unpublished Papers of Mme du Châtelet.* New York: Russell and Russell, 1967.

Wagener, Françoise. *Madame Récamier: 1777–1849.* Paris: Flammarion, 2000.

Waldron, Jeremy. *God, Locke and Equality: Christian Foundations of John Locke's Political Thought.* Cambridge: Cambridge University Press, 2002.

Wallace, John. 'John Dryden's Plays and the Conception of a Heroic Society.' In Perez Zagorin, ed., *Culture and Politics from Puritanism to the Enlightenment.* Berkeley: University of California Press, 1980.

Walpole, Horace. *Memoirs of the Reign of King George the Third.* London: Lawrence and Bullen, 1894.

Walsh, Jennifer M. *Edmund Burke and International Relations: The Commonwealth of Europe and the Crusade against the French Revolution.* New York: St Martin's Press, 1995.

Walter, Gerard. *Nero.* Trans. Emma Craufurd. London: Allen and Unwin, 1957.

Warren, Ann K. *Anchorites and Their Patrons in Medieval England.* Berkeley: University of California Press, 1985.

Waterbury, John. 'An Attempt to Put Patrons and Clients in Their Place.' In Ernest Gellner and John Waterbury, *Patrons and Clients in Mediterranean Societies.* London: Duckworth, 1977.

Weil, Simone. *The Need for Roots: Prelude to a Declaration of Duties toward Mankind.* Trans. Arthur Wills. Boston: Beacon Press, 1960.

Weinbrot, Howard D. *Augustus Caesar in 'Augustan' England.* Princeton, N.J.: Princeton University Press, 1978.

Weissman, Ronald. 'Taking Patronage Seriously: Mediterranean Values and Renaissance Society.' In F.W. Kent, Patricia Simon, and J.C. Eade, eds., *Patronage, Art, and Society in Renaissance Italy.* Oxford: Clarendon, 1987.

Westfall, R.S. *Never at Rest: A Biography of Isaac Newton.* Cambridge: Cambridge University Press, 1980.

Whelan, Frederick G. *Edmund Burke and India: Political Morality and Empire.* Pittsburgh: University of Pittsburgh Press, 1996.

Whelan, Ruth. *The Anatomy of Superstition: a Study of the Historical Theory and Practice of Pierre Bayle.* Oxford: Voltaire Foundation, 1989.

Wilcox, Derk Arend, Joshua Sheckman, and Penelope Naas, eds. *The Right Guide: A Guide to Conservative and Right of Centre Organizations.* Ann Arbor, Mich.: Economics America, 1993.

Wiles, Roy M. *Serial Publication in England before 1750.* Cambridge: Cambridge University Press, 1957.

Williams, Bernard. *Truth and Truthfulness: An Essay in Genealogy.* Princeton, N.J.: Princeton University Press, 2002.

Wilson, Arthur M. *Diderot: The Testing Years, 1713–59.* New York: Oxford University Press, 1957.

Wokler, Robert. *Rousseau.* Oxford: Oxford University Press, 1995.

Wollstonecraft, Mary. *A Vindication of the Rights of Men with a Vindication of the Rights of Woman and Hints.* Ed. Sylvana Tomaselli. Cambridge: Cambridge University Press, 1995.

Wood, Anthony À. *Athenae Oxonsienses.* London: T. Bennett, 1692.

Wood, Gordon S. *The Americanization of Benjamin Franklin.* New York: Penguin, 2004.

– *The Radicalism of the American Revolution.* New York: Alfred A. Knopf, 1992.

Wood, Marcus. '"The Abolition Blunderbuss": Free Publishing and British Abolition Propaganda.' In James Raven, ed., *Free Print and Non-Commercial Publishing since 1700.* Aldershot: Ashgate, 2000.

Woodward, W.E. *Tom Paine: America's Grandfather, 1737–1809.* New York: E.P. Dutton, 1945.

Wootton, David. 'David Hume, "the Historian."' In David F. Norton, ed., *The Cambridge Companion to Hume*. Cambridge: Cambridge University Press, 1993.

Worden, Balir. 'Marchamont Nedham and the Beginnings of English Republicanism, 1649–1656.' In David Wootton, ed., *Republicanism, Liberty and Commercial Society, 1649–1776*. Stanford, Calif.: Stanford University Press, 1994.

Wrightson, Keith. 'Class.' In David Armitage and Michael J. Braddick eds., *The British Atlantic World, 1500–1800*. New York: Palgrave Macmillan, 2002.

Xenophon. *Memorabilia*. Trans J.S. Watson. In A.D. Lindsay, ed. *Socratic Discourses*. London: J.M.Dent, 1954.

Yolton, Jean S., ed. *A Locke Miscellany: Locke Biography and Criticism for All*. Bristol: Thoemmes, 1990.

Young, B.W. *Religion and Enlightenment in Eighteenth-Century England*. Oxford: Clarendon, 1998.

Zaret, David. *Origins of Democratic Culture: Printing, Petitions and the Public Sphere in Early-Modern England*. Princeton, N.J.: Princeton University Press, 2000.

Zinsser, Judith P. 'Émilie du Châtelet: Genius, Gender and Political Authority.' In Hilda L. Smith, *Women Writers and the Early Modern British Political Tradition*. Cambridge: Cambridge University Press, 1998.

Zola, Émile. 'L'argent dans la Littérature.' In *Oeuvres Complètes*. Paris: Cercle du livres précieux, 1968.

Index

academy, academies, 6, 11, 33, 80, 106, 108–11, 185–6, 189–90; Académie Française, 43, 47, 105, 109–12, 186

Act of Union, 119, 120, 122, 123

Adams, John, 185

Adams, Robert, 24, 85

Addison, Joseph, 42, 43, 44, 57, 58, 97, 98

Agrippina, Julia Vipsania, 4, 68, 73

Aikenhead, Thomas, 54

Alembert, Jean Le Rond d', 21, 26, 29, 42, 50, 52, 67, 68, 69, 71, 76, 77, 80, 81, 100, 101, 107, 110, 111, 113, 114, 115, 118, 137–40, 142–4, 150, 153, 155, 171, 188; *Éloge de l'abbé de Saint-Pierre*, 77; *Essai sur la société des gens de lettres et des grands*, 21, 50, 67, 81, 137, 139, 142, 153

Alexander (the Great), 18, 38, 69, 70, 71

Alfieri, Vittorio, 114, 147–8

Algarotti, Francesco, 101

Allan, David, 122

Amato, Joseph, 72, 77

American War of Independence, 5, 59, 66, 171, 172, 174, 176, 180, 183, 189–90; effect on patronage, 190

Annandale, George Johnstone, 3rd Marquess of, 127

Argenson, Marc-Pierre de Voyer, Comte d', 28, 105, 136, 137

Argenson, René-Louis, Marquis d', 28, 105, 115, 137, 138, 143, 149, 151

Argyll, Archibald Campbell, 3rd Duke of, 9, 26, 27, 29, 30, 35, 48, 121–6, 129, 130, 132, 134, 192, 194

Aristophanes, 13, 15, 16

Aristotle, 3, 4, 5, 18, 38, 69, 70, 72

Augustus, Gaius Julius Caesar Octavianus, 70, 71, 72, 78

authors: age of, 21–2, 25, 38, 41, 157; consecration of, 8, 47, 49; as professionals, 6, 41, 45–7, 50, 56, 88, 141–2, 165, 186

authorship, work of isolated individual or collective project, 9, 191

Bacon, Francis, 19, 32, 39, 50, 188

Bailyn, Bernard, 6, 185, 189

Balcarres, Earl of, 125

Barbauld, Letitia, 7

Barbeyrac, Jean, 147

Barré, Colonel Isaac, 177, 181

Bassett, Thomas, 94

Virgil, Publius Vergilius Maro, 52,
71
Voltaire (Arouet, François-Marie), 3,
5, 8, 9, 10, 12, 20, 24, 26, 28, 33,
35, 36, 38, 41, 42, 43, 47, 49, 51,
52, 53, 55, 60, 61, 62, 64, 67, 68,
69, 70, 71, 74, 76, 77, 79, 80, 81,
82, 83, 88, 95, 97, 99, 101–18, 119,
129, 139, 142, 146, 148, 150, 152,
153, 155, 157, 158, 159, 164, 188,
191–2; preference for royal over
aristocratic patronage, 60–1, 70–1,
98, 109–10, 142, 159; *Essai sur les
moeurs*, 71; *La Henriade*, 42, 103;
Lettres philosophiques, 26, 60, 102;
Mahomet, 104, 112; *Philosophical
Dictionary*, 117, 118, 119; *Siècle de
Louis XIV*, 52, 81

Waldron, Jeremy, 93
Walpole, Horace, 114, 115, 118
Walpole, Robert, 56, 58
Warburton, William, 154–5
Warens, Françoise Louise de La
Tour, Mme de, 109, 135–6
Warham, William, Archbishop of
Canterbury, 38
Washington, George, 184
Waterbury, John, 31
Watt, James, 178
Wedgwood, Josiah, 178, 179
Weissman, Ronald, 63

Whig/Whigs, 25, 27, 29, 31, 34, 41,
42, 45, 55, 57, 58, 59, 82, 89, 91,
92, 95–8, 114, 120, 123, 124, 125,
127, 128, 165, 171, 173, 175, 184,
231n.37
Whitehead, Paul, 55
Wicksted, John Churchill, 5
Wilberforce, William, 155
Wilkes, John, 55, 157, 164, 172, 175
William of Orange, 83, 85, 86, 87, 97,
147
Williams, Bernard, 138–9
Wokler, Robert, 153
Wolff, Christian von, 70
Wollstonecraft, Mary, 6, 51, 100, 110;
A Vindication of the Rights of Women,
100
Wood, Anthony, 88, 89
Wood, Gordon, 5, 6, 33–4, 185,
189–90
Worden, Blair, 89
Wordsworth, William, 51
Wrightson, Keith, 7

Xenophon, 13, 15–18

Young, Brian, 24, 154

Zaret, David, 37
Zedlitz, Karl A., Count von, 7
Zinsser, Judith, 101, 116
Zola, Émile, 186–7